THE CATHOLIC UNIVERSITY OF AMERICA
CANON LAW STUDIES
No. 99

THE VALUE OF TESTIMONIAL EVIDENCE IN MATRIMONIAL PROCEDURE

AN HISTORICAL SYNOPSIS AND COMMENTARY

A DISSERTATION

Submitted to the Faculty of Canon Law of the Catholic University of America in Partial Fulfillment of the Requirements for the Degree of

DOCTOR OF CANON LAW

BY

DONALD WHALEN, M.A., J.C.L.
Priest of the Archdiocese of Boston

THE CATHOLIC UNIVERSITY OF AMERICA
WASHINGTON, D. C.
1935

Nihil Obstat:

VALENTINUS T. SCHAAF, O.F.M., J.C.D.,
Censor Deputatus.

Washingtonii, D. C., die XXV Maii, 1935.

Imprimatur:

GULIELMUS CARDINALIS O'CONNELL.

Bostoniensis, die XXV Maii, 1935.

Printed by
THE PAULIST PRESS
New York, N. Y.

VIRO . EMINENTISSIMO
GVLIELMO . CARDINALI . O'CONNELL
BONARVM . ARTIVM . FAVTORI . EGREGIO
HVNC . LIBRVM . QVALEMCVQVE
GRATO . ANIMO
D. D. D.

TABLE OF CONTENTS

CHAPTER VIII

PAGE

CHAPTER IX

FOREWORD

In the Fourth Book of the Code of Canon Law are rules for conducting a trial. Some of these rules which are not an unimportant part of the Code pertain to proof by testimonial evidence. The object of this work is to provide an additional facility in acquiring an accurate knowledge of the rules of testimonial evidence which have application to the marriage process.

The rules pertaining to the probative value of testimony which are expressed in the Code and in the recent jurisprudence of the Roman and Spanish Rotae are presented for this purpose. Chapter II, under Title X of the Fourth Book of the Code, is entitled, "On Witnesses and Attestations." These rules and the three introductory canons under Title X, "On Proofs," which are inseparably connected with them, are explained with special reference to the value of testimony in matrimonial causes.

The first four chapters are an historical synopsis based on sources of Roman, Germanic and Canon Law. The generic qualifications of witnesses are investigated in both Roman Law and in the early Councils of the Church. The origin of the *testimonium septimae manus* and its acceptance into Canon Law are indicated. Inquiry is also made into the concept of testimony which is found in the *Corpus Juris Canonici.* The last six chapters, following the order of the canons of the Code as far as is feasible, explain what is meant by testimonial evidence, indicate procedural rules which pertain to witnesses, state the generic human traits which affect probative value and explain the rules applicable to the examination and the evaluation of the testimony of witnesses in matrimonial procedure.

The writer is deeply appreciative of the assistance given him by Archbishop Philip Bernardini, S.T.D., J.U.D., who suggested the subject for this dissertation to be presented to the Faculty of the School of Canon Law of the Catholic University of America. He is also grateful to his other professors, the Rev. Dr. Valentine T. Schaaf, O.F.M., Dean of the School of Canon Law; Rev. Dr. Louis H. Motry; Rev. Dr. Edward G. Roelker; Rev. Dr. Francis J. Lardone; Professor John McDill Fox, School of Law. He is also indebted to Professor William B. Grogan of the School of Law, whose courses in Evidence were taken by the writer.

CHAPTER I

WITNESSES IN ROMAN CLASSICAL AND JUSTINIAN LAW

ROMAN LAW was not static at any period. Justinian not merely codified the laws but was also instrumental in gathering together a mass of legal literature which lay behind the laws in the *Corpus Juris Civilis.* Centuries of development can be traced in that collection. The subject, witnesses in Roman Classical and Justinian Law, considers one phase of the development As this subject is concerned with witnesses in Roman Law it naturally divides itself into two parts. Roman juridical trials were either civil or criminal. This topic is limited to a consideration of oral evidence in civil procedure as witnesses were employed differently in civil and in criminal procedure.

ARTICLE 1. CLASSICAL CIVIL LAW PROCEDURE

From our point of view, Roman civil procedure may be distinguished into the procedure of Classical and of Justinian Law. The Classical period, to which the present article is restricted, covered a cycle of years that stretched from about a century before Christ to the Later Empire at the end of the third century (A. D. 294).

This epoch witnessed the closing years of the statute process (*legis actiones*) which commenced under the Early Republic and terminated with the Republican era (B. C. ca. 449—ca. 130-180). It saw also the Formulary Procedure which began under the Republic and lasted during the Early Empire (B. C. ca. 130—A. D. 294). The Formulary System itself, after flourishing for nearly five hundred years, was discredited and came to the identical fate of the system it had displaced.

The old *legis actiones* are explained by Gaius [1] who composed his *Institutiones* about the time of Hadrian and the Antonines. These actions, five in number, were available only to Roman citizens. They were forms of procedure by means of which a dissatisfied person might

[1] G. 4, 11-31.

enforce a claim. The issue was decided (*in judicio*) by arbiters appointed by a magistrate (*in jure*) to try the case.[2] Not much is known about the original method of deciding disputes.[3]

Due, however, to their rigidity, statute actions fell, as Gaius remarks, into great discredit by reason of the excessive subtlety of the ancient *legis actiones.* This made the introduction of the system of formulae imperative.[4] The statute process, nevertheless, lasted during the entire Republican era until rendered optional to litigants by the Aebutian law (B. C. ca. 130-180) and suppressed by the *Legis Juliae* of Augustus.

The second great type of procedure during the Classical period was the Formulary System of Ordinary Procedure. Due to the causes enumerated by Gaius, which have been indicated, the Code of procedure changed. The Formulary System, under which Gaius wrote, derived its name from the description given to it in the sources. Gaius mentions the phrase, "litigate by formulas."[5]

Inaugurated not long before the advent of the closing century of the Republic, the new Formularly System outlived the Republic. It continued for three centuries of the Empire until the reign of Diocletian.

Compared with the old statute actions, this newer system possessed these two characteristics. In the first place, there was less formality. Besides this, such actions could be used by foreigners. The procedure was intended originally for aliens or *peregrini.* The Aebutian law made the formulae actions which could be used by foreigners available now also to Roman citizens in their own court of the city praetor.

The vehicle of expression, the formula, has been described by Gaius.[6] The Formula System took place in this manner. A preliminary hearing of the parties enabled the praetor to decide or pronounce an *arbitrium* that there was reason for an action. The praetor,

[2] G. 4, 82; Inst., 4, 10.

[3] G. 4, 16.

[4] G. 4, 30.

[5] G. 4. 30.

[6] G. 4, 30.

thereupon, appointed a judge-arbitrator, and acquainted him with the issues of fact to be tried. That no misunderstanding arise, the praetor gave the formula to the plaintiff in the presence of the defendant. Acceptance of the formula by the defendant constituted the *litis contestatio*.[7]

The arbitrator then tried the case. Technical knowledge of the law was often given by jurisconsults who instructed the arbitrators who frequently had no such knowledge of the law. An arbitrator could never deviate from the formula and the written instructions given him by the praetor. The case being tried, the praetor enforced the judgment (*sententia*) of the judge.

Commencing with Augustus, the Extraordinary Procedure came into being It came into vogue in the time of Diocletian. This latter Emperor, in A. D. 294, required that as a rule provincial governors hear and determine all causes themselves.[8]

From that time, it became the usual practice for a magistrate to judge a case in person by virtue of his extraordinary authority. He could, however, under certain circumstances, appoint an official, a *judex pedaneus,* as his substitute. In this manner, the Extraordinary procedure which in earlier times was occasionally employed in exceptional cases, became the rule. The Emperors Constantius and Constans (A. D. 342) entirely abolished the formulae, which as the Code reads: ". . . with their syllabic snares and pitfalls, are hereby abolished in every procedure."[9]

An era of highly developed Roman civil procedure came into being. A system of pleading was created which descended into the Justinian Law and thence into Canon Law and the modern civil procedure in Western Europe. The plaintiff and the defendant joining issue, the declaration or the complaint, confession and avoidance, re-

[7] G. 3, 180.

[8] The inferior judges, to whom, according to the Code, the governors used to refer their cases, do not signify the ordinary judges of the Formulary System, but subordinate officials to whom the governor delegated his extraordinary authority (*cognitio extraordinaria*) for trying cases. *Cf. Cod.*, III, 3, 2; *Cod.*, III, 3, 5.

[9] *Cod.*, II, 57, 1: "Juris formulae, aucupatione syllabarum insidiantes, cunctorum actibus radicitus amputentur."

joinder and surrejoinder, together with other pleadings, were seen for the first time in the Extraordinary period of Roman Law.

Article 2. Witnesses in Roman Classical Law

Having seen the general contour of the procedure in use during the Classical period, one turns to the matter of proofs. In Roman Law the testimony of witnesses possessed probative value.[10] Classical Law, with which this article is concerned, gave more importance to oral than to documentary evidence. Writings were not used in legal transactions as much as they were in later times. Hence, there was little need of written proof which was preferred to testimonial evidence in the Post-Classical period.[11] Cicero, in his oration *Pro Archia,* wrote that a reliable witness was preferable to a document.[12] Elsewhere, in his *Topica,* Cicero makes the further observation that one witness may be accepted and another refused.[13]

The preference of Classical Law for oral testimony may be explained historically. At that time, writing had not become common in legal transactions. Many litigants were unable to write. Furthermore, a considerable number of competent witnesses were required for legal transactions. In order to make a contract, for instance, substantive law provided only oral evidence with the exception of the contract *litteris.*

The last remark brings one to another fundamental consideration. Due to the arbitration system of the Classical period, there was no need of strict rules of procedure for estimating oral evidence. A few observations may help to clarify what is meant. Fundamental to an understanding of what follows is the principle that Roman Classical

[10] Rittershutii, Cunradi, *Expositio Methodica Novellarum Imperatoris Justiniani* (ed. Novissima, Florentia, 1839), par. 9, cap. 21, n. 2, col. 759. *Cf.* authorities quoted in par. 9, cap. 21, n. 2, cols. 759, 760.

[11] D. XXII, 3, 10; *Cod.,* IV, 19, const. 5-7.

[12] Cicero, *Pro Archia,* 4, 8: "Est ridiculum . . . cum habeas amplissimi viri religionem, integerrimi municipii iusuirandum fidemque, ea, quae depravari nullo modo possunt repudiare, tabulas quas idem dicis solere currumpi, desiderare."

[13] Cicero, *Topica,* XIX, 73: "Persona autem non qualiscumque est testimonii pondus habet."

Law, like all law, provided means for the vindication of a right. These means made up the body of adjective law. This was the law of procedure.

The ordinary procedure during the Classical period was guided, as mentioned above, by an arbitrator or a court-referee. He was an expedient appointed for the promotion of public order. Like a juror in the American and English systems of law, he was a private citizen. He had only the authority which was reposed in him. His duties terminated with the culmination of a case. The authority or power of such an appointee was great because of the implicit confidence reposed in him by the litigants.

From this point of view one cannot, consequently, expect to discover during the Classical period many rules of admissibility of testimony found in modern systems of law. Rules of admissibility of evidence are also outgrowths of tradition and litigious experience. By means of them a modern judicial tribunal, especially a jury, is guarded against erroneous persuasion.

What, then, do the sources specify concerning the evidence of witnesses in Classical Law? In Gaius, especially, one finds no rules pertaining to witnesses in adjective law. Although one does not discover any direct indications that the sources contemplated rules either for the qualifications of witnesses or for the evaluation of their testimony in adjective law, one cannot conclude that there are, consequently, no rules in Classical Law for estimating testimonial evidence.

The qualifications of witnesses found in the substantive code would, of course, be applied by the arbitrator. The praetors took cognizance of this. They proceeded as unobtrusively as possible to ameliorate the law under which the arbitrators decided cases. By tacit rather than by overt legislation, by innovations in the code of procedure rather than in the substantive code, they effected their purpose. The introduction of the Formulary System gave them authority to inaugurate new actions (*actiones utiles*). They were virtually invested with much legislative power.

In the Statute Process the legislator predominated; in the Formulary System the administrator predominated. In the *legis actiones* the legislator and the litigants alone appear to occupy the scene. The activity of the praetor is not so extensive. In the Formulary System the praetor had larger attributes. He appears to have stepped in front of the legislator and taken much of the initiative from the suitors.

It seems, therefore, that due to the latitude given the arbitrator, the sources do not enlarge upon the qualifications of witnesses under the law of procedure in the beginning of the Classical period. This is to be expected.

It is evident from explicit declarations found in the sources that witnesses were required in Classical Law.[14] At times, ten were required, as for confarreation.[15] At other times at least five witnesses were necessary for a transaction.[16]

Witnesses were used in *manumissio inter amicos* [17] as well as in other mancipations.[18] Witnesses were also requisite for wills. This rule applied not alone to wills *in pricinctu*, before the people,[19], but likewise to those *per aes et libram* and to praetorian wills. The procedure, moreover, necessitated the use of witnesses in the *litis contestatio.*

In Classical Law, furthermore, qualifications of witnesses are definitely indicated. They are based upon the status of persons in the Roman family. They included also citizenship, age, health and perception. Fundamentally they do not differ radically from the generic traits recognized in law as affecting the probative value of testimony.

Generic Traits Affecting Probative Value

1. Citizenship

In Classical Law citizenship was a decisive test in determining the extent of a person's private rights. The law applied exclusively to citizens. It was civil law in the literal meaning of the word. Consequently, the specifically Roman Law, which was known as the *jus civile,* was a law only for Roman citizens.

The *Institutes* of Gaius lay down the rule that a praetorian will is

[14] G. 2, 109; *cf. Inst.,* II, 11 pr.

[15] G. 1, 112.

[16] G. 1, 113; G. 1, 119; G. 1, 120; G. 2, 104; G. 3, 174.

[17] G. 2, 101; *cf. Inst.,* II, 10, 1.

[18] G. 1, 41.

[19] G. 2, 101; *cf. Inst.,* II, 10, 1.

invalid unless it is attested by the seals of seven witnesses.[20] More specifically, Gaius expresses the rule that witnesses for wills be Roman citizens.

There were certain species of property (*res mancipi*) which could not be sold effectually unless a formal proceeding called *mancipatio* was observed. Bearing this practice of *mancipatio* in mind, if the witnesses to the ceremony were not Roman citizens the deal was invalid.[21]

In early Roman Law a woman being married passed out of her own agnatic family into that of her husband. The person and the property of a woman came into the control of her husband (*in manum viri*) by ceremonies specially designed and used for the purpose of constituting the legal obligations of marriage. Among others was the *coemptio* or joint purchase with at least five citizens present, besides the balance holder (*libripens*) to witness it.[22] Finally, writing about the modes by which Latin freedmen became Roman citizens, Gaius states the qualification of citizenship for witnesses attesting the ceremony.[23]

2. Paterfamilias

The rule qualifying a Roman citizen to testify in the transactions enumerated and according to the tests brought forward to substantiate it, apply likewise to the *paterfamilias*. It is not thought feasible or necessary to repeat either.

In the Roman family the *paterfamilias* could not be a witness to the will of his *filiusfamilias*. Conversely, a *filiusfamilias* was excluded from being a witness to the will of his *paterfamilias*. The reason for this rule was that they were relations.[24]

3. Age

Gaius contains no criteria for estimating the testimony of the aged.

[20] G. 2, 119; *cf. Inst.*, II, 7, 4.
[21] G. 1, 119.
[22] G. 1, 113.
[23] G. 1, 29; *cf. Ulp.*, III, 3.
[24] G. 2, 105; G. 2, 106; *cf. Inst.*, II, 10, 9.

Classical Law divides the age of man into infancy, childhood (*impuberes*), puberty, and majority. Gaius lays down the rule that those who have not arrived at the age of puberty are rendered incapable of testifying.

Illustrative of this principle is the ceremony of adoption already described.[25] It was a rule that no child could witness a will.[26]

In coemption, all five witnesses had to be "above the age of puberty, besides the balance holder." [27]

4. Mental Health

In Classical Law, lunacy was considered either a temporary or a perpetual illness.[28] Persons of unsound mind were incapacitated from all juristic acts. The reason for this has been assigned by Gaius: "Furiosus nullum negotium gerere potest, quia non intellegit quid. agit." [29] Consequently, they could also testify.

5. Deaf and Dumb

Roman Classical Law took two testimonial elements into consideration. Recognizing that perception was of importance in testimony, it considered deafness and dumbness. Blindness was so apparently an element of the perceptive process that it was scarcely considered. Possessing no elaborate psychology making distinctions between illusions of sight and hearing, hallucinations and illusions, with which modern psychological research is still concerned, Roman Classical Law specified that deafness and dumbness affected testimony.

Deaf and dumb persons could neither make, nor be witnesses to a mancipatory will.[30]

[25] G. 1, 119.

[26] G. 2, 104.

[27] G. 1, 113.

[28] F. V., 183a; F. V., 238[2].

[29] G. 3, 106; *cf. Inst.*, III, 19, 8; G. 3, 109; *Inst.*, III, 19, 10.

[30] *Cf.* G. 1, 119.

Article 3. Witnesses in Justinian Law

In the last system of Roman civil procedure, the Extraordinary, the plaintiff's claim or bill of complaint was called a *libellus conventionis,* which was answered by a *libellum contradictionis.* The procedure of this period was more flexible than it was in Classical Law. The functions of the judges were included in those of the magistrate.[81]

Observing the subject of witnesses in the civil rather than the criminal law of this period (*ex legitimis et civilibus causis*) one perceives that although the system is less rigid than the Classical, the judges in the Extraordinary period did not possess the freedom to establish the value of evidence which was a characteristic of the preceding system. Judges were officials of a bureaucratic government which bound them by new rules and threatened them with penalties if they disobeyed. Cases were conducted by advocates (*oratores, patroni*). The litigants were present but assumed no formal part in the proceedings. It was a usual, but not a universal practice, to begin with speeches of the respective advocates. The evidence was then submitted. After discussion with the judge, the sentence of judgment was passed.

In Justinian Law documentary evidence was preferred to oral testimony.[82] Even before the hearing, the defendant could call on the plaintiff to exhibit the documents on which he based his claim. It appears that with the consent of the judge he could call for the plaintiff's accounts although the latter was not going to submit them. There was no right the other way.[83] Irrelevant facts were excluded.[84] Opinion evidence was admissible in exceptional cases, as for the comparison of writing.[85] Hearsay testimony, although admissible, was recognized as less weighty than direct evidence.[86] Under the influence of Christianity the oath was of great importance. Interrogations

[81] *Inst.*, IV, 5: "Extra ordinem jus dicitur qualia sunt hodie omnia judicia."

[82] D. XXII, 3, 10: "Census et monumenta publica *potiora* testibus esse, senatus censuit." *Cf.* Paulus, *Sent.*, V, 15, 4; *Cod.*, IV, 20, 1.

[83] *Cod.*, II, 1, 8.

[84] *Cod.*, IV, 19, 10, 17 and 22.

[85] *Cod.*, IV, 21, 1; *Nov.* 49, 2, 1 and 2.

[86] D. XXII, 3, 28.

and the judicial confession were also generalized and likewise assumed importance.

Proof by witnesses in Justinian Law is expounded clearly and in detail by Bethmann-Hollweg [37] who followed the legislative sources. The authors of manuals and recent special studies [38] have clarified the general rules and retraced the most important rules. For this reason a complete treatment of testimony in Justinian civil law is not given. A summary of the rules pertaining to the qualifications of witnesses in civil causes follows.

Some persons were absolutely disqualified from giving testimony. Under this classification were: (a) Infants and those bordering on infancy. Those who were not twenty years of age were disqualified to testify in *criminal matters.*[39] (b) Insane persons.[40] (c) Slaves.[41] (d) Infamous persons who had been declared such or were infamous by reason of their profession.[42]

Other persons, for reasons founded on equity, suffered relative incapacity to testify. Persons were disqualified from giving testimony due to the direct interest which they were presumed to have in the three following circumstances. First, sellers of goods and accomplices in the commission of delicts were incapacitated to testify.[43] Secondly, fathers could not testify on behalf of or against their sons.[44] Thirdly, witnesses were excluded from testimony on account of their enmity in civil as well as in criminal trials. If anyone should say that a witness who was about to provide testimony was hostile to him, and

[37] *Cf.* Bethmann-Hollweg, *Der Civilprozess des gemeinen Rechts in geschichtlicher Entwickelung* (Bonn, 1864-70), III, 272-289.

[38] *Cf.* Wenger, Leopold, *Institutionen Des Römischen Zivilprozessrechts* (München, 1925), 282-290; Fresquet, R. De, *Traité Élementaire De Droit Romain* (Paris, n. d.), II, 364, 365; Buckland, W. W., *A Text-Book of Roman Law from Augustus to Justinian* (Cambridge, 1932), 637; Colinet, Paul, *La Procédure Par Libelle* (Paris, 1934), II, 364, 365.

[39] *Cf.* D. XXII, 5, 20.

[40] *Inst.*, III, 19, 8.

[41] D. XXII, 5, 7; *Cod.*, IX, 41, 1.

[42] D. XXII, 5, 21, 1; *cf.* D. XXII, 5, 13.

[43] *Cod.*, IV, 20, 11.

[44] D. XXII, 5, 9.

he proved that at the very time that the witness was called upon to testify he was involved in criminal proceedings, the hostile witness, since the judge can admit a person to be a witness as suspect who *formerly* had an action against the accused, shall not be admitted to testify until the criminal case has been settled. When the witness is said to be hostile for some other reason, for instance, because he has been owed a sum of money, his testimony shall be taken, but it will not be available until the litigation between the witness and the party shall have been adjusted.[45]

[45] *Nov.* XC, 7. *Cf.* D. L, 16, 103.

CHAPTER II

TESTIMONY FROM THE APOSTOLIC AGE TO THE COUNCIL OF CHALCEDON

THE documents of ecclesiastical writers up to the Fourth General Council contain few direct references to the qualifications of witnesses. Allusions to a psychological evaluation of testimony during this period are indirect. Oral and documentary evidence together with an examination of the persons involved in litigation were the principal means of procuring evidence. Presumptions, visual inspection and the oath were not disregarded. Evidence presented to destroy or to weaken the effect of testimony was admissible.

ARTICLE 1. EPISTLES OF ST. PAUL

During the time of the Apostles, utterances of witnesses had importance. St. Paul reminded Timothy that two or three witnesses were required to make an accusation against a priest.[1] Notoriety was considered by the Apostle as a means of proof. It required no further evidence. This is evinced in the judgment of the incestuous man.[2]

Mindful of the injunction of the Apostle, the Christians of the primitive Church, cherishing truth, seldom swore oaths in courts of law. The Epistle to the Hebrews, nevertheless, permitted an oath to be taken.[3] What qualifications of witnesses in the primitive Church were required, cannot be stated with exactness. How extensive the Hebraic influence was upon the early documents of the Church is not determined.[4]

[1] 1 Tim. v, 19.

[2] 1 Cor. v, 1-9.

[3] Hebr. vi, 16.

[4] Among the Jews witnesses had to comply with four requirements: (1) Two had to testify to the same fact. The witnesses were required to be (2) Israelites; (3) men more than thirteen years of age who were not deaf, lunatic, and according to the better opinion, neither deaf nor blind. (4) A *wicked* man could not testify. *Cf. The Jewish Encylopedia,* art. "Evidence," V, 277-279.

Article 2. Provincial Councils Up to That of Constantinople

The acts of particular synods and of provincial councils which were held prior to the provincial synod of Constantinople (ca. 335) indicate that verbal and documentary evidence were admitted. Restricting investigation to the councils of this period which are authentic, one discovers few explicit references to witnesses from the Council of Jerusalem (ca. 51),[5] to the Synod of Constantinople (ca. 335). The qualifications of witnesses were not explicitly enumerated. The bishops who presided over these councils were concerned with the struggles being waged between the defenders of orthodoxy and the supporters of heresies. They exercised that arbitrative and judicial authority which is coeval with the Church in two principal ways, in disciplinary matters and in the determination of heresy,[6] the proponents of which were condemned.[7] Those accused of heresy had a

[5] Act. XV, 4-29; XXI, 25; Hefele-Leclercq, *Histoire des Conciles* (Paris, 1907-1930), I, 126; *Cod.*, I, 11.

[6] The repetition of baptism given by heretics was discussed at the (a) First Synod of Carthage. This was held ca. 198. *Cf. HL*, I, 154. Harduin and Mansi claim it was held ca. 218. The question was discussed at this council. *Cf. Cyprianus, Ep.*, LXXI, 4; *HL*, I, 154; *Hrd.*, I, Judex; *Msi.*, I, 733—*MPL.*, IV, 408; *C. Th.*, XVI, 6. (b) Synod of Iconia (ca. 230). *Cf. Cyprianus, Ep.*, LXXV, 7 and 19; Eusebius, *H.E.*, VII, 7; *HL*, I, 160; *Hrd.*, V, Judex; *Msi.*, I, 909 sqq. (c) Synod of Synadia (ca. 230). *Cf.* Eusebius, *H.E.*, VII, 7, 5; *HL*, I, 161; *Hrd.*, I, Judex; *Msi.*, I, 921.

[7] The heresy of Origen was denounced in the Synod of Alexandria (ca. 231). *Cf. Hieronimus in Rufinium*, II, 22; *Rufinus, Apol.*, II, 20; *HL*, I, 158; *Hrd.*, I, Judex; *Msi.*, I, 753. Of a general nature are the four provincial synods which concerned the *lapsi*, *viz.*, the First Synod of Carthage (ca. 251), the Synod of Rome (October, ca. 251), the Synod of Antioch (ca. 252), and the Synod of Carthage (15 May, ca. 252). Likewise, of a general nature were the three synods, *viz.*, the Third Synod of Carthage (ca. 253), which considered infant baptism, and the two Synods of Carthage, which considered heretical baptism (*i. e.*, ca. 256, the latter on 1 September, *cf. Hrd.*, I, 159; *Msi.*, I, 951; *HL*, I, 177, 1114). The Synod of Arsinoitisa (ca. 255) condemned the doctrine of the millennium. *Cf.* Dionysius, in Eusebius, *H.E.*, VII, 24, 6. Paulus Samosatenus was condemned at the Third Synod of Antioch (ca. 268) for his heresy. *Cf.* Eusebius, *H.E.*, VII, 30, 1; *Hrd.*, I, 195; *HL*, I, 199, 205. The Synod of Alexandria (ca. 306) condemned one Peter, an Egyptian Bishop for having im-

right to defend themselves. Mere accusation of teaching heresy was not sufficient proof for condemnation.[8] Documentary evidence was sometimes sufficient to effect a condemnation.[9] Although there was dependence upon witnesses, the early councils referred to do not specify the criteria which they should possess.

Circumstantial evidence was sometimes accepted as positive proof which was preferable to witnesses. This viewpoint is illustrated in the trials of St. Athanasius the Great, who is called "the Father of scientific theology."[10] Due to calumnies against him, St. Athanasius was repeatedly exiled.[11] A fourth and virulent charge of murder and of magic was made against him. The Miletians went about horrifying people by showing them a wooden box containing a black and withered hand of a dead man. They said that it was the hand of Arsenius, Bishop of Hypsele. Athanasius was accused of poisoning him and of using his remains for magical incantations. The Emperor Constan-

molated to idols. *Cf.* St. Athanasius, *Apologium contra Arianos*, LIX, *M.P.G.*, 25, 356; *HL*, I, 211; *Hrd.*, I, Judex; *Msi.*, II, 407. Synods which considered crimes, and those on behalf of Arius, although held, are of a general nature from the aspect of evidence.

[8] The Synod of Bastrenus (ca. 244) did not condemn Bishop Perillus of that city who was accused of heresy. *Cf.* Hieronimus, *De Viris Illustribus*, LX; *HL*, I, 162; *Hrd.*, V, 1495; *Msi.*, I, 787. Likewise there was no condemnation in the Synod of Arabia (ca. 249). *Cf.* Eusebius, *H.E.*, VI, 37; *HL*, I, 164; *Hrd.*, V, 1495; *Msi.*, I, 789; the Synod of Rome under Melchiadus (ca. 313) absolved Cecilionus. *Cf.* Augustinus, *Breviculus coll. cum Donatistis*, III, 12; *M.P.L.*, 43, 537; *Hrd.*, I, Judex; *Msi.*, II, 433.

[9] In the Fourth Synod of Carthage which Mansi refers to as the Second Synod of Africa, both Basilides and Marial were condemned on the strength of documentary evidence in the form of letters attesting their idolatry. *Cf.* *Cyprianus Ep.*, LXVII, 1, 6; *HL*, I, 172; *Hrd.*, I, 149; *Msi.* I, 905; *M.P.L.*, IV, 399.

[10] For his election, *cf.* The Synod of Alexandria (ca. 328) in *HL*, I, 636, 7; *Msi.*, II, 1085; Athanasius, *Apolog. c. Arianos*, 6—*M.P.G.*, 25, 260; *HL*, I, 638, 1.

[11] For the condemnation of St. Athanasius at Antioch (ca. 330) *cf.* Socrates, Scholasticus, *The Ecclesiastical History of Socrates* (London, 1853), I, 24—*M.P.G.*, 67, 144; Theodoret, *H.E.*, I, 20—*M.P.G.*, 25, 700; *HL*, I, 644; *Msi.*, II, 1085. For another condemnation at the Synod of Tyre (ca. 335) *cf. HL*, I, 656; *Msi.*, II, 1123; *Hrd.*, I, 539. For the condemnation at the Synod of Constantinople (ca. 335) *cf. HL*, I, 667; *Msi.*, II, 1167.

tine presided at a council summoned at Tyre (335). Eusebius of Caesarea was one of the judges. Athanasius was accused of the murder of Arsenius. The accusation was dissipated when Arsenius was produced in the council alive.[12]

Another charge against St. Athanasius, that he had destroyed a church, burned its books and broken a chalice in a hamlet named "The Peace of the Secontaruri" in the Mareotis was likewise refuted. It was proved by witnesses that the house was not a church, that Ischyras, allegedly in charge of it, was not a presbyter, and that no communion could have been given on the designated day which was neither a Saturday, a Sunday, or a festival day. Moreover, Ischyras made a judicial confession that he had been compelled to his criminal false-witness by the violence of three Miletian bishops.[13]

Besides witnesses and circumstantial evidence, presumptions pertaining to the mental state of those accused of professing heresy were employed. The production of witnesses against the Montanist or Cataphrygian heresy was difficult. The Montanists, wrote Eusebius in his *Ecclesiastical History*, had been excommunicated.[14] Their heresy was rejected by reason of presumptions rather than direct evidence.

Before turning to a consideration of the first Four General Councils from the aspect of testimony, one observes that Pope Felix II (d. 365) directly stated negative qualifications of witnesses. He expressed the rule that anyone who neglected the Christian religion could neither testify nor accuse.[15] The following were incompetent

[12] Socrates, *H.E.*, I, 24; Sozomen, *A History of the Church in Nine Books from A. D. 344 to A. D. 440* (London, 1846), II, 25. Eusebius, probably due to shame, does not record the incident.

[13] Letter of Ischyras to Athanasius, *Apol. c. Arian*, sec. 64. *Cf.* Farrar, *Lives of the Fathers, Sketches of Church History in Biography* (Edinburgh, 1889), I, 503-505.

[14] Eusebius, *H.E.*, V, 16; *cf. HL*, I, 128; *Msi.*, I, 724; *C. Th.*, XVI, 5, 34. For a synod held at Auchiale in France on the river Noire, *cf. HL*, I, 128. It is called Auchialus in *HL*, I, 24.

[15] Epistola I., Felicis Papae II (ca. 365), IX—*Msi.*, III, 411: "Ut testificandi, vel accusandi licentia denegetur his qui Christianae religionis et nominis dignitatem, et suae legis vel sui propositi normam, aut regulariter prohibiti, neglexerint."

to testify against a religious Christian, however humble or servile his condition be:

> Haeretici, a quibus nimium opprimimur, excommunicatique, homicidae, malefici, fures, sacrilegi, raptores, venefici, adulteri, et qui raptum fecerint, vel falsum testimonium dixerint, seu qui ad sortilegos magnosque concurrerunt, nullatenus ad accusationem vel ad testimonium erunt admittendi.[16]

Besides the aforementioned tests for judging witnesses, Pope Damascus I (ca. 304) required that witnesses who testified against bishops were to be without the stigma of infamy, and free from both suspicion and manifest fault. The witnesses were also to be instructed in the true faith.[17]

Article 3. First Four General Councils

The canons of the first Four General Councils do not directly consider the production or the qualifications of witnesses. The few canons which indirectly pertain to the qualifications of witnesses are understood from a comparison with other councils and historical incidents. The result of investigation is, consequently, of a negative character.

1. Canon 9 of the Council of Nicaea required an examination of the candidates for priesthood to be made.[18] For the nature of the examination one turns to the Council of Hippo (ca. 298) which decreed that no one was to be ordained unless approved by both the examination of the bishop and the testimony of the people.[19]

[16] Epistola I., Felicis Papae II (ca. 365), XV—*Msi.* III, 412.

[17] Epistola IV., Damasi Papae I (ca. 384), III—*Msi.*, III, 432.

[18] The Council was held in the summer of A.D. 325. *Cf. HL,* I, 326-332. The version of Dionysius Exiguus reads: "Si qui presbyteri sine examine sunt provecti, vel cum discuterentur, peccata sua, et homines contra canones commoti, manus confessis imponere tentaverunt; tales regula non admittit; quia quod irreprehensibile est, catholica defendit Ecclesia." *Cf. Hrd.,* I, 327; *Msi.,* II, 984, 985; *HL,* I, 587, 588; Lauchert, *Die Kanones Der Wichtigsten Altkirchlichen Concilien nebst Den Apostolischen Kanones* (Freiburg, 1896), 39, 40.

[19] *Cf.* Statutum 20—*Msi.,* II, 922: "Ut nullus ordinetur, nisi probatus vel

2. Canon 6 of the Council of Constantinople (May, 381), made regulations concerning charges brought against orthodox bishops.[20] The canon had the purpose of preventing persons from casting slurs on the reputations of bishops and thus upsetting the good order of churches administered by orthodox prelates.[21] In complaints involving personal injury, accusers were not to be questioned regarding their antecedents and their religious persuasion.[22] Regarding charges of an ecclesiastical nature, Canon 6 stated this testimonial qualification of witnesses. The status of a person who accuses was a test for estimating what he says. Hence it was that some persons, such as heretics, or those who professed the right faith but had fallen into schism in opposition to the canonical bishops, or those clerics who had not cleared themselves of a previous excommunication or accusation of a fault, were incompetent to testify.[23]

3. The Council of Ephesus, convoked by Theodosius II (d. 450), does not appear to contain anything pertaining to testimony.

4. Turning to the Council of Chalcedon, convoked by the Emperor Marcian (ca. 451),[24] it is observed that Canon 18 of this Coun-

episcoporum examine, vel populi testimonio." The ones who testified were to be from neighboring places. *Cf.* also Statutum 7—*Msi.*, III, 920.

[20] *Hrd.*, I, 811; *Msi.*, III, 559, 562, 563; Lauchert, *Die Kanones Der Wichtigsten Altkirchlichen Concilien nebst Den Apostolischen Kanones*, 85, 86.

[21] The atmosphere toward ecclesiastical authority about that time was one of suspicion. Bishops had to be circumspect as accusers were ready to strike at a weak point in their character or conduct. *Cf.* St. John Chrysostom, *Johannis Chrysostomi de Sacerdotio Libri Sex Graece et Latine* (Erhardus, 1725), III, 14.

[22] *Cf.* Eusebius, *H.E.*, I, 9; X, 5. The Council of Hippo made a rule that one whose conduct was blameworthy could not accuse a bishop unless he spoke on behalf of his own cause and not for ecclesiastical reasons. *Cf.* Statuta Concilii Hipponiensis (ca. 393), VI—*Msi.*, III, 920: ". . .; nisi ad causam suam dicendam. . . ."

[23] The provisions of Canon 6 of the Council of Constantinople are not dissimiliar to those of the Council of Carthage held under Bishop Genthilus (*i.e.*, ca. 389, 390). *Cf.* Caput 6, *Msi.* III, 694: "Si criminosus est non admittatur, ut accuset."

[24] Bright, William, *Canons of the First Four General Councils of Nicaea, Constantinople, Ephesus and Chalcedon with Notes* (Oxford, 2 ed., 1892), 140-144.

cil orders the deposition of clerics or monks who plot against their bishop or brother-clerics.[25]

The background of this canon suggests the case of Ibas, Bishop of Edessa. Having been a Nestorian, he reëntered the Church with Cyril of Antioch. Ibas was accused by four of his priests of Nestorianism, of simony and of general maladministration. Five witnesses joined the four accusers. Documentary and testimonial evidence were produced.[26] The evidence that Ibas had used blasphemous speech was disproved by the signed testimony of about sixty clerics of Edessa. These witnesses, whom the accusers themselves had said were present when the alleged blasphemy was uttered, disproved the malicious charges against the bishop. Besides this testimony, Ibas added a public confession of his faith. Notaries provided him with the interpretation of the disputed words *Deo amantissum* which he had given previously. Finally, Ibas acquainted the judges at Berytus with the information that [27] Maras, one of the more active accusers, had been excommunicated by an archdeacon of Ibas for insulting a presbyter.[28] The disqualification of interest or bias, however, is mentioned directly in neither the trial of Ibas nor in the Council of Chalcedon.[29]

[25] *Msi.,* VII, 378; Lauchert, *Die Kanones Der Wichtigsten Altkirchlichen Concilien nebst Den Apostolischen Kanones,* 93, 94.

[26] Actio Decima Chalcedonensis Concilii (ca. 451)—*Msi.,* VII, 206, 207.

[27] Actio Decima Chalcedonensis Concilii (ca. 451)—*Msi.,* VII, 212.

[28] Actio Decima Chalcedonensis Concilii (ca. 451)—*Msi.,* VII, 231, 232.

[29] The purpose of Canon 21 of the Council of Chalcedon was to prevent indiscriminate accusations against bishops; it required that a scrutiny of the reputations of accusers be made before their depositions were to be accepted. *Cf. Msi.,* VII, 379; Lauchert, *Die Kanones Der Wichtigsten Altkirchlichen Concilien nebst Den Apostolischen Kanones,* 94. Duchesne discovered a rule guarding bishops from the suspicion of biased persons in the Council of Toledo (636). *Cf.* Duchesne, L., *Le Liber Pontificalis* (Paris, 1886), I, 153, note 2.

CHAPTER III

INFLUENCE OF GERMANIC TESTIMONY ON CANON LAW

NOTHING is isolated in the history of a legal institution in the Occident. This is particularly true concerning the institutions of the Middle Ages. Scarcely any of them may be understood unless Teutonic customs be considered along with Roman classical antiquity.

From the fifth to the twelfth century there was little known about the genius of the lawmakers of Rome in the northern parts of what is now called Modern Europe. The customs of semi-barbarous peoples flourished in place of them. In a Germanic court, the litigants debated the case. Assertion was answered by formal negation. A trial of a question of fact as understood in modern courts of law was unknown. Germanic justice was summary and vindictive. The oath concerned the justice of the claim or of the defense as a whole rather than a decision based on the truth of specific facts.[1]

There emerged out of this epoch of seven centuries a species of the probative process which was incorporated into the common law of the Church. The title "*canonica purgatio*" is found in the Decretals.[2] The compurgation that influenced ecclesiastical legislation was of Germanic origin. As exemplified in the Code of Canon Law, it is a form of evidence compounded of the Germanic mode of proof called compurgation which is infused with invigorating principles adopted from the Roman concept of the oath. This element is firmly lodged in the matrimonial process. It has been adopted by the Church as an essential part of the testimonial proof of the non-consummation of a marriage in non-evident cases.[3]

The juridical institution of compurgation was adapted by the Church to the proof of both criminal and matrimonial causes. The

[1] *Cf.* Lingard, John, *Antiquities of the Anglo-Saxon Church* (Philadelphia, 1841), 185; *English Historical Review*, VIII (1893), 257.

[2] C. 1, X, *de purgatione canonica*, V, 34.

[3] Canon 1975, § 2; *cf.* C. 2, XXXIII, q. 1; c. 5, 7, X, *de frigidis, et maleficiatis et impotentia coeundi*, IV, 15.

present Code no longer puts it to use in criminal causes. The present legislation, nevertheless, retains the confirmatory oaths of seven witnesses as an integral part of the evidence required in causes involving impotence and non-consummation of a marriage. Before considering the Germanic testimony called compurgation and indicating how and when it was adapted into Canon Law, it will not be amiss to clarify what is meant by the Germanic element of compurgation.

Article 1. Meaning of Compurgation

The Decretals, the Decretalists, the Compilations and the old canonists distinguished vulgar (*purgatio vulgaris*) from canonical purgation (*purgatio canonica*).[4] The former, and especially ordeals,[5] were an abuse of rather than a contribution to the law of evidence.

A. Purgatio Vulgaris

The Germanic legal procedure insisted that a litigant prove his claim by a personal combat, by an ordeal, or by means of an oath with the aid of oath-helpers.[6] If a person did not wish to swear such an oath which is called compurgation, or could not secure the necessary number of compurgators who were neither strangers nor rejected because of their mendacious character, the ordeal was resorted to as subsidiary. Slaves, perjurers, poisoners and magicians were usually subjected to the ordeal.[7]

[4] C. 1, X, *de purgatione canonica,* V, 34; c. 8, *De Purgatione Canonica,* XXIX, I Comp.; cc. 1, 2, *De Purgatione Canonica,* XXX, I Comp.; Hostiensis, *Summa Aurea* (Lugduni, 1568), V, *De Purgatione Canonica,* 1.

[5] *Zeitschrift Der Savigny-Stiftung Für Rechtsgeschichte,* XXVIII, 236; Kirsch, "Ordeals," *The Catholic Encyclopedia,* XI, 276, 278. This contains a summary of conciliar legislation taken from Hefele. *Cf.* Reiffenstuel, Anacletus, *Ius Canonicum Universum* (Romae, 1838), t. XXXIV, l. V, n. 3; *The Continental Legal History Series,* VII, *A History of Continental Civil Procedure* (Boston, 1927), 155; c. (4), C. III, q. 2: ". . . exordio ultore gladio fereatur." For canonical teaching on confessions obtained through tortures, *cf.* Reiffenstuel, lib. II, tit. XVIII, nn. 137, 138; lib. II, tit. XX, n. 251.

[6] *Rerum Gallicarum et Franciscarum Scriptores* (H. Welter, Paris, 1738-1904), XIV, Introd. XXVII, n. 4.

[7] Meile, Joseph, *Die Beweislehre des Kanonischen Prozesses in Ihren Grundzügen Unter Beruchsichtigung Der Modernen Prozessrechtswissenschaft* (Paderborn, 1925), 8.

The judgment of God (*iudicium Dei*), which is said to be named after the Anglo-Saxon ordeal,[8] is found in the *Leges Burgundiorum*[9] and the *Lex Frisionum*.[10] The theory appears to have been that an All-Wise and an All-Powerful Being, solemnly invoked, would vindicate the innocent and avenge injustice.[11] An ordeal by fire was assigned to the accused who was constrained to either hold his hand over a fire or to carry a red-hot object in his bare hand.[12] In a plough-share ordeal[13] the accused was required to walk barefooted on red-hot plough-shares. Other ordeals were the water-ordeals in the process of which an object or objects were extracted from boiling water,[14] and the holding of a red-hot iron.[15] Prisoners, however, and necromancers were forbidden to undergo an examination by means of the burning iron.[16] Due to the influence of Christianity, the judgment of the cross (*iudicium crucis*) was sometimes employed.[17]

Besides these means of proof of innocence were also the bier-judgment by which the accused would touch the wounds of a murdered person. The observers would watch to see if the wounds bled. Sometimes lots were cast. At other times the accused, if a freeman, could avoid a one-sided ordeal by the duel or by a two-sided ordeal (*iudicium campi*). The unfit were replaced by substitutes (*campiones*). After jurisprudence had perfected the duel by numerous regulations, in the year 1301 limitations were put on it. Its use was restricted to capital cases and other means of evidence were pre-

[8] *Ibid.*

[9] These laws are commonly called *Gundobada* and *Papianus* by authors.

[10] *Lex Burgundiorum, M.G.H.*, Leges, III, 537; *Lex Frisionum, M.G.H.*, Leges, III, 6.

[11] Lea, Henry, *Superstition and Force* (Philadelphia, 1892), 25, 26.

[12] *Lex Ribuaria, M.G.H.*, Leges, V, 221, 222: "Quod si servus in igneum manum miserit, et lesam tullerit, dominus eius, sicut lex contenit, de furtu servi culpabilis iudicetur."

[13] *Lex Baiuwariorum, M.G.H.*, Leges, III, 486.

[14] *Lex Frisionum, M.G.H.*, Leges, III, 6; III, 8; XIV, 3; III, 9, for a water ordeal; *Lex Baiuwariorum, M.G.H.*, Leges, III, 485, for a *iudicium aquae.*

[15] *Lex Baiuwariorum, M.G.H.*, Leges, III, 486: *ferrum calidum. Cf. Lex Baiuwariorum, M.G.H.*, Leges, III, 475, 478; *ferrum candens.*

[16] *Lex Baiuwariorum, M.G.H.*, Leges, III, 475.

[17] *Lex Baiuwariorum, M.G.H.*, Leges, III, 474.

ferred. The Vehmic courts did away with auxiliary swearers. If the accused remained unscathed, this was accepted as conclusive proof of innocence. Failure in an ordeal was considered an infallible proof of guilt. Legal punishment followed.[18]

B. Purgatio Canonica

The least superstitious of the external sanctions surrounding the oath among the Germanic peoples was the rite of compurgation. It was proof of one's statement made under oath by the utterances of a group of friends, relatives or neighbors who also swore the same oath. It was from an ecclesiastical point of view canonical detection of the innocence of the accused.[19]

There is no formula extant in primitive codes of Germanic peoples embodying an oath of compurgation. The primitive laws were too chary of words in their skeleton codes to embody in them the formula usually employed for the oath of compurgation. It is assumed that at least in general outline there was little difference between the compurgation practiced by Teutonic tribes of remote and in later times.[20] In later times it is found in all the Germanic codes with the exception of the Visigoths who lived under Roman law.

Germanic trial procedure was summary in its process. It was arbitrarily decided that one of the litigants prove his case. After a preliminary judgment the litigant to whom proof was assigned attempted to purge himself with the aid of cojurors.

The cojurors were either eyewitnesses or auxiliary oath takers. The first class embraced those who were legally requested to be present at an event which was to take place or they were witnesses who chanced to be present at an occurrence which they were told to observe that they might later testify concerning it. It was regal jurisprudence which developed the evidence of eyewitnesses. Its development gradually opposed the abuses of the public law system.[21] Incidentally, it is the Salic law that mentions the accidental witnesses.

[18] *Cf.* Meile, *Die Beweislehre des Kanonischen Prozesses,* 89.

[19] Hostiensis, *op. cit.,* V, *De Purgatione Canonica* 1: ". . . Canonica purgatio est nocentis infamiae ecclesiasticae innocentiae canonice facta detectio."

[20] Lea, *Supersition and Force,* 58.

[21] *Cf. Meile, Die Beweislehre des Kanonischen Prozesses,* 9.

Besides eyewitnesses, there were also associate witnesses (*Erfahrungszeugen*). By reason of particular circumstances such as relationship or friendship they were presumed to possess a knowledge of long standing.

Qualified jurors were sometimes difficult to secure. Perjury was not infrequent. In such circumstances, the opposing party insisted on the rejection of the oath. An ordeal was resorted to for determination of guilt or innocence.[22] Compurgation, however, was allowed when the case appeared to favor greatly a litigant. Were he unable to procure the necessary number of compurgators, the litigant to whom the burden of proof was assigned was required to resort to an ordeal.[23]

The duty of becoming a compurgator was not to be undertaken lightly. It cannot be stated with exactness, however, that originally the selection of compurgators was left to the accused. Later, and certainly under the surveillance of the Church, a judge made the selection. A deficient number of compurgators was practically tantamount to a conviction.[24]

One must first of all keep clear in mind what was fundamental to the social life of the Germanic peoples. Each family was a unit. Every individual within a confederation was answerable to the general group as all in the group were responsible for each individual.[25]

Whenever an injury was done, the injured person called upon his kindred to aid him in compensating for the injury. The accused could, likewise, rally his kindred to resist an attack on him. He called upon and took some of his folks with him to court. It was usual for the kindred or friends of the accused to defend their relative or neighbor in court by means of their oaths.

Teutonic laws afford numerous illustrations of this procedure. The *Leges Alamannorum* give copious examples of it. The other Germanic laws contain the identical procedure. Seven to twelve witnesses usually sufficed, although the number was augmented. The

[22] Kirsch, *Ordeals*, 277.

[23] *The English Historical Review*, VIII (1893), 257-260; Lingard, *Antiquities*, 184.

[24] Hostiensis, *op. cit.*, V, *De Purgatione Canonica*, 7.

[25] *Cf.* Tacitus, *Germania* (Sidler's ed., Boston, 1893), XX, 21.

persons about to swear the oath are believed to have placed their hands together as a symbol of their trustworthiness. Having joined their hands the accused swore simultaneously with the compurgators.[26]

Turning to the *Leges Alamannorum,* it is observed that a large number of crimes were purged by compurgation. Among these may be mentioned murder. When the culprit denied such an allegation, he swore with a specified group of witnesses.[27] A woman whose child did not live eight days after its birth was cleared of the charge of murdering the child by compurgation with twelve witnesses.[28] For placing the corpse of a dead person in alien earth one was fined. He could deny the charge with twelve witnesses.[29] Twelve witnesses were employed when a person denied the charge that he had stabbed someone.[30] Legislation was stricter, however, for killing certain persons. The accusation of slaying a man of no particular station was purged with eleven witnesses;[31] whereas if one sent by the king into a province was slain the person who denied the murder had to provide twelve witnesses and twelve other witnesses were elected.[32] The charge of having neglected a mandate or sign given by the ruler of a province required five witnesses for a purgation.[33] Sometimes,

[26] The oath-takers were called *iuratores. Cf. Lex Alamannorum M.G.H.,* Leges, III, 59, 22; III, 128, 11; III, 131, 42; 133, 4.

[27] *Cf. Leges Alamannorum, M.G.H.,* Leges, III, 115, 1: "Si quis hominem occiderit et negare vorit, cum undecim nominatus iuret et alios tantos advocatos in arma sua sacramenta."

[28] *Leges Alamannorum, M.G.H.,* Leges, III, 160, 51: "Si qua mulier gravida fuerit et per factum alterius infans natu mortuus fuerit, aut si vivus natus fuerit et octo dies non vivit, cui imputatum fuerit 40 solidos solvat aut cum duodecim mediis electis iuret." *Cf. Leges Alamannorum, M.G.H.,* Leges, III, 72.

[29] *Leges Alamannorum, M.G.H.,* Leges III, 39, 14; III, 83, 8.

[30] *Leges Alamannorum, M.G.H.,* Leges, III, 35, 6; III, 35, 14.

[31] *Leges Alamannorum, M.G.H.,* Leges, III, 78, 6; *M.G.H.,* Leges, III, 78, 6, specifies the witnesses had to be named (*nominatus*).

[32] *Leges Alamannorum, M.G.H.,* Leges, III, 55, 2: "Si quis missum ducis infra provinciam occiderit, tripliciter eum solvat sicut lex habet. Si negare non fecisset, sicut lex . . . iuret cum duodecim nominatus et alios duodecim electos."

[33] *Leges Alamannorum, M.G.H.,* Leges, III, 54, 10. *Cf.* Du Cange, *Glossarium ad Scriptores et Infimae Latinitatis* (Ed. Nova, Parisiis, 1833), II, col. 1703, v. *dux.*

twenty-four, at other times, forty compurgators were required.[34] There were occasions when eighty witnesses provided by the accused or twenty-four selected ones were necessary for a compurgation.[35]

Theft from a church was purged by an oath of the accused who stood with his witnesses (*sacramentales*) before the altar in the presence of a priest.[36] Witnesses were required in cases involving the breaking of a betrothal agreement.[37]

In questions involving bequests of property, a definite number of witnesses who swore together was specified.[38] If the witnesses did not appear or a document was not found the natural heir swore with five oath-takers and "his own sixth hand" that his father neither made a will nor handed things over to another.[39] If a man wanted to bequeath something to the Church, six or seven witnesses were used and their names appended to the will which was drawn up before a priest, who put it upon the altar.[40]

The laws of the Barbarians were quite strict with reference to the moral qualifications of witnesses. Three or four witnesses could testify to homicide, theft or neglect, but they had to be of good repu-

[34] *Leges Alamannorum, M.G.H.*, Leges, III, 36, 15.

[35] *Leges Alamannorum, M.G.H.*, Leges, III, 37, 4. *Cf. M.G.H.*, Leges, III, 72, 16.

[36] *Leges Alamannorum, M.G.H.*, Leges, III, 133.

[37] *Leges Alamannorum, M.G.H.*, Leges III, 149: "Si quis filiam alienam desponsatam dimiserit et aliam duxerit, componat eam quod desponsavit et dimisit, cum 40 solidis et cum duodecim sacramentales iuret, cum quinque nominatos et septem advocatos, ut pro nullo vicio nec temptatam eam habuisset nec vitium in illa invenisset, sed amor de alia eum adduxit, ut illam dimisisset et aliam habuisset uxorem." *Cf. Leges Alamannorum, M.G.H.*, Leges, III, 62, 2.

[38] *Leges Alamannorum, M.G.H.*, Leges, III, 63, 5: "Si autem proximus mariti defuncti contradicere ipsam dotem ad illam mulierem voluerit quod lex non est, illa sequat cum sacramento cum nominatos quinque aut cum spata tracta pugna duorum. . . ."

[39] *Leges Alamannorum, M.G.H.*, Leges, III, 128, 11: "Si autem exinde nec carta nec testes apparuerint, tunc liceat illum heredem cum quinque iuratoribus electis et sua manu sexta per sacramento adfermare, quod pater ejus de praedictis rebus cartas neque traditiones non fecisset. Nam tamen si unum de istis apparuerit aut carta aut testes, sacramentum heres habere non potest."

[40] *Leges Alamannorum, M.G.H.*, Leges, III, 45; *cf. M.G.H.*, Leges, III, 46.

tation among the people, not swearers (*iuratores*), liars, nor acceptors of money for the purpose of speaking the truth. The judge took such things into consideration. One who lied a third time could not testify again.[41] There were occasions when twelve compurgators had to accompany the accused to a church where the oath was taken in the presence of the ruler of the province or his representative.[42] Reference is likewise made to an oath taken on one's breast.[43]

Other Germanic tribes had laws of a similar nature. The oath taken by compurgators is a Germanic legal institution. Without specifying the numerous examples of this, it may be noted that the *Lex Baiuwariorum*, among other laws, had one requiring that a person purge himself with twelve oath-helpers.[44] The *Lex Frisionum* required that a nobleman who denied the charge of murdering another nobleman should be purged of the accusation by eleven compurgators of like station. The number of compurgators varied in different regions inhabited by the Frisians.[45]

The *Lex Ribuaria* provides a long list of those required to purge the crimes alleged against them with the aid of compurgators. Specifically, if one denied slaying somebody in the service of the government (*in truste regia*), he swore with the aid of seventy-two witness.[46] Were a Ribuarian woman who was under forty years of age killed, the alleged crime was purged by a like number.[47] When a Ribuarian girl was killed, the accused of the murder swore with twelve witnesses.[48] Should a woman belonging to the court be attacked, or an ecclesiastical person be killed, thirty-six compurgators were needed.[49] Were a free (*ingenus*) Ribuarian killed by another

[41] *Leges Alamannorum, M.G.H.*, Leges, III, 59.

[42] *Leges Alamannorum, M.G.H.*, Leges, III, 53, 10.

[43] *Leges Alamannorum, M.G.H.*, Leges, III, 63, 9: ". . . iurare per pectus suum."

[44] *Lex Baiuwariorum, M.G.H.*, Leges III, 388, 48; for procedure in case of theft, *cf. Lex Baiuwariorum, M.G.H.*, Leges, III, 411, 2.

[45] *Lex Frisionum, M.G.H.*, Leges, III, 656, 657, 658.

[46] *Lex Ribuaria*, XI, 2, M.G.H., Leges, V ,216.

[47] *Lex Ribuaria*, XII, 1, *M.G.H.*, Leges, V, 216.

[48] *Lex Ribuaria*, XIII, *M.G.H.*, Leges, V, 217.

[49] *Lex Ribuaria*, XIV, *M.G.H.*, Leges, V, 217.

in similar condition, seventy were to aid in his vindication.[50] A man who denied that he had secretly burned a man by night was purged with seventy-two compurgators.[51] Had it been a serf who was charged with committing this crime, it was his master who purged him with six oath-takers.[52] Regarding a crime of theft purged by a serf, if he put his hand in fire and was burned, he was adjudged guilty of theft in spite of the previous testimony of his master.[53] The Ribuarian Laws contain numerous other laws pertaining to the compurgation of crimes.[54]

Article 2. Adaptation of Compurgation in Canon Law to Criminal Causes

Teutonic criminal procedure rested largely on negative proofs. Churchmen perceived the futility of attempting to vindicate an accused in accordance with such a procedure.[55] The Church was, consequently, compelled to tolerate abuses of the barbaric procedure for a time. During this period of the ordeal and compurgation, the barbarian would accept no other purgation of infamy. We necessarily find the cleric making his oath with three, five or seven of his colleagues.[56] Ultimately, however, through the influence of the Church, the burden of proof was thrown upon whomever made the accusation.

The influence of churchmen upon the Germanic law pertaining to

[50] *Lex Ribuaria,* XV, *M.G.H.,* Leges, V. 217. *Cf.* Du Cange, *Glossarium,* III, col. 1434, v. *ingenus.*

[51] *Lex Ribuaria,* XVII, 1, *M.G.H.,* Leges, V, 218.

[52] *Lex Ribuaria,* XVII, 2, *M.G.H.,* Leges, V, 218. The word *servus* was not used among the Germanic tribes as among the Romans. *Cf.* Du Cange, *Glossarium,* XI, col. 447-451, v. *servus.*

[53] *Lex Ribuaria,* XXX, *M.G.H.,* Leges, V, 221, 222.

[54] *Cf.* as examples: *Lex Ribuaria,* XVIII-XIX, *M.G.H.,* Leges, V, 218-220; *Lex Ribuaria,* XIV, 2, *M.G.H.,* Leges, V, 217.

[55] Engelmann-Millar, *The Continental Legal History Series,* VII, 57, 58.

[56] Hincmar Rhemensis, *Epis.* 34; *cf. M.P.L.,* 126, 255; Ivo Chartres, *Epist.,* 54, 206—*M.P.L.,* 162, 66; Van Espen, Z. B., *Jus Ecclesiasticum Universum* (Lugduni, 1778), pars III, t. VIII, c. IV, n. 43.

testimony cannot be stated with precision. If we look at the *Lex Baiuwariorum* some concept of this influence may be formed.[57] The bishops possessed discretionary power in their respective localities to mitigate the rigor of a sentence and to change the mode of proof. Nevertheless, it was quite natural that churchmen who administered the law of the land and who helped to shape ecclesiastical legislation be influenced by their environment. It was not, on the other hand, unusual that Germanic peoples would resent attempts to uproot immemorial customs and legal practices.[58]

It is an established fact that positions of trust were occupied by clerics under Christian emperors. Generally speaking, clerics were the sole leaders in the intellectual pursuits in the period following the debacle of the fifth and sixth centuries. Ecclesiastical judges, by reason of the Germanic principle of personality applied to laws,[59]

[57] The *Decreta Synodorum Bavaricarum:* "Si quis sacrilegium perpetraverit, si se iudiciaria lege expurgare volueret: si liber est, cum septuaginta duobus iudicium facere, si servus, super duodecim ferventes vomeres incendere aut calidum ferrum portare debet; si tamen hoc ex clementia episcopi permissum fuerit."—*Lex Baiuwariorum, M.G.H.*, Leges, III, 486.

[58] Four remote causes may be assigned for the inclusion of Germanic testimony in the *Decretum Gratiani* and the Decretals: (1) The fall of Rome and the consequent departure from Western Europe of the strength and military cunning of Rome. *Cf.* Gibbon, Edward, *The History of the Decline and Fall of the Roman Empire* (ed. by Dr. William Smith, New York, 1880), III, 36, 598-643, esp. 602-605; 654-656. (2) Organization of the Church for the civilization of the Western World. (3) Ascendency of Germanic customs. Germanic peoples supplied the vitalizing force liberating Roman law in Italy from the Byzantine manner. *Cf. M.G.H., Auct. Antiquiss.*, V, Pars Prior: Iordantis Romana et Getica, 94: "Gothi . . . usque sui iuri tenere." *Cf. Lex Ribuaria, M.G.H.*, Leges XXI, 3: "In iudicio interpellatus, sicut lex loci continet ubi natus fuit, respondeat." *Lex Ribuaria, M.G.H.*, Leges, XXXI, 4: "Quod si damus fuerit, secundum legem propriam, non secundum ribuariam damnum sustineat." For an analysis of Barbarian codes tracing the laws of personality, *cf. Institut de Grande Academie des Inscriptions et Belles-Lettres* (Paris, 1886-1891), XXXII, 311 sqq.; Vinogradoff, Paul, *Roman Law in Medieval Europe* (2 ed., Oxford, 1929), 15, 16. (4) Germanic tribal unit. The clergy, considered a quasi-family unit, forbidden to resort to the duel to compose their differences, were subjected to compurgation. *Cf.* Lea, *Superstition and Force*, 35.

[59] The Code of Theodotius II, the Younger, became a provincial law in the West. The private lives of Roman provincials were regulated by it. *Cf.*

administered Roman law to the clergy and Barbaro-Roman and Germanic law to the Germanic and Teutonic peoples.[60] In the administration of criminal procedure, at a time when churchmen were the principal dispensers of the law, due to the principle of personality laws, the same judges administered Canon Law and civil law. They applied Germanic law to the civilian; they applied Roman-Canon Law to the cleric and the *exempti.* In administrating personality laws, the clergy, giving voice to Roman ideals, embodied the process of compurgation into Canon Law. In the time of Gratian, as will be pointed out, compurgation was a common means employed for the vindication of the clergy suspected of crime.[61]

What is of importance from a legal and canonical point of view is that the affirmatory oath of Germanic compurgation was changed, due to the influence of the Church, into an oath of credibility. Compurgators swore that they believed the person defamed had sworn the truth.[62] In other words, the Church insisted that an oath of mere credibility was no proof of guilt or of innocence in itself. It was relegated to the place where it rightfully belongs. It became and has remained confirmatory or adminicular.

It is a matter of conjecture when the changed occurred. Gratian states that compurgation was required of clerics in the Council of Agatha (A. D. 506) when legitimate accusers could not prove the

Theiner, Augustinus, *Disquisitiones Criticae* (Romae, 1836), 222. Union of Church and State, a fundamental principle of Roman law, was the active agent in the legislation of Christian Emperors who, after the conversion of Constantine, perceived in the Church a powerful auxiliary to their own power. *Cf.* Gosselin, M., *Power of the Popes in the Middle Ages* (Translated by Matthew Kelley, London, 1853), II, 36.

[60] *Cf.* Gibbon, *The History of the Decline and Fall of the Roman Empire,* IV, 60-62, for privileges of Romans in Gaul.

[61] Schmalzgrueber, Franciscus, *Jus Ecclesiasticum* (Romae, 1845), pars III, tit. 24, nn. 13, 14. When positive evidence did not favor the accused, he was required to swear on the gospels or relics of a saint that the imputation was false. *Cf.* Duchesne, *Liber Pontificals,* I, 212, 232, 260, 261; II, 7; *Lex Frisionum, M.G.H.,* Leges, III, 666, which ordered theft to be purged by an oath taken on the relics of saints.

[62] Hostiensis, *op. cit.,* V, *De Purgatione Canonica,* 3. Note 3 in Rub. is omitted.

alleged crime of a priest.[63] A suspected bishop in kindred circumstances was required by the Council of Illerdia (A. D. 524) to undergo compurgation.[64] The researches of Charles Sebastian Berardi, however, have cast doubt on the authenticity of the second of these canons. Berardi was convinced that it was probably fabricated by Buchard of Worms who had used the Frankish capitularies of the first half of the ninth century.[65]

Granting that the second of these canons is of doubtful authenticity, one may not, nevertheless, unqualifiedly state that churchmen made no use of compurgation before the sixth century. St. Gregory of Tours (A. D. 539-595) in his *History of the Franks,* referred to the purgation of Queen Fredegundis. Three bishops, together with three hundred nobles, participated in that rite of compurgation in a synod composed of bishops.[66] The vindication of the Queen would naturally give impetus to the institution of compurgation. The Frankish capitularies gave at least a quasi-ecclesiastical sanction to the rite. After the ninth century, there appears to be no doubt about the universal acceptance of the rite of compurgation into the canons of the Church.

In the time of Gratian compurgation was solidly established in Canon Law. It was the prevalent mode of clearing a cleric *infamatus de delicto.*[67] It is now also part of a comparatively new process, the procedure for the dissolution of marriage on account of nullity. The historical evolution of compurgation tracing the history of the influence of the Frankish upon the Roman practice of separating married persons on account of impotence, and showing the establishment of the Gallican discipline at Rome has been eliminated, because its

[63] C. 12, C. II, q. 5.

[64] C. 13, C. II, q. 5.

[65] Berardi, Carolus, *Gratiani Canones* (Venetiis, 1787), I, P. I, cap. XXIII, 247-249: *De Concilio Agathensi:* I, P. I, cap. XXII, 263, 264: *De Concilio Ilerdensi; cf. Epis. Greg. ad Ioannem Ravennatum Episcopum,* in Burchardus Wormatiensis Ecclesiae Episcopus, *Decretorum Libri Viginti,* lib. IX, c. 40, 43—*M.P.L.,* 140, 821.

[66] *Hist. Franc.,* L. 8, c. IX; *cf. M.P.L.,* 71, 454; Van Espen *Ius Ecclesiasticum Universum,* IV, nn. 46, 140.

[67] Schmalzgrueber, *Ius Ecclesiasticum Universum,* par. III, t. XXXIV, nn. 13, 14.

inclusion would make this work too lengthy. In matrimonial procedure compurgation is now conventionally limited to seven witnesses on either side, whence arose its peculiar designation in matrimonial cases, the testimony of the seventh hand. Before considering the adaptation of compurgation to proof of marriage, the teaching of Gratian and of the Decretals regarding compurgation in its application to criminal causes may be summarized under three convenient headings, *viz.*, the general rules governing compurgation, the persons who underwent it, and the qualifications of the witnesses who took part in the rite.

A. General Rules for Compurgation

Compurgation was resorted to when there were legitimate accusers who were unable to prove the alleged crime of a priest who denied it.[68] It does not appear to have been a general rule that a man was coerced into purging himself when there was a deficiency of accusers.[69] There were occasions, as in litigation involving a benefice, when a legitimate accuser made no appearance. The suspect, because he was considered stained with crime, was required to submit to purgation. Thereafter, he was not molested.[70] Had a parish priest lost his reputation due to an alleged public crime, there being neither accuser nor witnesses, the bishop could compel him to purge himself unless the accused appealed to a superior judge.[71]

An oath was sufficient to purge a priest of a bad rumor when legal witnesses and accusers were lacking.[72] Accusation without proof was inadmissible. Whoever attempted to accuse without proof was suspended from his office and benefice until he canonically purged himself with an oath of compurgation.[73] In the time of the Decre-

[68] C. 12, c. II, q. 5.

[69] *Cf. Dictum Gratiani* ad (1 Pars), C. II, q. 5.

[70] C. 23, X, *de accusationibus inquisitionibus, et denunciationibus,* V, 1.

[71] *Cf. Glossa ad* c. 6, X, *de purgatione canonica,* V, 34: "Indicatis. ut infamia expurgetur."

[72] C. 16, C. II, q. 5.

[73] C. 2, X, *de calumniatoribus,* V, 2: "Quum autem processum negotii *et dicta testium* examinaverimus diligenter, nec intelligere potuerimus, probatum esse sufficienter aliquid de praedictis, eundem episcopum *de consilio fratrum*

tals, moreover, notorious simoniacs were not only deprived of their benefices, but were not permitted to undergo purgation.[74] Persons accused of apostacy during those times were compelled to purge themselves by canonical purgation.[75]

B. Persons Who Underwent Purgation

Various classes of persons were required to submit to purgation. The general principle was that no purgation was indicated when there was a merely probable violation of law. Were the probable crime noised about, the suspect had to purge himself.[76] A notorious simoniac was an exception to the rule. Such a one was not allowed to purge himself.[77]

Pope Sixtus (432-440), although he could not be compelled to submit to purgation, nevertheless purged himself before a council from a suspicion fomented by one Basso.[78] Under Pope Gregory I (d. 604), the priests and minor clerics who were defendants were ordered to swear on the Gospels or the relics of some saint and before the people that the charge was false.[79]

Besides the clergy and women dedicated to the service of God, a nobleman (*ingenuus*) who denied some accusation purged himself with the aid of twelve noblemen.[80]

nostrorum absolvendum decernimus ab obiectis, vobis *per apostolica scripta*, mandantes, quatenus memoratum magistrum scholarum, donec canonice suam purgaverit innocentiam, scilicet quod non calumniandi animo ad huiusmodi crimina proponenda processit, ab officio et beneficio suspendatis, ut coteri, simili poena perterriti, ad infamiam suorum facile non prosiliant praelatorum."

[74] C. 13, X, *de calumniatoribus*, V, 2; *cf.* c. 2, X, *de calumniatoribus*, V. 3.

[75] C. 3, X, *de apostatis et reiterantibus baptisma*, V, 9.

[76] *Cf.* Glossa ad c. 4, X, *de purgatione canonica*, V, 34: "Prodiderit in iudicio timore probationis: alias si occulte confiteretur sacerdoti, non repelleretur, dummodo esset occultum."

[77] C. 13, X, *de calumniatoribus*, V. 2.

[78] C. 10, C. II, q. 5. For examples of purgation undergone by the clergy, *cf.* c. 2, C. II, q. 4; c. 8, C. II, q. 5; c. 9, C. II, q. 5; c. 3, C. II, q. 4; c. 12, C. II, q. 5; c. 19, C. II, q. 5; c. 6, X, *de purgatione canonica*, V, 34; c. 12, C. II, q. 5; c. 17, C. II, q. 5; Duchesne, *Liber Pontificalis*, I, 212, 232, 260; II, 7.

[79] St. Gregory, L. 7, indict. 2, Epist. 80—*M.P.L.*, 77, 1012.

[80] C. 15, C. II, q. 5; *cf. Glossa* ad c. 1, X, *de purgatione canonica*, V, 34: "Expurget. Intellige de eo, qui infamatus est."

Looking at these various classes of persons from another aspect, it is observed that a quantitative rule of varying standard was applied to the number of those who were to be present at the purgation of the accused or the suspect.[81] A priest who was not believed by his bishop or fellow priests, and against whom suspicion was entertained by good and just men, purged himself with three or five, or seven good priests who resided in his vicinity. An instance of this occurred in the lifetime of Pope Leo III (d. 816), who employed twelve bishops in his own purgation.[82] If legitimate accusers could not prove the crimes charged to a priest who denied them, he purged himself together with seven of his companions if he could procure those who possessed the same order as he.[83] Gregory IX (d. 1241) modified this rule by permitting three witnesses to aid those believed to be in very bad repute.[84] Until he purged himself, an accused could, however, be suspended on account of the magnitude of a crime not only from his office but from his benefice. Scandalous familiarity with heretics required fourteen hands of the same order as the accused to purge him.[85]

[81] A cleric in exalted ecclesiastical position (*presul*) was not condemned without seventy-two witnesses. A like number of witnesses who agree (*contestes*) were required for the purgation of a Cardinal Bishop. A cardinal priest was not deposed without twenty-seven, and a subdeacon, acolyte, exorcist, lector or ostiarius was not purged of the imputation of a crime without seven witnesses. Witnesses and accusers were to be without infamy. *Cf.* cc. 2, 3, C. II, q. 4. A collegiate tribunal of twelve bishops or seventy-two who were qualified to accuse was required for the purgation of a bishop. *Cf.* c. 3, C. II, q. 4. Two or three suitable witnesses were needed to free clerics from the charge of fornication. A perusal of Gratian does not show that the testimony of two or three bishops, however, was enough to condemn a bishop. Pope Sylvester stated the opposite in a general synod. *Cf.* c. 1, C. II, q. 4; *cf.* c. 2, C. II, q. 4. The interpretation of the glossators indicates that these prescriptions were not literally observed. *Cf.* Reiffenstuel, *Ius Canonicum Universum,* lib. II, tit. XX, nn. 243, 244; Wernz, *Ius Decretalium,* V. 821.

[82] C. 19, C. II, q. 5; *cf.* c. 1, X, *de confessis,* II, 18: "Si tamen eos infamia hujusmodi laborare cognoveris, singulis eis adiunctis tribus sociis sui ordinis purgationem iniungas."

[83] C. 12, C. II, q. 5.

[84] C. 1, X, *de confessis,* II, 18.

[85] C. 10, X, *de purgatione canonica,* V, 34.

Religious priests and abbots were to consider themselves obliged to purge themselves of the imputation of simony. This was accomplished by the third hand of a lower order and by the fourth hand if the suspect be a religious priest or an abbot.[86] Deacons, denying an accusation of a crime, excused themselves from imputation of it with three witnesses who were also deacons.[87]

Gregory IX stated that if a noble or free-born man had been previously apprehended in theft, in perjury, or in the giving of false testimony, he was not to be admitted to take the oath. A purgation was indicated for him as though he was not a free-born man.[88]

C. *Qualifications of Compurgators*

A definite statement of the qualifications of witnesses for compurgation is found in the time of Gregory IX. An investigation preceded the rite. In the first place, the name of each co-jurator who wished to purge was ascertained. Diligent inquiry was made about the national origin of each co-jurator and regarding other circumstances which it was thought necessary to know. Provided that a witness admitted by the Church had a good reputation and that he had not been condemned for a crime, he could be a compurgator.[89]

Elsewhere the Decretals are more precise. Neighbors and honest men were admitted for the purpose of purgation.[90] The two qualifications of honesty and of good reputation were further explained. They denoted men who would be influenced by neither love, nor hatred, nor be the prospect of obtaining money to attest with an oath.[91]

An instruction of Pope Honorius III (d. 1227) to the Archbishop of London and his suffragans contained a rule that could the crime of a culprit be proved by witnesses worthy of credence, his own deposition to the contrary was inadmissible. Negative

[86] C. 17, C. II, q. 5.
[87] C. 12, C. II, q. 5.
[88] C. 1, X, *de pugatione canonica,* V. 34.
[89] *Cf. Glossa* ad c. 9, X, *de purgatione canonica,* V. 34.
[90] C. 11, X, *de purgatione canonica,* V. 34.
[91] C. 7, X, *de purgatione canonica,* V, 34.

proofs were worthless. It was, moreover, definitely stated that a man who was stained with infamy for a similar crime was hardly suitable to purge another canonically from a like crime.[92]

An accusation was definitely established. Inquiry was made about the fact that the crime had been committed. Relatives and associates of the accused were taken into consideration. Thereupon, suitable men who were not enemies or perjurers prosecuted the inquisition and were admitted to testify. Should the crime not be proved, canonical purgation was indicated.[93]

There were times, as in the case of a deacon accused of a crime, when a public examination was not believed to be necessary. Gratian alludes to a specific instance of this. When suitable witnesses and accusers were introduced and the deacon did not spontaneously confess the crime alleged against him, he was required to purge himself by an oath taken secretly before his archbishop together with some bishops and deacons of his church. This secret purgation was used when witnesses and accusers could not be found and the bad reputation of the deacon grew worse.[94]

The witnesses who were present also took an oath on the Gospels that they personally knew the truth of that to which they testified.[95] Gregory IX, more specific, calls attention to an epistle of Innocent III to the Patriarch of Aquila and to the Bishop of Mantua. A bishop swore on the Gospels first that he was innocent of a charge. The compurgators swore likewise that they knew that he spoke the truth.[96]

[92] C. 12, X, *de probationibus,* II, 19.

[93] C. 19, X, *de accusationibus, inquisitionibus, et denunciationibus,* V, 1.

[94] C. 1, C. XV, q. 5. The accused affirmed innocence by an oath when accusers and witnesses were not present. *Cf.* c. 5, C. II, q. 5. Uncautious oaths were prohibited. *Cf.* c. 2, C. II, q. 5. Priests took an oath "by the right faith." *Cf.* c. 1, C. II, q. 5. A layman in a controversy with a bishop purged himself with an oath; a bishop affirmed his innocence by his holy consecration. *Cf.* c. 4, C. II, q. 5. From the wording of this and similar passages in the Decretals one cannot state with exactness that they refer to the rite of compurgation. The accused could not criminate others unless he first purged himself. *Cf.* c. 1, C. II, q. 2; c. 2, C. III, q. 2; c. 3, C. III, q. 2.

[95] C. 20, C. III, q. 9.

[96] C. 5, X, *de purgatione canonica,* V. 34.

Besides an oath taken on the Four Gospels, one was taken by the "most holy body of Blessed Peter." At the suggestion of Pope Gregory, a Bishop Leo took such an oath to prove by purgation the falsity of a sinister rumor.[97] A Bishop Mena, likewise, took what was thought to be a satisfying oath.[98] A Bishop Maximum purged himself from the so-called simoniacal heresy before the body of St. Apollinaris.[99] The same oath was taken by a Bishop Marianus of Ravenna.[100]

In place of the requirement of taking such an oath it seems to have been a fact that either a bishop or a priest who was accused of a crime might celebrate Mass and communicate to show his innocence.[101] That this was an exception to the general mode of conducting purgation ceremonies appears to follow from the manner in which Gratian alludes to it. He calls attention to the fact that both Popes Sixtus and Leo III were unwilling that their example, which has been pointed out, be considered a precedent for prescribing any law exacting a purgation from others.[102]

Article 3. Adaptation of Compurgation to Proof of Marriage

The confirmatory oaths of seven witnesses became, in the time of Gratian and the Decretals, an integral part of the evidence required in causes involving impotence and non-consummation of marriage. The requirement of seven witnesses clothed this form of proof with the designation *testimonium septimae manus.* Gasparri and Feije, following Avanzinus, hold that the word "hand" connotes both the aid given to the spouses whose attestations were confirmed by these witnesses and the prevention of collusion between the married persons themselves.[103] Van Espen, one of the sources used by Avan-

[97] C. 7, C. II, q. 5.

[98] C. 7, C. II, q. 5.

[99] C. 8, C. II, q. 5.

[100] C. 9, C. II, q. 5.

[101] C. 26, C. II, q. 5.

[102] C. 26, C. II, q. 5.

[103] Gasparri, Petrus Cardinalis, *De Matrimonio* (1932), II, 295. *Cf.* Feije,

zinus, observes the Germanic origin of the use of the testimony of the seventh hand. He explains the word "hand" thus:

> Cum autem constet manum semper fuisse symbolum fidei; atque idcirco in iudiciis et contractibus, ubi fides addicitur, manus porrigi in signum fidei solitum quoque fuit; uti ut hodie porrectis manibus iuratur; indeque nihil frequentius in antiquis legibus quam manu quinta, manu sexta, septima vel duodecima se purgare; id est quinque, sex, septem vel duodecim adhibitis iuratoribus.[104]

In Germanic Law, the oath by the use of the hand had another and a legal connotation. It was said that an accused redeemed his hand with the aid of other compurgators. The conception was that one accused of a crime lost or forfeited his hand which signified his credibility. His relatives or neighbors restored his credibility by raising their hands. The text in the *Lex Frisionum,* Tit. X, *de testibus,* 1,[101] reads: "Si quis homo super reliquis sanctorum falsum sacramentum iuraverit, ad partem regis weregildum suum componat, et alio weregildo manum suam redimat; de coniuratoribus eius unusquisque weregildum suum persolvat."

The early history of the testimony of the seventh hand is a narrative of the practice of separating married persons by reason of impotence. The oath or *sacramentum* occupied the position of an adminicular or confirmatory proof in criminal causes. It was a last resort intended to either dissipate suspicion or to supply the lack of other direct testimony.[106] Applied to the testimony of the seventh hand the *sacramentum* became part of the probative process in the proof of impotence.

Passing over the reason for the difference in the theory and practice of the Roman and the Gallican Church, with which much of the scholarship of the old canonists was concerned, our conclusions may

Henricus J., *De Impedimentis et Dispensationibus Matrimonialibus* (Lovanii, 1885), 410, note 1.

104 Van Espen, *Ius Ecclesiasticum Universum,* III, tit. 8.

105 *M.G.H., Leges,* III, 665, 666.

106 Muscat, Remigius, *Institutiones Canonicae* (Romae, 1707), L. V, T. 34, n. 5.

be summarized in the following manner. The Gallican discipline was adopted by the Roman Church.[107] Pope Celestine III (A.D. 1191-1198), a great compromiser, gave expression to a conciliatory decision. It proposed that whenever the impotence of either spouse was proved, the married persons had the choice of living together as brother and sister or, should the party who was not impotent prefer the married state, both could separate.[108] Innocent III provided that should an error be made both parties were required to return to the former marriage which was considered valid.[109]

The development of the practice of separation due to impotence is the history of the testimony of the seventh hand. Until the revival of Roman jurisprudence gradually displaced it, compurgation was the prevalent means of establishing judicial truth. It was subsidiary in the probative process. In the twelfth century, however, compurgation was an essential element in ascertaining at least moral certainty about the truth of alleged facts known only to the spouses.[110]

From the Council of Trent to the Constitution *Dei miseratione* of Benedict XIV (3 November, 1741), there appear to have been two things that characterized the history of the testimony of the seventh hand. The Council of Trent instituted reform in the personnel of the matrimonial court. Duties were strictly delimited and processes involving marriages were couched in scientific form. The Constitution *Dei miseratione,* on the other hand, subjected matrimonial causes to strictly legal procedure. No marriages could be legally dissolved

[107] Freisen, Joseph, *Geschichte des Canonischen Eherechts bis zum Verfall der Glossenlitteratur* (Paderborn, 1893), 346, 347.

[108] C. 5, X, *de frigidis et maleficiatis, et impotentia coeundi,* IV, 15: "Quo lapso, si nec tunc cohabitare voluerint, et juxta decretum Gregorii mulier, si per justum judicium de viro probare potuerit, quod cum ea coire non possit, accipiat alium; si autem ille aliam acceperit, separentur. Quod si ambo consentiant simul esse, vir eam, etsi non ut uxorem, saltem habeat ut sororem." Compare with the *experimentum triennale* referred to by the old canonists and in S. R. R., *Nullit. Matrim.,* 15 November, 1909, *Coram Gustavo Persiani,* dec. XVI, n. 7—*Decisiones,* I (1909), 139.

[109] C. 6, X, *de frigidis et maleficiatis, et impotentia coeundi,* IV, 15.

[110] C. 5, X, *de frigidis et maleficiatis, et impotentia coeundi,* IV, 15.

thereafter without two conformable sentences in favor of the plaintiff.[111]

The only document since the Decretals of Gregory IX up to the second half of the nineteenth century which directly affected the testimony of the seventh hand was the Instruction of the Sacred Congregation of the Council on 22 August, 1840.[112] This instruction required that the spouses be examined. They were to be summoned before a *defensor vinculi* to be questioned. The married persons were permitted to name a number of relatives or friends of good reputation. These persons, having taken an oath of credibility, were interrogated about their knowledge of the lives of the married persons. Moreover, the instruction settled three things pertaining to the subject under investigation. In the first place, it eliminated the triennial experiment by failing to mention it.[113] Nevertheless, no law contemporaneous with the Instruction of 1840 is found which proves the displacement of the triennial experiment. In the second place, both spouses were required to take an oath of credibility regardless of their attitude toward the marriage bond.[114] Lastly, the scope of the testimony of the seventh hand was extended. It became a testimony concerning credibility, not of knowledge. It was directly concerned with the credibility of the persons who had contracted marriage. The testimony of the seventh hand could be exacted when an alleged fact was proposed by the unsupported deposition of the principals in the case. The testimony of the seventh hand was henceforth confined almost entirely to cases of impotence which were physically certain. The Sacred Congregation of the Council was alone the competent forum for adjudication of all other cases of impotence in which the indications were not physically certain.

[111] *Cf.* Santi, Franciscus, *Praelectiones Juris Canonici quas juxta ordinem decretalium Gregorii IX* (Ratisbonae, 1842), IV, 152.

[112] *Cf.* S. C. C., *Instr.*, 22 August 1840—*Fontes*, n. 4069.

[113] De Becker, Julius, *De Sponsalibus et Matrimonio* (Bruxellis, 1896), 160.

[114] The old discipline exacted the testimony of the seventh hand from the plaintiff (*actor*) or both spouses if they agreed on the petition to separate. *Cf.* Sanchez, Thomas, *De Sancto Matrimonii Sacramento Disputationum* (Lugduni, 1669), L. VII, d. 108, n. 7, 11.

CHAPTER IV

TESTIMONY ACCORDING TO THE CORPUS JURIS CANONICI

THE latitude permitted to judges by Roman Law tended toward subjectivism. The rigidity of the Teutonic system of evidence conduced to formalism. Canon Law endeavored to overcome these weaknesses by constraining subjectivism on the one hand, and by giving elasticity to arbitrary rules on the other hand. A fusion of the Germanic and Roman Law elements of evidence took place during the Middle Ages. A system of acquiring evidence was put upon a scientific basis. This was rendered possible through the wide prerogatives of Roman Pontiffs. The laws pertaining to evidence made by Innocent III (d. 1216), Honorius III (d. 1227), Gregory IX (d. 1241), Nicholas III (d. 1280), Boniface VIII (d. 1303), and Clement V (d. 1314), aided in systematizing the Canon Law of the Church. The subject-matter of this chapter embraces the rules of testimonial evidence found in the *Corpus Juris Canonici* which state the general qualifications of witnesses and specify the criteria which affect the probative value of their attestations.

In preference to considering each of the five compilations of the *Corpus Juris Canonici* as a unit by itself, it is believed desirable to present an analysis of their content which pertains to testimony. With the general criteria of testimony thus classified, exceptions incident upon the progression of thought upon the subject may be detected.

ARTICLE 1. GENERAL QUALIFICATIONS OF WITNESSES

The method used by Gratian was simple. He reassembled and compared two series of texts which appeared to be contradictory. He endeavored to establish a harmony between them, so that the discrepancies of one series would explain and justify the other. Profound in erudition, concise in style, the *Decretum Gratiani* was not, however, intended by its compiler to be an index of the evolution of ideas. This work is used as a basis for study. Changes in the concept of oral evidence found in the Decretals will be pointed out as occasion is thought to present itself.

One should not confuse the qualifications of witnesses with the rules forbidding some classes of persons from making accusations. Making explicit reference to the forty-eighth chapter of the *Digest*, Gratian summarizes the rules governing the accuser.[1]

In the time of Gratian, witnesses had to be qualified to testify. The preliminary qualifications of witnesses, perception, retention and narration, commonplace in modern studies of the principles of judicial proof, are found likewise in the *Corpus Juris Canonici.* Gratian states that:

> Witnesses may not proffer any written testimony, but present what pertains to what they saw and know, giving oral testimony truthfully. Nor shall they utter testimony about other causes or business unless it concerns what is known to be within the scope of their present acts.[2]

The preliminary qualifications of witnesses were likewise distinguished from the sanction given to the credibility of a witness.[3]

Witnesses testifying from hearsay (*de auditu et fama*) were not considered sufficient for proof.[4] As the tests for the credibility of a witness are not to be confused with the general qualifications of witnesses, so they are not to be confounded with the sanction given for the truth of utterances.

An analysis of the *Corpus Juris Canonici* shows that the necessity of witnesses was recognized. Manifest facts did not require accusation.[5] Of facts that are manifest, some are known to the judge but are unknown to others. Other things are hidden from the judge

[1] C. 14, C. II, q. 1. Compare with D. XLVIII, 2, 3.

[2] "Testes per quamcumque scripturam testimonium non proferant, sed presentes de his, que uiderunt et nonuerunt, ueraciter testimonium dicant. Nec de aliis causis uel negotiis testimonium dicant, nisi de his, que sub eorum presentia acta esse noscuntur."—c. 15, C. III, q. 9. *Cf. Nov.* XC, 2.

[3] *Cf.* c. 51, X, *de testibus et attestationibus,* II, 20.

[4] C. 33, X, *de testibus et attestationibus,* II, 20; *cf.* 47, X, *de testibus et attestationibus,* II, 20.

[5] C. 15, C. II, q. 1.

and known to others. Now, those things which only the judge knows, cannot be made public without an examination, because judiciary power is lost when one assumes the position of both accuser and judge. For no one can in one and the same cause be accuser and judge.[6] One cannot be simultaneously an accuser, a judge and a witness.[7]

Necessary as testimony is, not all witnesses were competent to give it. Only suitable (*idonei*) persons [8] or people innocent of blame,[9] the fitting (*congrui*) and the legitimate or qualified (*legitimi*)[10] were enabled to make depositions of a general nature. Such witnesses were to be examined diligently. Whoever impeded them from testifying was to be punished.[11]

As exemplified in the *Corpus Juris Canonici,* Canon Law followed the common experience of mankind in rejecting the testimony of various classes of persons who were deficient in understanding, insensible to the obligations incumbent on a witness and those whose primary interest was directly involved in the matter at issue. There appears to have been applied a principle analogous to that distinguishing a conclusive from a disputable presumption of law, to the effect that experience has taught that there is a relation between the condition or situation of a witness and the truth or falsity of his testimony. The law, consequently, excluded as unreliable those whose testimony was not considered credible. Obviously, no test of credibility could be infallible. A degree of certainty was approximated which was in accordance with the beliefs current at the time.

[6] *Dictum Gratiani* ad c. 17, C. II, q. 1.

[7] C. 1, C. IV, q. 4.

[8] C. 41, X, *de testibus et attestationibus,* II, 20; c. 16, X, *de praesumptionibus,* II, 23. This latter canon states that a witness is presumed to be suitable and is not held to prove it. The term *idonei* is explained as denoting suitable and faithful, *i. e.,* worthy of credence. *Cf.* Pirhing, Enricus, *Jus Canonicum in Quinque Libros Decretalium* (Dilingae, 1674-1678), lib. II, tit. XX, *de testibus et attestationibus,* sec. 1, §§ 1, 2, 3.

[9] C. 2, C. II, q. 1.

[10] C. 1, C. IV, q. 4. The words *idoneous, congruous, legitimos* are found in editions of Gratian.

[11] C. 37, X, *detestibus et attestationibus,* II, 20.

ARTICLE 2. SPECIFIC RULES FOR ESTIMATING TESTIMONY

Specific rules for estimating testimonial evidence are laid down in two different parts of the *Decretum Gratiani.* One of these parts mentions three,[12] the other, forty-three rules for estimating testimony.[13] Elsewhere, throughout this work, applications of these rules are made. The Decretals of Gregory IX (1241), and the glossators who emphasized the doctrine of Gratian, are more concise in their general divisions which pertain to evidence.

A concise exposition of the criteria for evaluating oral evidence is found in the Decretals of Gregory IX. Quoting the eighteenth chapter of the *Etymologies* of St. Isidore of Seville,[14] it is observed that witnesses are estimated by reason of their condition, their nature and their life. By their condition, is meant whether or not they are free. For often a dependent or serf suppresses testimony due to fear of the one who has him in power. By nature, the utterance of a witness is judged when it is asked whether the witness be man or woman. For the testimony of woman is vacillating and changeable. By one's life as a standard of the credibility of a witness is meant that inquiry is to be made whether the person be innocent in his personal conduct. A person whose life is not good lacks credibility.[15]

This outline of the norms for judging testimony is better understood by a perusal of Gratian. The forty-three rules of the Master are borrowed from Roman Law.[16] They are identical with those in force during the Extraordinary Period of Roman Law procedure. The forty-three rules of the Master will be summarized under the three convenient topics of condition, of nature and of life, which originate from St. Isidore. A second classification, proposed by Gratian, which is based on the disqualification of enmity in a witness, will be included under the topic of "life."

In some features, the criteria for judging testimony which were

[12] C. 2, C. III, q. 4.

[13] C. 3, C. IV, q. 2 and 3.

[14] *M.P.L.*, XVIII, col. 551; *cf.* Lindsay, W. M., *Isadori Hispalensis Episcopi Etymologiarum sive Originum* (Oxonii, 1910).

[15] C. 10, X, *de verborum significatione*, V, 40.

[16] *Cf.* D. XXII, 5, 21.

proposed by Gratian are similar to and in other respects they differ from the many rules and numerous exceptions which apply to criminal causes affecting the various classes of the clergy. These latter rules and exceptions apply to criminal rather than to civil and matrimonial causes. Irrelevant, and, perhaps confusing to one who would have to keep these distinctions constantly in mind, they are merely referred to in what follows.

A. Condition

1. Physical and Social Condition

The quantitative rule of evidence maintained its ascendancy throughout the Middle Ages. Gratian, however, did not hesitate to point out that such a rule was not conclusive. It is unbecoming, in the estimation of the Master, for a judge to consider merely the large number of those testifying. He should rather ponder the sincere credibility (*fides*) of the testimonies by which the light of truth is assisted.[17]

a. *Physical Condition*

The physical condition of a witness was taken into consideration. The aged and the sick, by reason of their infirmity, were not compelled to testify. Soldiers and those absent for reasons of state, were, as in the Extraordinary Period of Roman criminal procedure, also excluded from testifying.[18] Should the case, however, require them, not only private persons but even a magistrate was obliged to give testimony. In a cause involving adultery, the law specified that even a praetor ought to testify.[19] In the time of the Decretals, it was provided that the sick, the aged, the weak and the poor, who could not be brought into the presence of the judge to testify, were to be approached by a discreet examiner to take their depositions.[20] The sick and aged were admissible against the contumacious in a cause concerning freedom even when the issue was not contested.[21]

[17] C. 3, C. IV, q. 2.

[18] (C. 3), C. IV, q. 2 and 3. This is III Pars, § 10.

[19] (C. 3), C. IV, q. 2 and 3. *Cf.* III Pars, § 16.

[20] C. 8, X, *de testibus et attestationibus,* II, 20.

[21] C. 34, X, *de testibus et attestationibus,* II, 20.

b. *Social Condition*

The dignity, habits (*mores*) and the gravity of a witness should be made the subject of an examination. Those who vacillate against the credibility of their testimony were not to be heard.[22]

Speaking more directly, the social condition of a witness should be subjected to examination. Inquiry should be made whether the witness be a senator, a captain or plebeian. It should be asked whether he lead an honest and blameless life. Whether he be truly known and irreproachable in conduct, rich or poor, were to be subjects of inquiry. For some persons would easily admit a thing for money. Likewise, one should ascertain whether the witness be an enemy or a friend of the person against or on behalf of whom he will testify; for that testimony was to be admitted which lacked suspicion. It was devoid of suspicion if, in the first place, the person who gave it was an honest man. In the second place the motive of the witness in testifying was not suspect if he was not seeking money or favor. In the third place testimony was not suspect if it was not prompted by enmity towards the accused.[23]

Alluding to the *Lex Julia,* to which law reference has already been made, Gratian observes that a witness who was himself made a freedman or whose parent was freed by the accused, was inadmissible to testify on behalf of the benefactor.[24]

c. *Domestic Condition*

Testimony may also be evaluated from the aspect of domestic condition. It was a general principle that blood relations and those living in the home of either an accused or an accuser, could not testify against strangers.[25]

Passing over exceptions in criminal cases for a crime or an action of injury,[26] it is observed that a father was not a suitable witness

[22] (C. 3), C. IV, q. 2 and 3. This is rule § 1.

[23] (C. 3), C. IV, q. 2 and 3. This is rule § 2.

[24] (C. 3), C. IV, q. 2 and 3. This is III Pars, rule § 3.

[25] C. 1, C. III, q. 5; c. 24, X, *de testibus et attestationibus,* II, 20.

[26] *Dictum Gratiani* ad c. 18, C. III, q. 9; c. 23, X, *de sententia et re iudicata,* II, 27.

for his son, nor a son on behalf of his father.[27] But nothing prevented a son or two brothers under the control of their father from testifying concerning a transaction that did not pertain to their own father.[28] Serfs were not permitted to give testimony for or against their master.[29] Furthermore, stepfathers, stepsons, cousins on their mother's side and relations of a higher degree, could not testify against their fathers-in-law and mothers-in-law.[30] Sons and daughters-in-law could not be coerced into testifying unwillingly.[31] Finally, patrons could not be forced to testify against freedmen nor freedmen against their patron.[32]

Elsewhere, the Master assigns the reason for the exclusion of the aforementioned testimony. Such accusers and witnesses are suspect. Domestic affection arising out of blood relationship or by reason of the power possessed by the head of a family over witnesses in his power, is wont to impede the telling of the truth. Carnal love, fear and avarice, moreover, blunt the human perceptions. Opinions may be perverted so that witnesses may erroneously think that what they do is for the sake of piety, and that the money or reward which they receive for suborning themselves is a fitting reward for their prudence.[33]

B. Nature

Both the age and the sex of a witness were considered in evaluating testimony. Those who had not arrived at the age of puberty were inadmissible.[34] No one making an accusation could exact the testimony of somebody who was a minor of twenty years of age.[35]

In the time of Gratian, women were forbidden to testify.[36] An

[27] (C. 3), C. IV, q. 2 and 3. This is IV Pars, § 23.
[28] (C. 3), C. IV, q. 2 and 3. This is IV Pars, § 34.
[29] (C. 3), C. IV, q. 2 and 3. This is IV Pars, § 36.
[30] (C. 3), C. IV, q. 2 and 3. This is III Pars, § 4.
[31] (C. 3), C. IV, q. 2 and 3. This is III Pars, § 7.
[32] (C. 3), C. IV, q. 2 and 3. This is III Pars, § 6.
[33] C. 12, C. III, q. 5.
[34] (C. 3), C. IV, q. 2 and 3. This is III Pars, § 3.
[35] (C. 3), C. IV, q. 2 and 3. This is III Pars, § 14.
[36] The law of the Decretals which appears to exclude women from testifying because their testimony is changeable is not an inflexible rule and was interpreted by canonists before the Code as a simple admonition given to the judge.

exception was made for the graver crimes of simony and of *leze-majesty*. In these cases, witnesses were admissible who were less suitable.[37] Even the question of admitting an hermaphrodite to testify was taken into consideration.[38] In the time of the Decretals, women, besides being capable of testifying against clerics when there was question of a crime committed,[39] or a question involving an obstacle to an election,[40] could testify with the word of a man that a child was not theirs. Such testimony was accepted unless the contrary was established by circumstances and by witnesses who proved that both the child and its origin were known.[41]

The *Liber Sextus* of Boniface VIII,[42] (d. 1303) expressed the principle that women who were unwilling could not be coerced to testify for any cause not expressed in law. Should the testimony of women be necessary, the judges were obliged to see that the expenses of the women were defrayed. An exception to this was made concerning religious women. Even though they were willing to appear, religious women could not be brought outside their monastery personally for any cause.[43] Moreover, an abbess, in the time of the Decretals, could not testify in affairs pertaining to patrimony.[44]

C. *Life*

The personal habits and life of a witness were to be subjected to scrutiny. Honest persons of upright life and character were to be legitimately examined. Those whose personal conduct was reprehensible and infamous were not to give testimony. Even the laws of the governing secular affairs would not admit such.[45]

Cf. Wernz, *Ius Decretalium*, V, 608; Lega, Michael, *Praelectiones in Textum Iuris Canonici de Iudiciis Ecclesiasticis* (Ed. altera, Romae, 1905), I, n. 479, pp. 419, 420.

[37] *Dictum Gratiani* ad (c. 3), C. XV, q. 3; c. 4; C. XV, q. 3.

[38] (C. 3), C. IV, q. 2 and 3. This is IV Pars, § 22.

[39] C. 3, X, *de testibus et attestationibus*, II, 20.

[40] C. 33, X, *de testibus et attestationibus*, II, 20.

[41] C. 3, X, *qui filii sint legitimi*, IV, 17.

[42] *Cf.* Mourret, *Histoire Général de l'Eglise*, V, 31.

[43] C. 3, *de iudiciis*, II, 1 in VI°.

[44] C. 3, X, *de testamentis et ultimis voluntatibus*, III, 26.

[45] C. 2, C. III, q. 5.

The personal life of a witness could be suspect and blameworthy for one or both of two reasons. It could be blameworthy by reason of infamy.[46] A summary of persons excluded from testifying by reason of personal conduct may be made under two categories: (1) the infamous; and (2) those whose faith was accusable.

(1) *The Infamous.* A large classification of persons was considered infamous. Gratian classified them along with the suspect, the criminal, those who could be bribed (*gratiosi*), calumniators, the wicked and those who easily litigate.[47] A rather large classification [48] had application to accusers of bishops.

Infamous persons could not accuse those with a good reputation.[49] A witness, according to the Decretals of Gregory IX, had to be so suitable and faithful that no infamy could be charged against him by the person against whom he, who was also required to be fasting, was to utter his testimony.[50] As a general rule, consequently, the following could not give testimony: (a) Homicides, who were incidentally deprived of communion;[51] (b) those who committed rape;[52] (c) thieves;[53] (d) conspirators and the anathematized who were not permitted to harm anyone,[54] together with (e) perjurers were excluded from testifying.[55] Moreover, perjurers were required to submit to a forty-day fast of bread and water, obliged to perform penance during the seven years following a crime of perjury and were never to be without a penance. The perjurer was never to be received again as a

[46] C. 6, C. VI, q. 1; *cf.* 1 Cor. v, 11; c. 2, C. III, q. 7; *cf.* D. III, I, I.

[47] C. 10, C. III, q. 5. Another classification of the infamous is found in c. 17, C. VI, q. 1.

[48] C. 6, C. III, q. 5; c. 17, C. VI, q. 1.

[49] C. 16, C. VI, q. 1, *cf.* II Pars, § 1.

[50] C. 1, X, *de testibus et attestationibus,* II, 20.

[51] C. 20, C. XXIV, q. 3; c. 17, C. VI, q. 2.

[52] C. 7, X, *de testibus et attestionibus,* II, 20; c. 17, C. VI, q. 1, for application to the clergy.

[53] C. 7, X, *de testibus et attestationibus,* II, 20.

[54] C. 5, C. III, q. 4.

[55] (C. 3), C. IV, q. 2 and 3. This is III Pars, § 3. The stigma of perjury involved those who gave a bribe to a witness. *Cf.* (c. 3), C. IV, q. 2 and 3. This is III Pars, § 43. *Cf.* c. 1, X, *de crimine falsi,* V, 20; c. 7, X, *de testibus et attestationibus,* II, 20; c. 9, X, *de testibus et attestationibus,* II, 20.

witness.[56] (f) Calumniators who could not prove their accusation received punishment (*talio*).[57] Judges had competence to punish perjurers and those testifying in a vacillating manner.[58] (g) Soothsayers and diviners who could neither accuse nor act as witnesses;[59] (h) those in public bondage or who had hired themselves out to fight beasts could not testify.[60] Gladiators (*arenarii*) and the like were not allowed to make depositions without the torture.[61] Regarding the sordid history of the use of torture, it is observed that in the time of the Decretals the application of torture was considered improper by Canon Law.[62] (i) Besides these classes of persons, manifest enemies, were excluded from testifying.[63]

The classes of persons enumerated were excluded from giving testimony. The *Liber Sextus* of Boniface VIII laid down a rule that an advocate or a procurator who had taken part in a principal cause could not offer testimony if an appeal were taken.[64]

A much larger classification of infamous persons who were incompetent to testify applied to those infamous persons who were prevented from testifying against priests in high position and against bishops.[65] These included, besides those already mentioned, (a) those who had contempt for God's law and the statutes of the Church; (b) violators of sepulchres; (c) those who were considered of evil repute throughout the world; (d) the incestuous, adulterers

[56] C. 18, C. VI, q. 1.

[57] *Cf.* c. 2, C. II, q. 3. *Cf.* Du Cange, *Glossarium*, III, col. 972, v. *talio*.

[58] (C. 3), C. IV, q. 2 and 3. This is IV Pars, § 20.

[59] C. 9, C. III, q. 5.

[60] (C. 3), C. IV, q. 2 and 3. This is III Pars, § 3.

[61] (C. 3), C. IV, q. 2 and 3. This is III Pars, § 17.

[62] C. 6, X, *de reg. juris*, V, 41.

[63] C. 13, X, *de accusationibus, inquisitionibus et denunciationibus*, V, 1; (c. 3), C. IV, q. 2 and 3. This is IV Pars, § 42. Those coming from the houses of or associationg with enemies were excluded from testifying. *Cf.* (c. 3), C. III, q. 5.

[64] C. 3, *de testibus et attestationibus*, II, 10 in VI°.

[65] The ancient legislation concerning the incapacity of laymen to testify in criminal cases against clerics is of no more practical importance than the old laws concerning the incapacity of Jews and Infidels to testify. By its silence the Code has abrogated the canonical sanctions that had applied to those classes of persons.

and bigamists; (e) those fleeing to public wars and seeking to hold unworthy places, or unjustly appropriating the faculties of the Church; (f) calumniators and trouble-makers; (g) the anathematized, those repulsed from the Church for their crimes, slaves, penitents, those of unsound body, mind or intellect or not possessed of the right faith and conversation, domestics; (h) thieves; (i) those condemned for capital crimes;[66] (j) and finally, the sacrilegious.[67] Furthermore, for the condemnation of a bishop it was required that either the accused confess the crime alleged against him or be convicted by witnesses who were both innocent and canonically examined.[68]

(2) *Faith Accusable.* They whose conversation, life or faith was accusable were, like those who easily litigate, prevented from testifying.[69] Such persons embraced: (a) the anathematized;[70] (b) Jews and Pagans, who could not even accuse Christians.[71] Those Jews who a short while ago were Christians and became renegades were not allowed to testify. Having been suspected in the faith of Christ, the word of such people was doubtful when it came to a question of human testimony.[72] In all causes, a Christian was admitted to testify against a Jew.[73] (c) Apostates could neither accuse nor testify.[74] (d) Heretics and schismatics could not testify.[75] One suspect of heresy who did not purge himself of the suspicion and remained a

[66] C. 17, C. VI, q. 1; c. 9, C. III, q. 5.

[67] C. 2, C. III, q. 4. This latter law forbade the sacrilegious from testifying against religious Christians.

[68] C. 5, C. II, q. 1.

[69] C. 3, C. IV, q. 4.

[70] C. 5, C. IV, q. 4; c. 6, C. IV, q. 4; *cf.* c. 1, C. IV, q. 1: Whoever persevered in excommunication was not admitted to accuse another.

[71] C. 25, C. II, q. 7.

[72] C. 24, C. II, q. 7.

[73] C. 21, X, *de testibus et attestationibus,* II, 20.

[74] C. 2, C. III, q. 4. *Cf.* c. 1, X, *de haereticis,* V, 17: "Dubius in fide infidelis est, nec eis omnino credendum est, qui fidem veritatis ignorant. . . . " *Cf.* c. 2, C. III, q. 4.

[75] *Cf.* c. 36, C. XXIV, q. 3; c. 25, C. XXIV, q. 3, both of which are of a general nature.

year in excommunication, was condemned as a heretic.[76] An exception, however, was made. A heretic could accuse and testify against another heretic in litigation.[77] Other witnesses worthy of credence testified on behalf of the wives, sons, friends and the family of one who, while sick, received consolation from a heretic.[78] (e) Excommunicated persons could not testify. There are connotations and many species of excommunication found in the *Corpus Iuris Canonici,* which are not included in this chapter. The stigma of excommunication which was inflicted upon different crimes changed in different historical epochs.

[76] C. 13, X, *de haereticis,* V. 7.

[77] C. 26, C. II, q. 7.

[78] C. 4, X, *de accusationibus, inquisitionibus, et denunciationibus,* V, 1.

CHAPTER V

FUNDAMENTAL NOTIONS OF TESTIMONIAL EVIDENCE

THE terminology employed by the Code of Canon Law is to be understood according to the explanations given in the Code itself and in the works of canonists. The main methods of legal reasoning are not expounded in the Code. They are the untechnical ways of all sound reasoning in its normal manifestations. The general norms that govern it here are the ordinary rules of human thought and experience. They are to be sought in the ordinary sources and not in the Code. It will be of advantage to recall definitions and distinctions which pertain to the proof of a marriage, as the words "proof," "testimony," and "evidence" may be used in various senses. For the sake of clearness the meaning of these various terms will be indicated.

ARTICLE 1. THE NATURE OF PROOF OR JUDICIAL EVIDENCE

The Code uses the term "proof" (*probatio*) in a restricted sense.[1] On the one hand, it means the presentation of some fact in a court of law. Something objective, whether it be animate or inanimate, has to be shown (*demonstratio*). On the other hand, the word "proof" denotes that the manifestation of the objective fact is to be made to an ecclesiastical judge in such a way that his mind is convinced of the truth or of the existence of the alleged fact. The fact itself must be analyzed before the eyes of the judge so that from

[1] The word *probare* signifies examine, investigate. If a thing or action stands this test of its genuinity and worth, it is considered proved (1544, § 1). In another sense it signifies establish (determine), and corroborate. The qualities of a thing or of a person or of an action are established and found correct. (1707.) An authoritative ratification or approval is based on it. *Cf. Reg.* 29, R. J., in VI°. In its third meaning the word signifies display, show, exhibit, expose, explain, expound, interpret, and convince. *Cf.* Meile, *Die Beweislehre Des Kanonischen Prozess,* 20; Eichmann, Eduard, *Das Prozessrecht des Codex Iuris Canonici* (Paderborn, 1921), § 42, p. 133. In the American common law, proof in a general sense concerns the "ratio cinative process of contentious persuasion,—mind to mind, counsel to juror, each partisan seeking to move the mind of the tribunal." *Cf.* Wigmore, John Henry, *The Principles of Judicial Proof as given by Logic, Psychology, and General Experience and Illustrated in Judicial Trials* (Boston, 1913), 1.

what he perceives he may proceed by inferences [2] to a conclusion (*probatio*).

In ecclesiastical trials there is a main contention which has to be proved by evidence and assailed by opposing evidence. Evidence, a term used in the Anglo-American system of proof in trials at common law,[3] generally speaking, means information. The information or evidence is presented for the purpose of convincing a judge concerning the truth of an alleged fact. In an ecclesiastical trial, there is discussion about a cause (*causa*). This term is more restrictive than the word "case" as it designates a question or a matter submitted to adjudication.[4] In order to avoid error, the judge must first accurately perceive and mentally recognize the facts which are adduced. Thereupon, he must draw inferences from the separate evidentiary facts. In other words, the judge must give a correct interpretation of the significance or meaning of the information presented in court. This is not a precise but a restricted meaning of the canonical expression "proof" (*probatio*) which is rendered into English by the term "judicial evidence" which is used in the Anglo-American systems of law.[5]

[2] An inference is "the persuasive effect of each evidentiary fact, regarded separately, as to its *Probandum.*" *Cf.* Wigmore, *The Principles of Judicial Proof,* 5, § 1. An inference is from a fact (*probans*) to a proposition to be proved (*probandum*). Cf. Wigmore, *op. cit.,* 5, § 2.

[3] The German language, like the English, has a word for evidence, *viz., Beweis,* which denotes both *demonstratio* and *probatio,* although these latter terms are sometimes used as synonyms in German. The Code does not give a definition of either proof or of evidence. The Code is reluctant to define controverted words, being mindful of the Roman legislator who wrote: *"Omnis definitio in iure periculosa est: parum est enim ut non subverti possit."* *Cf.* D. L, 202, 17.

[4] "Causa est res, seu ius deductum in iudicum."—Vives, *Compedium Iuris Canonici* (4 ed. Romae, 1905), p. 409; *cf.* G. IV, 15, 53; D. V, 8, 5.

[5] In Anglo-American common law, a workable definition of "judicial evidence" represents "any knowable fact or group of facts, not a legal or a logical principle, considered with a view to its being offered before a legal tribunal for the purpose of producing the effect of persuasion, positive or negative, not of law or of logic, on which the determination of the tribunal is to be asked." *Cf.* Wigmore, *The Principles of Judicial Proof,* 5, § 1; Thayer, James Bradley, *A Preliminary Treatise on Evidence at the Common Law* (1 ed., Cambridge, 1898), 263-270.

The Definition of Proof or Judicial Evidence in Canon Law

The classical and the modern canonists have accepted the definition of proof applied to the evidence given in ecclesiastical courts which was proposed by Mascardus.[6] According to Mascardus, proof is defined as "a presentation of something doubtful, which is to be made to a judge by legitimate means in causes which are controverted before the judge himself." [7] This definition of proof,[8] which is of little practical consequence, nevertheless settles an intricate problem. The perfection of the definition has been determined by the progress of a people in civilization.[9] The expression "something doubtful" in the definition means that a fact is doubtful, not a right or a law.[10] By "means" one is to understand probatory means, such as documents, witnesses, and the like. One can understand this

[6] The three volumes of Joseph Mascardus (d. 1588), *Conclusiones Omnium Probationum quae in Utroque Jure Quotidie Versantur* (Venice, 1588) show methods of proof and contain numerous maxims on legal reasoning. *Cf.* Rittershutii, *Expositio Methodica Novellarum,* par. 9, cap. 21, n. 5, col. 759.

[7] "Probatio est ostensio rei dubiae per legitimos modos iudici facienda in causis apud ipsum iudicem controversis." *Cf.* Mascardus, *Conclusiones Omnium Probationum,* I, q. II, n. 17. This definition is accepted by Lega, *Praelectiones,* I, 391; Noval, P. Josephus, *Commentarium Codicis Iuris Canonici,* IV, *De Processibus* (Romae, 1920), I, n. 439; A Coronata, M., *Institutiones Iuris Canonici ad Usum Utriusque Cleri et Scholarum, De Processibus* (Taurini, 1933), III, n. 1272; Wernz-Vidal, *Jus Canonicum* (Romae, 1927), VI, *De Processibus,* n. 432; Roberti, Franciscus, *De Processibus* (Romae, 1926), II, n. 324; Vermeersch-Creusen, *Epitome Juris Canonici* (Altera editio, Romae, 1924), III, n. 163. A more specific definition of judicial proof is, "Probatio est actus judicialis, quo per instrumenta, aut testes, aut idonea argumenta judici de re, aut facto dubio, et controverso fit fides." *Cf.* Schmalzgrueber, *Ius Ecclesiasticum Universum,* lib. IV, tit. XIX, n. 1.

[8] From a different aspect, proof (or disproof) may be said to be the persuasive effect of an entire mass of evidential facts (inference) taken in globo and pertaining to some proposition. *Cf.* Wigmore, *The Principles of Judicial Proof* (2 ed., Boston, 1931), 9, 10.

[9] For an appraisal of the definitions of proof given by Azone, Accursius, Hostiensis, Godfredus and others, *cf.* Mascardus, *Conclusiones Omnium Probationum,* I, 7-27.

[10] Reiffenstuel expressed this by stating that "Probatio versantur circa facta, et quidem incerta seu dubia."—Reiffenstuel, *Ius Canonicum Universum,* lib. II, tit. XIV, n. 36; *cf.* also lib. II, tit. XIX, n. 36.

when he realizes that the term "proof" or "judicial evidence" embraces all means whereby an alleged matter of fact, the truth of which is submitted to investigation, is established or disproved. The means employed must be "legitimate." They are to possess the approbation of law. The knowledge in accordance with which a judge is obliged to decide a controversy ought to be public. It should be obtained from sources which the public authority recognizes to be suitable. Moreover, the manner in which the information is obtained is to be acknowledged by public authority as suitable. Private knowledge is insufficient because it is derived in a private manner and from sources that are not public. Testimony, for instance, when given by witnesses who lack legal qualifications, is produced by illegitimate means. Moreover, a witness is insufficient as a rule to prove past acts which require writing for the substance of the act or the contract.[11] It is illegal proof. Furthermore, a witness who is not examined in the manner laid down by the law gives illegal or illegitimate proof. The phrase "to a judge" denotes that the evidence must be sufficient to influence the judge so that he may form a definite opinion or come to a conclusion.[12]

Article 2. Classification of Proofs or of Judicial Evidence

There are, according to Mascardus, twelve species of proofs. These, he believes, are preferably reduced to nine which are enumerated in the verse:

> Aspectus, sculptum, testis, notoria, scriptum.
> Iurans, confessus, praesumptio, fama probavit.[13]

[11] *Cf.* S. R. R., *Londonen. Incardinationis,* 9 Januarii, 1912, *Coram R. P. D., Antonio Perathoner,* Dec. 11, n. 9—*Decisiones,* IV (1912), 18, 19:—"Idem valet de Archiepiscopi MacEvay testimonio, quod ceterum iurantum non est, et insuper in discrimen vitae prolatum fuit . . . Quando autem scriptura necessaria est ad substantiam actus, necessaria quoque est, ut probati docent auctores, ad probationem actus, ita ut testes tantummodo haud sufficiant . . . Ceterum, etsi detur scripturam in casu posse suppleri per testes, tamen unicum Praesule MacEvay testimonium haud sufficit. *Nam vox unius, vox nullius.* Unicus scilicet testis satis est ad probandum, tantum quando eius depositio nemini nocent et alteri prodest."

[12] *Cf.* Noval, *De Processibus,* I, 439.

[13] Mascardus, *Conclusiones Omnium Probationum,* I, q. IV, nn. 1, 2.

Looking at these from a limited point of view, one may restrict them for practical purposes to five divisions of proof.

A. Natural and Artificial

An Aristotelian division based on the means used to establish a fact distinguishes between natural (*inartificialis*) and artificial proof. The former proves a controverted thing directly and immediately. It is derived principally from extrinsic considerations such as the testimony of two or three credible witnesses, a presumption of law or of fact, the oath and public or authentic documents. Artificial proofs, on the other hand, include the extra-judicial confession, the statement of one witness worthy of credence, a private document, the comparison of signatures, one's reputation and, finally, unsubstantial presumptions. Artificial proof, conceived by the art or by the industry of the one attempting to prove something, is insufficient to terminate a controversy with moral certitude.[14]

B. Judicial and Extra-Judicial

By reason of its form, proof is divided into judicial and extra-judicial in accordance with whether or not it is presented in or outside of a court of law. The judicial proof takes place after, and the extra-judicial is presented before, the *litis contestatio.*[15]

C. Full and Incomplete

Due to the effect which is produced, proof is also distinguished into full or complete (*plena*) proof, which is satisfactory to the judge so that he is enabled to proceed without further inquiry to pronounce a definite opinion or sentence,[16] and incomplete proof. This dis-

[14] Schmalzgrueber, *Ius Ecclesiasticum Universum*, lib. IV, tit. XIX, n. 7; Soglia, Joannis Cardinalis, *Institutiones Juris Publici et Privati Ecclesiastici* (10 ed., Boscocia, 1842), II, lib. III, cap. 1, 353, § 149.

[15] Schmalzgrueber, *ibid.*

[16] "Probatio plena ita definiri solet, quod illa fit, quae tantam fidem faciat, quantum ad finiendam controversiam sufficiat."—Mascardus, *Conclusiones Omnium Probationum*, I, q. IV, n. 15; *cf.* Schmalzgrueber, *Ius Ecclesiasticum*

tinction is also expressed by saying that evidence may be complete and incomplete.[17] Mascardus distinguished full proof into these species, namely, writings, the confession, evidence of fact, the oath, presumptions that are just, and reputation.[18] Incomplete (*semiplena*) proof has less probative force in a court of law. It does not possess the full certitude that persuades. Expressed in mathematical computation it is described as half-proof.[19] Although the principle is thus stated, it admits exceptions in Canon Law. Two incomplete or "half full" proofs, whether they be of the same kind or different, that tend toward the same purpose, can aid one another collectively in spite of the fact that they do not prove by themselves.[20] There is no unanimity of opinion among writers on evidence about the feasibility of the distinctions between natural and artificial proof on the one hand and between full and incomplete proof on the other. Writers are not uniform in their explanation of what constitutes artificial proof.[21] Schmalzgrueber sustained the distinction between full and incomplete proof, notwithstanding the fact that the jurists Duarenus, Donellus, Pacianus and Giphani, arguing from the Justinian Code, maintained that there is no justification for the division.[22] The view of Aristotle was that the only incontestible kind of proof is "complete proof," which may be called "full proof." This philosopher was of the opinion that the fallible kind of proof has no specific

Universum, lib. IV, tit. XIX, n. 8. Compare with S. R. R., *Impedimenti Ad Matrimonium,* 22 Januarii, 1911, *Coram R. P. D., Aloisio Sincero,* dec. IV, n. 7—*Decisiones,* III (1911), 35, 36; S. R. R., *Nullit. Matrim.,* 17 Januarii, 1912, *Coram R. P. D., Michaele Lega,* dec. XX, n. 23—*Decisiones Coram Lega,* 261.

[17] Meile, *Die Beiweislehre des Kanonischen Prozesses,* 23.

[18] Mascardus, *Conclusiones Omnium Probationum,* I, q. IV, n. 16.

[19] In defining half-proof Mascardus uses the term *res gestae* which is ambiguous. *Cf.* Mascardus, *Conclusiones Omnium Probationum,* I, q. IV, n. 17; Schmalzgrueber, *Ius Ecclesiasticum Universum,* lib. IV, tit. XIX, n. 8.

[20] S. R. R., *Proprietatis,* 16 Augustii, 1916, *Coram R. P. D., Gulielmo Sebastianelli,* dec. XXVI, n. 2—*Decisiones,* VIII (1916), 279. Compare S. R. R., *Nullit. Matrim.,* 22 Februarii, 1921, *Coram R. P. D., Ioanne Prior,* dec. I, n. 6—*Decisiones,* VIII (1921), 7; S. R. R., *Nullit. Matrim.,* 12 Novembris, 1921, *Coram R. P. D., Ioanne Prior,* dec. XXVIII, n. 4—*Decisiones,* XIII (1921), 265.

[21] Wernz-Vidal, VI, *De Processibus,* n. 433, note 7.

[22] Schmalzgrueber, *Ius Ecclesiasticum Universum,* lib. IV, tit. XIX, n. 8, 25.

name.[23] The Code also employs the phrase "fuller proof" (*plenior probatio*).[24] Such a phrase is intended to make it evident that some causes require full and conclusive proof which excludes a prudent doubt. This term is found in the Code [25] and in decisions of the Roman Rota.[26]

Indifferent to the opinions of some of the old canonists and the modern jurists who expressed a proposal to discard the distinction between full or complete and imperfect or incomplete evidence, the Code established the division. Canon 1829 treats of incomplete or imperfect evidence. Incomplete or imperfect proof may be the deposition of one witness, unless he be qualified to testify about his official duties,[27] the supplementary oath,[28] a private document,[29] a simple presumption,[30] rumor,[31] the testimony of the seventh hand in matrimonial procedure,[32] inquisitorial evidence,[33] or an extra-judicial confession.[34] Full or complete evidence is expressed in a negative way in Canon 1791, and in a positive manner in Canon 2019. Full or complete proof is usually effected by two or three sworn witnesses who have the necessary qualifications,[35] by public records or documents,[36] legal presumptions,[37] and the oath of decision.[38] The completeness

[23] Aristotle, *Rhetorica*, I, 2; *cf.* Aristotle, *Analytica Priora*, II, 27.

[24] Canon 1810; *cf.* A Coronata, *De Processibus*, III, n. 1322, p. 228; Roberti, *De Processibus*, II, n. 354, p. 77.

[25] *Cf.* Canon 1810; Roberti, *De Processibus*, II, n. 365, p. 93.

[26] S. R. R., *Parisien. Nullit. Matrim.*, 3 Julii, 1922, *Coram R. P. D., Petro Rossetti*, dec. XXII, n. 4—*Decisiones*, XIV (1922), 218; S. R. R., *Nullit. Matrim.*, 19 Decembris, 1922, *Coram R. P. D., Friderico Cattani Amadori*, dec. XXXVIII, n. 13—*Decisiones*, XIV (1922), 352.

[27] Canon 1791, § 1.

[28] Canon 1829.

[29] Canon 1827.

[30] Canon 1828.

[31] Canon 1939.

[32] Canon 1975, § 2.

[33] Canon 1946, § 2, 2°.

[34] Canon 1753.

[35] Canon 1791, § 2.

[36] Canon 1816.

[37] Canon 1827.

[38] Canon 1836, § 2.

of the proof is not absolute but only relative. The law can demand a stronger proof inasmuch as it excludes the weaker means of evidence. The moral certainty which suffices for the completion of evidence does not exclude every possibility of a doubt. For this reason, evidence which is full or complete under usual circumstances can become heightened. From a procedural aspect proofs must be full (a) in beatification and canonization processes, in which no proof is admissible which is not elicited from witnesses and documents;[39] (b) in criminal causes, which require full proof produced by suitable witnesses, by the clearest documents or by indications which point to the proof of something doubtful and making the thing evident;[40] (c) and in matrimonial causes. Accusation made against a marriage already contracted[41] or against its non-consummation must be fully proved.[42] The usual means employed for this purpose are[43] the

39 Canon 2019; *cf.* Eichmann, *Das Prozessrecht,* § 42, p. 135; Meile, *Die Beweislehre, des Kanonischen Prozesses,* 23.

40 *Cf.* S. R. R., *Exercitiorum Spiritualium et Suspensionis,* 16 Junii, 1910, *Coram R. P. D., Josepho Mori,* dec. XXII, n. 4—*Decisiones,* II (1910), 212, 213; *Cod.,* IV, 19, 25: "Sciant cuncti accusatores eam se rem in publicam notionem deferre debere, quae munita sit idoneis testibus, vel instructa apertissimis documentis, vel indiciis ad probationem indubitatis et luce clarioribus expedita." *Cf.* Meile, *Die Beweislehre des Kanonischen Prozesses,* 23: "The criminal procedure demands: 'probationes luce meridiana clariores.' "

41 *Cf.* Canon 1014.

42 Cf. Canon 1015, § 1. "In iudicio de nullitate matrimonii, non sufficit quaelibet probatio, sed *plena* probatio necessaria est," Santi, *Praelectiones Iuris Canonici,* IV, t. XIX, n. 47; *cf.* S. R. R., *Nullit. Matrim.,* 17 Januarii, 1912, *Coram R. P. D., Michaele Lega* dec. XX, n. 23—*Decisiones Coram Lega,* 261. Simulated consent requires full proof. *Cf.* S. R. R., *Impedimenti ad Matrimonium,* 22 Januarii, 1911, *Coram R. P. D., Aloisio Sincero,* dec. IV, n. 7—*Decisiones,* III (1911), 35, 36. Affinity is to be proved "rigorously" when there is a question of dissolving a marriage already contracted. *Cf.* S. R. R., *Nullit. Matrim.,* 4 Julii, 1913, *Coram R. P. D., Ioanne Prior,* dec. XXXV, nn. 5, 6—*Decisiones,* V (1913), 427. A violent presumption suffices in the proof of affinity *ex copula illicita.* *Cf.* S. R. R., *Imolen. Nullit. Matrim.,* 2 Augustii, 1913, *Coram R. P. D., Antonio Parathoner,* dec. XLIII, n. 4—*Decisiones,* V (1913), 501.

43 Compare with Meile, *Die Beweislehre des Kanonischen Prozesses,* 39, 40.

examination of the married persons,[44] the examination of witnesses,[45] the production of sworn documents [46] and the findings of experts.[47] Expert advice must be consulted in all causes pertaining to impotence and defect of consent.[48]

D. Direct and Indirect

Judicial investigation looks exclusively to the past for facts from which to reason and for the experience which enables it to reason with accuracy. There are two ways by which a past fact may, when knowledge of it cannot be acquired by personal observation, be ascertained. In the first place, the information may be obtained from persons who have mediate or immediate knowledge of the fact. In the second place, conclusions or inferences may be elicited from other facts related to the principal one which can itself thereby be sufficiently established. In the former case, the inference is founded on the philosophic principle, sanctioned by experience, that trust can be put in human veracity.[49] In the latter case, the conclusion is de-

[44] Canons 1742-1746; 1750 to 1753. *Cf.* S. C. De Disciplina Sacramentorum —*Regulae Servandae in Processibus Super Matrimonio Rato Et Non Consummato, Cum Appendice Praecipuorum Actorum Formularum, Quae Utiliter Et Opportune Adhibentur in His Causis* (Romae, 1923), nn. 50-57.

[45] Canons 1756-1791. *Cf.* S. C. De Disciplina Sacramentorum—*Regulae Servandae In Processibus Super Matrimonio Rato Et Non Consummato,* nn. 39-47; compare with the Instruction of the Ordinary of Maintz for commissarial hearings on matrimonial causes, 25 February, 1927, in *Archiv für katholisches Kirchenrecht* (Mainz, 1885-) LV (1886), 107, 689.

[46] Canons 1812-1824; *cf.* S. C. De Disciplina Sacramentorum—*Regulae Servandae In Processibus Super Matrimonio Rato Et Non Consummato,* nn. 75-78.

[47] Canons 1792-1805; S. C. De Disciplina Sacramentorum—*Regulae Servandae In Processibus Super Matrimonio Rato Et Non Consummato,* nn. 84-95; *Regulae Servandae in Iudiciis Apud S. Romanae Rotae Tribunal* (Romae, 1910), §§ 120-136.

[48] Canons 1976; 1982; *cf.* Linneborn, Johannes, *Grundriss Des Eherechts Nach Dem Codex Iuris Canonici* (Paderborn, 1932), § 62, 1, p. 461.

[49] "Ad primum ergo dicendum, quod quia homo est animal sociale, naturaliter unus homo debet alteri id, sine quo societas humana servari non posset: non autem possent homines ad invicem convivere, nisi sibi invicem crederent, tamquam sibi veritatem manifestantibus; et ideo virtus veritatis aliquo modo

rived through the aid of experience and by reasoning from previous experience with the nexus between known and disputed facts.

In judicial inquiries inferences differ. They fall under two divisions. One class embraces inferences from an assertion, whether oral or documentary. It concerns the truth of what was stated. The other class comprises inferences from facts that are considered to exist. On the strength of them one may proceed to a knowledge of the facts whose existence has thus been indicated. The distinction is usually expressed by stating that all evidence is either direct or indirect.[50] Direct proofs in Canon Law concern positive facts.[51] A direct proof means that a given fact is proved either by its actual production, or by an admissible declaration (*confessio*) or by the testimony of a person who has himself perceived it. Indirect proofs are, according to Noval, explained in the following manner: "*Indirecte* autem probari possunt nonnulla facta negativa, seu aliquae negationes facti, videlicet, negatio aut negativa (propositio) facti *coarctata* (ad tempus, locum, etc.), negativa *iuris*, negativa *qualitatis*, non autem omnes, scilicet, negativae *facti puri*." [52] By indirect evidence or proof is meant that there are other facts proved by direct evidence from which the existence of the given fact is logically inferred.[53]

E. *Testimonial and Circumstantial*

Testimonial evidence or proof is the assertion of a person who is not one of the litigants concerning the thing at issue. Such a person is called a witness, that is, a suitable person legitimately summoned into court, whose testimony is used for the purpose of proving that a fact happened and moving the judge to credence concerning it.[54] In

attendit rationem debiti."—St. Thomas, *Summa Theol.*, II-II, q. 109, a. 3, ad. I. *Cf.* Wernz-Vidal, VI, *De Processibus,* n. 466, p. 402.

[50] *Cf.* Wigmore, *The Principles of Judicial Proof,* 7.

[51] Noval, *De Processibus,* n. 440, p. 307.

[52] *Ibid.*

[53] *Cf.* Phipson, Sidney L.—Ilbert, Sir Courtenay Peregrine, "Evidence" in *The Encyclopaedia Britannica* (14 ed., London, 1929), VIII, 906; Meile, *Die Beweislehre des Kanonischen Prozesses,* 22.

[54] *Testis iudicialis* est persona idonea legitime in iudicum vocata, cuius testimonio ad probandum factum, et fidem iudici faciendam utimur."—Zallinger,

the pages that follow, the word "witness" will be used in this sense, although the term "witness" (*testis*) has been used in the decisions of the Roman Rota for any proof and is not understood exclusively as proof by witnesses.[55]

Circumstantial evidence is any fact other than the utterance of a person regarding the existence of the thing disputed. The task of the judge is to infer from what he sees and hears in court to the existence of facts which he neither sees nor hears.[56] Circumstantial evidence and the evidence of ponderable things are sometimes in conflict with the evidence of witnesses. No logical process, but only an act of sense apprehension as to the existence or the non-existence of the thing as alleged arises with reference to the mode of producing persuasion by circumstantial evidence.[57]

Presentation of a document in court is not, strictly speaking, submission of evidence to the existence of it. The presentation is a way of permitting the court to proceed to a conviction concerning the existence of the document. In this sense, it is a means of producing persuasion. The presenting of evidence from this aspect is not asking the judge to perform a process of inference. Nevertheless, ecclesiastical courts are not hidebound by numerous rules of admissibility of proof. Trained judges decide upon both points of law and of fact. There is little probability of erroneous inference as a jury of un-

Jacobus Ant., *Institutiones Juris Ecclesiastici Maxime Privati Ordine Decretalium* (Romae, 1823), lib. II, tit. 20, § 237, p. 177.

[55] *Cf.* S. R. R., *Privationis Parochiae et Exeratiorum Spiritualium, Stanislaopolitana,* 7 Augustii, 1913, *Coram R. P. D., Michaele Lega,* dec. XLVI, n. 16—*Decisiones,* V (1913), 560; S. R. R., *Heliopolitana. Iuspatronatus,* 22 Novembris 1913, *Coram R. P. D., Michaele Lega,* dec. XLIX, n. 26—*Decisiones,* V (1913), 602.

[56] Wigmore, *Principles of Judicial Proof* (Boston, 1913), 6; *ibid.* (2 ed., Boston, 1931), 10-13; Wigmore, *Select Cases on the Law of Evidence* (3 ed., Boston, 1932), 15-28. Professor Wigmore coined the excellent term *auctopic proference* which avoids the fallacy of attributing an evidential quality to what is merely the thing itself. It cannot be used whenever there is a dependence upon witnesses to prove a thing.

[57] Evidence of a fact and inspection by the eyes fully proves and relieves of the necessity for other proofs. *Cf.* Mascardus, *Conclusiones Omnium Probationum,* I, q. VIII, n. 20.

trained men, unused to distinctions, are not admitted to ecclesiastical trials for the purpose of deciding upon questions of fact submitted to their judgment.

The admixture of both kinds of evidence is neither necessary nor inevitable. On the one side is a circumstance given as a basis for an inference without the intervention of an assertion. On the other, there is an assertion, as for example, that this woman remarked that she was going to marry because she was actuated by fear. This latter statement posits the main thing to be proved in the case. It requires no intervening inference apart from the fact of the assertion. Between these two extremes is a mass of ordinary evidence. What is of concern, however, is the nature of the particular evidentiary fact presented, whether it be assertive or circumstantial.[58]

Article 3. General Applications of the Term Proof or Evidence

A. In the Science of Law

The numerous distinctions found in the Code show the purport and indicate the importance of proof in legislation and in jurisprudence. The science of law is a moral science which takes human relations into consideration. One estimates the motives of men from their actions. External, human actions are the evidence by which the motives of men are estimated.

This observation is of importance in considering the motives that influence legislation. Things may occur in the soul of man or in a manner difficult of access.[59] The administration of justice can be confronted with this difficulty. The validity of evidence may, when public interest demands it, be safeguarded, circumvented or facilitated.[60]

[58] For the distinction between principal and contrary evidence, *cf.* Meile, *Die Beweislehre des Kanonischen Prozesses*, 23, 24; for simple, affirmative and negative evidence, *cf.* Meile, *op. cit.*, 24.

[59] Proof of one's intention is almost impossible. *Cf.* Mascardus, *Conclusiones Omnium Probationum*, I, concl. XCIX, n. 2. Such an intention, however, may be proved by conjectures, presumptions, and the like. *Cf. op. cit.*, I, concl. XCIX, n. 3.

[60] Canon Law obliges that a record of public acts be kept. The bishop is

B. In Court Procedure

The regulations which have been indicated have a negative or preventive character in the material law. They do not, however, clarify the indefiniteness nor settle the difficulties that come up in jurisprudence. Intricate cases require judicial solution. It is imperative that the various kinds of processes embody the essentials required for the production of moral certitude by means of positive evidence. Legal formalities and complex conditions should be no obstacle to this.

The competence of evidence frequently depends on the locality of the object, the contract or the crime which requires examination. The proximity of the incident facilitates the acquisition of the truth concerning it. The regulations of the Code which govern the necessary forum for marriage causes and for affairs involving tutorship and inheritance have the purpose of localizing, as far as possible, what requires investigation.[61]

In selecting judges, the Church lays special emphasis on an efficient general and juridical education. Conscientiousness, wisdom and experience are not overlooked.[62] Punctuality and exactitude in the observance of all legal details pertaining to the production of evidence are thus promoted. In this manner, the Church strives to prevent trickery, machinations and arbitrariness. The Church protects its members from such abuse of the office of judge by requiring judges

custodian of the secret archives of the diocese. *Cf.* Canons 379-382. He is custodian of all diocesan records. *Cf.* Canons 383, 384. It is obligatory to record promises of marriage, Canon 1017; publication of banns of marriage, Canons 1022-1026; form of marriage, Canon 1103, §§ 1, 2. Marriages are to be recorded in the baptismal record, Canon 470, § 2; marriages of conscience are recorded, Canons 1106, 1107; baptisms are recorded, Canons 761, 777-779; records of baptism and confirmation are required, Canon 1021, §§ 1, 2; the recording and proof of confirmation, Canons 798-800; subdiaconate and solemn profession are recorded in the baptismal book, Canon 470, § 2. The Code specifies forms of evidence: for example, the sworn affirmation, *cf.* Canon 1019, § 2; one reliable witness, *cf.* Canon 779.

[61] *Cf.* Meile, *Die Beweislehre des Kanonischen Prozesses,* 1.

[62] Canons 1574, § 3; 1623-1625.

to take an oath.[63] It insists that exceptions against a judge on account of blood relationship and affinity or for other reasons must be heard and settled before the trial begins.[64] Fidelity in the consigning of evidence to writing is insured by the presence of a trusted notary [65] together with the presence of a *promotor iustitiae* or a *defensor vinculi,* all three of whom are required to be guided by ethical principles.

C. *In the Order of Processes*

In the order of processes [66] the presenting of evidence takes highest rank. It comprises the principal part of the procedure. The decision (*sententia*) of the judge is actuated by it.

Having a central position, the law of evidence is concerned with both the individual and with society. Obedience to public law frequently depends on the possibility of making this part of the process an actuality. In the last analysis judicial evidence governs this directly. Law and jurisprudence do well to develop an understanding of the law of evidence.[67]

[63] Canon 1621, §§ 1, 2.

[64] *Cf.* Canons 1613, § 1; 1614, § 2.

[65] *Cf.* Canon 1585.

[66] A person is a subject of rights and duties in the Church by baptism. *Cf.* Canon 87. By separating one's self from the Church or by censures and vindictive penalties one is deprived of ecclesiastical rights. Although such persons retain a radical capacity for enjoying rights they lack a *facultas agendi* until, the obstacle being removed, they are restored to the use of the rights. *Cf.* Chelodi, *Ius de Personis* (Tridenti, 1927), n. 91; Wernz-Vidal, II, *De Personis,* n. 1. A right is guarded by an action unless it is expressly stated otherwise. *Cf.* Canon 1667. The exercise of such an action in court, *viz., ad ius suum in iudicio persequendum* (Canon 1668, § 1), may involve a canonical process, which is concerned with an action (*actio*), the "right" to which is to be understood in the sense indicated. In Roman Law, from which Canon Law derives its concept, an action was both the power of having recourse to a public authority to redress a grievance and the process or suit itself employed for this purpose. Celsus defined *actio* as a *jus persequendi in judicio quod sibi debetur. Cf.* D. XLIV, 7, 51. Another accepted definition is *jus petendi judicio quod sibi debtur. Cf. Inst.,* IV, 6.

[67] Meile, *Die Beweislehre des Kanonischen Prozesses,* 2.

Article 4. Three Canonical Viewpoints Regarding Evidence

A. The Ideal System

Prior to the Code of Canon Law, some canonists formed an ideal system of their own regarding evidence. They adopted the viewpoint of the legislator (*de lege ferenda*). Since the promulgation of the New Code scientific explanation centers within the limits of positive rules (*de lege lata*). Most of these norms are found in Title Ten of the Fourth Book of the Code.[68]

In addition to positive, ecclesiastical law, the natural and divine law retain their full force.[69] Moreover, a series of basic principles governing the law of evidence, whether they are legally arranged or not, are dictated by common sense. The right of an accused to be heard and to offer proof of his innocence is one of them.

B. Theoretico-Practical System

A study of evidence which explains judgments and the logical process of proceeding to a conclusion so that the truth may be attained has a close relationship to philosophical methods of cognition found in both logic and in criteriology.[70]

Although judicial evidence enters into the speculative domain of sound reasoning, it is concerned with the concrete, practical affairs of life. Modern jurists lay special emphasis on this. Nevertheless, when individual recognition of evidence degenerates into casuistry or one-sided specialization, the abuse of evidence works to the disadvantage of those whom it should aid or protect.[71] The spirit behind the technical elegancies and varieties of the process involving the production of evidence is soon caught, when uniform principles are at the basis of evidence.[72]

[68] Canons 1747-1836. *Cf.* Canons 1974-1982; 2019-2036. More specific rules are pointed out in the treatment of the marriage process.

[69] Canon 6, 5°.

[70] Meile, *Die Beweislehre des Kanonischen Prozesses*, 2.

[71] *Ibid.*, 2, 3.

[72] The basic truths used in the demonstrative sciences are common only in the sense that they are analogous. *Cf.* Aristotle, *Analytica Posteriora*, I, 10.

C. *Historico-Modern System*

Both the natural-positive and the theoretico-practical doctrines of evidence were the result of a long development. An explanation of the canons of the Code involves both the perusal of the words of each canon and an exposition of the historical origin and application of canons to present conditions.[73] Some authorities would give an exposition of evidence apart from controversial and difficult cases. In various cases the burden of proof, the production of evidence and the means of proof differ greatly. The Code takes the standpoint which puts the basic principles of evidence in norms which are placed, with modifications, in the general part concerned with the process. The Code provides for exceptions. They are found in supplements for vincular, for criminal and for beatification processes. This standpoint sets evidence in contentious and in criminal causes in less opposition. It rather serves to group definitions and rules in an official manner.[74]

[73] *Cf. S. Congregatio De Seminaris et De Studiorum Universitatibus—A. A. S.*, IX (1917), 439.

[74] Meile, *Die Beweislehre des Kanonischen Prozesses*, 2, 3.

CHAPTER VI

ESSENTIAL RULES FOR PRESENTATION OF TESTIMONY IN MATRIMONIAL PROCEDURE

THE Fourth Book of the Code is entitled *De Processibus*. It includes several kinds of procedure, whether judicial or non-judicial.[1] Title Ten of the Fourth Book is "Concerning Proofs." The inscription "Concerning Proofs" does not have the force of law nor does it summarize the context of the canons under it. It, nevertheless, furnishes, as such rubrics do, an authentic indication of the content of the canons under it. "A rubro nigrum valet illatio."[2] Title Ten is divided into eight chapters or captions. The second of these, "On Witnesses and Attestations,"[3] will be considered in this and in the following chapters. This chapter restricts itself to an explanation of the basic rules of the Code which are replies to six following questions:[4] When is the testimony to be presented? What facts and matters need no proof? By whom must the evidence be presented? What are the means employed to renounce proofs? Is testimonial evidence admitted in all ecclesiastical trials? What persons are excused from giving testimony? The six articles which follow endeavor to indicate the answers to these questions.

ARTICLE 1. DIVISION OF THE PROBATORY PERIOD

The probatory period officially opens immediately after the *litis contestatio*[5] and continues up to the close of the trial (*conclusio in causa*).[6] No canonical text exists, however, which expressly permits, obliges or forbids a judge to divide this period into two parts, one of which is devoted to the production of the proofs and another to the

[1] Noval, *De Processibus,* IV, n. 1, 5, pp. 1, 2.

[2] *Cf.* Maroto, Philippus, *Institutiones Iuris Canonici* (Matriti, 1919), I, 155.

[3] Canons 1754-1791.

[4] *Cf.* Canons 1747, 1748, 1749, 1754, 1755.

[5] *Cf.* Canon 1731, 2°.

[6] *Cf.* Canon 1860, § 1; Roberti, *De Processibus,* II, n. 227, 1, p. 30.

evaluation of them. Archbishop T. Muniz, formerly Auditor of the Supreme Tribunal of the Rota at the Apostolic Nunciature in Madrid, drew up the following useful rules which were formulated from a consideration of both Canon 1731, 2°, and the practice of the Spanish ecclesiastical tribunals:[7]

1. In trials of minor importance the judge can decide upon the day when the parties are obliged to appear immediately to propose their proofs and to verify those that are legitimate. If the parties do not terminate the task in one session they can continue the business on the following *legal* day. Inasmuch as the petitioner is the first who speaks, he is required to be the first who furnishes proof unless the judge finds a reasonable cause for changing the order.

2. In trials of major importance, either by reason of the matter involved or because of the difficulty entailed in the proof, the judge can divide the probatory period into two parts. The first of these, the shorter, is devised for the purpose of proposing the whole proof. The second, designates the time during which one should verify the proposed proof. It is convenient, in the estimation of Archbishop Muniz, always to divide the probatory period in this way.

3. Extension of time must be asked by either or by both of the parties during the time specified.[8] The judge may be more indulgent in granting a prorogation of the time if both parties rather than one of them ask for it. Equity is the norm for conceding such extensions in order that the parties may not be left without an opportunity to defend themselves. The judge is not, unless it be important, allowed to grant extensions of time beyond the period required.

4. Should the judge divide the probatory period into the aforementioned parts and one of the litigants propose a new proof in the second period, it is possible for four situations to arise: (a) In procedure involving the nullity of a marriage or in causes pertaining to

[7] The Spanish Rota was the court of third instance in Spain. *Cf.* Wernz-Vidal, VI, *De Processibus,* n. 605, n. 557. The Spanish Rota was suppressed 1 August, 1933. *Cf. Periodica de Re Canonica et Morali* (Romae et Bruges, 1905-), XXII (1933), 207. A treatment of the former Austrian concession is found in the *Archiv für katholisches Kirchenrecht,* LV (1886), 353-356.

[8] For example, if two days remain before the date of the trial, either litigant or both parties may petition for four more days.

Sacred Orders, the judge should admit a new proof immediately.[9] (b) If an oath be the proof which one of the parties wants admitted, it is to be admitted because the necessity or the convenience of this proof is apparent when one adverts to the deficiencies of verified proofs. (c) Should one kind of pertinent proof be offered and the opposing party does not object to the admission of it, the judge may admit it. (d) Should the opposing party, however, object to the admission of the pertinent proof, the proof is admissible only for a grave reason because it can be admitted after the conclusion of the cause.

5. Rather than determine upon the two parts of the probatory period from the beginning, it is more advantageous and practical to settle the two following things. First, when the question presents itself, it is well to determine the date for the presenting of proof and the time during which the proof will be accepted. In the second place, in the time during which the proposed proof is admitted, it is helpful to fix the number of days during which the proofs must be substantiated. This is practical because the judge can thereby know the greater or less difficulty that can exist in the verification of statements.[10]

Article 2. Facts and Matters Which Need No Proof

Canon 1747. Non indigent probatione:

1°. Facta notoria, ad normam Canon 2197, nn. 2, 3.

2°. Quae ab ipsa lege praesumuntur;

3°. Facta ab uno ex contendentibus asserta et ab altero admissa, nisi a iure vel a iudice probatio nihilominus exigatur.

Facts are the object of judicial proof. Those facts which are controverted by parties, and which appear doubtful to the judge and relevant to the determination of the cause must be proved.[11] The things which a judicial confession of a litigant [12] or the visual inspec-

[9] Canons 1969, 1983.

[10] Muniz, T., *Procedimientos Eclesiásticos* (2 ed., Sevilla, 1930), III, n. 275, pp. 218, 219.

[11] Roberti, *De Processibus*, II, n. 325, p. 25.

[12] *Cf.* Canon 1750.

tion of the judge himself [13] or a presumption of law [14] have evidently established do not have to be proved again. Proof substantiating such things is superfluous,[15] because what is seen and heard is sufficient.[16] Due to the limitation made by this essential principle, some facts need not be proved. The litigants, consequently, can refuse to propose and may renounce the verification of proofs in the three following circumstances mentioned in the canon.

A. Notorious Facts

Canon 1747, 1°. Non indigent probatione:
"Facta notoria, ad normam Canon 2197, nn. 2, 3."

Notorious facts, provided that they be notorious either by notoriety of law or of fact, do not require proof.[17] *Notoriety of law* is present when something has become an adjudged matter,[18] or a judicial confession [19] has been made. A judicial confession is an admission made in court before a competent judge and during judicial proceedings by either the defendant or plaintiff against himself in favor of the other party or by both litigants against the truth or justice of their claims. An extra-judicial confession takes place outside of court.[20]

The doctrine on the confession is not developed in this chapter because on the one hand, the confession is considered to be not proof

[13] *Cf.* Canons 1807, 1808, 1810.

[14] *Cf.* Canons 1825, § 2; 1826.

[15] Wernz-Vidal, VI, *De Processibus*, n. 437, pp. 379, 380.

[16] "Cum itaque nec cetera probationum iudicia reprobentur, iure competente praediorum, quae in quaestionem veniunt, dominium ad te ostende pertinere. Nam res vindicantem ab emptore suos numeratos nummos adservantem erga probationem laborare non convenit, si quidem huiusmodi, licet probetur, factum intentioni nullum praestet adminiculum."—*Cod.* IV, 19, 21.

[17] *Cf.* Pirhing, *Ius Canonicum*, lib. II, tit. XIX, § 4, n. 31.

[18] *Cf.* Canon 1902.

[19] *Cf.* Canons 1750, 2197, 2°.

[20] *Cf.* Reiffenstuel, *Ius Canonicum Universum*, lib. II, tit. XVIII, n. 4; Eichmann, *Das Prozessrecht*, § 45, 1, p. 139.

properly so called,[21] and on the other hand because the litigants are not and cannot be witnesses on their own behalf at the same time.[22] Hence, the statements of the defendant and the plaintiff are, despite the misuse of terms by some authors, called "depositions" whereas the testimonies of third parties or witnesses are called "attestations." Unless there was a sentence or unless a judicial confession was admissible, circumstantial evidence did not, according to the Decretals,[23] excuse one from proof. *Notoriety of fact* is present when something is so publicly known or has occurred in such circumstances that it cannot be concealed by any artifice or be excused by any favor of the law.[24] Factual notoriety exists with relation to the things which are known by everybody, *e. g.*, well-known historical events, common occurrences in the natural order, and the like. A judge is obliged to admit such facts even though he himself had not referred to them during the process, as a judge is not deprived by his office of common

[21] In one place Reiffenstuel referring to the maxim, "Propria confessio est optima probatio," calls the judicial confession fullest proof. *Cf.* Reiffenstuel, *Ius Canonicum Universum*, lib. II, tit. XVIII, n. 12; Schmalzgrueber, *Ius Ecclesiasticum Universum*, lib. II, Pars III, tit. XVIII, n. 20; S. R. R., *Nullit. Matrim.*, 15 Novembris, 1909, *Coram R. P. D., Gustavo Persiani*, dec. XVI, n. 7—*Decisiones*, I (1909), 139; c. 2, *de capellis monachorum et aliorum religiosum*, III, 37; c. 10, X, *de cohabitatione clericorum et mulierum*, III, 2. In another place, Reiffenstuel states that properly speaking the confession is rather a revelation of the proof: "Unde consequens est, quod confessio proprie non sit probatio, sed potius revelatio probationis; adesque quod in statuto faciente mentionem de probationibus, in materia odiosa non comprehendatur confessio."—*Ibid.*, n. 14.

[22] *Cf.* S. R. R., *Mediolanen. Nullit. Matrim.*, 23 Februarii, 1909, *Coram R. P. D., Ioanne Prior*, dec. VII, n. 14—*Decisiones*, II (1910), 65; S. R. R., *Limburgen. Nullit. Matrim.*, 2 Januarii, 1913, dec. I, n. 8—*Decisiones*, V (1913), 7; S. R. R., *Nullit. Matrim.*, 8 Martii, 1915, *Coram R. P. D., Seraphino Many*, dec. VIII, n. 5—*Decisiones*, VII (1915), 85; S. R. R., *Iniuriarum. Sententia Super Quaestione Incidentali*, 2 Julii, 1915, dec. XXVI, n. 6—*Decisiones*, VII (1915), 281; S. R R., *Moguntina. Nullit. Matrim.*, 14 Julii, 1921, *Coram R. P. D., Friderico Cattani Amadori*, dec. XVII, n. 8—*Decisiones*, XIII (1921), 167, 168.

[23] *Cf.* "Nos igitur consultationi tuae taliter respondemus, quod si crimen eorum ita publicum est, ut merito debeat appellari notorium, in eo casu nec testis nec accusator est necessarius, quum huiusmodi crimen nulla possit tergiversatione celari."—C. 8, X, *de cohabitatione clericorum et mulierum*, III, 2.

[24] Canon 2197, 3°.

knowledge. Moreover, it is supposed that such things are known by him. Nevertheless, a judge cannot admit facts which are, perhaps, known to himself but are not common knowledge because the parties have a poor estimation of them. Judicial reasoning is not to be concerned with them.[25] Viewing the basic rule laid down in the canon under consideration from another aspect, the notoriety or evidence of publicly known facts is concerned with those permanent facts, the only proof of which is based on the mere looking at them without the need of any other instrument or proof. The canon is not concerned with transitory facts the remembrance of which vanishes and which although they be alleged as notorious, are not truly such.[26] The attestations of witnesses and a judicial process (*ordo judiciorum*) are not needed for the declaration of a fact which is notorious. Such a fact ought not to be proved, but merely alleged.[27]

In matrimonial procedure, there may come to the attention of the ordinariate a case of a ratified but non-consummated marriage dissolved by a subsequent religious profession. The curia makes the observation that such a marriage may be presumed "ratum et non consummatum" if the spouses had not cohabited after the celebration of the marriage.[28] Consequently, inquiry must be made of the curia of the place in which the marriage took place regarding the non-consummation of the marriage and the testimony of the declaration concerning it. Archbishop Muniz writes that [29]

> . . . in this case when the Holy See has not decided anything, the non-consummation of the marriage could be declared in an administrative way only if it is evidently established, and

[25] Roberti, *De Processibus,* II, n. 325, pp. 25, 26.

[26] Muniz, *Procedimientos Eclesiásticos,* III, n. 276, 2a, p. 220; *cf.* "Sed cum multa dicantur notoria, quae non sunt, providere debes, ne quod dubium est pro notorio videaris habere."—C. 14, X, *de appellationibus, recusationibus, et relationibus,* II, 28; Wernz-Vidal, VI, *De Processibus,* n. 437, p. 380.

[27] Reiffenstuel, *Ius Canonicum Universum,* lib. II, tit. IX, n. 37. *Cf.* Noval, *De Processibus,* IV, n. 444, pp. 311, 312; Wernz-Vidal, VI, *De Processibus,* n. 437, pp. 379, 380; A Coronata, *De Processibus,* III, n. 1273, p. 180.

[28] Canon 1015, § 2.

[29] Translated from Muniz, *Procedimientos Eclesiásticos,* II, n. 258, 5°, pp. 309, 310.

> it is public and notorious that the spouses had not cohabitated; in all other cases of this nature one has to proceed in a judicial way, and therefore, with the intervention of the defender of the marriage bond, because the presumption of law established by Canon 1015, § 2, has to be destroyed.

Also in the marriage process regarding the existence of the impediment of crime,[80] if it be established that a civil marriage was celebrated while the other spouse was living, the impediment of crime arising out of adultery exists because of the violent presumption of adultery. In cases like this it does not seem possible that any proof can destroy such a presumption. The notoriety or clandestinity surrounding the circumstances of the marriage makes no difference as the fact of a civil marriage, even before a justice of the peace in this country, is sufficient.[81] It is, however, possible that no impediment exists in the internal forum if adultery did not take place. Nevertheless, the marriage cannot be authorized to take place in the external forum without a dispensation. The same can be said if the attempted marriage had been celebrated by some other public action. If the attempt was made by a secret action one must believe the depositions of the contracting parties for the reason that the attempt cannot be proved in the external forum. The proofs of the marriage may be summarized in the following manner:

1. Before the marriage
   a. Record of marriage.
   b. Any means to supply record.
      (1) Depositions of Spouses—Confession of one alone suffices for proof.
      (2) Record of their children as legitimate.
2. After the marriage—External Forum only.
   a. Same proofs as above (*i. e.*, before the marriage).
   b. Proof of cohabitation.
   c. Proof of attempted marriage while legitimate spouse lived.

[80] Canon 1075. For a treatment of the subject from the aspect of proof when there is murder before the second marriage, or adultery with promise to marry after the death of a spouse, *cf.* Donohue, John H., *The Impediment of Crime* (The Catholic University of America Canon Law Studies, No. 69, 1931), pp. 73-79.

[81] *Cf.* Decretum S. C. de Sacram., *A. A. S.*, IV (1912), 403.

d. Proof of attempted marriage while *knowing* legitimate spouse lived. This can be proved by indications—not by a confession.[32]

On the other hand, facts that are manifest but not notorious must be proved by demonstrating that some public and well-known proclamation exists concerning them.[33] For example, in the marriage process it is to be observed that in the impediment of crime arising from adultery and conjugicide, the latter delict is not presumed in the external forum but must be proved by a sentence because it is a public fact. Even though the conjugicide is established, the adultery is not presumed; but if the murderer was not the spouse of the dead person but the party who wanted to contract marriage, it is necessary to prove that the object of the conjugicide was not marriage but another object. There is a presumption of fact that the object of the murder was marriage, inasmuch as the natural repugnance to contract marriage with the murderer of the spouse cannot be overcome if it is not already overcome by illicit relations which were forbidden before.[34]

In a question involving the commission of a notorious crime, when the evidence against the culprit is evident, neither citation nor process is necessary.[35]

B. *Matters Presumed by the Law Itself*

Canon 1747, 2°. "Quae ab ipsa lege praesumuntur."

Neither direct nor indirect proof is required for matters which are presumed by the law itself. The inclusion of the word "law" (*lege*) implies two things. In the first place, it implies that proof against a simple presumption is not excluded inasmuch as Canon 1747 merely states that simple presumptions do not need proof, and, moreover, a simple presumption sometimes admits of proofs to the contrary provided that they are convincing ones. Thus, the father of a child is

[32] *Cf.* Muniz, *Procedimientos Eclesiásticos,* II, n. 306, 1°, pp. 365, 366.

[33] *Cf.* Reiffenstuel, *Ius Canonicum Universum,* lib. II, tit. IX, n. 42.

[34] Muniz, *Procedimientos Eclesiásticos,* II, n. 306, 3°, p. 367.

[35] *Cf.* S. R. R., *Pharen. Iurium et Poenarum,* 10 Junii, 1910, *Coram, R. P. D., Gulielmo Sebastianelli,* dec. XX, n. 7—*Decisiones,* II (1910), 195, 196.

he whom legitimate marriage designates as such, unless the contrary be proved by conclusive arguments. Children born at least six months after the celebration of the marriage or within ten months of the dissolution of conjugal life are presumed to be legitimate.[36] The parties do not need judicial proof if their allegations are presumptions of law that are not impugned. If it is certain and it is not disputed that Titus, for example, was born of a legitimate marriage, it does not have to be proved that he is a legitimate son.[37] Secondly, questions which pertain to the common law, written or unwritten, do not constitute the object or purpose of judicial proof in any inferior or superior court. Ecclesiastical curias have knowledge of the rights of moral and physical persons, of what is conformable to law and do not make them the subject matter of proof.[38] Consequently, evidence contrary to a simple presumption is admissible. Thus it appears that contrary proof may be admitted against those things which have been proved in court by reason but not in a clear and evident manner.[39]

An inferior judge should, of necessity, know the particular laws and universal customs observed in the diocese or province where he functions. Particular rights involving them in their respective regions are not to be proved. However, this specific knowledge cannot be supposed to be the possession or be exacted from superior judges. This is the reason why particular laws and customs are to be proved before a superior judge.[40] Likewise, the laws and particular customs known in other dioceses and even the local statutes and customs of one's own diocese should not be proved for the benefit of an inferior judge. Individual or singular privileges are, however, to be not merely alleged in court, but must be proved.[41] With regard to the

[36] *Cf.* Canon 1115; Gasparri, *De Matrimonio* (1932), II, n. 1113, pp. 194, 195.

[37] *Cf.* Muniz, *Procedimientos Eclesiásticos*, III, n. 276, 3°, p. 220. For the manner of proof of filiation, age and virginity, *cf.* Schmalzgrueber, *Ius Ecclesiasticum Universum*, lib. II, Pars III, tit. XX, n. 57; S. C. Consilii Instr., 22 Augusti, 1840—*Coll.* n. 1840 which considers the proof of virginity.

[38] *Cf.* c. 44, X, *de appellationibus, recusationibus, et relationibus*, II, 28; Reiffenstuel, *Ius Canonicum Universum*, lib. II, tit. IX, n. 36; Wernz-Vidal, VI, *De Processibus*, n. 438, p. 380.

[39] Wernz-Vidal, VI, *De Processibus*, n. 437, note (28), p. 380.

[40] *Cf.* c. 1, *de constitutionibus*, I, 2 in VI°.

[41] *Cf.* cc. 13, 21, 24, X, *de privilegiis et excessibus privilegiatorum*, V, 33; c. 1,

individual privileges referred to, the judge can always supply the parties with proofs and make use of private knowledge.[42] Hence, to summarize this, the principals can renounce the proposal and verification of proof because they do not dispute the fact but a right or the application of the law in a proposed case. However, if the disputed right originates from a particular custom, local statute, privilege, pious foundation or from a contract, it is necessary to prove to the judge that the custom, statute, privilege or foundation exists as inferior judges cannot be compelled to have more than a knowledge of general laws, laws of provincial councils, synodal statutes, and diocesan dispositions of a general nature. Likewise, a metropolitan judge cannot be compelled to possess more than a knowledge of the same provisions of the law.[43]

Nevertheless, should a direct or an indirect proof be adduced in opposition to presumptions, it is required that the facts upon which the presumptions rest be established by proofs;[44] for the facts presumed by the law or in the law itself vouch for the proof. Properly speaking, facts which are presumed are not proved facts, but are accepted as proved. They relieve the party on behalf of whom they militate from the burden of proof. However, it is possible to break down a presumption of law to which the Code refers in this canon by any clear and full proof. The person whom a presumption of law favors is sometimes said to have his intention founded in law.[45] Judicial decisions which constitute the foundation of a presumption certainly are to be proved in court.[46]

In matrimonial procedure, the purpose of the evidence is the proof or disproof of the validity of a contracted marriage. To prove the invalidity of a marriage contract, it is necessary to prove that a diriment impediment [47] obstructed it at the time of the celebration. The

de constitutionibus, I, 2 in VI°; c. 1, *de praescriptionibus,* II, 13 in VI°; Wernz-Vidal, VI, *De Processibus,* n. 438, p. 380.

[42] Roberti, *De Processibus,* II, n. 325, p. 26.

[43] Muniz, *Procedimientos Eclesiásticos,* III, n. 276, 1°, pp. 219, 220.

[44] Roberti, *De Processibus,* II, n. 326, b, n. 26.

[45] A Coronata, *De Processibus,* III, n. 1273, II, 2°, pp. 180, 181.

[46] *Ibid.,* 181.

[47] *Cf.* Canons 1036, § 2; 1067-1080.

proofs must be confined to the particular impediment alleged as the reason for the nullity which was claimed. Moreover, although a former marriage be invalid or dissolved for some cause, it is illicit to contract another before it shall have been legitimately and certainly established that the prior marriage is null or has been dissolved.[48]

The reason for this is that once a marriage has been validly contracted it remains valid and is not necessarily affected by an obstacle which arises after it.[49] A marriage enjoys the favor of law [50] when it possesses the appearance of a true marriage which was celebrated in accordance with the established form.[51] The principle, *matrimonium gaudet favore iuris,* signifies that in doubt of law or of fact about a marriage the validity of the marriage stands until the contrary be proved. The rule suffers an exception in favor of the faith as Canon 1127 states that in doubt the privilege of faith enjoys the favor of law.[52] By reason of this the marriages of converted infidels are declared null if their validity be prudently doubted.[53] Once persons are married according to the legitimate form their marriage absolutely enjoys the favor of law so that it cannot be declared null until it be fully [54] or evident [55] proved. The marriages

[48] Canon 1069, § 2.

[49] For example, a legitimate marriage between two infidels is valid. If consummated in infidelity it is not dissolved by religious profession. *Cf.* Chelodi, Joannes, *Ius Matrimoniale Iuxta Codicem Iuris Canonici* (ed. altera, Trento, 1921), n. 153. Positive arguments should demonstrate the opposite opinion which was held by Wernz, *Ius Decretalium,* IV, 699. A marriage, however, consummated by two infidels, one of whom remains in infidelity and wishes neither to be converted nor to live peacefully with the other party who is converted, receives baptism, and fulfills the necessary conditions, can be dissolved. *Cf.* Gasparri, *De Matrimonio,* II, n. 1131, pp. 206, 207; for the dissolution of such a marriage when unconsummated, *cf.* Gasparri, *De Matrimonio,* n., 1155, n. 2°, p. 231.

[50] *Cf.* Canon 1014.

[51] *Cf.* Canons 1094-1103.

[52] Canon 1127; *cf.* Chelodi, *Ius Matrimoniale,* n. 7, b, p. 6.

[53] *Cf. Benedictus* XIV, Ep. *Probe te,* 15 Decembris, 1751—*Fontes,* n. 418; Dubium, *A. S. S.,* XXXI (1899), 694.

[54] *Instructio Austriaca,* § 147; S. R. R., *Nullit. Matrim.,* 1 Augusti, 1913, *Coram R. P. D., Michaele Lega,* dec. XLII, n. 11—*Decisiones,* V (1913), 495;

of the faithful and of infidels enjoy this favor of the law so that the contrary must be proved conclusively by a trial (*iudicium*) in the proper sense of the word.[56] The principle that a marriage enjoys the favor of law had been received in the old jurisprudence of the Sacred Congregations [57] and is accepted by the more recent jurisprudence of the Roman Rota. On account of insufficient proofs, actions commenced for declarations of nullity have been frequently rejected.[58] Nevertheless, another exception to the presumption of the validity of a contracted marriage exists besides the one involved in Canon 1127.

ibid., dec. XXXIX, n. 11—*Decisiones Coram Lega,* 485; S. R. R., *Nullit. Matrim.*, 19 Januarii, 1910, *Coram R. P. D., Gustavo Persiani,* dec. III, n. 7—*Decisiones,* II (1910), 24; S. R. R., *Parisien. Nullit. Matrim.*, 23 Januarii, 1920, *Coram R. P. D., Petro Rossetti,* dec. III, n. 5—*Decisiones,* XII (1920), 14.

[55] S. R. R., *Moguntina. Nullit. Matrim.*, 14 Julii, 1921, *Coram R. P. D., Friderico Cattani Amadori,* dec. XVII, n. 5—*Decisiones,* XIII (1921), 166; *cf.* S. R. R., *Nullit. Matrim.*, 11 Augusti, 1921, *Coram R. P. D., Francisco Solieri,* dec. XXIII, n. 3—*Decisiones,* XIII (1921), 231.

[56] *Cf.* S. R. R., *Nullit. Matrim.*, 15 Decembris, 1915, *Coram R. P. D., Gulielmo Sebastianelli,* dec. XLI, n. 8—*Decisiones,* VII (1915), 460, 461; S. R. R., *Neo-Eboracen. Nullit. Matrim.*, 1 Martii, 1913, *Coram R. P. D., Friderico Cattani Amadori,* dec. XVI, n. 17—*Decisiones,* V (1913), 191.

[57] *Cf.* S. C. Off., Instr., 24 Januarii, 1877 (Ad Ep. Nesquallien), *Coll.* n. 1465; "In dubio standum est pro validitate matrimonii, praesertim quando constat matrimonium fuisse contractum. Imo etiam si hoc non constaret, sed matrimonium possessionem pro se ostendere posset, quod verificatur quando coniuncti bona fide putant se in vero et legitimo coniugio vivere, et ceteri nullum ex illa coniunctione scandalum patiuntur, quia arbitrantur eam esse legitimam: etiam in hoc casu praedictum principium valeret, et ab eodem recedere non liceret."—S. C. S. Off., Instr. (Ad Vic. Ap. Oc. Cen.), 18 Decembris, 1872, n. 2—*Coll.*, n. 1392. Compare with S. R. R., *Nullit. Matrim.*, 30 Junii, 1910, *Coram R. P. D., Michaele Lega,* dec. XXIII, n. 6—*Decisiones,* II (1910), 223.

[58] See also S. R. R., *Nullit. Matrim.*, 6 Decembris, 1909, *Coram R. P. D., Gustavo Persiani,* dec. XVIII, n. 9—*Decisiones,* I (1909), 159, 160; S. R. R., *Nullit. Matrim.*, 19 Januarii, 1910, *Coram R. P. D., Gustavo Persiani,* dec. III, n. 7—*Decisiones,* II (1910), 24; S. R. R., *Nullit. Matrim.*, 17 Martii 1919, *Coram R. P. D., Iosepho Mori,* dec. XII, n. 6—*Decisiones,* II (1910), 119; S. R. R., *Ugentina. Nullit. Matrim.*, 22 Martii, 1910, *Coram R. P. D., Aloisio Sincero,* dec. XIII, nn. 5, 6—*Decisiones,* II (1910), 124, 125; S. R. R., *Parisien. Nullit. Matrim.*, 13 Junii, 1911, *Coram R. P. D., Francisco Heiner,* dec. XXIV, nn. 4, 7—*Decisiones,* III (1911), 260-262; S. R. R., *Trinocomalien. Nullit. Matrim.*, 1 Februarii, 1913, dec. VIII, n. 4—*Decisiones,* V (1913), 88.

A clandestine marriage has to be proved.[59] A truly clandestine marriage, although it be validly contracted by Christians under certain conditions without the required form is subject to the application of the two general principles for the proof of a fact: (a) If witnesses were present at the marriage they plainly prove it in spite of the denial of both spouses. The reason for this is that the proofs of a diriment impediment are confined to the time during which the marriage was allegedly contracted.[60] (b) If no witnesses were present, and one of the married persons admits the fact of marriage, the validity of it is recognized unless it prejudice against another marriage which was publicly celebrated. Should both parties deny that a clandestine marriage occurred, it is accepted that it was not contracted. If one party affirm and the other deny, the party affirming the fact of a clandestine marriage, has to prove it. Deficient in proof, the validity of the alleged marriage is not sustained because in doubt that a clandestine marriage took place, it does not enjoy the favor of law.[61]

Facts freely asserted in the admission or confession of one of the parties [62] properly speaking do not constitute proof. A confession or admission does not free one from the burden of proving because the burden of proof, with which the following canon is concerned, flows from the confession.

C. *Facts Asserted by One of the Litigating Parties and Admitted by the Other*

Canon 1747, 3°. "Facta ab uno ex contendentibus asserta et ab altero admissa, nisi a iure vel a iudice probatio nihilominus exigatur."

[59] *Cf.* S. R. R., *Nullit. Matrim.*, 28 Maii, 1909, *Coram R. P. D., Aloisio Sincero,* dec. VI, n. 2—Decisiones, I (1909), 58, 59.

[60] Feije, *De Impedimentis et Dispensationibus Matrimonialibus,* n. 84, 4°, p. 56.

[61] Chelodi, *Ius Matrimoniale,* n. 128, p. 139.

[62] *Cf.* Canons 1750 to 1753; Roberti, *De Processibus,* II, nn. 329-333, pp. 32-39.

Unless the law or the judge demand it, proof of facts asserted by one of the litigants and denied by the other is not required. Such facts are not further controverted. The judge can assume that they are a basis for his decision. A fact, moreover, need not be explicitly admitted by the adverse party. It is sufficient that from the acts it be accepted as admitted. The rule has weight absolutely in causes involving private welfare as in this the parties can renounce their right. It relaxes in great measure in causes which involve the public welfare as the law is made to safeguard this. Nevertheless, in causes pertaining to the bond of marriage the judge can always require the prescription of the law which demands the proof.[63] The law makes this disposition

> because the facts affirmed by one party and admitted by the other in the acts (*acta*), in the petition, the answer, the reply, the duplicate, the absolution of the propositions or in any other judicial act may not be accepted by the judge as a renunciation of the proof in so far as he fears collusion between the parties, *e. g.*, in the case of a trial for divorce. Or the judge must ask for proof because the law itself demands it, *e. g.*, in a trial for the nullity of a marriage,[64] and in general in causes of the public good,[65]

as has been stated.

Facts freely asserted in the admission or confession of one of the parties [66] do not, properly speaking, constitute proof. For an admission is not a relaxation from the burden of proof, as the burden of proof follows from it. A confession is not a manner of arrangement which concerns one's own substantial or processul rights because the process is arranged neither to assume obligations nor to make it licit for parties to derogate from processual law. Likewise, properly speaking, a confession or admission is not proof as it restricts the will of a judge. Consequently, it is reduced to legal proof because the legislator considers the facts asserted by either litigant

[63] Roberti, *De Processibus,* II, n. 325, c., p. 26.

[64] *Cf.* Canon 1747 with Canon 1975, § 2.

[65] Translated from Muniz, *Procedimientos Eclesiásticos,* n. 276, p. 219.

[66] *Cf.* Canons 1750-1753; Roberti, *De Processibus,* II, nn. 329-333, pp. 32-39.

against himself. Hence, after a judicial confession it is not permitted to adduce a contrary proof to destroy it.[67] Nevertheless, if the confession be judicial and the admission pertains to private business, it fully proves and relieves the plaintiff from the burden of proof.[68] In the latter instance, a judge cannot exact further proof as the judicial admission fully proves. He can, nevertheless, require further proofs if the confession be extra-judicial or if the judicial confession was not elicited freely and with deliberation.[69]

Article 3. By Whom Evidence Must Be Presented

Canon 1748, § 1. Onus probandi incumbit ei qui asserit.

§ 2. Actore non probante, reus absolvitur.

Having considered general rules for the admissibility of evidence, the Code proceeds to point out by whom the evidence is to be presented, or to dispose of the burden of proof. The content of the burden of proof is, as the wording of the canon shows, characterized by a juxtaposition of an affirmative and a negative. The Roman jurist Paulus made such a distinction when he expressed the principle: "Ei incumbit probatio qui dicit non qui negat." [70] The Code does not, however, expressly put affirmative and negative in juxtaposition, but assertion and burden of proof are placed together. The legislator seems to have intended to disregard questions which have been disputed by canonists for centuries. The Code, consequently, takes the position that a party who makes a charge must, by assuming the burden of proof, prove the whole legal claim, whereas the party who asserts nothing positive assumes no responsibility for the substantiation of facts.

First, the burden of proof will be deliberated upon, and then, the proof of negative statements will be discussed.

[67] *Cf.* Roberti, *De Processibus,* II, n. 329, pp. 33, 34.

[68] *Cf.* Canon 1751.

[69] *Cf.* Canons 1751 and 1753; Reiffenstuel, *Ius Canonicum Universum,* lib. II, tit. XVIII, n. 62. For exception in criminal causes see *ibid.,* n. 65.

[70] Paulus, D. XXII, 3, 2.

A. The Burden of Proof

Modern scholars hold contrary and paradoxical opinions on the burden of proof. With laconic brevity the Code expresses the rule that the burden of proof in judicial proceedings, either contentious or criminal, lies on him who makes the claim in court.[71] The subjective claim of the principle upon law is ideal. The human mind can only recognize and understand it from the legal facts. These must be called to the attention of the judge for the purpose of acquainting him with them.

1. *Generally speaking, the burden of proof rests on the plaintiff (actor)*.[72] The silence of a litigant does not diminish the burden of proof on the part of the plaintiff.[73] The plaintiff generally asserts something detrimental to the defendant, and, consequently, the burden of proof falls on him.[74] The burden is imposed in accordance

[71] *Cf.* Canon 1748. Compare "Quod autem postulas, ut illuc personam dirigere debeamus, qua de his, quae dicuntur, possit esse probatio, esset utcumque excusabile, si umquam ratio ei, qui accusatur, necessitatem probationis imponeret. At postquam non tibi, sed accusantibus hoc onus incumbit, ad nos, sicut praefati sumus, dilatione cessante uenire non desinas."—C. 1, C. VI, q. 5; *cf.* c. 1, *de confessis*, II, 9, in VI°; *Cod.* IV, 19, 1, 9.

[72] *Cf.* S. R. R., *Nullit. Matrim.*, 17 Januarii, 1912, *Coram R. P. D., Michaele Lega*, dec. V, n. 5—*Decisiones*, IV (1912), 37. Compare with the principle, "Quod omnes attigit, ab omnibus debet probari," in S. R. R., *S. Angeli De Lombardis*, 22 Februarii, 1919, *Coram R. P. D., Friderico Cattani Amadori*, dec. VI, n. 3—*Decisiones*, XI (1919), 62. For the burden of the proof of custom, *cf.* S. R. R., *Mediolanen*, 18 Julii, 1914, *Coram R. P. D., Gulielmo Sebastianelli*, dec. XXVI, n. 5—*Decisiones*, VI (1914), 278, 279; S. R. R., *Segusina. Iuris Canendi Missas Adventicias*, 12 July, 1913, *Coram R. P. D., Antonio Perathoner*, dec. XXXVI, n. 3—*Decisiones*, V (1913), 434. In litigation regarding the right of a church to a sodality, the burden of proof was thus expressed: "Sodalitate in themate actrici onus incumbit probandi se habere legitimum acquisitionis titulum seu legitime acquisivisse patronatum quem sibi vindicat supra ecclesiam, quod non praestet neque praestare valet."—*Cf.* S. R. R., *Theatina. Iurium*, 23 Martii, 1911, *Coram R. P. D., Iosepho Mori*, dec. XIV, n. 2—*Decisiones*, III (1911), 136. See also S. R. R., *Solutionis*, 10 Julii, 1915, *Coram R. P. D., Petro Rossetti*, dec. XXX, n. 20—*Decisiones*, VII (1915), 323.

[73] *Cf.* S. R. R., *Nullit. Matrim.*, 18 Augusti, 1916, *Coram R. P. D., Seraphino Many*, dec. XXVIII, n. 22—*Decisiones*, VIII (1916), 324, 325.

[74] *Cf.* Eichmann, *Das Prozessrecht*, § 43, pp. 135-137; Meile, *De Beweislehre des Kanonischen Prozesses*, 27, a.

with a principle of natural justice. The party who affirms a fact denied by the other party has the affirmative, regardless of how much literal negation there may be in what he says.[75] If the plaintiff fails to prove his claim the defendant wins, although he has not disproved anything.[76] Moreover, the defendant called into court is not, except in cases defined by law, obliged to exhibit his documents (*instrumenta*) to the plaintiff in order to substantiate an action of the plaintiff against himself.[77]

This rule applies fully to matrimonial procedure. In matrimonial causes of nullity the burden of proof falls on the person petitioning for a declaration of the invalidity of a contracted marriage. The rule holds although only a probable reason for the validity of the marriage exists and although it be controverted that the marriage was contracted.[78]

[75] *Cf.* S. R. R., *Nullit. Matrim.*, 17 Januarii, 1912, *Coram R. P. D., Michaele Lega,* dec. XX, n. 5—*Decisiones Coram Lega,* 251. In defamation cases, the judge can impose continued silence when the defamer does not prove his detraction. *Cf.* S. R. R., *Diffamationis,* 12 Decembris, 1910, *Coram R. P. D., Michaele Lega,* dec. XXXIII, n. 4—*Decisiones,* II (1910), 352. Compare especially with S. R. R., *Diffamationis,* 8 Martii, 1913, *Coram R. P. D., Michaele Lega,* dec. XVII, n. 7—*Decisiones,* V (1913), 203, 204. A person asserting *iuspatronatus* has the burden of proof. *Cf.* S. R. R., *Isclana. Iurispatronatus,* 8 Junii, 1916, *Coram R. P. D., Iosepho Mori,* dec. XVI, n. 5—*Decisiones,* VIII (1916), 176.

[76] C. 26, X, *de sententia et re iudicata,* II, 27; c. 36, X, *de iureiurando,* II, 14; c. un., X, *ut ecclesiastica beneficia sine diminutione conferantur,* III, 12; Pirhing, *Ius Canonicum,* lib. II, tit. XIX, § 2, nn. 5-8; Bouix, Marie Dominique, *De Iudiciis Eccelsiasticis* (3 ed., 2 vols., Pariis, 1883) pp. 305, 306; S. R. R., *Refectionis Damnorum,* 4 Aprilis, 1916, *Coram R. P. D., Ioanne Prior,* dec. VII, n. 21—*Decisiones,* VIII (1916), 83.

[77] Schmalzgrueber, *Ius Ecclesiasticum Universum,* lib. II, Pars III, tit. XIX, n. 41; *cf.* Wernz-Vidal, VI, *De Processibus,* n. 436, note (16), p. 378; Wernz, *Ius Decretalius,* V, n. 172; c. 5, X, *de renunciatione,* I, 9; c. 3, X, *de causa possessionis et proprietatis,* II, 12.

[78] *Cf.* S. R. R., *Nullit. Matrim.*, 30 Junii, 1910, *Coram R. P. D., Michaele Lega,* dec. XXIII, n. 12—*Decisiones,* II (1910), 221; *ibid.,* dec. IX, n. 2—*Decisiones Coram Lega,* 133. In doubt regarding promises (*sponsalia*) they must be fully proved as there is a presumption of liberty. *Cf.* S. R. R., *Impedimenti et Damnorum,* 1 Augusti, 1913, *Coram R. P. D., Aloisio Sincero,* dec. XLI, n. 3—*Decisiones,* V (1913), 479. Consent given externally is always pre-

It was stated that generally speaking the burden of proof is on the plaintiff. The plaintiff, however, is freed from the burden of proof in those cases in which the Code prescribes the contrary,[79] which cases fall back into cases of presumptions of law.[80]

2. *Inversion of the burden of proof: It may fall on the defendant.* It has been seen that the burden of proof usually falls on the plaintiff. The defendant who disavows or denies something is free from the burden of proof. This follows from the principle, "He who asserts, must prove; he who does not assert, need not prove." Usually the burden of proof falls on the plaintiff. It seems that only obvious impracticality on the one hand, and evident feasibility on the other, can authorize the invention of exceptions to release a party from the duty of proving the facts essential to his case. There are, nevertheless, cases in which the burden of proof falls on the defendant, not upon the plaintiff. These are chiefly:

a. When the defendant by taking exception, affirms some fact and thus becomes, as it were, a plaintiff, *e. g.*, if the defendant state that he was induced to enter into a contract through the influence of grave fear.[81] In matrimonial procedure, a defendant may make an

sumed true until evidently proved otherwise. *Cf.* S. R. R., *Nullit. Matrim.*, 19 Januarii, 1910, *Coram R. P. D., Gustavo Persiani*, dec. III, n. 8—*Decisiones*, II (1910), 27; S. R. R., *Nullit. Matrim.*, 16 Junii, 1916, *Coram R. P. D., Seraphino Many*, dec. XVIII, n. 2—*Decisiones*, VIII (1916), 201, 202; *ibid.*, 29 Februarii, 1916, dec. IV, n. 8—*Decisiones*, VIII (1916), 53, 54. The one alleging *metus* is obliged to prove it. *Cf.* S. R. R., *Nicien., Nullit. Matrim.*, 15 Martii, 1915, *Coram R. P. D., Gulielmo Sebastianelli*, dec. X, n. 2—*Decisiones*, VII (1915), 112; S. R. R., *Nullitatis vel Dispensationis Matrimonii*, 27 Aprilis, 1915, *Coram R. P. D., Iosepho Mori*, dec. XIX, n. 4—*Decisiones*, VII (1915), 209; S. R. R., *Parisien., Nullit. Matrim.*, 4 Novembris, 1915, *Coram R. P. D., Gulielmo Sebastianelli*, dec. XL, n. 2—*Decisiones*, VII (1915), 446; S. R. R., *Nicien., Nullit. Matrim.*, 30 Decembris, 1915, *Coram R. P. D., Petro Rossetti*, dec. XLII, n. 6—*Decisiones*, VII (1915), 468, 469. Revalidation is not presumed, but has to be proved. *Cf.* S. R. R., *Neo-Eboracen., Nullit. Matrim.*, 1 Martii, 1913, *Coram R. P. D., Friderico Cattani Amadori*, dec. XVI, n. 21—*Decisiones*, V (1913), 194.

[79] For example, Canons 1454, 1536, § 1.

[80] *Cf.* Eichmann, *Das Prozessrecht*, § 43, pp. 135-137.

[81] "Si quis id quod traditur ex iusta causa non a domino et nondum usucaptum petet, iudicium dabo. Merito praetor ait 'nondum usucaptum' nam si

exception by which he affirms something by setting up three defenses or exceptions pertaining to a former marriage: (1) That the former marriage was invalid because of a diriment impediment. In the marriage process the burden of proof may occasion difficulty under this category in the proof of the impediment of abduction (*raptus*).[82] In the proof of the existence of the impediment of abduction, if the marriage has been *already* contracted, the proof of the impediment and of the nullity of the marriage will have to be stronger to prove it in the external forum. It is necessary to prove that the forcible abduction (*raptus*) took place and that the marriage was celebrated in an unsafe place or at least in a locality which was not conducive to freedom of the woman. The intention to contract a marriage is easily presumed in the abductor if there is an indication of the impediment as the marriage followed the abduction or the retention of the intended spouse and it is logical to think that those acts were done for the purpose of marriage. The obligation to prove that there is no relation between the abduction and the marriage devolves upon the party denying it and on the defender of the marriage bond.[83] The general rule is that the petitioner capable of accusing a marriage may be either the contracting party in all causes involving separation or nullity unless the married persons themselves were the cause of the impediment, or the promoter of justice in the case of impediments which are by their nature public so that they can be proved by testimonial or documentary evidence.[84] The assertion of such petitioners to the invalidity of the marriage does not enjoy the favor of law. (2) That the spouse of the former marriage died before the second marriage was contracted. (3) That the spouse of the former marriage died after the second marriage took place. In each of these

usucaptum est, habet civilem actionem nec desiderat honorariam."—Ulpianus, D. VI, 2, 1, 2; *cf.* Reiffenstuel, *Ius Canonicum Universum*, lib. II, tit. XIX, nn. 128, 129; Wernz, *Ius Decretalium*, V, n. 596.

[82] Canon 1074.

[83] Muniz, *Procedimientos Eclesiásticos*, II, n. 294, pp. 352, 353.

[84] *Cf.* Canon 1971, 1°, 2°. The person accusing the marriage has the burden of proof. *Cf.* S. R. R., *Transilvanien. Nullit. Matrim.*, 5 Julii, 1921, *Coram R. P. D., Raphaelo Chimenti*, dec. XVI, n. 6—*Decisiones*, XVI (1921), 159.

cases the defendant spouse becomes the plaintiff with reference to the exception. He or she has the burden of proving what he or she states.

b. When the law assists the plaintiff and resists the defendant, by reason of the fact the plaintiff has an intention founded in law, the defendant has the burden of proof, *e. g.*, the law assists bishops and pastors; also, if a minor takes exception to a superior (*maior*) for selling an immovable thing, the superior must prove his right.[85]

c. When the defendant, confident of the issue, voluntarily assumes the burden of proof. Nevertheless, if the defendant be deficient in proof he is not condemned on that account unless he, perhaps, had expressly obliged himself to the loss of the cause. The principle is always true, that the plaintiff not proving, the defendant is absolved.[86]

d. When the judge for a good reason transfers the burden of proof to the defendant.[87] The exceptions made to the principle "onus probandi incumbit ei qui asserit" lead some [88] to observe that the principle is not to be accepted absolutely but with restrictions so that it can be substituted for another: "onus probandi dividendum esse aequo modo inter partes." Roberti [89] observes that the plaintiff should both prove his right and that it still exists. He ought to prove, first, the existence of all conditions which are required to establish a right, and secondly, the lack of any ground on account of which the right would be deficient. For example, the plaintiff ought to prove two things, first, that an obligation was contracted, the consent being

[85] *Cf.* "Qui a pupillo emit, probare debet tutore auctore lege non prohibente se emisse, sed et si deceptus falso tutore auctore emerit, bona fide emisse videtur."—D. VI, 2, 13, 2.

[86] *Cf.* Gaius, D. VI, 2, 14; Reiffenstuel, *Ius Canonicum Universum*, lib. II, tit. XIX, nn. 135-140; Wernz, *Ius Decretalium*, V, n. 596, nota (15).

[87] *I. e.*, by a *iuramentum delatum*, *cf.* Wernz-Vidal, VI, *De Processibus*, n. 435, p. 378.

[88] *Cf.* Roberti, *De Processibus*, II, n. 326, p. 27; Muniz, *Procedimientos Eclesiásticos*, III, n. 280, pp. 221, 222; by implication, Wernz-Vidal, VI, *De Processibus*, nn. 435, 436, pp. 377-379; A Coronata, *De Processibus*, III, n. 1274, p. 182, makes the above statement in the text.

[89] *Cf.* Roberti, *De Processibus*, II, n. 326, p. 27.

truly given without fraud, invalidating fear, and the like; and secondly, that the obligation still exists. Therefore, a very grave obligation is imposed on the plaintiff which might jeopardize the defense of a right. Hence, equity persuades that the burden of proof should be divided between the parties. A distinction is made between facts which are constitutive of law and facts extinctive of the same (*facta constitutiva iuris et extinctiva*). The former are either generic or specific conditions which are required for the purpose of creating a right. The plaintiff is held to prove only the specific conditions of fact, *e. g.*, that consent had been truly given. The defendant is obliged to prove that some generic condition may be lacking. Since generic conditions are usually present, their existence is presupposed unless the defendant objected that they were defective, *e. g.*, that consent was vitiated by a deliberate will of transgressing the law (*dolus*).[90] Unless the plaintiff had proved that the specific conditions were present, his petition is rejected according to the principle enunciated in the Code: "Actore non probante, reus absolvitur." But if the plaintiff had proved that these specific conditions were present and the defendant had objected that some generic condition is lacking, the defendant is held to prove that the defect is present and thus, "reus excipiendo fit actor."

With reference to this explanation one must first of all make a fundamental distinction between two different senses of the phrase *onus probandi* or be led into the error of imposing an obligation where it does not belong. In its true sense, the burden of proof denotes a risk of non-persuasion upon the evidence of a legal controversy. In this sense of the term the burden of proof remains once it is established. In a secondary sense, the phrase means the duty of producing evidence.[91] In the first sense, the burden of proof, in matrimonial procedure at least, does not change once it has been settled. The plaintiff in the matrimonial process states that a valid marriage was not contracted and does not exist at the present time.

[90] *Cf.* Savigny, Friedrich C. von, *System des Heutigen Romischen Rechts* (Berlin, 1841), § 225, pp. 423-433.

[91] *Cf.* Wigmore, John H., *A Treatise on the Anglo-American System of Evidence in Trials at Common Law* (2 ed., Boston, 1923) IV, § 2489.

Expressed in the affirmative, the plaintiff alleges that he or she was and is free from the obligations arising from a matrimonial contract at the time of the marriage ceremony. The obligation on the plaintiff is a grave one. It is true that it might jeopardize a declaration of nullity to which the plaintiff considers he or she has a right in justice or in equity, and hence believes that the burden of proof should be divided between the defendant and the plaintiff. This manner of reasoning, however, does not appear to be applicable in matrimonial procedure not only because the risk of non-persuasion is on the plaintiff, but also because theoretical considerations of equity and justice are not to lead one to tamper with a sacrament inasmuch as the reason behind such explanations from justice and equity appears to be the difficulty and facility of furnishing proof. In the secondary sense of the phrase "burden of proof," it is admitted that it can and does change during the progress of a trial.

No rule or group of harmonious principles will provide a sure and universal test for a definite apportionment to each party of specific facts for which he will be responsible as a prerequisite of obtaining action by the tribunal on his behalf. This is a question of policy and fairness based on past experience and canonical equity. The Code does not justify one in stating that it has accepted such a test as this is a matter of jurisprudence. There are rules for specific cases which rely for their ultimate reasons upon the undefined reasons of fairness and experience.

The partition of proof should not, however, be materially considered so that the judge ought first to elicit respective proofs from the plaintiff and then from the defendant. Any party can enforce the "controversial sphere," partially recognizing the right of the adversary. The old *positiones,* which are explained in the next chapter, are directed to this purpose. The same purpose is attained today especially through the interrogations. Thus, for example, whoever alleges prescription implicitly admits the preceding existence of the law. Hence a plaintiff is not compelled to prove this further. The same is to be said of a plaintiff who had partially admitted an exception or *"reconventio."* [92]

[92] *Cf.* Roberti, *De Processibus,* II, n. 226, p. 28.

B. The Proof of Negative Statements

The proof of negative facts presents a peculiar difficulty. The impossibility of the proof of a negative was, as pointed out, recognized in the Middle Ages. The principle, "negativa non sunt probanda" was accepted. This principle was derived from sources of Roman Law which are not well understood. The general principle is: "Ei incumbit probatio qui dicit, non qui negat." [93] This text does not, in the first place, specify what is denied. Secondly, it does not designate whether it is the plaintiff or the defendant who does not have to prove his claim when he makes a denial. Hence, one turns to the following text taken from Justinian Law which restricts the general principle that the burden of proof is on the one who asserts something, not on the one who denies it. The text follows: "Actor quod adseverat probare se non posse profitendo reum necessitate monstrandi, contrarium non adstringit, cum per rerum naturam factum negantis probatio nulla est." [94] Roberti [95] is of the opinion that "these two texts allude to a case in which one pretends that a right comes to him from a fact; in which case he and not the adverse party evidently ought to prove the fact; as when the plaintiff does not prove, the defendant (*reus*) is absolved." The text from the *Digest* states a general principle. The text from the *Code* is a restriction made on the general principle. The text from the *Code* is worded in an indirect manner. The rendition of Roberti is direct. A plaintiff (*actor*) alleges something and cannot prove his claim. This does not compel the defendant to prove the contrary, for in accordance with the nature of things, denial of a fact is no evidence. The doctrine which was accepted into Canon Law is that whoever denies a fact cannot be compelled to assume the obligation of proving the negative. Even though the plaintiff state that he cannot prove the fact which he alleges to have happened, he cannot shift the burden of proof on the defendant (*reus*) who denies the fact. This is more clearly expressed in the following gloss to the *Code of Justinian:*

[93] Paulus, D. XXII, 3, 2.

[94] *Cod.* IV, 19, 23.

[95] *Cf.* Roberti, *De Processibus,* II, n. 226, note 2, p. 28.

> "Licet actor dicit se non posse probare, onus tamen probationis non refunditur in reum, hoc dicit secundum Bald. & salice. & not. Vel sic, Actori asserenti incumbit onus probandi, reo uerò neganti non incumbit, etiam si actor dicat se probare non posset nec propter hoc conuenit in eum onus probandi transferre: quia negativa probari non potest. h. d. Pau. de Castro." [96]

Furthermore, it is only a negative fact which need not be proved, and not a negation of a right.[97] Finally, in accordance with the nature of things, certain negatives, such as infinite things, cannot be proved.[98]

The Code of Canon Law omits the proof of negative facts because every negation involves some affirmative.[99] Even when two things attributed to something are different, the exclusion of one is an implicit affirmation of the other. Although one of them be indeterminate, it can, by a denial, be determined. Thus, if some one denies that a color is white, he affirms that it has another color which can be determined. In the second place, as often as negatives are to be proved, especially if the proof involves something which happened within certain limits of place and time, one can gather the elements of proof from which, according to various cases, a defect of an existing law may appear. Thus it can be proved that some one who was close to the scene of a crime at the time of its commission had committed a definite delict. In this manner, likewise, a defect of existing servitude (*actio negatoria*) or a defect of the verification of a negative, and the like, are proved.[100]

[96] *Glossa ad Cod.*, IV, 19, 13. *Cf.* c. 11, X, *de probationibus*, II, 19.

[97] "Factum: secus si ius."—*Glossa ad Cod.*, IV, 19, 13.

[98] "Quando actor dicit probare se intentionem suam non posse, Quaeritur: *an contrarii probatio incumbit Reo?* Negat*ur per 1 ult. C. de R. V.* et ob hanc rationem: quia per rerum naturam negativa non potest probari, scil. infinita, nam restricta ad quanitatem, qualitatem, locum et tempus potest probari, arg. 1, 77, § 25, *de Legat.*, 2, 1, optimam."—*Glossa ad Cod.*, IV, 19, 13.

[99] "Certe si diligenter attendas, non est aliqua negativa, quae tacitam non habeat affirmationem."—*Glossa ad* D. XXII, 3, 2.

[100] *Cf.* Roberti, *De Processibus*, n. 326, 3, p. 29.

In matrimonial as well as in criminal procedure, one of the litigants, either the plaintiff or the defendant, may deny facts which are directly or indirectly pertinent to the issue. In matrimonial causes the presence of an alleged diriment impediment may be denied. Whoever denies an allegation is generally dispensed from the burden of proof. The four following classes of negations must, however, be distinguished to ascertain whether one is obliged to prove a denial and to determine when a negation can be proved.

1. *Negation of a Fact.* A negative of fact is a denial that something has been done or has taken place.[101] For the sake of precision and clarity negations of fact are divided into two kinds of negatives:

a. A *pure and simple denial* is unqualified as to time, place or other circumstances, *e. g.*, the statements, "I did not enter into a marriage contract; I was never cited into court; I did not resign my ecclesiastical office." It is impossible to prove these denials wholly, either directly or indirectly. In any case the proof must be produced by the one who makes an affirmation.[102] What does not exist cannot be proved. Such a fact or act which is denied absolutely is supposed to have no existence.[103] Moreover, it is the doctrine of Pirhing [104] that an assertion or a proposition pertaining to some negative fact cannot be directly proved by witnesses or documents (*instrumenta*). It can, nevertheless, be proved by a confession or admission of the thing in question.

b. A *qualified denial* is a negation circumscribed as to time, place or other circumstances, *e. g.*, the statements, "I deny that I contracted a marriage with that person, in that place or at that hour; I

[101] *Cf.* Noval, *De Processibus*, n. 440, p. 307.

[102] *Cf.* Muniz, *Procedimientos Eclesiásticos*, III, n. 281, p. 222. Reiffenstuel distinguishes a negation of fact into pure and simple (*non coarctata*) and a negation which is determined as to place, time or circumstances (*coarctata*). The latter alone can be proved indirectly. The burden of the proof of the former is on the adverse party. *Cf.* Reiffenstuel, *Ius Canonicum Universum*, lib. II, tit. XIX, nn. 45, 46.

[103] Referring to the question of evidence of proof, *cf.*, "Actor quod adseverat probare se non posse profitendo reum necessitate monstrandi contrarium non adstringit, cum per rerum naturam factum negantis probatio nulla sit."—*Cod.* IV, 19, 23.

[104] Pirhing, *Ius Canonicum*, lib. II, tit. XIX, § 2, n. 9.

did not commit that delict." These statements may be proved indirectly by proving an alibi (*coarctata*) that the person involved was elsewhere at the time the fact is alleged to have happened.[105] It is said that these statements *may* be proved in this manner indirectly to indicate that the negation need not necessarily be proved by him unless he makes it the basis of an action, since in the latter case the rule applies that everyone is obliged to prove what is the basis of his action or what he demands, because, as Schmalzgrueber observes,[106] proof is only a true definition and a demonstration of some fact.

2. *Negation of a Law.* A negative of law is a denial that a certain thing can be or has been lawfully and validly done, *e. g.*, a person denies that his marriage took place in a valid manner, before a priest and two witnesses. The legality or validity of acts under this category is to be distinguished in this manner. (a) A negation of a law in a matter which is generally permitted by the law as legal and valid must be proved by the person denying, who must allege the defect of liceity or of validity. For example, an allegation that an election was not licit or valid must be proved by showing the defect of liceity or of validity.[107] The reason for this is that the presumption of law in the case is that the act which took place can be and has been done lawfully and validly. Such negations, moreover, imply an affirmation that the act was accomplished in an unjust or invalid manner.[108] (b) On the contrary, a negation of law in a matter generally forbidden by law need not be proved by the person denying it, *e. g.*, the statement, "I deny that he committed homicide in self-

[105] *Cf.* Muniz, *Procedimientos Eclesiásticos,* III, n. 281, p. 222; c. 35, X, *de testibus et attestationibus,* II, 35; Pirhing, *Ius Canonicum,* lib. II, tit. XX, n. 10. The statement of Wernz-Vidal that there is no lack of cases in which at least indirect proof of a negative assertion can, and therefore, ought to be produced, properly belongs under this category of a qualified rather than a pure and simple denial. *Cf.* Wernz-Vidal, VI, *De Processibus,* n. 436, p. 378. Compare also Pirhing, *Ius Canonicum,* lib. II, tit. XIX, § 2, nn. 8-13.

[106] Schmalzgrueber, *Ius Ecclesiasticum Universum,* lib. II, Pars III, tit. XIX, n. 38.

[107] *Cf.* Muniz, *Procedimientos Eclesiásticos,* III, n. 281, p. 222; Wernz-Vidal, VI, *De Processibus,* n. 436, pp. 378, 379; Pirhing, *Ius Canonicum,* lib. II, tit. XIX § 2, n. 12.

[108] *Cf.* Reiffenstuel, *Ius Canonicum Universum,* lib. II, tit. XX, n. 51.

defense." The burden of proof of a defect of legality or of validity devolves on him who affirms it.[109]

3. *Negation of a Quality.* A negative of quality is a denial that a certain person has certain perfections or qualities. It may be (a) the denial of the existence of a substantial quality with which nature commonly endows men or which the generality of men possess, *e. g.*, legitimacy. Such a denial must be proved.[110] The burden of proof of qualities which are naturally and commonly possessed by all men, such as sanity of mind, eyesight and hearing, lies on him who denies their presence. The law presumes that they are the possession of everybody. (b) The denial may be a negation of an accidental quality which is not possessed by the majority of men, *e. g.*, a doctorate in some science or an expert witness. The person who affirms that he has the quality which is denied has the burden of proof. But if the law presumes it, it is already considered proved; it is unnecessary to prove it for the effects which the law attributes to it. Such a negation must be proved by the one who denies the quality when there is question of the liceity or the validity of the appointment of an official to an office.[111]

4. *Pregnant Negation (negativa praegnans).* A pregnant negation is a denial which virtually and implicitly contains an affirmative assertion, *e. g.*, the statement, "He did not contract a marriage of his own free will." It is evident that such a denial is equivalent to or an implication of an affirmation that the person contracted a marriage through the influence of violence, fear or deception which can be the object of proof. This disjunctive negation contains first, an absolute or pure denial and, secondly, a pregnant negation. With reference to the former, the burden of the proof of the absolute denial falls on the plaintiff who affirms what is denied. The plaintiff must first prove

[109] *Cf.* Muniz, *Procedimientos Eclesiásticos,* III, n. 281, p. 222; Pirhing, *Ius Canonicum,* lib. II, tit. XIX, § 2, n. 12.

[110] *Cf.* Muniz, *Procedimientos Ecclesiásticos,* n. 281, p. 222; Reiffenstuel, *Ius Canonicum Universum,* lib. II, tit. XIX, n. 50.

[111] Muniz, *Procedimientos Eclesiásticos,* III, n. 281, p. 222; Pirhing, *Ius Canonicum,* lib. II, tit. XIX, § 2, n. 13. Compare c. 2, X, *de testibus et attestationibus,* II, 20; Schmalzgrueber, *Ius Ecclesiasticum Universum,* lib. II, Pars III, tit. XIX, nn. 33-36, 50; Pirhing, *Ius Canonicum,* nn. 17, 18.

what is absolutely denied, and only after he has proved it is the defendant obliged to prove his pregnant denial or the second part of his disjunctive answer or denial.[112]

Article 4. The Means Employed to Renounce Proofs

Canon 1749. Probationes quae ad moras iudicio nectendas postulari videntur, ceu examen testis longe dissiti, cuius domicilium nescitur, vel cognitio documenti quod cito haberi non potest, iudex ne admittat, nisi hae probationes necessariae videantur quia ceterae deficiant aut satis non sint.

The obvious purpose of this canon is to terminate trials as quickly as possible. The judge should not admit any evidence which is presented merely to delay the trial unless the evidence is necessary because of insufficiency or deficiency of other proofs.

In the practice of the Roman Rota, the judge may not curtail the controversy (*litis*) in criminal trials until the proofs and legitimate defenses are admitted.[113] The testimonial evidence of a witness who lives far from the court or whose place of residence is unknown and documentary evidence cannot be readily produced (*futilia documenta*) have a dilatory effect. Such evidence is suspect of being demanded for a trivial or an evil purpose and should be rejected.[114] The application of this provision of the law and jurisprudence requiring trials to be terminated quickly can give rise to an "incident," or fact which the litigants are not agreed upon, if one of the principals objects to the admission of this proof.[115]

Examining the canon from another aspect, if *both parties agree* that the proof is not necessary, they will ask the judge to declare the

[112] *Cf.* Pirhing, *Ius Canonicum,* lib. II, tit. XIX, § 2, n. 2; Schmalzgrueber, *Ius Ecclesiasticum Universum,* lib. II, Pars III, tit. XIX, n. 34; Wernz-Vidal, VI, *De Processibus,* n. 436, p. 379; Muniz, *Procedimientos Eclesiásticos,* III, n. 281, p. 222.

[113] S. R. R., *Alexandrina. Expensarum Iudicialium,* 14 Junii, 1909, *Coram R. P. D., Michaele Lega,* dec. VII, n. 3—*Decisiones,* I (1909), 62, 63.

[114] *Cf. Regulae Servandae in Iudiciis Apud S. R. Rotae Tribunal,* § 27, 3.

[115] Muniz, *Procedimientos Eclesiásticos,* III, n. 284, p. 224.

conclusion of the cause (*conclusio causae*),[116] assigning the motives on which they found the renunciation of the proof. The judge will examine the motives and if he finds them conformable with Canon 1747 he will declare the cause concluded. If the renunciation is done by *one of the parties*, the judge should wait until the case is presented by the other party. If this party asks the opening of the probatory period because the disputed facts need proof, the judge may provide for the opening of the probatory period, putting away the first thing, *i. e.*, the renunciation.[117]

Article V. Admission of Testimonial Evidence

Canon 1754. Probatio per testes in quibuslibet causis admittitur, sub iudicis tamen moderatione, secundum modum praefinitum in canonibus qui sequuntur.

After considering the judicial confession, the Code takes up the subject of witnesses and their attestations (*De testibus et attestationibus*). Canon 1754 expressly states that witnesses are to be considered as a means of evidence. The general principle is that witnesses are admitted in all ecclesiastical causes. By the phrase, *sub iudicis tamen moderatione*, the canon declares that the judge should regulate what pertains to witnesses and should admit only as many of them as are necessary to discover the truth. Pius VII (1740-1823), in 1800, said that if a fact to be proved has been conclusively demonstrated by witnesses, further examination of any witnesses on that particular point should be omitted for the sake of brevity and the expedition of justice.[118] The bare assertions of a witness whose testimonial status is not well known may be admissible in Canon Law. On the simple doctrine of probabilities one usually, however, gives credence to the greater number of witnesses who consistently agree about the existence of a fact.[119] Not infrequently a large number of

[116] Canon 1860, § 2.

[117] Muniz, *Procedimientos Eclesiásticos*, III, n. 277, p. 220.

[118] Benedictus XIV, *Opera Omnia et Bullarii Romani Continuatio* (Prati, 1844), VII, Pars I, n. XXII, p. 61.

[119] "Non enim ad multitudinem respici oportet, sed ad sinceram testimoniorum fidem et testimonia, quibus potius lux veritatis adsistit."—D. XXII, 5, 21, 3.

witnesses adds nothing to the discovery of truth. Many witnesses may be dependent upon the testimony of one person.[120]

The second part of Canon 1754 and the canons which are expounded in the chapters which follow are restrictions of the general rule which admits witnesses in all judicial proceedings. The limitations are established by the Church to preclude the danger of error and corruption.

Article VI. Persons Excused from the Obligation of Giving Testimony

Canon 1755, § 1. Testes iudici legitime interroganti respondere et veritatem fateri debent.

§ 2. Salvo praescripto Canon 1757, § 3, n. 2, ab hac obligatione eximuntur:

1°. Parochi aliique sacerdotes quod attinet ad ea quae ipsis manifestata sunt ratione sacri ministerii extra sacramentalem confessionem; civitatum magistratus, medici, obstetrices, advocati, notarii aliique qui ad secretum officii etiam ratione praestiti consilii tenentur, quod attinet ad negotia huic secreto obnoxia;

2°. Qui ex testificatione sua sibi vel consanguineis vel affinibus in quolibet gradu lineae rectae et in primo gradu lineae collateralis, infamiam, periculosas vexationes, aliave mala valde gravia obventura timent.

§ 3. Testes iudici legitime interroganti scienter falsum affirmantes aut verum occultantes puniantur ad normam Canon 1743, § 3; eademque poena mulctentur omnes, qui testem vel peritum donis, pollicitationibus aut alio quovis modo inducere praesumpserint ad falsum testimonium dicendum aut ad veritatem occultandam.

One credible witness suffices for light causes in which there is a modicum of prejudice to a third party as in summary causes. *Cf.* Reiffenstuel, *Ius Canonicum Universum*, lib. II, tit. XX, n. 280.

120 *Cf.* S. R. R., *Nullit. Matrim.*, 23 Martii, 1915, *Coram R. P. D., Aloisio Sincero*, dec. XII, n. 10—*Decisiones*, VII (1915), 127.

The first paragraph of this canon considers the admission of witnesses; the second gives consideration to persons who are excused from the obligation of assuming the office of witness. Regarding the admission of witnesses, the first paragraph indicates that all who are not exempted by the second paragraph of the canon and who have been legitimately cited [121] to appear before the judge, or his auditor [122] or his legitimate delegate [123] are obliged to answer and to speak the truth when interrogated in the lawful place and time concerning facts which pertain to the cause. The office of witness affects the public welfare. As this duty is one of public interest those who are called upon to provide testimony are to comply with it rightfully. Nevertheless, the necessity of testifying is not absolute since it can be supplied by other means. Consequently, the law does not insist on it if the observance of it would impede a greater good or if it could not be fulfilled without a grave inconvenience.[124]

Not all witnesses who are otherwise qualified are to be coerced to provide testimony. Limitations or exceptions to the general rule requiring all persons to tell the truth when they are lawfully interrogated are established by the second paragraph of the canon. The following are exempt:

1. *Priests and others with regard to Confidential Communications.* The phrase, *salvo praescripto,* is to be interpreted as denoting the word "besides" (*praeter*) so that priests, whether they be pastors,

[121] *Cf.* Canons 1715-1723, 1765. Nullity of a citation frees a witness from the obligation to appear. *Cf.* Muniz, *Procedimientos Eclesiásticos,* III, n. 312, p. 248; III, n. 311, note 2, p. 247. If the party cited does not appear, it should be imputed to him; the validity of the process is not thereby doubtful and another citation is not needed. *Cf.* Reiffenstuel, *Ius Canonicum Universum,* lib. II, tit. XX, nn. 418-430; A Coronata, *De Processibus,* III, n. 1294, p. 206. In the citation generally the questions or articles proposed must not be indicated but only the generic object of the requisite attestation is declared. *Cf. Regulae Servandae in Iudiciis apud S. R. Rotae Tribunal,* § 114, n. 8.

[122] *Cf.* Canon 1582.

[123] Canon 1773.

[124] *Cf.* Roberti, *De Processibus,* II, n. 336, pp. 42, 43; Wernz-Vidal, VI, *De Processibus,* n. 460, pp. 397, 398; Augustine, *A Commentary,* VII, pp. 202, 203; Noval, *De Processibus,* IV, n. 461, p. 326; Muniz, *Procedimientos Eclesiásticos,* III, n. 318, p. 253.

vicars-general, professors or engaged in any other capacity, are incapable of giving direct or indirect testimony about anything learned through a sacramental confession.[125] They are not merely exempted from the obligation of replying to questions regarding matters learned outside of confession but are also held to maintain silence regarding them in an ecclesiastical court.[126]

The Code enumerates a group of others who are exempt from the obligation of giving testimony. The list is not exclusive of those who may be bound by a professional secret (*demonstrativa non taxativa*).[127] Hence, besides civil magistrates, physicians, midwives, lawyers and notaries who are enumerated in the canon, procurators, pharmacists, nurses and everybody to whom a secret was committed for the purpose of obtaining advice are exempt from the obligation of testifying.[128] This law was formulated to safeguard the confi-

[125] S. R. U., Inquisit. Instr., 9 Junii, 1915—*Period.*, VIII (1915), 183. This instruction was not printed in the *A. A. S. Cf.* "Sacerdotibus omnibus in memoriam revocamus prohibitionem ne quid unquam attingant pertinens ad materiam confessionis sacramentalis. sub nulla forma nulloque praetextu, ne obiter quidem, nec directe nec indirecte, neque in publicis neque in privatis sermonibus, praesertim occasione Missionum et exercitiorum spiritualium."—(S. C. S. Off., Instr., 9 *iunii,* 1915)—Decretum 268, *Acta Et Decreta Concilii Provincialis Portlandensis in Oregon Quarti* (Portlandiae, 1932).

[126] In trials at common law and in equity as established in the United States confidential communications to clergymen or medical men in their professional capacity are not privileged but are made so by statute in some states. *Cf.* Reynolds, William, *The Rules of Evidence and the Conduct of the Examination of Witnesses in Trials at Common Law and in Equity as Established in the United States, with the Reasons for Them* (Chicago, 1912), § 101, p. 262.

[127] Roberti, *De Processibus,* II, n. 336, p. 43; A Coronata, *De Processibus,* III, n. 1282, p. 191; Noval, *De Processibus,* IV, n. 462, p. 327.

[128] For a consideration of secrets from the aspect of moral theology, *cf.* De Lugo, Joannes, *Disputationes Scholasticae et Morales* (Parisiis, 1869), VI, Disp. XIV, sec. IX, nn. 135-143; Lehmkuhl, Augustinus, *Theologia Moralis* (Friburgi Brisgoviae, 1914), I, nn. 1196-1198; Noldin, II, *De Praeceptis,* nn. 666-670; Prummer, Dominicus M., *Manuale Theologiae Moralis Secundum Principia S. Thomae Aquinatis In Usum Scholarum* (Friburgi Brisgoviae, 1928), II, nn. 175-181; Vermeersch, Arthurus, *Theologiae Moralis Principia, Responsa, Consilia* (Bruges, 1926), II, nn. 697-701.

dence people have or should have in persons who occupy public or semi-public positions.[129]

2. *Persons Who Would Sustain Injury.* By reason of the grave private loss that they would suffer, all persons who reasonably fear that their testimony will render themselves or their relatives in every degree of the direct line and up to the first degree of the collateral line infamous,[130] or occasion dangerous vexations, are exempt from the obligation of giving testimonial evidence. The probable evils which are feared can be of a material nature, such as confiscation of one's property, or they may be in the moral order, such as the vexation of one's family that would result from giving evidence.[131] All persons who are excused from the obligation of giving testimony must, nevertheless, appear before the judge if they are legitimately cited and declare that there is a sufficient reason for their exemption in order that it may be verified by him.[132] The judge can be told by the witnesses who have sufficient reason for exemption from testifying that they will not reply to questions regarding such things.[133] Those who are exempted are, however, constrained to testify about other facts with regard to which there is no reason for exemption. Likewise, if they have been freed by the parties from the obligation of keeping a secret known through a confidential communication or if the evils which are feared can otherwise be averted, they are held to give testimony.[134] It has happened that in matrimonial causes and in those pertaining to the validity of a ratified marriage, lawyers and physicians have refused to give testimony even when the parties themselves had freed them from the obligation of keeping a professional secret pertaining to them in order that the physicians and lawyers may be produced as witnesses. There is no foundation for such

[129] *Cf.* Roberti, *De Processibus,* II, n. 336, p. 43; Augustine, *A Commentary,* VII, 203.

[130] *Cf.* Reiffenstuel, *Ius Canonicum Universum,* lib. II, tit. XX, n. 24.

[131] A Coronata, *De Processibus,* III, n. 1282, p. 191; *cf.* Augustine, *A Commentary,* VII, 203, 204; Roberti, *De Processibus,* II, n. 336, p. 43.

[132] Wernz-Vidal, VI, *De Processibus,* n. 463, p. 401; Roberti, *ibid.;* A Coronata, *ibid.*

[133] *Cf.* Muniz, *Procedimientos Eclesiásticos,* III, n. 319, pp. 253, 254.

[134] *Cf.* Roberti, *De Processibus,* II, n. 336, pp. 43, 44.

refusals to testify in an ecclesiastical court.[135] When the testimony of a physician is admitted, the court is to consider not merely his character but also whether his testimony is suspect by reason of his enmity or friendliness toward the parties or members of their families.[136]

3. *Penal Sanctions against Perfidious Witnesses.* The third paragraph of this canon establishes that witnesses questioned by the judge in a lawful manner who knowingly make a false statement or conceal the truth are to be punished with the same penalties as are threatened in Canon 1743, § 3; the same penalty may be meted out also to those who would presume to bribe witnesses or experts with gifts and promises, or in any way endeavor to induce them to tell a falsehood or to hide the truth. Canon 1755, § 3, is divided into two parts. The first part refers to the witnesses themselves who have been lawfully interrogated. The second part applies to those persons who have the presumption to induce witnesses or experts to tell a falsehood or to hide the truth by gifts, promises or in any other manner. With regard to the first classification, witnesses who have been lawfully interrogated, and who knowingly affirm what is false or conceal the truth, are punished in accordance with Canon 1743, § 3, by the same penalties which are threatened agains the parties who refuse to answer without a lawful reason who have been caught in a lie. According to the various circumstances the judge may inflict the penalty at a time defined by himself. The three penalties referred to in Canon 1743, § 3, are removal from legitimate ecclesiastical office, the personal interdict and suspension. These penalties are *ferendae sententiae.* They can be inflicted by the judge in the principal trial (*iudicio*), or even by the delegated judge (*judex delegatus*) who must question witnesses in order to attain the truth.[137] In Canon 1755, § 3, the words *eademque poena* with reference to those who

[135] *Cf.* Wernz-Vidal, VI, *De Processibus,* n. 463, note 24, p. 401; A Coronata, *De Processibus,* III, n. 1282, p. 101.

[136] *Cf.* S. R. R., *Nullit. Matrim.,* 25 Februarii, 1911, *Coram R. P. D., Iosepho Mori,* dec. X, n. 3—*Decisiones,* III (1911), 95, 96; S. R. R., *Nullit. Matrim.,* 1 Augusti, 1913, *Coram R. P. D., Michaele Lega,* dec. XXXIX, n. 3—*Decisiones Coram Lega,* 477, 478.

[137] A Coronata, *De Processibus,* III, n. 1270, p. 176.

try to induce witnesses and experts to tell a falsehood or hide the truth by bribes, promises or in any other manner, do not refer to one penalty as the singular would indicate. These words should be interpreted as referring to three penalties in accordance with the diversity of cases.[138] Three penalties are mentioned in the canons referred to, namely:

a. *Removal from Legal Ecclesiastical Acts.* The first penalty mentioned is removal from legal ecclesiastical acts. The general principle is that witnesses who have been lawfully interrogated and affirm a falsehood or hide the truth are punishable. The Code does not distinguish between the obligation of testifying in criminal and in civil causes. It seems that the obligation must be recognized for criminal causes.[139] A witness who refuses to answer can be coerced by penalties and taxed in proportion to the damage which accrues to the principals as a consequence of his disobedience.[140] The canon under consideration assumes that the witness has no legal reason for refusing to answer as he should have made known such an excuse to the judge.[141] In private causes one does not usually proceed to inflict penalties on disobedient witnesses except at the instance of the parties.[142] When perjury has been committed, the penalties must be imposed by the judge.[143]

Removal from legal ecclesiastical acts at a time which is defined by the judge in conformity with the circumstances of the case is the penalty to be inflicted on clerics and lay persons who unlawfully refuse to answer a question or who are afterwards discovered to have lied in answer to a question. Thus lay persons who are guilty of these delinquencies are deprived of the right to be sponsors either personally or through a procurator at baptism[144] or confirmation; [145] they

[138] *Cf.* A Coronata, *De Processibus,* III, n. 1282, note 1, p. 192.

[139] Reiffenstuel held a contrary opinion which should be sufficient to persuade a judge to employ sparingly his right to compel a witness to testify. *Cf.* Reiffenstuel, *Ius Canonicum Universum,* lib. II, tit. XXI, nn. 18-27.

[140] Canon 1766, § 2.

[141] *Cf.* Canons 1757, 1766, § 1; 1770.

[142] *Cf.* Muniz, *Procedimientos Eclesiásticos,* n. 313, p. 248.

[143] A Coronata, *De Processibus,* III, n. 1282, p. 192.

[144] *Cf.* Canons 765, 2°, 5°; 766, 2°.

[145] *Cf.* Canon 795, 2°.

cannot be official administrators of ecclesiastical property, couriers or beadles.[146] Clerics who are culpable are forbidden to be employed in an ecclesiastical court as judge, auditor, relator, defender of the bond, fiscal promoter, and promoter of the faith; they are also deprived of an active voice or right of voting at ecclesiastical elections, including those held by monastic chapters and chapters of religious communities and acts of actual exercise of *iuspatronatus* or advowson.[147]

b. *Personal Interdict.* The second penalty mentioned is a personal interdict. This is the heaviest penalty of the three. It is to be inflicted upon a lay person who swears falsely after having taken an oath to tell the truth and nothing but the truth. Lay persons who have been personally interdicted are forbidden to receive sacraments and sacramentals.[148]

c. *Suspension.* Should a cleric tell a falsehood after having taken an oath he is to be suspended [149] totally in virtue of Canons 1743, § 3, and 1755, § 3, *i. e.*, from office as well as from benefice.[150] It is evident that the penalties mentioned in Canon 1743, § 3, are *ferendae sententiae* which are to be imposed by the judge although in this case the penalty of suspension on the delinquent cleric is laid down by law.[151]

[146] *Cf.* Canon 2256, § 2.

[147] Canon 2256, § 2; Augustine, *A Commentary,* VIII, 167, 168.

[148] Canons 2275, 2°; 2260, § 1; 1144, 1152, 1240, § 1, 2°. *Cf.* Devoti, Ioannes, *Institutionum Canonicarum* (Venetiis, 1860), IV, tit. XIX, n. 2; Chelodi, *Ius Poenale,* n. 41, p. 53; Conran, Edward J., *The Interdict* (The Catholic University of America Canon Law Studies, No. 56, Washington, D. C., 1930), 8; Cerato, P., *Censurae Vigentes Ipso Facto A Codice Iuris Canonici Excerptae Cum Suspensionibus Ferendae Sententiae Poenis Vindicativis Remediis Poenalibus Et Irregularitatibus* (2 ed., Patavii, 1921), n. 91, p. 195.

[149] *Cf.* Canon 2278, § 1; Cocchi, Guidus, *Commentarium In Codicem Iuris Scholarum* (Taurini, 1928), V, *De Delictis Et Poenis,* n. 91, p. 154; n. 98, p. 169; Cerato, *Censurae Vigentes,* nn. 3, 4, pp. 7, 8; Ayrinhac, H. A., *Penal Legislation in the New Code of Canon Law* (New York, 1920), n. 78, pp. 88, 89.

[150] Compare *Il Monitore Ecclesiastico,* Serie V, Vol. II, Fasc. VI (1930), 251-254; *Ius Pont.,* IV (1924), 11-20; X (1930), 211; Eichmann, *Das Prozessrecht,* § 46, VII, p. 145.

[151] A personal interdict cannot be imposed on a lay witness or expert who

The last part of Canon 1755, § 3, prescribes that penalties identical with those mentioned in the first part of the canon must be inflicted on those who shall have had the presumption to induce witnesses or experts to give false testimony or to conceal the truth. The word *praesumpserint* is not employed here in the sense in which it is used in the Fifth Book of the Code. These delicts require full imputability and must have been consummated when the crime had taken place.[152] The penalties which have been mentioned are also among those which are to be inflicted on those who fraudulently substitute one person for another in causes involving the non-consummation of a marriage.[153]

committed perjury, nor can a cleric be suspended by a judge for perjury in causes pertaining to marriage *ratum et non consummatum,* unless he consult the Ordinary. *Cf. Regulae Servandae in Processibus super Matrimonio Rato et Non Consummato,* n. 40—*A. A. S.,* XV (1923), 389. For the application of the principle to clerics in causes involving validity of sacred orders, *cf.* n. 31—*A. A. S.,* XXIII (1931), 457.

[152] Canon 1755, § 3; Roberti, *De Processibus,* II, n. 336, p. 44.

[153] "Ad compescendum huiusmodi facinus, iudices instructores et Ordinarii prae oculis habeant praescripta canonum 1743, § 3; 1755, § 3 et 2362, eaque applicent, congrua congruis referentes."—S. C. de Disc. Sacram., *Normae Observandae In Processibus Super Matrimonio Rato et Non Consummato Ad Praecavendum Dolosam Personarum Substitutionem,* n. 7—*A. A. S.,* XXI (1929), 490.

CHAPTER VII

RULES EXCLUDING TESTIMONIAL EVIDENCE

Having designated the general rules for the admissibility of evidence, the Code logically and in conformity with the judiciary form or order followed by the Decretals [1] specifices three things in the canons which follow: (a) what precedes the admission of witnesses; (b) the things which constitute and accompany the production of the proof; and (c) the examination of witnesses, which legitimately follows their reception. This chapter confines itself to the first two of these. It is concerned with first, the rules of a generic nature which the Code lays down for the estimation of the worth of various witnesses, and secondly, the procedural norms which are introductory to the examination of the witnesses.

Article 1. Who Can Be Witnesses

Canon 1756. Omnes possunt esse testes, nisi expresse a iure repellantur vel in totum vel ex parte.

In determining what testimony shall be admitted and evaluated by the ecclesiastical judges, and what is inadmissible, or in other words, in distinguishing between persons who are competent and those who are incompetent to testify, the law excludes as incompetent those persons whose testimony, in general, is found more likely than otherwise to be false. No test of credibility can be infallible. An approximation to a degree of certainty that will ordinarily conform to the requirements of a cause is all that can be attained. This canon, consequently, expresses the general principle that all can be witnesses unless they are excluded wholly or partially by law. This principle was laid down in the Austrian Instruction.[2] A matrimonial tribunal is to estimate the credibility of witnesses from the

[1] *Cf.* Zallinger, *Institutiones Iuris Ecclesiastici,* lib. II, tit. XX, § 247, pp. 183, 184.

[2] *Instructio Austriaca,* § 151.

point of view of their natural fitness to testify and from the aspect of their generic legal qualifications found in individual cases and in accordance with what the nature of the cause postulates.

Some persons, as the canon under consideration states, are absolutely (*ex toto*) disqualified from testimony in any trial. They are juridically incapable of making an attestation because they lack the three preliminary qualifications of any witness, observation, retention and narration. These are called witnesses who are incapable of testimony (*incapaces*). There are other persons who are partially (*ex parte*) or relatively excluded from giving testimony. These persons are called either unacceptable (*non-idonei*) or suspect (*suspecti*) witnesses.[3] The following canon names the classes of witnesses who are totally or partially disqualified. It expresses the generic legal qualifications which enable a judge to reject some witnesses and evaluate the attestations of others.

Article 2. Rules Defining the Generic Qualifications of Witnesses

Canon 1757, § 1. Ut non idonei repelluntur a testimonio ferendo impuberes et mente debiles.

§ 2. Ut suspecti:

1°. Excommunicati, periurii, infames, post sententiam declaratoriam vel condemnatoriam;

2°. Qui ita abiectis sunt moribus ut fide digni non habeantur;

3°. Publici gravesque partis inimici.

§ 3. Ut incapaces:

1°. Qui partes sunt in causa, aut partium vice funguntur, veluti tutor in causa pupilli, Superior aut administrator in causa suae communitatis aut piae causae, cuius nomine in iudicio consistit, iudex eiusve assistentes, advocatus aliique qui partibus in eadem causa assistunt vel astiterunt;

[3] *Cf.* Leccisi, Giacinto, *La Prova Testimoniale nel Codice Di Diritto Canonico* (Romae, 1926), 11; A Coronata, *De Processibus*, III, n. 1283, p. 192.

2°. Sacerdotes, quod attinet ad ea omnia quae ipsis ex confessione sacramentali innotuerunt, etsi a vinculo sigilli soluti sint; imo audita a quovis et quoquo modo occasione confessionis ne ut indicium quidem veritatis recipi possunt;

3°. Coniux in causa sui coniugis, consanguineus et affinis in causa consanguinei vel affinis, in quolibet gradu lineae rectae et in primo gradu collateralis, nisi agatur de causis quae ad statum civilem aut religiosum personae spectant, cuius notitia aliunde haberi nequeat, et bonum publicum exigat ut habeatur.

Canon 1756 contains a general rule that all can be witnesses unless they be expressly excluded by law either wholly or partially. This precept regarding witnesses is prohibitory. An individual need not prove that he is a suitable witness. A person can be excluded from testifying either officially or by a litigant who should establish or prove the lack of a quality which is required by law. A deficiency of such a juridical quality can refer on the one hand either to the duty or to the exercise of it which a witness must perform. On the other hand, the deficiency may refer to a definite person on behalf of or against whom he is to testify.[4]

This general rule would sometimes exclude a credible witness. Justice as well as the sacredness of the sacraments, requires that the decision of causes be not embarrassed by statements generally found to be deceptive or totally false. There should be, then, rules which designate the classes of testimony which should be excluded as valueless or admitted as suspect. The Code, adhering to the view that it is expedient to retain at least one exclusionary rule, distinguishes among witnesses who are unacceptable, suspect and incapable of testifying. Children who have not arrived at the age of legal puberty, and persons deficient in understanding, are inadmissible. Other classes of persons are admitted to testify as suspect witnesses. A third group of witnesses are incapable of making an attestation in specified causes. Canon 1757 should, consequently, be considered under its threefold division.

[4] Wernz-Vidal, VI, *De Processibus,* n. 464, pp. 401, 402.

A. Persons Disqualified from Testimony as Unacceptable

The law of the Decretals, as was indicated, excluded either absolutely or relatively for definite causes many classes of persons from giving testimony. No precise distinction between the various cases can be stated. Before the Code, canonists did not agree among themselves. Some understood that the exclusionary rules were absolutely invalidating (*inhabilitantes*).[5] Others, and perhaps more rightly, believed that only the persons prohibited by the natural law are incapable of testifying (*inhabiles*). The other persons whom they estimated preferably as suspect were to be removed at the instance of a litigant. Absolute disqualification to testify was expressed in the Rules of the Roman Rota.[6]

The Code opportunely decides who are incapable of testifying by distinguishing the unacceptable from the suspect and the incapable witnesses. Weakness of mind renders the first class incapable of testifying. Presumption of a perverse will makes the second group suspect. A policy of law to safeguard the social order places the third classification among those incapable of testifying. The exclusion is not, however, equal for all, as the exclusion may be only partial.[7] Witnesses who are incapable of making an attestation can never be called upon to testify. If called upon the stand they are not obliged to reply. If they respond to a question, their testimony, being valueless, is not considered.[8] Non-suitable and suspect witnesses on the contrary, who are now to be considered, are usually excluded, but, from a disposition of the law, they can be admitted by a decree of the judge. In such a case they are admissible when the judge declares it expedient, but generally they are heard without taking an oath and their testimony has only the value of a disclosure (*indicium*) and as an auxiliary to the proof.[9]

[5] *Cf.* Lega, *Praelectiones,* I, n. 478, pp. 419-423.

[6] *Regulae Servandae In Iudiciis Apud S. R. Rotae Tribunal,* § 114, n. 1; *cf.* Roberti, *De Processibus,* II, n. 337, p. 44.

[7] Canons 1757, § 2, 3°, and 1757, § 3.

[8] *Cf.* Roberti, *De Processibus,* II, n. 337, pp. 44, 45.

[9] *Cf.* Canon 1758. Canon 1755, § 2, mentions the persons who cannot be obliged to assume the duty of witnesses. Canon 1757 contains a list of those

Canon 1757, § 1. Ut non idonei repelluntur a testimonio ferendo impuberes et mente debiles.

A suitable witness [10] is said to be one who is not prevented by nature or prohibited by law from testifying.[11] A witness is presumed to be suitable as long as legitimate exception is not taken against him by the episcopal curia.[12] Persons in whom knowledge or understanding is supposed to be lacking, are considered unsuitable to give testimony. Such persons do not have even the power of actually possessing the preliminary qualifications which any witness must have, *viz.*, perception, retention and narration. It is absurd, in the opinion of the Roman Rota,[13] to admit those witnesses to whom the authors exclude.

1. *Witnesses under the Age of Puberty.* Deficiency of understanding or knowledge is judged to be present in infants. They cannot, consequently, testify.[14] This exclusion is considered to be a pre-

who ought to be excluded. There is a relation between these canons so that those who should be excluded *a fortiori* must be said to be exempted unless a decree of the judge admitting them should intervene.

[10] Examples of the use of this expression are found in S. R. R., *Stanislaopolitana. Privationis Parochiae et Exercitiorum Spiritualium,* 7 Augusti, 1913, *Coram R. P. D., Michaele Lega,* dec. XLVI, n. 4—*Decisiones,* V (1913), 551, 552; S. R. R., *Nullit. Matrim.*, 6 Aprilis, 1914, *Coram R. P. D., Seraphino Many,* dec. XV, n. 4—*Decisiones,* VI (1914), 183; S. R. R., *Nullit. Matrim.*, 23 Martii, 1915, *Coram R. P. D., Aloiso Sincero,* dec. XII, n. 4—*Decisiones,* VII (1915), 124; S. R. R., *Nullit. Matrim.* (no date), 1909, *Coram R P. D., Seraphino Many,* dec. III, n. 3—*Decisiones,* I (1909), 25; S. R. R., *Nullit. Matrim.*, 10 Februarii, 1912, *Coram R. P. D., Friderico Cattani Amadori,* dec. VIII, n. 4—*Decisiones,* IV (1912), 86.

[11] Zallinger, *Institutiones Iuris Ecclesiastici,* lib. II, tit. XX, § 237, p. 177.

[12] S. R. R., *Nullit. Matrim.*, 29 Iulii, 1911, *Coram R. P. D., Francisco Heiner,* dec. XXXVI, n. 4—*Decisiones,* III (1911), 408; S. R. R., *Nullit. Matrim.*, 11 Aprilis, 1911, *Coram R. P. D., Iosepho Mori,* dec. XVI, n. 9—*Decisiones,* III (1911), 167.

[13] *Cf.* S. R. R., *Nullit. Matrim.*, 18 Augusti, 1916, *Coram R. P. D., Seraphino Many,* dec. XXVIII, n. 19—*Decisiones,* VIII (1916), 324.

[14] *Cf.* Wernz-Vidal, VI, *De Processibus, n.* 466, p. 402; S. R. R., *Nullit. Matrim,* 21 Decembris, 1912, *Coram R. P. D., Michaele Lega,* dec. XLI, n. 4—*Decisiones,* IV (1912), 471.

scription of the natural law.[15] The law excludes boys who have not completed their fourteenth year and girls who have not completed their twelfth year of age from testifying.[16] The foundation of the distinction is, as pointed out, found in Gratian and in the Decretals.[17] Minors who have arrived at the age of puberty (*impuberes puberes facti*) can testify about the facts which they had perceived before puberty, especially if what they had perceived happened close to that age.[18] The reason for this disposition of the law is that some maturity of judgment is presumed after the legal age of puberty. A defect of understanding begets an obstacle to marriage as well as an exclusion from testifying based on the natural law, whereas lack of puberty, being temporary, begets an impediment of ecclesiastical law as well as an exclusion from testimony which is ecclesiastical.[19]

Puberty can be proved by a certificate of baptism or by the parents or other persons who possess information about the age of the person.[20] A difficulty may arise in matrimonial procedure, how-

[15] Reiffenstuel, *Ius Canonicum Universum,* lib. II, tit. XX, n. 15; *cf.* Lega, *Praelectiones,* I, n. 479, p. 419.

[16] Canon 88, §§ 2, 3; *cf.* Eichmann, *Das Prozessrecht,* § 46, p. 142.

[17] *Cf.* also c. 15, C. XXII, q. 5.

[18] Schmalzgrueber, *Ius Ecclesiasticum Universum,* lib. III, tit. XX, n. 7; *cf.* Reiffenstuel, *Ius Canonicum Universum,* lib. II, tit. XX, n. 78; Wernz, *Ius Decretalium,* V, 608, nota 14; Muniz, *Procedimientos Eclesiásticos,* III, n. 302, p. 239; Wernz-Vidal, VI, *De Processibus,* n. 466, pp. 402, 403; A Coronata, *De Processibus,* n. 1284, p. 193; S. R. R., *Nullit. Matrim.,* 21 Decembris, 1912, *Coram R. P. D., Michaele Lega,* dec. XLI, n. 4—*Decisiones,* IV (1912), 471. Witnesses were not permitted to testify in causes involving the beatification and canonization of the Servants of God if their testimony concerned what they observed before the age of puberty. *Cf.* S. R. R., *Nullit. Matrim.,* 21 Decembris, 1912, *Coram R. P. D., Michaele Lega,* dec. XXXI, n. 4—*Decisiones Coram Lega,* 353, 354; S. R. R., *Nullit. Matrim.,* 21 Decembris, 1912, *Coram R. P. D., Michaele Lega,* dec. XLI, n. 4—*Decisiones,* IV (1912), 472. Two minors, however, near the age of puberty, were admitted to testify to a miraculous fact in the canonization process of St. Raymond. *Cf.* S. R. R., *Nullit. Matrim.,* 21 *Decembris,* 1912, *Coram R. P. D., Michaele Lega,* dec. XLI, n. 4—*Decisiones,* IV (1912), 471; Muniz, *Procedimientos Eclesiásticos,* n. 302, 1ª, p. 239.

[19] *Cf.* S. R. R., *Nullitatis vel Dispensationis Matrimonii,* 27 Aprilis, 1915, *Coram R. P. D., Iosepho Mori,* dec. XIX, n. 5—*Decisiones,* VII (1915), 210.

[20] *Cf.* Canons 772, § 2; 779; S. C. S. Off., Instr. (*Ad Ep. Rituum Orient.*) a. 1883—*Fontes,* n. 1076, 35—"Quare in hoc casu inquirendum erit de aetate

ever, with regard to determining the date of the birth of abandoned children. If the baptismal record states nothing clearly, two or three days are to be added to the date on which the children were found because a presumption of fact exists that the abandoned children were born a few days before they were abandoned. If, however, they were abandoned during the first years of their childhood, but the day of their birth is not established, and their present appearance does not indicate that they have already passed the canonical age, it is necessary to forward the case to the Ordinary. This is to be done in order that he may gather information to ascertain the date on which the person was abandoned and find out an approximation of the age of the person at the time of his abandonment. If the doubt persists (that is, in case of a marriage), the Ordinary can grant a dispensation for doubtful cases. When the child is a son or daughter of a well-known family and the baptismal certificate (or birth record from the register of vital statistics) is not recorded, the testimony of the family is sufficient to determine the age, if there are no presumptions against the fact.[21]

Besides these general rules to be considered in the evaluation of the testimony of those who have not arrived at the age of puberty, more specifically in matrimonial causes children must not in practice be repelled by the judge from testifying on account of an absolute defect of the required age. If, however, exception may be taken to them by reason of their age, their attestations can only attain the force of an auxiliary to the proof.[22] In marriage procedure adults can testify about things which they perceived during pubescence. Such witnesses are worthy of credence, and are considered by the Roman Rota to enjoy credibility and must, consequently, be considered credible witnesses.[23] Although the Code estimates that those

legitima eorum, a quibus sponsalia fuerunt contracta, quod facile fiet petitis documentis ex libris baptizatorum atque ex testimonio parentum, sive aliorum, qui personas, de quibus agitur cognoscant." Roberti, *De Processibus,* II, n. 337, p. 45.

[21] Muniz, *Procedimientos Eclesiásticos,* II, n. 239, p. 284.

[22] S. R. R., *Nullit. Matrim.,* 21 Decembris, 1912, *Coram R. P. D., Michaele Lega,* dec. XLI, n. 4—*Decisiones,* IV (1912), 472.

[23] S. R. R., *Nullit. Matrim.,* 21 Decembris, 1912, *Coram R. P. D., Michaele Lega,* dec. XXXI, n. 4—*Decisiones Coram Lega,* 355.

who have not arrived at the age of puberty are non-suitable as witnesses, nevertheless Canon 1758 permits them to be heard and their testimony has the value of auxiliary proof.

2. *The Mentally Weak.* Among persons who are weak in mind are those who suffer from some disease on account of which they are incapable of either rightly perceiving facts or of communicating their perceptions to others. Witnesses must be of sound mind, on the one hand, at the time during which they had observed the facts, and on the other hand, at the time when they narrate their testimony.[24] The time during which witnesses make their attestations must be considered. Consequently, persons who do not enjoy the use of their mental faculties are inadmissible to testify about things which occurred before they lost the use of their mind.[25] Among the weak in mind must certainly be enumerated those who are permanently deprived of the use of reason, morons, the feeble-minded, mentally deranged maniacs, the demented, monomaniacs, imbeciles, those in second childhood and idiots.[26] Canon Law excludes these classes of people from making an attestation as unsuitable, that is, as persons who should not be admitted to testify. Moreover, it is a rule that those who are drunk, or under the influence of drugs, and those subject to illusions or hallucinations while suffering from a fever, are temporarily rendered unfit for testimony and are inadmissible to attest concerning what happened in their presence during those periods of temporary derangement.[27]

The deaf, the dumb and the blind are not specifically mentioned in this canon. They are not absolutely unsuitable to testify. They have some fitness for making an attestation. In individual cases one

[24] *Cf.* Roberti, *De Processibus,* II, n. 337, p. 45.

[25] Pirhing, *Ius Canonicum,* lib. II, tit. XX, sec. I, § 1, n. 5.

[26] *Cf.* Meile, *Die Beweislehre des Kanonischen Prozesses,* 50; A Coronata, *De Processibus,* I, n. 121; III, n. 1284, p. 193; Muniz, *Procedimientos Eclesiásticos,* III, n. 302, 2a, p. 239.

[27] *Cf.* Reiffenstuel, *Ius Canonicum Universum,* lib. II, tit. XX, n. 15; Lega, *Praelectiones,* n. 479; Wernz, *Ius Decretalium,* V, 608; Schmalzgrueber, *Ius Ecclesiasticum Universum,* lib. II, tit. XX, nn. 3, 4; Augustine, *A Commentary,* VII, 207; Noval, *De Processibus,* IV, n. 464, pp. 327, 328; Wernz-Vidal, VI, *De Processibus,* n. 466, pp. 402, 403; Muniz, *Procedimientos Eclesiásticos,* n. 302. p. 239.

should consider the nature of the facts, the time during which the facts occurred, as also the culture of mind which the persons have.[28] Because of an impairment of their organs of perception, the color blind cannot describe color nor can nearsighted persons naturally perceive distant objects. The deaf cannot make an attestation about anything that entails sound.[29] In practice, however, the deaf can read written interrogations; a mute can write replies to questions; the deaf and dumb can ask questions and make replies in writing. If they can neither read nor write, they can communicate their testimony through an interpreter. The blind are able to narrate what they saw before they lost their power.of vision or what they had perceived with other senses.[30] Pirhing makes a trenchant observation regarding the value of the testimony of the deaf and dumb.[31] The judge is to estimate prudently with regard to a blind person testifying, whether or not he is perhaps deceived by the sound of a voice, as this can easily happen. Likewise, a deaf witness may be easily deceived by sight unaccompanied by sound. This observation is based upon the fact that the perception required in judicial proceedings is not mere comprehension but also judgment whereby the reason can determine whether the mental representation is compatible with the external object.

3. *Admissibility of Women to Testimony.* Some texts of Gratian and the Decretals, as pointed out, appeared to exclude the attestations of women.[32] It is thought that these texts were rather an admonition made to the judge than a prohibition, [33] because women are admitted by other texts. Hence, in the present legislation, there

[28] Roberti, *De Processibus,* II, n. 337, p. 45; Wernz-Vidal, VI, *De Processibus,* n. 466, p. 402; A Coronata, *De Processibus,* III, n. 1284, p. 193.

[29] *Cf.* Meile, *Die Beweislehre des Kanonischen Prozesses,* 50.

[30] Roberti, *De Processibus,* II, n. 337, pp. 45, 46.

[31] Pirhing, *Ius Canonicum,* lib. II, tit. XX, sec. I, § 1, nn. 6, 7.

[32] *Cf.* also c. 17, C. XXXIII, q. 5: "Mulierem constat subiectum domino iure esse, et nullam auctoritatem habere; nec docere potest, nec testis esse, neque fidem dare, nec iudicare." Women are, nevertheless, admissible in c. 3, 33, *X, de testibus et attestatinibus,* II, 20; c. 3, X, *qui matrimonium accusare possunt, vel contra illud testari,* IV, 18; c. 2, *de iudiciis,* II, in VI°.

[33] Ferraris, *Bibliotheca Canonica Iuridica,* VII, v. "Testis," art. 1, nn. 41-43, p. 463.

is no limitation restricting women from giving testimony.[34] They cannot be excluded in criminal or contentious causes.

In matrimonial causes women not rarely are preferable witnesses and are admitted by the express sanction of the law.[35] In matrimonial procedure, the testimony of women is of great importance, especially in force and fear (*vis et metus*) cases.[36] A woman servant testified in a Roma Rota case that she had received a blow and been upbraided by the father of the woman petitioning for a declaration of annulment of her marriage. She had been struck because she spoke to the victim of her father's brutality. The witness told that she had seen the father strike a table in a fit of rage. She heard him try to influence his daughter to marry against her will. Other facts were added by the testimony of another woman.[37]

Among the extraordinary proofs for the absence of the diriment impediment of religious profession [38] is the testimony of the superior. It may be well to clarify this point by indicating the extraordinary proofs of this impediment. The extraordinary proofs of the absence of sacred orders as well as of religious profession are four. They are considered in this place from the aspect of a person dedicated to religion who is restrained from marrying by a solemn vow of virginity. The proofs are:

(a) A rescript of the Holy Office or of the Sacred Congregation of the Sacraments which establishes the nullity of the ordination or of

[34] Roberti, *De Processibus,* II, n. 337, p. 46; Meile, *Die Beweislehre des Kanonischen Prozesses,* 50.

[35] Schmalzgrueber, *Ius Ecclesiasticum Universum,* lib. II, Pars III, tit. XX. n. 56; Pirhing, *Ius Canonicum,* lib. II, tit. XX, sec. I, § 7, n. 72; *A. F. K. K.*, XLV, p. 199; Wernz-Vidal, VI, *De Processibus,* n. 466, p. 403; *cf.* Canon 1648, § 3; Roberti, *De Processibus,* II, n. 337, p. 45.

[36] *Cf.* Canon 1087.

[37] S. R. R., *Nullit. Matrim.*, 16 Maii, 1912, *Coram R. P. D., Michaele Lega,* dec. XXIV, n. 3—*Decisiones Coram Lega,* 294. In another case two women testified that the father of the petitioner was tyrannical and that he would stop at nothing right or wrong to attain his purpose. *Cf.* S. R. R., *Veszprimien. Nullit. Matrim.*, 2 Junii, 1911, *Coram R. P. D., Michaele Lega, Videntibus omnibus,* dec. XIII, n. 8—*Decisiones Coram Lega,* 177, 178.

[38] *Cf.* Canon 1073.

the obligations resulting from it. This is the proof if the case is treated in a disciplinary manner or process.

(b) The execution of a sentence by the ecclesiastical tribunal which the Holy See has sent to take the case under consideration. This is the manner of handling such a case if it is considered in a judicial manner.[39]

(c) What is more pertinent to the testimony of a superior is the rescript of the Sacred Congregation of Religious in which the solemn profession was declared null. Whenever this is at hand, the Ordinary is to admit no other proof than the pontifical dispensation or testimony to its existence if the religious superior has already certified to the fact of solemn profession.

(d) The last proof is the pontifical indult of secularization because by it the religious is freed from his or her vows. The religious who have taken perpetual vows, solemn or simple, who have been dismissed from their institute (*i. e., religio*),[40] remained obliged by their vows if the constitutions of their communities or the indults of the Holy See do not dispose something to the contrary. Consequently, if someone who took a solemn vow invoke these privileges of his religious institute (*religio*), he has the obligation of proving them. The procedure or mode of acting by a diocesan curia is always to question the authenticity of a pontifical rescript when one of the aforementioned kinds is presented to it, if it has not received the rescript directly from the Sacred Congregations, or if the curia does not receive authentic testimony of the superior of the former religious. Outside of these two cases the curia should always ask *directly* for proofs or indications of their authenticity.[41]

Likewise, a woman superior of a religious community may give testimony in the solution of a valid marriage by religious profession. When a spouse enters religion and the husband remains in the world, he has to prove nothing unless he desires to contract a marriage, enter a religious community or receive sacred orders. If he intends to remarry, the dissolution of the first marriage must be

[39] Canons 1993; 1998.

[40] *Cf.* Canon 488, 1°.

[41] *Cf.* Muniz, *Procedimientos Eclesiásticos,* II, n. 286, pp. 343, 344.

established by the authentic testimony of solemn profession which is given by the superior who received it as well as by the proof of the consummation of the marriage. If there be no contradiction, it is not necessary to consider this proof judicially.[42]

B. Persons Who Can Be Disqualified as Suspect

Canon 1757, § 2. Ut suspecti:

1°. Excommunicati, periurii, infames, post sententiam declaratoriam vel condemnatoriam.

The law calls attention to the danger of admitting persons to testify whose credibility is doubtful. When special circumstances justify their admission, the judge can permit them to appear in court as suspect witnesses. They are suspect because it is presumed that they have so perverse a will that their testimony cannot be heeded. Theirs is a defect of probity which exposes a person who accepts their veracity to the danger of deception.[43]

1. *Excommunicated, Perjurers and Infamous Persons.* The excommunicated, perjurers and infamous persons are suspect after a declaratory or condemnatory sentence has been passed against them.[44] Looking at this general rule more closely, the following is to be observed:

a. Excommunicated persons who are to be shunned (*excommunicatus vitandus*) but against whom no sentence is passed [45] are un-

[42] Muniz, *Procedimientos Eclesiásticos,* II, n. 501, p. 625. The testimony of a superior and the sisters in her community is less suitable or invalidating (*inhabiles*) in litigation for legacies left to their community, but they are admissible in things difficult to prove because they are not directly interested in the cause and because they know what is usually of private knowledge in their communities. *Cf.* S. R. R., *Deposite PII,* 18 Januarii, 1921, *Coram R. P. D., Ioanne Prior,* dec. III, n. 8—*Decisiones,* XIII (1921), 26.

[43] *Cf.* Wernz-Vidal, VI, *De Processibus,* n. 466, p. 403.

[44] For a long list of other persons who were excluded from testifying before the Code, see Chapter IV. supra and Reiffenstuel, *Ius Canonicum Universum,* lib. II, tit. XX, n. 39; Lega, *Praelectiones,* n. 479, pp. 419, 420.

[45] *Cf.* Canons 2258, 2343, § 1, 1°; Pirhing, *Ius Canonicum,* lib. III, tit. XX, sec. I, § 2, n. 31; Chelodi, *Ius Poenale,* n. 36, p. 44; Augustine, *A Commentary,* VIII, pp. 173-175.

doubtedly to be considered suspect on account of the reasons embraced under this general topic in spite of the fact that they are not comprehended in this part of the canon.[46] The judge can also exclude the excommunicated persons who are called tolerated (*tolerati*).[47] He should not do this, however, unless one of the principals propose such an instance.[48]

b. Perjurers who deliberately violate their oath are excluded from giving testimony. They offend against the reverence due to God, the dignity of judicial tribunals and the right of the litigants.[49] The Ordinary can deprive them of the right and capacity to testify if he thinks it fit. He may mete out a special or indeterminate penalty against those who perjure themselves outside of a trial court.[50] It appears that a declaration stating that perjury was committed and that the perjurer will be inadmissible as a witness, is to be issued by the Ordinary or the judge.[51] In matrimonial procedure no one is presumed to be a perjurer unless it is proved, which can happen if the witness contradicts himself.[52] In the practice of both the Spanish tribunals [53] and of the Roman Rota the testimony of perjurers lacks all probative value, in spite of the fact that the witnesses per-

[46] *Cf.* Roberti, *De Processibus,* II, n. 337, p. 46.

[47] Canon 2258, § 1; *cf.* Canon 1654, § 1.

[48] *Cf.* Schmalzgrueber, *Ius Ecclesiasticum Universum,* lib. II, Pars III, tit. XX, n. 27; *cf.* Wernz-Vidal, VI, *De Processibus,* n. 466, p. 403.

[49] Schmalzgrueber, *Ius Ecclesiasticum Universum,* lib. II, Pars III, tit. XX, nn. 24, 25; *cf.* Campegius, Joannes, *Tractatus et Regulae de Testibus* (Venetiis, 1508), Regula XXXV, fol. 16, in which ten reasons are assigned for the inadmissibility of perjurers.

[50] Canon 2323; *cf.* Chelodi, *Ius Poenale,* n. 63, p. 79. Punishments for perjurers in ecclesiastical trials are indicated in Canons 1743; 1755, § 3.

[51] *Cf.* Augustine, *A Commentary,* VII, p. 208; A Coronata, *De Processibus,* III, n. 1285, note 6, p. 193.

[52] "Nemo praesumitur periurus, nisi probetur, praesertim non in casu, cum agatur de accusando de illicitis relationibus non solum actorem, cuius interest, ut matrimonium dissolvatur seu declaretur nullum, sed etiam Castriciam quae certo illis contradixisset, si contra veritatem talia contra ipsam deposuisset."—S. R. R., *Nullit. Matrim.,* 29 Julii, 1911, *Coram R. P. D., Francisco Heiner,* dec. XXVI, n. 4—*Decisiones,* III (1911), 408.

[53] Muniz, *Procedimientos Eclesiásticos,* III, n. 302, 3a, p. 239: perjurers and infamous persons are inadmissible without an indult.

jured themselves before a civil magistrate in a divorce case and appear before a matrimonial tribunal to tell the truth under oath. The Roman Rota made the following decision in reply to its own question summarizing this doctrine:

> Quaenam ut vera est retinenda depositio? Non constat. Sed certum est periurium in uno vel in alio iudicio admissum: testibus periuriis nulla fides potest haberi.[54]

c. Infamous persons are inadmissible as witnesses until the infamy of law as well as in fact [55] is absolved. The infamy understood by the canon is infamy of law. Infamy in fact, although it is not a penalty, can be embraced under the canon.[56] The infamous in fact can be included among the suspect by reason of infamy when they have sustained a condemnatory or declaratory sentence to that effect, as it is not clearly established that factual infamy alone renders a witness suspect. A sentence is required for the declaration of infamy of law or infamy in fact.[57] The rejection of excommunicated witnesses vanishes with absolution from excommunication. The rejection of infamous persons is removed by an indult which frees them from the cause of suspicion.[58] Archbishop Muniz [59] expresses the opinion that perjured persons are not rejected by reason of their perjury if this, also, is removed by an indult. A Coronata [60] observes that according to Archbishop Muniz, infamous and perjured persons can never be admitted unless they can present an indult. The scholarly Archbishop speaks in the whole chapter about the legal rejection or reprobation of witnesses. He does not state that infamous and perjured persons are always inadmissible to testify

[54] S. R. R., *Parisien. Nullit. Matrim.*, 12 Junii, 1919, *Coram R. P. D., Petro Rossetti*, dec. XI, n. 16—*Decisiones*, XI (1919), 108; *cf.* Noval, *De Processibus*, IV, n. 466, pp. 328, 329.

[55] Canon 2293. *Cf.* Chelodi, *Ius Poenale*, n. 50, p. 62.

[56] *Cf.* Pirhing, *Ius Canonicum*, lib. II, tit. XX, sec. I, § 2, n. 18.

[57] Noval, *De Processibus*, IV, n. 466, p. 329; A Coronata, *De Processibus*, III, n. 1285, p. 193.

[58] Roberti, *De Processibus*, II, n. 337, p. 46; Eichmann, *Das Prozessrecht*, p. 142.

[59] Muniz, *Procedimientos Eclesiásticos*, III, n. 302, 3ª, p. 239.

[60] A Coronata, *De Processibus*, III, n. 1285, note 1, p. 194.

without an indult, but remarks that the rejection of such persons does not disappear except by an indult. His statement that the rejection "does not disappear except by an indult" [61] appears to provide latitude of the positive idea of A Coronata and other authors [62] that perjurers, in spite of the fact that they have been reinstated or reformed, do not cease to be suspect. Moreover, Reiffenstuel [63] taught that a witness who was not suspect when he took the oath but became such before he gave testimony can be or ought to be excluded by the judge unless the cause of suspicion were concealed at the time the testimony was given. The capacity of witnesses to testify should be considered with reference to the time during which they made their attestations. But if a witness were capable of testifying at the time when he took the oath and was incapable just before or while giving testimony, he is excluded because the capability to testify is considered at the time the attestation was made.

2. *Moral Incapacity for Testimony.*

Canon 1757, § 2, 2°. Qui ita abiectis sunt moribus ut fide digni non habeantur.

The second class of persons excluded from testimony as suspect are those who are stigmatized for want of integrity. It is no small difficulty to determine precisely what crimes render a person so unprincipled in morals that he cannot be accepted as worthy of credence. The rule is justly stated to require that the persons be not merely unprincipled but "so unprincipled in morals that they are not to be believed." This implies such a dereliction of moral principles that one may infer a conclusion of entire disregard of the sacredness of an oath. The difficulty rests in the specification of offenses.

[61] " . . . la tacha de la excomunión se borra con la absolución de ésta, pero la de infamia o periurio no desaparece sino con el indulto."—Muniz, *Procedimientos Eclesiásticos*, III, n. 302, 3a, p. 239.

[62] *Cf.* A Coronata, *De Processibus,* III, n. 1286, p. 194; Noval, *De Processibus,* IV, n. 466, pp. 328, 329; Roberti, *De Processibus,* II, n. 337, p. 46.

[63] Reiffenstuel, *Ius Canonicum Universum*, lib. II, tit. XX, nn. 17-21, 47, 48, 54.

The older canonists included among the usual or more general enumeration of delicts or indications of depraved morals those persons who were either very poor and vile [64] or engaged in employments, such as executioners and the like, which were considered debasing. The Code rightly pays attention only to moral capacity,[65] and considers suspect those who, because of the commission of a delict or their moral depravity, have been declared infamous in fact as long as the sentences to that effect had not been revoked or the penalties remitted.[66] The Holy See formerly delegated guardians (*conservatores*) who were obliged to defend miserable persons from manifest injuries and violence.[67] The present law, mindful of the helplessness of the very poor, specifies that ecclesiastical judges must pronounce sentence in accordance with equity which is deduced from written law.[68] Consequently, a judge who ignores the comment of St. James [69] and gives a more favorable decision to a man or woman because he or she is rich or prepossessing and is biased against somebody whose background is humble and clothing poor, is an unjust judge deserving of the contempt of honest men.

Among those who should be enumerated as suspect witnesses to be excluded by reason of their moral depravity because a sentence to that effect was not revoked or penalties against them were not remitted,[70] are habitual drunkards, those who live in or frequent

[64] "Personas valde pauperes et viles"—*Cf.* D. XXII, 5, 3; Schmalzgrueber, *Ius Ecclesiasticum Universum,* lib. II, Pars III, tit. XX, n. 28; Reiffenstuel, *Ius Canonicum Universum,* lib. II, tit. XV, n. 98; Ferraris, *Bibliotheca,* VII, v. "Testis," art. 1, nn. 37-40, pp. 462, 463, esp. n. 40; Zallinger, *Institutiones Iuris Ecclesiastici,* lib. II, tit. XX, § 238, pp. 177, 178; Campegius, *De Testibus,* Regula CXIII, fol. 39.

[65] Roberti, *De Processibus,* II, n. 337, p. 46.

[66] *Cf.* c. 18, C. VI, q. 1; Wernz-Vidal, VI, *De Processibus,* n. 466, pp. 403, 404.

[67] *Cf.* S. R. R., *Michoagen. Crediti.,* 7 Januarii, 1913, *Coram R. P. D., Michaele Lega,* dec. II, n. 6—*Decisiones,* V (1912), 13.

[68] S. R. R., *Diffamationis,* 19 Juniis, 1911, *Coram R. P. D., Francisco Heiner,* dec. XXVI, n. 16—*Decisiones,* III (1911), 281.

[69] James ii, 2, 3, 9.

[70] *Cf.* c. 18, C. VI, q. 1; Wernz-Vidal, VI, *De Processibus,* n. 466, pp. 403, 404.

places of corruption, thieves, gaolbirds, and the like. The existence of this disability depends on no one person, but rather on public opinion. Consequently, the disability cannot be proved apart from notorious facts, but is established by the judgment of prudent people.[71]

Canon 1757 mentions nothing about heresy, lese majesty, slavery and other disqualifications of a kindred nature which were mentioned in Chapter IV. These crimes are usually accompanied by infamy or excommunication so that they may be included in this category. As a rule heretics and the unbaptized (*infideles*) are admissible in beatification processes.[72]

The Roman Rota has admitted the testimony of non-Catholics who make their attestations under oath. The jurisprudence with regard to the juridical value of their testimony was summarized in this opinion concerning a force and fear case:

> Etiam protestantes, si sub fide iuramenti deponunt, credibiles sunt ideoque audire debent, praesertim si, uti in casu, fere unici testes sint, qui depositiones facere valent.[73]

A Protestant mother refused to appear in court because she would not acknowledge the competence of a matrimonial tribunal over the marriage of a Protestant. She wrote the court that she was opposed to the marriage of her daughter to a Catholic. Her letters were received as testimony. The Rota was of the opinion that citation of her had not been absolutely useless because of her disobedience or contumacy, because her letters manifested that she had a stubborn mind and was bitterly obstinate in her intention to influence her daughter.[74] A Protestant who was also a Mason, whose knowledge is

[71] Muniz, *Procedimientos Eclesiásticos,* III, n. 302, 4a, pp. 238, 239. Compare Reiffenstuel, *Ius Canonicum Universum,* lib. II, tit. XX, nn. 55-57. For exclusion of various kinds of criminals in Roman Law under the Principate, *cf.* Mommsen, Theodore, *Le Droit Penal Romain,* Traduit de L'Allemand par J. Duquesne (Paris, 1907), II, p. 77.

[72] Canon 2027, § 1. *Cf.* Meile, *Die Beweislehre des Kanonischen Prozesses,* 52.

[73] S. R. R., *Osnabrugen., Nullit. Matrim.,* 11 Januarii, 1912, *Coram, R. P. D., Francisco Heiner,* dec. III, n. 6—*Decisiones,* IV (1912), 22.

[74] S. R. R., *Nullit. Matrim.,* 21 Decembris, 1912, *Coram R. P. D., Michaele Lega,* dec. XXXI, n. 5—*Decisiones Coram Lega,* 355, 356.

unquestioned and whose sincerity is undoubted is, with a letter of credibility, admissible as an expert witness in matrimonial procedure. In a vitiated consent case a letter of credibility was given to a Mason enabling him to act in the capacity of an expert witness. The vicar general of the diocese testified to the man's knowledge and sincerity.[75] The practice of the Roman Rota, as seen, has been to require that the testimony of Protestants be given under oath. It would seem that an affirmation made by a credible member of the Society of Friends would suffice.

A reply of the Pontifical Commission for the Authentic Interpretation of the Canons of the Code affirmed that members of atheistic sects and those who formerly belonged to one or more of them are to be considered, as far as all juridical effects are concerned, in the same manner as former members of non-Catholic sects or those who are actually non-Catholics.[76] The reply mentions sacred ordination and matrimony. This does not, however, exclude an atheist from the right to testify as the word "*etiam*" implies that such atheists enjoy the more usual effects of the law. One of such effects of the law which results from the reception of baptism,[77] and which is enjoyed by baptized non-Catholics, is the right of standing in court unless prohibited by the sacred canons.[78] Until a decision adverse to this reply of the Pontifical Commission is made, atheists can appear in ecclesiastical courts as witnesses as do non-Catholics. As the reply states nothing further, the general law expressed in Canon 1757, § 2, 2°, must be observed. Consequently, if atheists be admitted into court as witnesses their profession of atheism warrants a

[75] S. R. R., *Nullit. Matrim.*, 23 Martii, 1914, *Coram R. P. D., Gulielmo Sebastianelli,* dec. XII, n. 6—*Decisiones,* VI (1914) 146, 147.

[76] D. An ad normam Codicis iuris canonici, qui sectae atheisticae adscripti sunt vel fuerunt, habendi sint quoad omnes iuris effectus etiam in ordine ad sacram ordinationem et matrimonium, ad instar eorum qui sectae acatholicae adhaerent vel adhaeserunt.

R. Affirmative.—Responsa Ad Proposita Dubia. 1. De Sectae Atheisticae Adscriptis, *Pontificia Commissio Ad Codicis Canones Authentice Interpretandos,* 30 Julii, 1934, *A. A. S.*, XXVI (1934), 494.

[77] Canon 87.

[78] Canon 1646.

presumption that they are unworthy of credibility. The judge does not require them to take an oath as they are suspect.

3. *Emotional Incapacity to Testify: Enmity.*

Canon 1757, § 2, 3°. Publici gravesque partis mimici.

Emotion may affect the three testimonial elements of perception, recollection and narration so that some aberration from exactness may take place. The strong feeling of enmity as distinguished from perception and conscious reasoning is a source of illusion as it disturbs intellectual operations. When the mind is under the temporary sway of anger, or a man is under the control of enmity which has been nursed a long while, there will be a readiness to interpret objects with the assistance of real or fancied representations of objects congruent with the emotion.

Public and violent enemies of either defendant or plaintiff are excluded from testimony as suspect witnesses.[79] The enmity must be public, grave, and limited to one of the litigating parties.

a. Enmity is *public* when not only the reason for it, but also the circumstances of it are known.[80] The circumstances of the case can make this known, *e. g.*, a former lawsuit, a threat of assault or serious quarrels.[81]

b. Animosity is *grave* when it takes rise from a serious cause

[79] Canon 1757, § 2, 3°; *Cod.* IV, 20, 17; cc. 13, 19, X, *de accusationibus, inquisitionibus et denunciationibus,* V, 1. Other causes of suspicion in force before the Code have been abolished. The law of the Decretals prohibited laymen from testifying against clerics in criminal causes. Laymen could accuse, but were not permitted to calumniate clerics who had injured them. *Cf.* c. 14, X, *de testibus et attestationibus,* II, 20. Those living in the houses of or consorting with enemies were not to be believed. *Cf.* c. 3, C. III, q. 5. Canonists excluded domestics from testifying against their employers, friends or companions against others and enemies in a cause against an enemy. *Cf.* Lega, *Praelectiones,* I, *De Iudiciis,* n. 480, p. 421; Wernz, *Ius Decretalium,* V, 463; Zallinger, *Institutiones Iuris Ecclesiastici,* lib. II, tit. XX, § 243, VII, pp. 179, 180.

[80] Muniz, *Procedimientos Eclesiásticos,* III, n. 302, 5ª, p. 240; *cf.* Canon 2197, 1°.

[81] *Cf.* Augustine, *A Commentary,* VII, p. 210.

or is intended to inflict great injury on another's reputation, life or possessions.[82] Violent hatred, however, is no longer considered to exist between those who merely do not foster mutual relations. In the old legislation, light enmity was insufficient to discredit a witness to render him incapable of testifying.[83] In the new law, a judge ought, nevertheless, to take it into consideration.[84] Exception to the rule is made in the case of a former enemy who was reconciled,[85] because the cause of suspicion ceases with the termination of the enmity. Intimate friendship is not included among the reasons for suspicion. Nevertheless, the judge is to weigh these elements in the proofs.[86]

c. The enmity must, lastly, be *restricted* to the litigant against whom testimony is to be given, for if a witness be an enemy to both defendant and litigant, his testimony could not be rejected.[87]

The practice of the Roman Rota provides a suggestion of practical importance in evaluating the testimony in matrimonial procedure. A witness may not be an avowed enemy of either the defendant or the plaintiff and yet one of the litigants, apprehensive of an adverse decision, may try to divine what the nature of his testimony will be. In a force and fear case the plaintiff, a woman, felt that a priest would testify against her. She sent a lay lawyer to ascertain if he was to be called into the case. The priest testified that the attorney appeared to be desirous of penetrating his intention with regard to the attestation he was going to make. The father of the woman corroborating this, added that his daughter persauded her mother not to oppose the declaration of nullity. He made the further attestation that his son, the brother of the plaintiff, came a long distance for the purpose of reproaching him for demanding a hearing and retard-

[82] Muniz, *ibid.*

[83] Pirhing, *Ius Canonicum,* lib. II, tit. XX, sec. I, § VI, n. 54; *cf.* Reiffenstuel, *Ius Canonicum Universum,* lib. II, tit. XX, nn. 135-138.

[84] A Coronata, *De Processibus,* III, n. 1285, p. 194.

[85] *Cf.* Reiffenstuel, *Ius Canonicum Universum,* lib. II, tit. XX, n. 137.

[86] Roberti, *De Processibus,* II, n. 337, pp. 46, 47; *cf.* Muniz, *Procedimientos Eclesiásticos,* III, n. 302, 5ª, p. 240.

[87] Augustine, *A Commentary,* VII, p. 210; *cf.* A Coronata, *De Processibus,* III, n. 1285, p. 194; Reiffenstuel, *Ius Canonicum Universum,* lib. II, tit. XX, nn. 138-140.

ing a solution of the case favorable to the wishes of the plaintiff. The Rota concluding that there had been collusion between the parties, added this observation on such practices:

> Equidem hi praevii tractatus cum testibus, etsi non eo spectant ut attestationes favorabiles comparentur, tamen semper perturbant genuinam factorum recordationem, quae facile in memoria, seu phantasia, subvertitur ex eiusmodi collationibus.[88]

C. Persons Disqualified from Testimony as Incapable

> **Canon 1757, § 3, 1°. Qui partes sunt in causa, aut partium vice funguntur, veluti tutor in causa pupilli, Superior aut administrator in causa suae communitatis aut piae causae, cuius nomine in iudicio consistit, iudex eiusve assistentes, advocatus aliique qui partibus in eadem causa assistunt vel astiterunt.**

The most important, because extensive, ground of incapacity is that supposed inclination to falsify which arises from the prospect of gaining or losing by the issue of the proceedings. This canon declares incapable of making an attestation those whose duties are believed incompatible with their testimony and those whose spiritual ministrations prevent them from testifying lest the spiritual welfare of others suffer.

1. *Interest in the Litigation.* In the early development of canonical jurisprudence the testimony of all interested witnesses was excluded. The theory of the original disqualification appears to be that due to the weakness of human nature there is more reason to distrust such a biased testimony than to believe it, because interested witnesses were likely to bear false witness. It was a dictum of Roman Law that no one is a suitable witness in a thing pertaining to himself.[89] The disqualification of interest as a source of incompetency

[88] S. R. R., *Nullit. Matrim.*, I Augusti, 1913, *Coram R. P. D., Michaele Lega*, dec. XXXIX, n. 9—*Decisiones Coram Lega*, 483, 484.

[89] "Nullus idoneus testis in re sua intelligitur."—Pomponius, D. XXII, 5, 11.

was long allowed to perpetuate its principle in criminal causes with rigorous literalness.

The general disqualification by reason of interest in litigation includes a mass of detailed rules depending on the principle which rests on the supposed emotional incapacity of interested persons to testify. The phrase, *aut partium vice funguntur,* indicates the general rule that persons engaged in the place of the litigating parties are prevented from testifying because they restore or supply the incapacity of the parties. The parties or those who represent them are admitted during the proceedings of the court. The witnesses provide the testimonial proof (*partes contestatio; testes, probatio*). Thus in civil causes those who may have either a moral or a patrimonial interest are excluded from testimony.[90] The rest of the canon specifies the persons who cannot play the double part of representing in two parts of a probatory process at the same time. For, abstractly, testimony refers to some extraneous object and nobody can, as seen, testify on his own behalf (*in re sua*) or for himself (*pro se*). These persons, for example, include:

a. A tutor or curator in a cause involving his charge.

b. A superior or administrator in a cause pertaining to his college, community or a pious cause in which he has an interest.[91] Pastors litigating in favor of their parishes, holders of benefices while engaged in contention for their benefices and rectors of colleges during the time when they argue on behalf of those under them are also in this category.[92] As plaintiff or defendant and witness are different,

[90] S. R. R., *Salutarum. Iurium.*, 5 Julii, 1915, *Coram R. P. D., Guilielmo Sebastianelli,* dec. XXVII, n. 9—*Decisiones,* VII (1915), 290.

[91] *Cf.* Eugene III. "Insuper *etiam auctoritate nostra* statuimus, ut liceat vobis in causis ecclesiae vestrae ferre testimonium, dummodo unus ex vobis vel duo ad agendum et respondendum instituantur, quorum testimonium in causis, in quibus actores vel responsales sunt instituti, non debet admitti."—c. 6, X, *de testibus et attestationibus,* II, 20.

[92] *Cf.* "*Praeterea* non lateat prudentiam vestram quod clerici non sunt a ferendo testimonio super *proprio* negotio ecclesiae suae, nisi alia rationabilis causa impediat, repellendi."—c. 12, X, *de testibus et attestationibus,* II, 20; Reiffenstuel, *Ius Canonicum Universum,* lib. II, tit. XX, nn. 197-199; Lega, *Praelectiones,* I, n. 481, pp. 421, 422; Muniz, *Procedimientos Eclesiásticos,* III, n. 302, 6ª, p. 239; Noval, *De Processibus,* IV, n. 467, pp. 329-331; Wernz-Vidal, VI, *De Processibus,* n. 466, note (33), p. 405.

it is possible for the administrator of a religious institution to be a litigating party and the rector of the institution to be a witness. Furthermore, a prelate, either diocesan or regular, may testify in a case involving his own church or community; canons and capitulars also can testify in civil matters involving their chapters, provided that no personal interests, but only the chapters as such are directly involved.[93] Noval [94] admits this in spite of the contrary opinion of Reiffenstuel,[95] because if the legislator had intended that moral noncollegiate persons be disqualified he should have expressed this, even as in Canon 1572, § 2, the legislator declared that a bishop is an incompetent judge in three distinct things. These things are cases involving first, the rights or temporal property of the bishop; secondly, the episcopal revenues (*mensa*); and thirdly, the revenues of the diocesan curia. Noval [96] and Roberti [97] are of the opinion that the rights and temporal property (*iura et bona*) mentioned include also spiritual rights. These, however, do not have application to the United States at the present time. The Code prevents a bishop from sitting in judgment on the three things mentioned because he would be a judge in his own cause.[98] These cases may be tried by the diocesan tribunal in a body consisting of the official and two senior synodal judges longest in office,[99] or they may be brought before the court of the immediate superior and independently of the consent of the bishop.[100] If the metropolitan is a party to the trial the imme-

[93] *Cf.* Augustine, *A Commentary,* VII, pp. 210, 211.

[94] Noval, *De Processibus,* IV, n. 467, p. 331; *cf.* Muniz, *Procedimientos Eclesiásticos,* III, n. 302, 6ª, note (2), p. 240; Meile, *Die Beweislehre des Kanonischen Prozesses,* 50.

[95] Reiffenstuel, *Ius Canonicum Universum,* lib. II, tit. XX, n. 207.

[96] Noval, *De Processibus,* IV, n. 110, p. 59.

[97] Roberti, *De Processibus,* I, n. 96, p. 162.

[98] Before the Code a bishop could legally take cognizance of fiscal causes. *Cf. Il Monitore Ecclesiastico,* XXXIII (1921), 24, 25.

[99] Augustine, *A Commentary,* VII, p. 29; Roberti, *De Processibus,* I, n. 96, p. 163. If judges were nominated at the same time their seniority is computed in accordance with Canon 106, § 3.

[100] *Cf.* A Coronata, *De Processibus,* III, n. 1115, p. 24; *cf. Designatio Ordinariorum Pro Appellatione In Secundo Grado—A. A. S.,* XX (1928), 359.

diate superior is the Apostolic Delegate of the Holy See.[101] Finally, members of an association are admitted more or less in so far as they and their interests are distinct from the moral person and its interests. On the contrary, the promoter of justice and the defender of the marriage bond who defend the public welfare in court are excluded.[102]

c. The disqualification of interest embraces those who represent the parties in court (*procuratores*) or who aid them as counsel. These are disqualified from acting as witnesses.[103]

d. Judges, assessors, auditors, notaries, messengers and apparators are disqualified by reason of interest.[104]

2. *Privileged Communications between Confessor and Penitent.*

> **Canon 1757, § 3, 2°. Sacerdotes, quod attinet ad ea omnia quae ipsis ex confessione sacramentali innotuerunt, etsi a vinculo sigilli soluti sint; imo audita a quovis et quoquo modo occasione confessionis ne ut indicium quidem veritatis recipi possunt.**

The divine law forbids every use of any knowledge learned from sacramental confession as the information is obtained as the representative of God.[105] The canon under consideration expresses a general disqualification which is wider than the mere seal of con-

[101] Augustine, *A Commentary,* VII, 29; *cf.* Roberti, *De Processibus,* I, n. 92, p. 163; Canons 285 and 1594, §§ 1-3.

[102] Roberti, *De Processibus,* II, n. 337, p. 47; *cf.* Wernz-Vidal, VI, *De Processibus,* n. 466, p. 404.

[103] *Cf.* c. 3, *de testibus et attestationibus,* II, 10, in VI°; *cf.* Muniz, *Procedimientos Eclesiásticos,* III, n. 302, 7ª, p. 240. For beatification and canonization causes compare Canon 2027.

[104] Roberti, *De Processibus,* II, n. 337, p. 47; A Coronata, *De Processibus,* III, n. 286, p. 195; Meile, *Die Beweislehre des Kanonischen Prozess,* 50, assigns the reason for the disqualification of judges as the fact that they would not appraise their own testimony objectively. For the disqualification against judge and defender of the marriage bond (a) in case of non-consummation of marriage *cf. Regulae Servandae in Processibus Super Matrimonio Rato et Non Consummato,* n. 16, §§ 1, 2; Decretum., S. Congr. De Disciplina Sacram., 7 Maii, 1923, *A. A. S.,* XV (1923), 389. (b) In case of trial of validity of sacred orders, *cf.* Canon 1993, and n. 8—*A. A. S.,* XXIII (1931), 457.

[105] *Cf.* Canons 888-890, 2269, §§ 1, 2.

fession. The disqualification includes all persons, priests and lay persons, who intentionally, that is through malice, curiosity or in the capacity of interpreter, or accidentally in any manner whatsoever, came either mediately or immediately, directly or indirectly, to the knowledge of something, not only sins but all information, made known orally or by writing or by signs to any priest in confession. The incapacity primarily affects priests and secondarily and accidentally all those who learned anything made known in confession.[106] The ecclesiastical law laid down in this canon determines that attestations which mention anything pertaining to sacramental confession cannot be received as an indication of the truth and are devoid of value, although the penitent releases the person who heard what he said in confession,[107] because no one can take advantage of or interpret a violation of the seal for his own use.[108] Even a written confession which was lost and found by another has no value as evidence although the one reading it is not bound to keep silent by the seal of confession but by a natural secret. The reason for this is that due to the sacredness of the sacrament of penance what is heard in confession will not be brought into the external forum lest aversion from the sacrament arise.[109] The practice of the Roman Rota has been to

[106] *Cf.* S. C. C. Off., decr., 18 Novembris, 1682—*Fontes*, n. 758; Cappello, Felix M., *Tractatus Canonico-Moralis De Sacramentis* (Romae, 1929), II, Pars I. *De Poenitentia*, nn. 891-895, pp. 736-741; Noldin, H., *De Sacramentis* (19 ed., Oeniponte, 1929), III, *De Sacramentis*, n. 8, pp. 416-418; n. 417, pp. 426-428; Claeys Bouuaert-G. Simeon, *De Sacramentis* (Liege, 1931), II, nn. 137, 138, pp. 119-121; Muniz, *Procedimientos Eclesiásticos*, III, n. 302, 8ª, p. 240.

[107] Compare c. 13, X, *de excessibus praelatorum et subditorum, V*, 31. In the filiation case of Duke Sforza-Cesarini before the Roman Rota, 1834-1837, the Tribunal rejected the attestation of a confessor who testified with the permission of the mother of the infant whose origin was questioned, that she had accused herself of adultery committed about the time the child was conceived. *Cf.* Lega, *Praelectiones*, I, n. 459, p. 406.

[108] Schmalzgrueber, *Ius Ecclesiasticum Universum*, lib. II, Pars III, tit. XVIII, n. 31.

[109] *Cf.* Reiffenstuel, *Ius Canonicum Universum*, lib. II, tit. XVIII, nn. 133-136; Schmalzgrueber, *Ius Ecclesiasticum Universum*, lib. II, Pars III, tit. XVIII, nn. 29-32; Wernz-Vidal, VI *De Processibus*, n. 366, pp. 405, 406.

exclude testimony referring to the sacrament of penance. It does not countenance reference to the confessional for the purpose of keeping matters referred to in letters secret. In a cause of simulated consent it was declared that one of the reasons for the rejection of testimony, which itself was open to suspicion, was that a letter written by the mother of a man who was known to be of bad character lacked probative value because she wanted the facts narrated therein to be kept under the seal of confession.[110] More specifically, the testimony of the pastor on behalf of a plaintiff was rejected by the Rota because sacramental confessions are made to God and not to man and, moreover, for the following reason:

> Verum an falsum dixerit Confessarius, et recte an non egerit in vulganda sacramentali confessione de mandato licet confitentis, sed ad propinquorum ipsius causam iuvendam in alterius perniciem, quod execrandum videtur, . . . non putarunt Patres inquirere, quippe abundans erat responsio, quod confessio matris, licet sacramentalis, vim nullam recipit a iure in praeiudicium legitimae filiationis.[111]

But as a confessor is also a public magistrate in the external forum, he enjoys credibility when, with the permission of a penitent, he attests that he himself gave absolution from censures.[112] The secrecy safeguarding what is heard in the confessional must be sharply distinguished from the secrecy which surrounds the avocations of clerics and laymen. These avocations do not disqualify from testimony in ecclesiastical courts.[113] Hence, officials, physicians, midwives, lawyers, notaries and other persons, whether ecclesiastical or lay, can legally refuse to testify. Likewise those who would suffer

[110] S. R. R., *Nullit. Matrim.*, 30 Augusti, 1911, *Coram R. P. D., Michaele Lega,* dec. XVII, n. 12—*Decisiones Coram Lega,* 227.

[111] This reason was also assigned by the Roman Rota in *Romana-Filiationis die 20 ianuarii 1834,* coram D'Avella, n. 23, quoted in S. R. R., *Nullit. Matrim.*, 8 Martii, 1913, *Coram R. P. D., Ioanne Prior,* dec. XVIII, n. 8—*Decisiones,* V (1913), 214.

[112] *Cf.* Canon 2251, S. Poenitentiaria Apostolica, Monita de usu facultatum confessariis per annum sanctum tributarum . . . , 31 Julii, 1924—*A. A. S.*, XVI (1924), 337-344; Roberti, *De Processibus,* II, n. 337, p. 48.

[113] Meile, *Die Beweislehre des Kanonischen Prozesses,* 50.

dire consequences to themselves or their families are excused from testimony.[114]

3. *Domestic Relationship.*

> **Canon 1757, § 3, 3°. Coniux in causa sui coniugis, consanguineus et affinis in causa consanguinei vel affinis, in quolibet gradu lineae rectae et in primo gradu collateralis, nisi agatur de causis quae ad statum civilem aut religiosum personae spectant, cuius notitia aliunde haberi nequeat, et bonum publicum exigat ut habeatur.**

Canon 1757, § 3, 3°, contains two parts which are corollaries to the general rule of exclusion from interest. Husband and wife cannot be admitted as witnesses for or against each other. Persons related to one another by consanguinity or affinity of the direct line and in the first degree of the collateral line are excluded from testimony. The last part of the canon gives an exception to the general rule.

a. *Marital Relationship.*

> **Canon 1759, § 3, 3°. "Coniux in causa sui coniugis . . ."**

The incompetence of husband and wife to be witnesses for one another seems to rest on the identity of interest and consequent danger of perjury.[115] It is a policy of law which is intended to guard

[114] Koeniger, Albert M., *Katholisches Kirchenrecht mit Berücksichtigung des Deutschen Staatskirchenrechts* (Freiburg Im Breisgau, 1926), p. 415.

[115] Compare with S. R. R., *Nullit. Matrim.*, 16 Maii, 1914, *Coram R. P. D., Petro Rossetti*, dec. XVIII, n. 6—*Decisiones*, VI (1914), 210; *ibid.*, 3 Augusti, 1914, dec. XX, n. 10—*Decisiones*, XIII (1921), 193. *Cf.* Knecht, August, *Handbuch Des Katholischen Eherechts auf Grund Des Codex Iuris Canonici Und Unter Berücksichtigund Des Bürgerlichen Eherechts Des Deutschen Reiches, Österreichs, Ungarns Der Tschechoslowakei Der Schweiz* (Freiburg Im Greisgau, 1928), 773. The Code does not extend privileged relations to future spouses and those living in concubinage. *Cf.* Reiffenstuel, *Ius Canonicum Universum*, lib. II, tit. XX, nn. 114, 115. The judge may, nevertheless, inquire into the reason for their relationship.

the security and confidence of marital life because its admission would lead not so much to domestic disunion but harm to the public good.[116]

b. *Family Relationship.*

> **Canon 1757, § 3, 3°. " . . . consanguineus et affinis in causa consanguinei vel affinis, in quolibet gradu lineae rectae et in primo gradu collateralis, nisi agatur de causis quae statum civilem aut religiosum personae spectant, cuius notitia aliunde haberi nequeat, et bonum publicum exigat ut habeatur."**

The general principle stated in this part of the canon is that relatives by consanguinity and affinity in every degree of the direct line together with brothers and sisters, brothers-in-law and sisters-in-law who are those in the first degree of the collateral line are disqualified for testimony whenever their relatives are involved.[117] Exceptions to the rigorous literalness of the rule were carved out of this disqualification. They were made because first, the reason for the disqualification appears to be true only in a limited sense as no exclusion could be so defined as to be consistent, simple and practical; and secondly, because the hardship of the exclusion is intolerable in matrimonial causes as relatives naturally know more about an ordinary marriage than strangers. Hence, exception was made, as the part of the canon following the word *nisi* indicates, in causes involving the civil and religious status of persons provided that information which is indispensable to the public welfare cannot be obtained elsewhere.[118] Hence,

[116] Canon 1751; *cf.* article, Pellegrini, B., "De Intentione Bono Sacramenti Adversa Eiusdem; Probatione in Iudiciis ad normam Canon 1886," *Ius Pontificium,* X (1930), 57.

[117] Meile, *Die Beweislehre des Kanonischen Prozesses,* 51; Muniz, *Procedimientos Eclesiásticos,* III, n. 302, 9ª, p. 240. Compare D. XXII, 5, 4, and 9; "Parentes et liberi invicem adversus se nec volentes ad testimonium admittendi"; *Cod.* IV, 20, 6; c. 1, C. III, q. 5; c. 37, X, *de testibuset attestationibus,* II, 20; c. 3, X, *qui matrimonium accusare possunt, vel contra illud testificandi,* IV, 18; Schmalzgrueber, *Ius Ecclesiasticum Universum,* lib. II, Pars III, tit. XX, n. 30.

[118] *Cf.* Roberti, *De Processibus,* II, n. 337, p. 48; Eichmann, *Das Prozessrecht,* § 46, 3, p. 143; Pirhing, *Ius Canonicum,* lib. II, tit. XX, sec. I, § 3, nn.

the testimony of relatives and relations is admissible in causes pertaining to both the beatification and the canonization of the servants of God [119] and in matrimonial causes, especially those involving the validity of the marriage bond.

Canon 1974. Consanguinei et affines de quibus in Canon 1757, § 3, 3°, habentur testes habiles in causis suorum propinquorum.

In matrimonial causes all are admitted who have knowledge about the marriage and are not suspect. This canon puts its sanction on the admission of blood relatives and relations by marriage who are declared capable of testimony. This is an exception to the rule.[120] The term "blood relatives" naturally embraces those who are related to the married persons,[121] and hence the parents of the principals,[122]

35-40. Reverence for the sacrament of matrimony, and the avoidance of sin by their children are the reasons why parents can testify against their children in matrimonial causes. *Cf.* Reiffenstuel, *Ius Canonicum Universum,* lib. II, tit. XX, nn. 572, 573.

[119] Canon 2027. Heretics and infidels are admissible but not a confessor of the person to be beatified or declared a saint. *Cf.* Canon 1757, § 3, 2°. The ponens, advocate or procurator as long as they are interested parties in the cause or anyone who acted as judge during the process is inadmissible. *Cf.* Canon 2027, § 2.

[120] Gasparri, *De Matrimonio* (1932)., II, n. 1263, p. 294; Chelodi, *Ius Matrimoniale,* n. 177, p. 193; Payen, G., *De Matrimonio in Missionibus ac Potissimum in Sinis Tractatus Practicus et Casus* (Zi-ka-wei, 1928), III, n. 2686, p. 505; Wernz-Vidal, V, *Ius Matrimoniale,* n. 700, II, p. 837; *Regulae Servandae In Processibus Super Matrimonio Rato Et Non Consummato,* n. 58. *Cf.* Feije, *De Impedimentis,* n. 685; Schmalzgrueber, *Ius Ecclesiasticum Universum,* lib. II, Pars III, tit. XX, nn. 30-33; Mansella, Josephus, *De Impedimentis Matrimonium Dirimentibus ac De Processu Iudiciali in Causis Matrimonialibus* (Romae, 1881), 188.

[121] S. R. R., *Nullit. Matrim.,* 8 Januarii, 1921 (Chancery, 22 Februarii, 1921), *Coram R. P. D., Ioanne Prior,* dec. I, n. 2—*Decisiones,* XIII (1921), 2; *ibid.,* 12 Novembris, 1921, dec. XXVIII, n. 3—*Decisiones,* XIII (1921), 264, 265.

[122] *Cf.* S. R. R., *Nullit. Matrim.,* 27 Augusti, 1912, *Coram R. P. D., Michaele Lega,* dec. XXXVIII, n. 7—*Decisiones,* IV (1912), 443; S. R. R., *Nullit. Matrim.,* 18 Decembris, 1913, *Coram R. P. D., Friderico Cattani Amadori* dec. LII, n. 10—*Decisiones,* V (1913), 643, 644.

especially the mother whose testimony has great weight,[123] brothers and sisters,[124] uncles and aunts.[125] There is no reason why the judge should not estimate the testimony of other grades of relationship, *e. g.*, cousins.[126] Blood relatives and relations by marriage are not rejected from testimony because they are usually more familiar with the domestic and intimate affairs of the principals than others are.[127] More-

[123] *Cf.* S. R. R., *Nullit. Matrim.*, 18 Decembris, 1913, *Coram R. P. D., Friderico Cattani Amadori*, dec. LII, n. 7—*Decisiones*, V (1913), 642. S. R. R., *Nullit. Matrim.*, 11 Maii, 1910, *Coram R. P. D., Michaele Lega*, dec. VIII, nn. 3 and 9—*Decisiones Coram Lega*, 126 and 129. In this latter case on the form of marriage the decision, due to legal reasons, was against the plaintiff although her mother's testimony was excellent regarding specific facts. *Ibid.*, 30 Junii, 1910, dec. IX, n. 7—*Decisiones Coram Lega*, 136; S. R. R., *Nullit. Matrim.*, 11 Augusti, 1910, *Coram R. P. D., Antonio Perathoner*, dec. XXX, n. 4—*Decisiones*, II (1910), 302; S. R. R., *Nullit. Matrim.*, 30 Augusti, 1911, *Coram R. P. D., Michaele Lega*, dec. XVII, n. 11—*Decisiones Coram Lega*, 226, 227.

[124] *Cf.* S. R. R., *Nullit. Matrim.*, 30 Augusti, 1911, *Coram R. P. D., Michaele Lega*, dec. XVII, n. 16—*Decisiones Coram Lega*, 229.

[125] *Cf.* S. R. R., *Nullit. Matrim.*, 30 Augusti, 1911, *Coram R. P. D., Michaele Lega*, dec. XVII, n. 16—*Decisiones Coram Lega*, 229.

[126] *Cf. ibid.* A cousin of remote degree gave valuable testimony in a case involving simulated consent because "de visu et auditu." C. 3, X, *qui testimonium accusare possunt, vel contra illud testari*, IV, 18; *Instructio Austriaca*, §§ 155, 156, 157; Reiffenstuel, *Ius Canonicum Universum*, lib. II, tit. XX, nn. 116-120.

[127] *Regulae Servandae In Processibus Super Matrimonio Rato Et Non Consummato*, n. 60, § 2, n. 70; S. R. R., *Parisien., Nullit. Matrim.*, 26 Aprilis, 1916, *Coram R. P. D., Gulielmo Sebastianelli*, dec. XII, n. 8—*Decisiones*, VIII (1916), 138, 139; S. R. R., *Separationis quoad thorum et cohabitationem*, 20 Aprilis, 1912, *Coram R. P. D., Michaele Lega*, dec. XXII, n. 2—*Decisiones Coram Lega*, 274; *ibid.*, 8 Aprilis, 1913, dec. XXXVI, n. 3—*Decisiones Coram Lega*, 433; S. R. R., *Trinomalien. Nullit. Matrim.*, 1 Februarii, 1913, *Coram R. P. D., Aloisio Sincero*, dec. VIII, n. 2—*Decisiones*, V (1913), 84; S. R. R., *Nullit. Matrim.*, 8 Martii, 1913, *Coram R. P. D., Ioanne Prior*, dec. VIII, n. 9—*Decisiones*, V (1913), 215; S. R. R., *Nullit. Matrim., Vic. Apost. Tonkin. Orientalis.*, 18 Augusti, 1921, *Coram R. P. D., Friderico Cattani Amadori*, dec. XXVI, n. 2—*Decisiones*, XIII (1921), 252; S. R. R., *Nullit. Matrim.*, 9 Januarii, 1922, *Coram Iosepho Florczak*, dec. 1, n. 13—*Decisiones*, XIV (1922), 6; S. R. R., *Camenecen. Nullit. Matrim.*, 17 Maii, 1922, *Coram R. P. D., Ioanne Prior*, dec. XVI, n. 6—*Decisiones*, XIV (1922), 149; Knecht, *Handbuch Des Katholischen Eherechts auf Grund Des Codex Iuris Canonici*, p. 773.

over, consanguinity and affinity does not diminish but increases credibility, unless the relations be suspect because of special reasons, as there is a presumption in favor of their knowledge and veracity.[128] A Rota decision previous to the Code summarized the accepted juridical doctrine with regard to relatives in these words:

> Singulare est in causis matrimonialibus, ob eorum naturam ut, qua testes, fidem mereantur ii qui in aliis iudiciis repelluntur propter affectum et coniunctionem sanguinis: ita pater, mater, fratres, sorores nedum admittuntur sed pro comprobandis impedimentis aliquando sunt testes necessarii, quippe qui maxime edocti de factis domesticis unde impedimenta enascuntur.[129]

Another Rota decision made before the Code mentioned the admission of relations by marriage together with friends who might know about the marriage. "At in causis admittitur testimonium consanguineorum, affinium, vel amicitiae vinculum cum actore coniunctorum, praesertim in re facti, quod ex sese difficillimum est probatu." [130] An example of the use of the testimony of relatives in matrimonial procedure is found in the juridical proof of the presumed death of a spouse.[131] As the special testimonial proofs of this are fully explained in Chapter X, in this place the general rule for the establishment of the proof is indicated inasmuch as it refers to the testimony of relatives. After the deposition of the surviving spouse is taken, the Ordinary will require the pastor of the plaintiff to inquire prudently among the blood relatives concerning their opinion [132] about

[128] *Cf.* cc. 5, 22, 47, X, *de testibus et attestationibus,* II, 20; *Instructio Austriaca,* § 151; S. R. R., *Varsavien seu Lublinen. Nullit. Matrim.*, 21 Julii, 1910, *Coram R. P. D., Gulielmo Sebastianelli,* dec. XXVIII, n. 5—*Decisiones,* II (1910), 291: "Testimonia haec attendenda maxime sunt, quia consanguinitas non minuit, imo auget fidem, ratione praesumptae scientiae et veritatis."

[129] S. R. R., *Nullit. Matrim.*, 21 Decembris, 1912, *Coram R. P. D., Michaele Lega,* dec. XLI, n. 5—*Decisiones,* IV (1912), 472; *cf.* S. R. R., *Osnabrugen. Nullit. Matrim.*, 11 Januarii, 1912, dec. III, n. 6—*Decisiones,* IV (1912), 28-30.

[130] S. R. R., *Nullit. Matrim.*, 29 Julii, 1911, *Coram R. P. D., Francisco Heiner,* dec. XXXVI, n. 4—*Decisiones,* III (1911), 408.

[131] *Cf.* S. C. S. Off., Instr., a. 1868—*Fontes,* n. 1002; *cf. A. F. K. K.*, XLVIII (1882), 56.

[132] The word "conjecture" is used for presumption: "Quaero septimo, an interse differant praesumptio, indicium, coniectura, signum, suspicio et ad-

the death of the missing party. At the same time a notification can be published in the official announcements of the diocese and in some newspaper requesting that the curia be acquainted with information about the missing person. The notices can even be opposite to what is desired. The publicity may occasion difficulties as the person may not want the fact of his marriage known. The Ordinary may demand the information or refuse to publish the notice. After the deposition of the living partner and the investigation by the pastor, and when the time given in the published edict has passed, the Ordinary will proceed to the establishment of the proof.[133]

In the category of domestic relationship, employees or domestics are to be included. It is hardly possible to give a general rule covering their anomalous position. They are admissible to testimony in beatification processes.[134] They are admissible to testify in matrimonial procedure,[135] although, by reason of their dependence, they are sometimes considered suspect.[136] The judge is to inquire diligently whether any reason for suspicion exists. He should obtain the testimony of the pastor or of another priest who performed a marriage which is accused for alleged force and fear.[137]

miniculum? Et multum inter se differre scribunt omnes. Nam Praesumptio illa est, quae (ut suis locis diximus) interdum oritur a probabilibus, et tunc appellatur praesumptio iuris, vel hominis, ut explicavimus supra quaest. 4 et 5. Interdum oritur a necessariis, et tunc appellatur praesumptio iuris et de iure, de qua quidem egimus supra quaest. 3. Et praesumptio dicta a dictione prae, id est, ante et sumptio, hoc est, ante sumptio: quia ante legitimas probationes aliquid sumet pro vero."—Menochius, Jacobus, *De Praesumptionibus, Coniecturis, signis, et indiciis* (Sumptibus Samuelis de Tournes; Coloniae Allobrogum; 1686), lib. I, Quaestia 7, §§ 1-5.

[133] *Cf.* Muniz, *Procedimientos Eclesiásticos,* II, n. 259, p. 310.

[134] Canon 2027, § 1.

[135] S. R. R., *Nicien. Nullit. Matrim.,* 22 Junii, 1921, *Coram R. P. D., Friderico Cattani Amadori,* dec. XIV, n. 2—*Decisiones,* XIII (1921), 137, 138; S. R. R., *Nullit. Matrim., Vic. Apost. Tonkin Orientalis,* 18 Augusti, 1921, *Coram R. P. D., Friderico Cattani Amadori,* dec. XXVI, n. 2—*Decisiones,* XIII (1921), 252; S. R. R., *Nullit. Matrim.,* 11 Aprilis, 1922, *Coram R. P. D., Ioanne Prior,* dec. XI, n. 5—*Decisiones,* XIV (1922), 95.

[136] S. R. R., *Nullit. Matrim.,* 19 Junii, 1909, *Coram R. P. D., Gulielmo Sebastianelli,* dec. VIII, n. 5—*Decisiones,* I (1909), 70.

[137] S. C. S. Off. Instr. (*ad Ep. Rituum Orient.*) a. 1883—*Fontes,* n. 1076, n. 39.

ARTICLE 3. GENERAL DIFFERENCES BETWEEN SUITABLE, SUSPECT AND INCAPABLE WITNESSES

Canon 1758. Non idonei et suspecti audiri poterunt ex decreto iudicis, quo id expedire declaretur; sed eorum testimonium valebit tantummodo ut indicium et probationis adminiculum, et generatim iniurati audiantur.

The Code terminates the article, *Qui testes esse possunt*, with this canon determining the value of the testimony of non-suitable and suspect witnesses. They can be heard upon a decree of the judge declaring their admission expedient. Their testimony, however, has only the worth of something corroboratory and confirmative of the proof (*indicium et adminiculum*). As a rule, they are heard without the oath.[138]

In the first place, the distinction between unsuitable, suspect and incapable witnesses which is new, appears to be a deduction from the nature of the defects with which certain people are encumbered relative to their testimonial capacity.[139] The cases of non-suitableness and suspicion appear to be mentioned in the Code demonstratively (*demonstrative*) whereas those relative to incapacity are exclusive (*taxative*).[140]

There is no express text in the Code which enumerates other reasons for which a witness can be rejected. Other reasons which were mentioned above are interested parties as friends of the accused and

[138] *Cf.* Muniz, *Procedimientos, Eclesiásticos,* III, p. 240.

[139] Before the Code, many authors distinguished witnesses into *habiles simpliciter* and *omni exceptione maiores,* the latter being *habiles* in a positive and a comparative grade, *i.e.,* something more than merc *habiles.* *Cf.* Reiffenstuel, *Ius Canonicum Universum,* lib. II, tit. XX, n. 10. Others distinguished *inhabiles* into "absolute," for any cause, and "relative" for definite causes. *Cf.* Lega, *Praelectiones,* I, nn. 479, 480, pp. 419-421. Another distinction of *inhabiles* was with reference to natural defect, moral turpitude and interest or affection. Witnesses were also distinguished into *remissibiles* by the litigants and *irremissibiles.* The last distinction does not appear to be current since the Code. *Cf.* Reiffenstuel, *Ius Canonicum Universum,* lib. II, tit. XX, nn. 17, 18.

[140] *Cf.* Noval, *De Processibus,* IV, n. 369, p. 332; A Coronata, *De Processibus,* III, n. 1287, p. 198.

servants of the litigant who presents them. Those who have been deceived or menaced into giving a declaration may be mentioned. The qualifications of witnesses enumerated in Canon 1757 are those which the law itself considers. The other qualifications can be called *ab homine* to distinguish them from the legal requirements of witnesses, as they are insufficient to prevent witnesses from being received and making an attestation. These reasons are insufficient to diminish the value of their testimony and to remove the efficacy of it from the mind of the judge. This is the case because these reasons are presumptions of fact against the impartiality of the witnesses. The last of the general questions in Canon 1774 [141] is intended to discover some of these reasons.[142]

Strangers whose credibility is above reproach and who are cognizant of the circumstances surrounding a case are to be admitted to testify when relatives are heard. Strangers may also be omitted.[143] The Code has not received the old regulation, already explained in Chapter IV, which excluded laymen from testifying against clerics in criminal procedure. It forbids clerics to testify against laymen in secular criminal causes without the permission of the Ordinary.

Article 4. Conditions to be Fulfilled in the Production of Witnesses

Having considered what persons are legally excluded from testimony and distinguished rules of admissibility which are peculiar to matrimonial causes, the Code proceeds to consider the conditions necessary for the induction of witnesses. What immediately follows is a consideration of, first, the production of witnesses; secondly, the presentation of them, and thirdly, the rejection of the witnesses who lack the generic qualifications explained in Article 1 of this Chapter.

[141] Canon 1774: " . . . deinde deferendae sunt interrogationes quae causam ipsam respiciunt et sciscitandum unde et quomodo ea quae asserit, habeat cognita."

[142] *Cf.* Muniz, *Procediemientos Eclesiásticos,* III, n. 303, p. 241.

[143] Knecht, *Handbuch Des Katholischen Eherechts auf Grund Des Codex Iuris Canonici,* 773; *cf.* Linneborn, *Grundriss Des Eherechts,* § 62, 2, p. 46.

A. The Production of Witnesses

Witnesses are to be produced legitimately. The production of witnesses is a petition by a litigant to the judge asking that he cite and examine the witnesses named individually (*testes inducere*) in proof of an action or exception within a determined time. Presentation is the designation of the witnesses to be cited.[144] The postulation or asking of proof by witnesses (*postulatio*) precedes the production of them and hence is distinct logically, if not in practice, from the production of the witnesses.[145] For practical purposes the production of witnesses is the request made by the litigant, the promoter of justice or the defender of the bond asking the judge to summon witnesses before him. It is called such, not because by it the party actually produces the witnesses, but because by it he does what he can to present them before the judge.

The purpose of the legitimate production of witnesses is expressed in the following canon:

> **Canon 1760, § 1. Si quis sponte compareat testimonii reddendi gratia, iudex poterit eius testimonium admittere vel repellere prout expedire censuerit;**
>
> **§ 2. Debet autem testem, qui se sponte obtulerit, repellere cum comparere sibi videatur moras iudicio nectendi causa vel iustitiae et veritati quoquo modo officiendi.**

They are called voluntary or self-appointed witnesses who spontaneously offer themselves to state something without being presented by those who have the right of presentation and without being invited to testify by the judge. According to the former discipline their testimony was considered suspect; the party who would be put at a disadvantage by it could take exception to it. Nevertheless, if this party were present when the testimony was given or at the spontaneous presentation of the witness and he did not take exception to such a witness, the testimony had the value of the attestation of a presented wit-

[144] *Cf.* Roberti, *De Processibus,* II, n. 338, p. 49; Noval, *De Processibus,* IV, n. 471, p. 333; A Coronata, *De Processibus,* III, n. 1288, p. 198.

[145] *Cf.* Canon 1761, § 1; Lega, *Praelectiones,* I, n. 483, p. 424.

ness.[146] Canon 1760 provides the judge with the power to admit the self-appointed witnesses if he deem it opportune. Since such witnesses are frequently suspect,[147] the Code commands the judge invariably to reject those suspects who evidently offer themselves for the purpose of delaying the trial or in some way obstructing the attainment of justice and truth. The judge does this not because there is a presumption of law but due to a ***presumptio hominis*** which proceeds from the judge and insinuates into his mind the fact that a self-appointed witness is suspect of being actuated either by the prospect of his own advantage or undue interest toward the party against or on behalf of whom he intends to testify.[148]

1. *The Time for Production of Witnesses.*

> **Canon 1761, § 1. Cum probatio per testes postulatur, eorum nomina et domicilium tribunali indicentur; praeterea exhibeantur positiones seu articuli argumentorum super quibus testes sint interrogandi.**
>
> **§ 2. Si ne intra diem quidem peremptorium a iudice praestitutum, obtemperatum fuerit, postulatio deserta censetur.**

The time during which the production of witnesses takes place is usually between the *litis contestatio*[149] and the conclusion of the cause.[150] Thereafter, they are inadmissible except in causes which do not become adjudged matters (*res iudicata*), or in causes in which, due to something legitimately preventing it, they could not be produced during the "useful time."[151] The litigant who wishes to prove

[146] Wernz, *Ius Decretalium,* V, n. 612; Reiffenstuel, *Ius Canonicum Universum,* lib. II, tit. XX, n, 416.

[147] Roberti, *De Processibus,* II, n. 338, p. 49; Augustine, *A Commentary,* VII, p. 213.

[148] Reiffenstuel, *Ius Canonicum Universum,* lib. II, tit. XX, n. 415; Lega, *Praelectiones,* n. 477, p. 418; Augustine, *A Commentary,* VII, p. 213; Muniz, *Procedimientos Eclesiásticos,* III, n. 301, pp. 238, 239.

[149] Canons 1730, 1731, 2°; *cf.* Muniz, *Procedimientos Eclesiásticos,* III, n. 298, p. 237.

[150] *Cf.* Canons 1860-1862.

[151] Canon 1861, § 1.

his action or exception by witnesses petitions the judge to admit proof by witnesses. The party should send a judicial petition to the judge.[152] Names of witnesses together with their domiciles should be mentioned in the petition. The *positiones* or articles of the arguments upon which the witnesses are to be interrogated should be mentioned [153] The judge is asked to make these inquiries. Witnesses should be designated by their full names and, if there be need of it, other necessary indications should be added. When there is no domicile, the quasi-domicile or place of actual residence can be mentioned.[154] The judge is to examine the petition. He is to exclude the witnesses who are incapable of testimony (*inhabiles*). He is to take cognizance of the witnesses who are unacceptable (*non-idonei*) or suspect and admit the rest. If the occasion present itself, the judge can add to, correct, or change the articles. The litigant who proposed the articles can, nevertheless, appeal against the judge for the reason that he either did not admit the postulation or because he arbitrarily corrected the articles and substituted others.[155] Finally, the judge publishes or edits a decree for the admission or the rejection of the witnesses.

Leaving the consideration of this decree for the moment, and looking at the time for the production and verification of proofs more closely, it may be helpful to indicate briefly in this place the practice of the Spanish tribunals with regard to the time when witnesses are to be produced and when the proofs afforded by them are to be verified. These tribunals divide the probatory period into two parts. In the first part, proofs are proposed and witnesses must be presented. In the second period the proof must be verified. An analysis of this practice follows:[156]

[152] *Cf.* Canon 1761, § 2. The Code does not require it to be in writing but this is the better practice. *Cf.* A Coronata, *De Processibus,* III, n. 1290, note 4, p. 200.

[153] Canon 1761, § 1. In matrimonial causes of nullity the defender of the bond prepares questions in accordance with Canon 1968, 1°.

[154] Roberti, *De Processibus,* II, n. 339, p. 51.

[155] Lega, *Praelectiones,* I, n. 384, pp. 424, 425; A Coronata, *De Processibus,* III, n. 1290, p. 200.

[156] *Cf.* Muniz, *Procedimientos Eclesiásticos,* III, n. 296, pp. 234, 235, for a development of the division of the probatory period.

If Probatory Period is divided for Production and Verification of Proofs.

1. Production.
   a. Formulation of testimonial proof.
   b. Production of witnesses
      (1) During peremptory time determined by judge: if petition offered relevant or other facts.
      (2) Not during peremptory time determined by judge: Assumed litigants renounced privilege of proof. (Canon 1761, § 2.)
   c. Presentation of witnesses not in same document with proposed proofs.

   If judge did not determine time for presenting, must take place by last day.
2. (Verification.)

If Probatory Proof is not Divided.

1. Production of witnesses has two terms appointed by judge in
   a. Important Causes:
      (1) Party requests admission of testimonial proof.
      (2) Citation and presence of witnesses.
   b. Minor Causes:
      (1) Verbal treatment allowed.
      (2) Production of witnesses before examination permitted by Code.
2. (Verification.)

2. *By Whom Witnesses are Produced.* The witnesses employed to convince the judge are naturally to be produced before him. This is done by: (a) the parties themselves in private civil causes inasmuch as these take place at the insistence of the litigants.[157] The party who produced the witness can renounce examination of him; but the adverse party can ask (*postulare*) that, notwithstanding the renunciation, the witness be subjected to examination.[158] (b) The promoter

[157] Canon 1759, § 1; *cf.* cc. 24, 35, 37, 46, X, *de testibus et attestationibus,* II, 20; Canon 1619, §§ 1, 2.

[158] Canon 1759, § 4.

of justice or the defender of the bond also has the right to produce witnesses in causes pertaining to the public welfare.[159] They present the names of the witnesses whom they wish the judge to summon. They likewise petition him to summon them to appear and be interrogated before him.[160] (c) The judge also has the right and an obligation of officially producing witnesses as frequently as a cause involves minors or those juridically equivalent to them, and generally speaking, as often as the public good requires.[161]

B. *The Presentation of Witnesses*

1. *The Number of Presentations in Ordinary Cases.* Five different normal presentations of witnesses can take place with regard to each fact subjected to demonstration. The five presentations are first, that of the party who disputes the fact; secondly, that of the other litigant, be he defendant or plaintiff; thirdly, that of the one who denies or explains it in his own manner; fourthly, that of the promoter of justice or of the defender of the bond in causes pertaining to them respectively, and, fifthly, that which can be decided upon officially by the judge in minor causes affecting moral persons and in causes involving the public welfare.[162]

It was a common doctrine found in the Decretals [163] that litigants may produce witnesses three times. According to the present discipline of the Code, in ordinary cases the following are to be observed:

[159] Canon 1759, § 2; *cf. Regulae Servandae in Iudiciis apud S. R. Rotae Tribunal,* § 114, n. 3.

[160] *Cf.* Roberti, *De Processibus,* II, n. 338, p. 49.

[161] Canon 1759, § 3; *cf.* cc. 2, 3, X, *de testibus et attestationibus,* II, 20.

[162] *Cf.* Canon 1759; Muniz, *Procedimientos Eclesiásticos,* III, n. 297, p. 236.

[163] The number of witnesses was reduced. *Cf.* cc. 36, 37, X, *de testibus et attestationibus,* II, 20. Three productions were regularly admitted. *Cf.* cc. 15, 36, 55, X, *de testibus et attestationibus,* II, 29; *Nov.* XC, 4. Four productions were conceded exceptionally. *Cf.* c. 55, X, *de testibus et attestationibus,* II, 20; Reiffenstuel, *Ius Canonicum Universum,* lib. II, tit. XX, nn. 445-449; Lega, *Praelectiones,* n. 497, p. 436; Roberti, *De Processibus,* II, n. 338, p. 50; Wernz-Vidal, VI, *De Processibus,* n. 469, p. 407. A fourth production was permitted in Justinian Law for the reason that the religion of the one swearing an oath was believed to abolish all sinister suspicion. *Cf.* Rittershutii, *Expositio Methodica Novellarum Imperatoris Justiniani,* par. 9, cap. 22, n. 17, col. 770.

a. When the time for formulating the proof is conceded, the list of witnesses to be produced can be augmented within the specified time as frequently as he wishes, provided that the judge does not limit the time according to the power given him. For, in order to prevent unnecessary prolongation of a trial the judge has a right and an obligation to restrict a too large number of witnesses.

b. When the peremptory time for presentation of witnesses is conceded in the same circumstances, the list of witnesses can be increased.

c. When the time for formulation of the proof and the peremptory term for presentation of witnesses are not specified, only two limitations restrict the production of witnesses: (1) when new witnesses would be presented regarding the same fact after the publication of the attestations;[164] (2) inasmuch as the judge, as seen above, must restrict an excessive number of witnesses, he can decide upon the limit. The promoter of justice can suggest that the judge summon witnesses officially in the trials wherein this is possible. The defender of the bond, on the other hand, has the privilege of making a new presentation at any time as the peremptory terms have no value with regard to him.[165]

2. *The Number of Presentations in Extraordinary Cases.* There are four extraordinary cases when the presentation of witnesses can take place. These are:

a. Before the reply to the petition, the presentation of witnesses can be done when there is contumacy or when it appears necessary to take the testimony because there is danger that the witness is likely to die or is going away or because there is some other just cause which renders the taking of his testimony afterwards impossible or difficult.[166]

b. In causes which have no definite term for appeal against them, as in causes involving the nullity of a marriage or of sacred ordination, a new presentation of witnesses can be made after the publication of the attestations if the cause be a grave one. For example, presentation can be made because the attestations which were re-

[164] Canon 1786.

[165] Canon 1969, 3°; *cf.* Muniz, *Procedimientos Eclesiásticos,* III, n. 297, p. 236.

[166] Canon 1730.

ceived previously were null; for the reason that they did not prove anything for or against the cause and the juridical status of the persons involved was doubtful; or because of the existence of some reasonable indications that the new witnesses will bring forward new proofs which it was impossible to present before.

c. In any other civil or criminal cause, a new presentation can be admitted after the publication of the depositions, if a reason for doing such is sufficiently grave.[167]

d. After the conclusion of the cause, witnesses can be presented and admitted if it is proved that it was impossible to admit them previously.[168] This same criterion must be adhered to in the admission of new witnesses, in the re-examination of witnesses who were already examined and whenever the declarations are something new for the litigants.[169]

3. *The Quantitative Rule for Presentation of Witnesses.* Regarding the total number of witnesses admissible, Canon 1762 merely states that the judge has the right and the obligation to restrict a too large number of them.[170] There is no other positive disposition made by the Code. The judge possesses discretionary power to limit an excessive number.

Turning to matrimonial procedure, from the aspect of the number of witnesses of the seventh hand that are to be presented, there are rules to be observed.

> **Canon 1975, § 1. In causis impotentiae vel inconsummationis, nisi de impotentia vel inconsummatione aliunde certo constet, debet uterque coniux testes, qui septimae manus audiunt, inducere, sanguine aut affinitate sibi coniunctos, sin minus vicinos bonae famae, aut**

[167] Canon 1786.

[168] Canon 1861, § 1.

[169] *Cf.* Muniz, *Procedimientos Eclesiásticos,* III, n. 298, p. 237, with Canon 1781.

[170] The Decretals fixed the admissible number of witnesses as forty for each party. *Cf.* c. 37, X, *de testibus et attestationibus,* II, 20. The text, however, may be interpreted as a regulation of the number of times a witness may be produced.

> **alioquin de re edoctos, qui iurare possint de ipsorum coniugum probitate, et praesertim de veracitate circa rem in controversiam deductam; quibus iudex ad normam Canon 1759, § 3 alios testes potest ex officio adiungere.**

The presentation of witnesses of the seventh hand, whether they be blood relatives or relations by marriage or, when it is impossible to summon these, neighbors [171] of the married persons, can take place after the verification of the proofs. Each of the married persons must present his witnesses of credibility who are technically called *testes septimae manus*. As the term indicates, the testimony must be furnished by seven witnesses introduced by each party. That is, seven witnesses are to be presented by each litigant, which makes fourteen in all. If this number cannot be produced, fewer will suffice, but the reason for a reduction in the number is to be mentioned in the acts of the trial.[172] It was stated that these witnesses can be produced after the verification of the proofs. This is so because the testimony of the seventh hand is a species of suppletory proof, as shown in Chapter III, which is inadmissible if the case of impotence or of inconsummation of the marriage is evidently proved. This hybrid form of testimony is an argument of credibility that strengthens the value of the depositions of the married persons. Even fourteen such witnesses prove nothing by themselves without the support of other arguments, conditions and presumptions. Moreover, although they can be proposed from the beginning of the trial or after it has begun, the party who is interested can, if he or she sees that his or her testimony has no value by itself, renounce it.

4. *The Form for the Presentation of Witnesses.* The strictly canonical form in which to make the presentation of witnesses is the following:

a. The judge is petitioned in writing to admit the witnesses.

b. The list of the witnesses together with their full written names, and residence is sent with the petition.

[171] C. 5, X, *de frigidis et maleficiatis, et impotentia coeundi,* IV, 15.

[172] *Cf. Regulae Servandae in Processibus Super Matrimonio Rato et Non Consummato,* n. 58.

c. The interrogation to be made or an enumeration of the facts which are to be the subject of the examination are added to the list.

d. The original or master-copy of the list of the witnesses is signed by the party who presents it. It is placed in the custody of the notary. In his presence the parties exchange a copy of their respective list. The notary makes a marginal note on the original list to the effect that the lists have been exchanged.[173]

When the judge receives this petition he can weigh its content, admit or reject it orally in the presence of the parties while the tribunal is convened. A notary consigns this to writing.[174] This old practice of giving the list to the judge is observed in both the Roman and Spanish curias. At the request of the party the judge is empowered to keep the names of one or more of the witnesses secret; he can withhold the names of the witnesses from the adverse party before the examination takes place, or if he prudently think that the witnesses should be safeguarded from corruption or other grave difficulty, he can refuse to divulge their names at least before the publication of the testimony.[175]

Article 5. The Rejection of Witnesses (*Reprobatio Personae Testis*)

Canon 1764, § 1. Testes debent ex officio excludi, si iudici liquido constet eos a testimonio ferendo prohiberi, salvo praescripto Canon 1758.

§ 2. Ast etiam, postulante adversario, testes excludendi sunt, si iusta exclusionis causa demonstretur, quae exclusio dicitur *reprobatio personae testis*.

§ 3. Pars nequit reprobare personam testis quem ipsa induxit, nisi nova reprobationis causa supervenerit, quamvis possit eius dicta reprobare.

§ 4. Reprobatio testis fieri debet intra triduum postquam testium nomina cum parte communicata fuerunt,

[173] *Cf.* Canons 1761, 1763; Muniz, *Procedimientos Eclesiásticos,* III, n. 299, p. 237.

[174] Roberti, *De Processibus,* II, n. 339, p. 52.

[175] Canon 1763.

nec postea facta admittatur, nisi a parte demonstretur vel saltem iuramento affirmetur defectum testis antea sibi notum non fuisse.

§ 5. Iudex autem reprobationis discussionem in finem litis reservet, nisi contra testem stet praesumptio iuris, aut defectus sit notorius vel statim ac facile probari possit vel postea probari nequeat.

The reprobation of a witness is an exception proposed by either the party who produced the witness or his adversary against the person of a witness when a just reason has been demonstrated so that he is excluded from testimony in a certain cause.[176] It tends to impede a witness from being admitted to testimony by making an exception against him as incapable, unsuitable or suspect. Even in cases in which the exclusion should have been absolutely made by the judge, the party whose interest it is can make it if the judge has been negligent.[177] Unless the judge think it expedient it would seem superfluous to make it after the testimony was given.

A. When Reprobation Takes Place

Reprobation of a witness should regularly be made within three days after the names of the witnesses are made known to the party concerned. Facts are not admissible afterwards unless the party shows or at least affirms, under oath that the defect of a witness was unknown to him previously.[178] The reason for this prescription is

[176] Canon 1764, § 2; *cf.* Roberti, *De Processibus,* II, n. 340, p. 52; A Coronata, *De Processibus,* III, n. 1293, pp. 203, 204; Wernz-Vidal, VI, *De Processibus,* n. 479, p. 417. Before the Code the unfit for testimony were called either those "remissible" or "non-remissible" by the parties. *Cf.* Lega, *Praelectiones,* I, n. 482, p. 422; Reiffenstuel, *Ius Canonicum Universum,* lib. II, tit. XX, n. 17, n. 540.

[177] A Coronata, *De Processibus,* III, n. 1293, p. 204; Leccisi, *La Prova Testimoniale,* n. 12, p. 18.

[178] Canon 1764, § 4. In the Decretals an exception was to be proposed before the publication of attestations. Thereafter, ignorance of a defect in a witness and reservation to himself of the power to propose an exception were the only cases in which it could be made. *Cf.* c. 9, X, *de probationibus,* II, 19.

a presumption of law that the person who thus takes exception to a witness is acting maliciously and reprobates a witness after he knows from his published attestation that he testified against him.[179] Consequently, before hearing witnesses, or at least before publishing attestations, the judge ought to make an allowance of three days. Otherwise the time for exercising the privilege of reprobating a witness should either be declared closed because it is after the publication of the testimony [180] or it should be admitted during a time that is suspect. But if the adverse party show or affirm under oath that the defect of a witness either did not exist before, or at least that he was ignorant of it, the exception is admissible not only after three days or after the publication of the attestations, but even in the court of second instance in so far as a sentence can be impugned.[181] This is a limitation on a party preventing him from rejecting a witness he himself introduced unless he later find a new reason for reprobating him, although he can take exception to the statements made by the witness,[182] because "*quod semel* placuit amplius displicere non potest." [183] A Coronata holds what appears to be a preferable opinion,[184] that when there is a question of absolute unfitness of a witness (*inhabilis testis*) which the parties cannot remove by their own consent, reprobation of the witness is always admissible because of the public welfare.[185] If the witnesses were not rejected by the party they were considered to have been admitted by the litigants and the defects are accepted as having been removed. Nevertheless, regarding the value of the testimony of unsuitable witnesses it seems that one should say that they are not deserving of full credibility, even granting that the judge must not neglect to hear their attestations.

The Code restored the law of the Decretals in this respect rather than *Regulae Servandae in Iudiciis apud S. R. Rotae Tribunal*, § 115.

[179] A Coronata, *De Processibus*, III, n. 1293, p. 205; *cf.* Reiffenstuel, *Ius Canonicum Universum*, lib. II, tit. XX, n. 537.

[180] Canon 1783, 1°.

[181] Roberti, *De Processibus*, II, n. 340, pp. 52, 53.

[182] Canon 1764, § 3.

[183] Reg. 21, R. J., in VI°.

[184] *Cf.* A Coronata, *De Processibus*, III, n. 1293, pp. 204, 205.

[185] Compare Noval, *De Processibus*, IV, pp. 479, 336.

B. How Reprobation Takes Place

Witnesses can be rejected in the following ways after a petition has been submitted to the judge:

1. In virtue of Canon 1764, § § 1, 2, 3, the judge himself who has a clear knowledge of the legal qualifications of witnesses must *ex officio* reject a witness who lacks one of them.

2. The party against whom the witnesses are presented can for a just cause reject them.[186]

3. The party who presents them can impugn the witnesses after their testimony if a cause for the rejection becomes apparent after their presentation.

4. The promoter of justice and the defender of the bond can reject the witnesses who were presented by the parties as the parties can reject the witnesses presented by them.

5. If the judge officially summon witnesses all the persons interested in the trial can reject them.

The judge reserves discussion of the reprobation of witnesses *in finem litis.*[187]

[186] In the Decretals, witnesses called *testes reprobatorii* were admissible to contradict witnesses. Others called *testes reprobatorii reprobatorum* could in turn contradict the *testes reprobatorii. Cf.* c. 39, X, *de testibus et attestationibus,* II, 20; *cf.* Reiffenstuel, *Ius Canonicum Universum,* lib. II, tit. XX, n. 553.

[187] Canon 1764, § 5. *Cf.* Blat, Albert, *Commentarium Textus Codicis Iuris Canonici* (Romae, 1927), IV, *De Processibus,* n. 270, pp. 287-290; Roberti, *De Processibus,* II, n. 341, p. 53; *cf.* c. 1, X, *de exceptionibus,* II, 25: ". . . antequam causa per sententiam terminetur." Reiffenstuel, *Ius Canonicum Universum,* lib. II, tit. XX, n. 541. Noval holds that it should be done after the examination of witnesses but not after the publication of their testimony—*cf.* Noval, *op. cit.,* IV, n. 479, pp. 335, 336. Vermeersch-Creusen, *Epitiome,* lib. IV, *De Processibus,* pars I, sec. I, n. 176 following *Il Monitore Ecclesiastico,* XXXIII (1921), 153, 154, object to this opinion and grant that the examination of the *motives* of reprobation can be made after the publication of the testimony: "Anche pero se fosse provato il motivo, non cesserebbe per cio nel giudice la facolta di ordinaire la deposizione del teste dimostrato sospetto (c. 1758), quindi il § 5 di questo canone (1764) stabilisce che la discussione dei motivi, debba riservasi di regula *in finem litis,* cioe dopo pubblicate le deposizioni (*cfr.* 1783, § 1), salvo che il motivo sia notorio, favorito da presunzione di diritto, o la prova debba farsi subito perche soggetta altrimenti a perire."

The reprobation of the person of a witness is to be made in writing, which specifies the names of the rejected witnesses, together with the cause of the rejection and the proof of it. The written statement must be presented to the tribunal during the three days following the notification of the last of the witnesses. This must be done even though the judge has not appointed this time, because it is the legal time for the rejection of witnesses.[188] Because this is a peremptory term, the notary records the date on which the document for the reprobation was presented. In admitting the judicial petition containing the qualifications of witnesses the judge reserves the decision of this incidental question which comes up in the trial, until after the question immediately in the following circumstances found in the Code:[189]

a. If the exception is a legal objection by a presumption of law against the witness.

b. If the defect of a witness is notorious and could be proved easily and immediately.

c. If the lack of the generic qualifications for the rejection of a witness can be proved with facility. In this case it is not necessary to prove the qualifications. The testimony of other witnesses is unnecessary to prove the inadmissibility of such a witness.

d. If there be a reasonable fear that the defect cannot be proved afterwards because of the absence or the death of those who are to give the proof, or, for instance, if the witness were seriously ill or about to leave for a distant country and it is feared that this proof may disappear.[190]

In any event this incidental question must be resolved after hearing the party who presented the rejected witnesses. The judge cannot reject the witnesses until he hears the parties.

[188] Canon 1764, § 4.

[189] Canon 1764, § 5; *cf.* Roberti, *De Processibus,* II, n. 341, p. 54; Muniz, *Procedimientos Eclesiásticos,* III, n. 304, p. 342.

[190] Canon 1764, § 5.

CHAPTER VIII

THE EXAMINATION OF WITNESSES

ARTICLE 1. PROCEDURAL RULES PRELIMINARY TO THE ADMINISTRATION OF THE OATH

Following the issuance of the decree of admission of the witnesses two things should take place before the oath to tell the truth under judicial examination is given.

A. Exchange of Names of Witnesses between Litigants

The decree issued by the judge which specifies the peremptory time and the names of the witnesses is sent to both of the litigants.[1] If, however, the judge adverts to the fact that this cannot be done without gave difficulty, *e. g.*, without danger of corruption or of violence, he may defer it until after the examination of witnesses, but before the publication of the testimony.[2] The reason for this mutual notification of the names of the witnesses is that an opportunity is thus given to the adverse party to propose exceptions against the witnesses. For if a just reason is shown for the exclusion of a witness, he must be declared inadmissible. This exclusion is called the "reprobation of the person of a witness."[3]

[1] Roberti, *De Processibus,* II, n. 339, p. 51.

[2] Canon 1763; Roberti, *ibid.*

[3] Canon 1764, § 2; *cf.* Reiffenstuel, *Ius Canonicum Universum,* lib. II, tit. XX, nn. 418-421; Droste, Francis-Messmer, Sebastian G., *Canonical Procedure in Disciplinary and Criminal Cases of Clerics* (New York, 1887), 67*, p. 114. In practice the names of witnesses are made known only after the examination. *Cf.* A Coronata, *De Processibus,* III, n. 1291, p. 202. Especially in criminal causes names of witnesses cannot be communicated to the accused, or should not be, by reason of the danger of infamy, grave molestation by enemies, etc. *Cf.* Wernz-Vidal, VI, *De Processibus,* n. 480, p. 420. Wernz-Vidal say that the obligation of communicating the names urges at least before the publication of the attestation. *Cf.* Wernz-Vidal, *ibid.*, n. 470, p. 408.

B. Legitimate Citation of Witnesses

Witnesses must be legitimately cited.[4] If the adverse party does not make an objection, the judge commands each witness to be cited for examination at determined hearings of the trial.[5] If, on the other hand, the adverse party made an objection against a witness, an incidental question arises [6] which must be decided according to the norms.

The citation of witnesses is made by the official or the auditor after the names of the witnesses are presented to and accepted by the court.[7] A preliminary investigation having shown that some proof of the asserted impediment exists, the accuser of the marriage has the right to produce juridical proofs of the asserted impediment. The written citation must mention what judge serves it, give the general reason for it,[8] at least in a general way, contain the full names of the litigants, the place and precise time for appearance, be signed by the official or his auditor and the notary and must have the seal of the tribunal on it.[9] The validity of a citation depends on these elements. Nullity of a citation frees a witness from the obligation of appearing in court.[10] The name of the person cited is, according to the Roman Rota, necessary for a valid and juridical citation because it prevents fraud and substitution by a plaintiff and makes citation easier against

[4] Citation of the adverse party is unnecessary if there is danger of delay, a cause of heresy, or in delicts belonging to the competency of the Holy Office. *Cf.* c. 20, *de haereticis,* V, 2 in VI°; Wernz-Vidal, VI, *De Processibus,* n. 470, p. 408.

[5] *Cf.* Canons 1715-1723, 1765. The judge has the right and should prevent others from impeding the production of witnesses even by penalties. *Cf.* Canons 1762, 2145; 1; A Coronata, *De Processibus,* III, n. 1290, p. 200; Eichmann, *Das Prozessrecht,* § 46, p. 141.

[6] *Cf.* Roberti, *De Processibus,* II, n. 339, pp. 51, 52.

[7] Canon 1765 together with Canons 1715-1723.

[8] *Regulae Servandae in Iudiciis apud S. R. Rotae Tribunal,* § 114, n. 8.

[9] *Cf.* Canon 1715.

[10] Muniz, *Procedimientos Eclesiásticos,* III, n 312, p. 248. *Cf.* Canons 1723, 1724.

the contumacious.[11] When the name of a private individual is unknown to the judge, in order to cite that person, the qualities or duties which he has and which characterize him individually, should be expressed in the citation.[12] The spontaneous appearance of witnesses may take the place of a citation, but the notary records this in the acts,[13] as the disposition of the law regarding such witnesses must, as explained, be taken into consideration.[14] It seems, with deference to better judgment, that the practice of the Spanish courts of not citing witnesses to court but of inviting them through the party who requires them is applicable to the United States, especially in regions where the competency of the ecclesiastical courts is questioned by non-Catholics and Catholics of weak faith.[15] If it is necessary to cite a non-Catholic, rather than a formal citation it is, it seems, preferable to mail a courteous and formal letter requesting his appearance. A witness duly and properly cited is bound to appear or acquaint the judge with the reason for his absence.[16] Because the duty of appearing in court is a public or quasi-public one,[17] witnesses are obliged to conform to it.[18] A legitimate reason excuses non-appearance; a grave reason frees one from not answering questions when cited; a most grave reason is necessary to excuse one from not signing his testimony.[19] In private causes, however, penal-

[11] *Cf.* S. R. R., *Treviren. Diffamationis,* 7 Februarii, 1913, *Coram R. P. D., Seraphino Many,* dec. X, n. 8—*Decisiones,* V (1913), 121, 122.

[12] S. R. R., *Treviren. Diffamationis,* 7 Februarii, 1913, *Coram R. P. D., Seraphino Many,* dec. X, n. 9—*Decisiones,* V (1913), 122.

[13] *Cf.* Canon 1711, § 2.

[14] *Cf.* Canon 1760. Older canonists before the Code applied to cases of spontaneous witnesses, Reg. 43, R. J., in VI°: *"Qui tacet, consentire videtur." Cf.* Reiffenstuel. *Ius Canonicum Universum,* lib. II, tit. XX, n. 417.

[15] *Cf.* Muniz, *Procedimientos Eclesiásticos,* III, n. 311, n. 2, p. 247.

[16] Canon 1766, § 1.

[17] Wernz-Vidal, VI, *De Processibus,* n. 460, pp. 397, 398; A Coronata, *De Processibus,* III, n. 1294, p. 206.

[18] Whoever spurns a citation is to be declared guilty of contumacy. He may suffer a penalty and be fined. *Cf.* Canon 1766, § 2; S. R. R., *Diffamationis,* 18 Martii, 1913, *Coram R. P. D., Michaele Lega,* dec. XVII, n. 12—*Decisiones,* V (1913), 207.

[19] *Cf.* nevertheless, Canons 1755, § 2, 1°, 2°; 1755, § 3, and 1743, § 3.

ties are not inflicted except at the instance of a litigant,[20] but all are held not to impede the cited person from appearing.[21] The obligation to appear when cited applies not only in contentious causes but also in criminal causes.[22]

Article 2. Rules for the Administration of the Oath

The oath is an expedient intended to eliminate any motives which a witness may have to falsify by calling God to his attention and reminding him of divine vengeance which provides a motive of fear which should be stronger than the influence of other motives.[23] The law insures the utterance of truth by appealing to the conscience and sense of accountability which a witness has. Even in cases when the oath is remitted, the judge should always impress a witness with the gravity of the obligation to manifest the truth.

After the witness has been duly cited and immediately before his judicial examination, he appears before the judge or his auditor to take an oath. In matrimonial procedure the Code distinguishes four important kinds of oaths,[24] which are considered under the four following headings: (1) The oath *de veritate dicenda;* (2) the oath *de veritate dictorum;* (3) the oath *ad secretum servandum,* and (4) the oath *testimonium septimae manus.* The oath of purgation (*ius purgatorium*) is not mentioned here because it is not considered in the Code. The fourth of these oaths, the testimony of the seventh hand, which is an oath of credibility has practical importance in matrimonial procedure.

20 Muniz, *Procedimientos Eclesiásticos,* III, n. 313, p. 248.

21 *Cf.* Canon 2209, §§ 3, 4, 1755, § 3, 1743, 2256; Reiffenstuel, *Ius Canonicum Universum,* lib. II, tit. XX, nn. 432, 433; A Coronata, *De Processibus,* III, n. 1294, p. 206.

22 The contrary opinion was held by Reiffenstuel who, nevertheless, seemed to advise the judge to exercise his right sparingly in compelling witnesses to testify in criminal causes. *Cf.* Reiffenstuel, *Ius Canonicum Universum,* lib. II, tit. XX, nn. 18-27.

23 *Cf.* Canon 1316, § 1.

24 Canon 1767, § 3, S. C. de Prop. Fide Instr., "Causae Matrimoniales," a. 1883, n. 15—*Coll.,* n. 1587.

A. The Oath de veritate dicenda

Canon 1767, § 1. Testis, antequam testimonium edat, iusiurandum praestare debet de tota ac sola veritate dicenda, salvo praescripto Canon 1758.

§ 2. Partes earumve procuratores praestationi iurisiurandi testium assistere possunt, salvo praescripto Canon 1763.

§ 3. Testibus, si de iure partium mere privato agatur, poterit iusiurandum, utraque parte consentiente, remitti.

§ 4. Sed etiam cum iusiurandum a teste non exigitur, iudex testem commonefaciat gravis obligationis, qua semper tenetur, veritatem dicendi.

1. The law of the Decretals imposed on witnesses an oath to tell the truth and nothing but the truth because an unsworn witness proved nothing.[25] This oath was usually given before the testimony was received.[26] The general rule expressed in Canon 1767, § 1, obliges all witnesses to tell the truth and nothing but the truth. Canon 1758, however, exempts the unfit and the suspect from taking it. Such an oath is promissory. Witnesses oblige themselves to declare the whole and nothing but the truth.[27]

The oath to tell the whole truth (*de tota veritate dicenda*) includes or implies an obligation to reply truthfully when under oath. The possibility of restricting such an oath to only some points or articles is excluded. The oath, however, does not oblige a witness to amplify his testimony unless asked, provided that he states the whole truth implied by the questions, whether the entire truth was

[25] Cc. 5, 39, 47, X, *de testibus et attestationibus*, II, 20.

[26] This is implied in cc. 17, 19, X, *de testibus et attestationibus*, II, 20. Canonists, however, did not reprobate the custom of giving the oath after the testimony provided that the witness had been forewarned regarding it. *Cf.* Pirhing, *Ius Canonicum*, lib. II, tit. XX, sec. I, n. 117.

[27] S. C. S. Off. Instr. (ad Ep. Rituum Orient.), a. 1883—*Fontes*, n. 1076.

asked for or not.[28] The oath to tell only the truth (*de sola veritate dicenda*) explicitly excludes the assertion of any falsehood in an attestation.[29]

2. The litigants or their procurators can be present when the oath is administered, provided that they come before the examination begins. No plea of exception can be construed from their voluntary or involuntary absence.[30]

3. The custom of excusing all witnesses from an obligation to take an oath is not admitted except in the case of certain persons, like bishops, whose credibility is presumed to be excellent by reason of their nobility of character or of their status. The omission of the oath is, nevertheless, to be recorded, sealed and forwarded to the judge.[31] As a rule, the consent of both parties is necessary for the omission of the oath as detriment can happen to both plaintiff and litigant from a false attestation.[32] The canon under consideration [33] confines itself to the observation that the oath can be omitted with the consent of both litigants, in merely private causes. Hence, in other causes, especially in criminal and matrimonial causes, which pertain to the public welfare, the oath cannot be omitted.[34] These conditions when the oath *de veritate dicenda* may be dispensed with are: (a) In causes of private good but not contentious causes involving the public welfare. (b) In criminal causes the oath cannot be given to the culprit lest he be forced to degrade or betray himself.[35]

4. Even when a witness is not obliged to swear an oath the judge

[28] *Cf.* Reiffenstuel, *Ius Canonicum Universum*, lib. II, tit. XX, nn. 465, 468; Augustine, *A Commentary*, VII, pp. 219, 220; Vermeersch-Creusen, *Epitome*, IV, pars. I, sec. I, n. 178, p. 69.

[29] *Cf.* Reiffenstuel, *Ius Canonicum Universum*, lib. II, tit. XX, n. 466.

[30] Canons 1767, § 2, 1763; *cf.* Augustine, *A Commentary*, VII, p. 219.

[31] *Cf.* Reiffenstuel, *Ius Canonicum Universum*, lib. II, tit. XX, nn. 477-480.

[32] *Cf.* Reiffenstuel, *Ius Canonicum Universum*, lib. II, tit. XX, n. 482.

[33] *I. e.*, Canon 1767, § 3; *cf.* c. 39, X, *de testibus et attestationibus*, II, 20.

[34] *Cf.* c. 30, X, *de testibus et attestationibus*, II, 20. Reiffenstuel wrote that when a cause involves the dissolution of a marriage, one cannot be excused from taking an oath. *Cf. ibid.*, nn. 485-487, esp. 487; Lega also includes causes pertaining to benefices and criminal causes. *Cf.* Lega, *Praelectiones*, I, n. 486, p. 425.

[35] Canon 1774.

must admonish him that there is always a serious obligation for him to tell the truth.[36] This suggests the question of a refusal to testify. Most canonists have adopted the principle, *"testis non iuratus non probat. Testi non iurato non creditur."* A judicial attestation is valueless from a probatory aspect unless elicited under oath.[37] In trials of common law and in equity as established in the United States, all oral evidence must be given under oath; if there be alleged conscientious scruples a solemn religious affirmation involving a like appeal to God is accepted. The court may inquire of the witness what form of oath is binding on his conscience. The proper time for the inquiry is before the witness is sworn.[38] In the common law of the Code refusal to take an oath is equivalent to the withdrawal of a deposition [39] because the rule is that an unsworn witness does not possess credibility.[40] The present law provides a judge with

[36] Canon 1767, § 4.

[37] "Iusiurandi religione testes, priusquam perhibeant testimonium, iam dudum artari praecimus et ut honestioribus potius fides testibus habeatur."—*Cod.* IV, 20, 9; *cf. Nov.* 90; Rittershutii, *Expositio Methodica Novellarum,* par. 9, cap. 21, n. 4, col. 759.

[38] Reynolds, *Trial Evidence,* § 110, pp. 270, 271; Omichund *v.* Barker Chancery, 1744, Willes, 538; 1 *Atk.* 45; 1 Wils. 84; Wigmore, *A Treatise on the American System of Evidence in Trials at Common Law,* III, § 1817. The oath is made optional by statutes in: (1) *Massachusetts* (a) Declaration of conscientious scruples permits affirmation as prescribed by Quakers, if the Court or magistrate on inquiry is satisfied with the truth of the declaration. *Cf. Masaschusetts* (Gen. L. 1920, c. 233, § 18); Norman, Edwin Gates and Houghton, Arthur Stillman, *Massachusetts Trial Evidence Including Citations from Massachusetts Reports* (New York, 1911), § 1792, p. 1793. (b) Believers in non-Christian religions may be sworn according to their religious ceremonies. Penalties of perjury require unbelievers in any religion to testify truly. Their disbelief in the existence of God may be accepted to affect their credibility. (2) *Illinois.* Liberty of conscience shall not be construed to dispense with oaths or affirmation. *Cf. Illinois* (Const. 1870, Art. II, § 3). (3) *California.* No person shall be rendered incompetent to testify on account of an opinion on matters of religious belief. *Cf. California.* (Const., 1879, Art. I, § 4). Wigmore, *op. cit.,* III, § 1828.

[39] Wernz-Vidal, VI, *De Processibus,* n. 471, p. 409.

[40] Reiffenstuel, *Ius Canonicum Universum,* lib. II, tit. XX, nn. 463, 491; (c. 3), C. IV, q. 3.

discretionary power to bind a witness by penalties if he has no legitimate excuse for refusing to swear an oath.[41] Authorities on the fourth book of the Code like Roberti,[42] A Coronata [43] and Muniz,[44] are of the opinion, which is a practical norm guiding the procedure of many tribunals, that a judge can hear an unsworn witness and estimate accordingly the value of this testimony. This opinion was forecasted by the juris-consult Rittershutius [45] when he observed that the oath is, properly speaking, not proof, but rather a relief from the burden of proof so that one should not oblige a witness to make an oath who has sufficient proofs of his intention.[46] It diminishes the value of testimony to make an unsworn statement and refusal to take the oath can render a declaration inefficacious.[47]

The common law of the Code prescribes no formula for the swearing of this oath. Any tribunal can follow its own practice. In Spain some tribunals require the recitation of the formula, "I swear that I will tell the whole and nothing but the truth regarding the things concerning which I shall be interrogated." [48] In other Spanish tribunals the formula is recited in interrogatory form. The deponent or witness replies in the affirmative.[49] Whenever the oath is taken by the litigants, witnesses and experts, it must be preceded by the invocation of the Holy Name of God. Lay people should touch the book of the Gospels with the right hand. Priests should place their right hand upon their breasts, as the content of the Gospels is written on the "fleshy tablets" of their hearts.[50]

[41] Canons 1766, § 2, 2242, § 2. *Cf.* Chelodi, *Ius Poenale,* n. 31, p. 35.

[42] Roberti, *De Processibus,* II, n. 342, 1, p. 55.

[43] A Coronata, *De Processibus,* III, n. 1297, p. 209.

[44] Muniz, *Procedimientos Eclesiásticos,* III, n. 314, 1, 2, p. 249.

[45] Rittershutii, *Expositio Methodica Novellarum,* par. 9, cap. 21, n. 4, col. 751.

[46] The suppletory, estimatory and decisive oaths and the *testimonium septimae manus* are *means of proof* in Canon Law.

[47] *Cf.* Canons 1622, 1743, § 3, 1755, § 3, 1758, 1791, § 2.

[48] A. Coronata, *De Processibus,* III, n. 1295, p. 208.

[49] Muniz, *Procedimientos Eclesiásticos,* III, n. 314, p. 249.

[50] Canon 1622, § 1; *cf.* Muniz, *ibid.;* S. C. S. Off. Instr. (ad Ep. Rituum Orient.), a. 1883, n. 12—*Fontes,* n. 1076, S. C. de Prop. Fide, Instr., a. 1883—*Coll.,* n. 1587, n. 12; S. R. R., *Impedimenti ad Contrahentium,* 11 Martii, 1910,

B. *The Oath de veritate dictorum*

Canon 1768. Testes, tametsi iusiurandum praestiterint de veritate dicenda, poterunt nihilominus pro prudenti iudicis arbitrio, absoluto examine, adigi ad iusiurandum de *veritate dictorum* sive circa omnes positionum articulos sive circa aliquos tantum, quoties gravitas negotii et editae testificationis adiuncta id postulare videantur.

The oath *de veritate dictorum* which Archbishop Muniz calls an "oath of ratification" [51] is an assertory oath by which a witness confirms as true what he testified before the judge. This oath is found in the Decretals,[52] in Instructions of the Holy See [53] and in rules laid down for the guidance of ecclesiastical tribunals.[54] The Rules of the Roman Rota [55] commanded that this oath be given to all deponents and witnesses. It left to the discretion of the judge whether he should require the taking of the oath *de veritate dictorum* after the examination. It commanded that the oath to tell the truth before the examination be taken by all. The Code confirms this regulation by requiring the oath *de veritate dicenda*.

The oath regarding the truth of everything said can refer to all the articles in the list of questions (*i. e., positiones*) or only to some.

Coram R. P. D., Gustavo Persiani, dec. X, n. 19—*Decisiones,* II (1910), 104; *Regulae Servandae in Processibus Super Matrimonio Rato et Non Consummato,* n. 39; Appendix, nn. XVIII, XXIX.

[51] Muniz, *Procedimientos Eclesiásticos,* III, n. 314, 2ª, p. 249.

[52] C. 5, X, *de testibus et attestationibus,* II, 20. The oath was used in a case involving consanguinity.

[53] *Cf.* S. C. Concilii, Instr., 22 Augusti, 1840 (De causis matrimonialibus recte pertractandis)—*Coll.,* n. 911; *Instructio Austriaca,* § 146; S. C. de Prop. Fide, Instr., a. 1883 (De Iudiciis ecclesiasticis circa causas matrimoniales)—*Coll.,* n. 1587, n. 12; S. C. S. Off. Instr. (ad Ep. Rituum Orient.), a. 1883, n. 15—*Fontes,* n. 1076.

[54] *Cf. Regulae Servandae in Iudiciis apud S. R. Rotae Tribunal,* § 114, n. 2; *Regulae Servandae in Processibus Super Matrimonio Rato et Non Consummato,* n. 39.

[55] *Ibid., cf.* S. R. R., *Solutionis et Refectionis Damnorum,* 7 Decembris, 1914, *Coram R. P. D., Iosepho Mori,* dec. XXXVI, n. 2—*Decisiones,* VI (1914), 333.

The judge should order it to be taken when the gravity of the business, a suspicion about the veracity of some testimony, or a contradiction is apparent between the various attestations or depositions or other similar circumstances seem to postulate it.[56]

C. *The Oath ad secretum servandum*

The oath to keep the questions proposed and the answers given secret until the whole proceedings are published, or forever, if the reputation of others is jeopardized or quarrels, scandals or other disadvantages are to be feared from a divulgation,[57] can be included included in the formula used for the oath taken before the examination (*de veritate dicenda*) or after it (*de veritate dictorum*).[58] This oath is promissory until the matters pertaining to the trial are published (*acta et allegata*) and become a matter of public knowledge.[59] The litigants or their procurators may be present at the oath to tell the whole truth and nothing but the truth, as well as be present at the oath *de veritate dictorum* and the oath to keep the proceedings secret.[60] As a matter of fact, today the parties are not always cited to be present at the giving of the oath. Their presence is required neither at the interrogations of witnesses in court nor at the appearance of the witnesses in court in order to give juridical value to the

[56] *Cf.* Roberti, *De Processibus,* II, n. 342, p. 55; Augustine, *A Commentary,* VII, p. 220; Muniz, *Procedimientos Eclesiásticos,* III, n. 314, 2ª, p. 249; A Coronata, *De Processibus,* III, n. 1296, p. 210; *cf.* S. C. EE. et RR., Instr., 11 Junii, a. 1880, n. 18—*Coll.,* n. 1534 (for criminal and disciplinary causes); Schmalzgrueber, *Ius Ecclesiasticum Universum,* lib. II, pars. III, tit. XX, nn. 86, 87.

[57] Canon 1623, § 3; *cf.* Canon 1944, § 1 for criminal causes; "Este juramento de secreto perpetuo se exige a los que testifican en los processos *contra sollicitantes in confessione.*"—Muniz, *Procedimientos Eclesiásticos,* III, n. 314, note 1, p. 250.

[58] A Coronata, *De Processibus,* III, n. 1297, note 5, p. 210. Older authors held the opinion that this oath was contained in the oath *de veritate dicenda. Cf.* Reiffenstuel, *Ius Canonicum Universum,* lib. II, tit. XX, n. 470. Reiffenstuel gives the following examples of this: (a) When the judge receives information on something notorious for his full instruction, *cf. ibid.,* n. 472; (b) Proof of custom of a people, *cf. ibid.,* n. 473; (c) Generally when witnesses are received for the information of the judge alone, *cf. ibid.,* n. 474.

[59] Canon 1769; Roberti, *De Processibus,* n. 342, p. 55.

[60] Canon 1767, § 2.

attestations of the witnesses.[61] Should the litigants, however, want to be present, they must be admitted, unless there be the difficulty contemplated by Canon 1763.[62] The promoter of justice or the defender of the bond, if the causes require either, is always present at the giving of the oath. Many witnesses can simultaneously swear, but it is expedient that each take his oath individually. A record of the full name and signature of each witness who took the oath should be made. If the oath were not imposed, as generally happens in the case of non-suitable and suspect witnesses, the fact must be recorded.[63]

D. The Oath Testimonium septimae manus

Canon 1975, § 2. Testimonium septimae manus est argumentum credibilitatis quod robur addit depositionibus coniugum; sed vim plenae probationis non obtinet, nisi aliis adminiculis aut argumentis fulciatur.

The oath or testimony of the seventh hand is peculiar to the procedure in causes for the dissolution of a marriage by reason of impotence or non-consummation. As shown in Chapter III, this type of testimony originated from the old Germanic law.[64] The fourteen witnesses of the seventh hand [65] appear on the stated day.[66] They

[61] Muniz, *Procedimientos Eclesiásticos,* III, n. 314 1ª, a, p. 248.

[62] A Coronata, *De Processibus,* III, n. 1295, p. 209.

[63] *Cf.* Roberti, *De Processibus,* II, n. 343, p. 56.

[64] Knecht, *Handbuch Des Katholischen Ehrechts auf Grund Des Codex Iuris Canonici,* pp. 786, 787; Meile, *Die Beweislehre,* 8, 55; Haring, *Der Kirchliche Eheprozess,* pp. 29, 63, 64; Eichmann, *Das Prozessrecht,* § 83, p. 215.

[65] The phrase *testimonium septimae manus* technically designates a number of witnesses. The number is not certainly absolute. *Cf.* S. R. R., *Nullit. Matrim.,* 15 Novembris, 1909, *Coram R. P. D., Gustavo Persiani,* dec. XVI, n. 5—*Decisiones,* I (1909), 138, 139. Variety in the number has ranged from eleven and fourteen in *Seinen. Matrim.,* 15 Februarii, 1884—*A. S. S.,* XVII (1884) 3-15; *Dispensationis Matrim.,* 14 Decembris, 1878, et 25 Januarii, 1879 (Hispaniae Diocesi)—A. A. S., XII (1879), 342 to one witness. *Cf. Mediolanen. Matrim.,* 9 Augusti, 1890—*A. A. S.,* XXIII. (1890), 474. In this case, one Augustinus Rosa was the witness of the seventh hand on one side. *Cf. Regulae Servandae in Processibus Super Matrimonio Rato et Non Consummato,* n. 59.

[66] "Moderatoris actorum erit tribunal convocare partes et testes citare."

are preferably the relatives or relations of the principals. If no one or an insufficient number of these be available, neighbors or friends of unimpeachable character,[67] who are cognizant of the marital difficulty in question, may replace the relatives or relations.[68] Nevertheless, those who are not relatives or relations may be omitted. The judge may, however, officially add other witnesses.[69] He has the obligation of doing this if a party did not introduce witnesses of the seventh hand or if they produced only three or four, or if the witnesses, although they be seven or more for each party, are not sufficient to establish the truth of the matter at issue.[70] Under pain of invalidity of the process the judge cannot omit the testimony of the seventh hand in any case.[17]

In court before they give the testimony of the seventh hand, the witnesses take the oath to tell the truth and nothing but the truth, as do all witnesses testifying from their knowledge (*de scientia propria*). Following their testimony they also take the double oath that they spoke the truth and that they will keep their testimony secret.[72] Here one must make a sharp distinction between the

—S. C. de Prop. Fide, Instr., a. 1883, n. 9—*Coll.*, n. 1573. If distance, occupation or other legitimate reason prevent a desirable witness from appearing the judge may delegate someone to receive, juridically, the attestation. Signed and sealed it can be admitted in the acts of the process. *Regulae Servandae in Processibus Super Matrimonio Rato et Non Consummato,* nn. 23, 24; *cf.* S. C. Concilii, Instr., 22 Augusti, 1840—*Coll.*, nn. 1571, 1573.

67 "Quoad singulos in judicium vocatos vel vocandos, actorum moderator inquirere debebit probitatem et credulitatem et ad hoc curabit ut ab eorum parochiis, sin minus a personis fide dignis, litterae testimoniales exhibeantur quae etiam in actis referendae."—S. C. S. Off., Instr., (ad Ep. Rituum Orient.), a. 1883, n. 16—*Fontes,* n. 1076, n. 14, *Coll.*, n. 1572.

68 Eichmann, *Das Prozessrecht,* § 83, p. 216.

69 Knecht, *Handbuch,* p. 773.

70 S. C. De Disciplina Sacram., *Regulae Servandae in Processibus Super Matrimonio Rato et Non Consummato,* n. 61.

71 *Strigonien. Matrim.*, 16 Decembris, 1893—*A. S. S.*, XXVI (1893), 584. Such exceptions are rare. Sometimes this testimony can be overwhelming. *Cf. Leopolien. seu Premislien. Dispensationis* Matrim., 13 Julii, 1896—*A. A. S.*, XXIX (1896), 542. *Cf.* Canon 1975.

72 *Regulae Servandae in Processibus Super Matrimonio Rato et Non Consummato,* nn. 39, 46.

testimony of the seventh hand and the testimony which they may adduce as witnesses testifying to what they saw or heard (*de visu et de auditu*). The Rules of the Sacred Congregation of the Sacraments published in 1923 state that in the examination of the witnesses of the seventh hand, the judge shall ask general questions and finally the particular questions drawn up by the defender of the bond which were given to the judge.[73] Following this examination, they perform their special duty of taking the oath of credibility. Regarding the latter testimony, that of the seventh hand, it is, as the canon cited states, an argument of credibility in the veracity of the principals.[74] By itself, it produces no evidence. As Haring [75] succinctly expresses it, the testimony of these witnesses stands or falls with their integrity. Two remarks are important here. The first is, that

[73] *Regulae Servandae in Processibus Super Matrimonio Rato et Non Consummato,* n. 67; *cf.* "Seorsim erunt hi quatuordecem confiantes septimum manum examini subjiciendi designatis diebus et horis delato prius juramento singulis."—S. C. Concilii, Instr., 22 Augusti, 1840—*Coll.,* n. 1571.

[74] S. R. R., *Nullit. Matrim.,* 16 Maii, 1914, *Coram R. P. D., Petro Rossetti,* dec. XVIII, n. 13—*Decisiones,* VI (1914), 214; S. R. R., *Nullit. Matrim.,* 23 Martii, 1915, *Coram R. P. D., Aloisio Sincero,* dec. XII, n. 10—*Decisiones,* VII (1915), 127; S. R. R., *Nullit vel Dispensationis,* 27 Aprilis, 1915, *Coram R. P. D., Iosepho Mori,* dec. XIX, n. 8—*Decisiones,* VII (1915), 213; S. R. R., *Nullit. Matrim.,* 25 Martii, 1920, *Coram R. P. D., Petro Rossetti,* dec. X, n. 7—*Decisiones,* X (1920), 74; S. R. R., *Nullit. Matrim.,* 17 August, 1920, *Coram R. P. D., Iulio Grazioli,* dec. XXV, n. 10—*Decisiones,* XII (1920), 242, 243; S. R. R., *Nullit. Matrim.,* 3 Augusti, 1921, *Coram R. P. D., Petro Rossetti, dec.* XX, n. 7—*Decisiones,* XIII (1921), 191; S. R. R., *Dispensationis Matrim.,* 30 Decembris, 1921, *Coram R. P. D., Maximo Massimi,* dec. XXXII, n. 3—*Decisiones,* XIII (1921), 296, 297; S. R. R., *Nullit. Matrim.,* 3 Augusti, 1921, *Coram R. P. D., Petro Rossetti,* dec. XX, n. 8—*Decisiones,* XIII (1921), 192; S. R. R., *Nullit. Matrim.,* 6 Decembris, 1921, *Coram R. P. D., Raphaelo Chimenti,* dec. XXX, n. 7—*Decisiones,* XIII (1921), 282; S. R. R., *Nullit. Matrim.,* 10 Augusti, 1922, *Coram R. P. D., Francisco Solieri,* dec. XXX, n. 14—*Decisiones,* XIV (1922), 285.

[75] "Ihr Zeugnis steht und fällt mit ihrer Redlichkeit. Sie können förmlichs Zeugen de scientia werden, wenn sie z. B. aussagen können, da sie zu einer unverdächtigen Zeit, als noch nicht an die Lösung der Ehe gedacht wurde, von dem Nichtvollzug der Ehe hörten." Haring, *Der Kirchliche Eheprozess,* p. 29; *cf.* Linneborn, *Grundriss Des Eherechts,* § 62, I, p. 462.

the precept of the Instruction of 1840 expressly ordains [76] and the Rules of 1923 imply by the use of singular number [77] that individual examination must be adhered to strictly. They must not be examined in a body.[78] In the second place, they must take the oath as to the veracity of the parties.

The Rules of 1923 do not directly state that the oath of credibility must be given in a separate exclusive process for each witness when the oath of the seventh hand is taken. Nevertheless, after they are examined regarding their perception and knowledge of the case, these rules do [79] command that after the testimony is read to the witness (*legitur testis*), that is, read successively, the witnesses are to take the oath and sign the document. Moreover, as they also answer the questions put to them, it is possible that they may become formal witnesses (*de scientia*) when they are in a position to assert what they saw or heard about the marriage in a time that is not suspect, that is before the dissolution of the marriage was considered.[80] This is borne out by the more recent decisions of the Roman Rota.[81]

[76] S. C. Concilii, Instr., 22 Augusti, 1840—*Coll.*, n. 1571.

[77] *Cf. Regulae Servandae in Processibus Super Matrimonio Rato et Non Consummato*, nn. 66, 67.

[78] " . . . compleantur actus processus per examen septimae manus, non vero globatim."—*Decretum*, 24 Martii, 1871—*A. S. S.* (1871), VI, 461.

[79] *Regulae Servandae in Processibus Super Matrimonio et Non Consummato*, n. 69.

[80] *Ibid.*, n. 60, n. 2; n. 70.

[81] "Testes praeterea septimae manus ex utraque parte, quos fide dignos esse declarant eorum Rectores Curati, iuratam confessionem coniugum de non consummatione matrimonii veracem esse attestantur. Neque proli ex illicito commercio natae providere voluit actor, quamobrem in carcerem coniectus est. Carolus interrogationi, 'Arripiebatur quia proli non providerat?' respondit: 'Ita per duas noctes commorabatur in carcere; per istas noctes tantum a cubiculo absens fuit.' "—S. R. R., *Nullit. Matrim.*, 9 Junii, 1911, *Coram R. P. D., Ioanne Prior*, dec. XXII, n. 13—*Decisiones*, III (1911), 243. "Nam testes (septimae manus) a Caia inducti non solum testati sunt de veracitate huius mulieris, sed etiam de matrimonii inconsummatione. Ita Clotildis, Philumena, Maria, Thomas, Metalis, qui duo postremi testes matrimonium non fuisse consummatum dixerunt ex rumore publico, qui circumferebat quaedam facta turpia viro adscripta, quibus arguebatur eius ad opus coniugale impotentia."—S. R. R., *Nullit. Matrim. vel Dispensationis*, 15 Julii, 1911, *Coram R. P. D., Gulielmo Sebastianelli*, dec. XXXI, n. 9—*Decisiones*, III (1911), 344.

Regarding the value of the testimony of these witnesses, their competency for testimony seems to be unquestionable. They know the character and the conduct of the married persons better than anyone else. The deposition of a plaintiff strengthened by the testimony of the seventh hand and placed in a setting of favorable circumstances (*adminicula*) implies a moral certainty of the truthfulness of it. In particular cases, however, the very will to further the interests of a relative or friend may become a strong incentive to deception. As no human testimony is absolutely unimpeachable, both the judge and the defender of the bond must be discreet in the examination of the witnesses of the seventh hand and view their testimony in the light of the circumstances surrounding the case. The value of this type of testimony is enhanced when, together with the oath of credibility, these witnesses also possess a personal knowledge of facts which is not to be suspected.[82]

Article 3. The Obligation of Witnesses to Be Present in the Tribunal

A. The General Rule

In Justinian law, witnesses were generally produced before the judge at the seat of the tribunal.[83] In the Middle Ages, as the letter of Pope Callistus I (d. ca. 223) to the bishops of Gaul shows, the witnesses were to appear before the tribunal where the court sat.[84] The present law lays down a general rule that witnesses must be examined in the place where the court convenes.[85] As there is no restriction expressed in the law, the value of testimony does not depend on the place where it is received.[86] The judge can interrogate

[82] The mother of a plaintiff said: " . . . se vidisse virum nudum, occasione ebrietatis, et insuper subjecisse eumdem judicio medico qui retulit virum haud esse aptum."—*Mediolanen. Nullit. Matrim.*, 9 Augusti, 1890—*A. S. S.*, XXIII (1890), 465.

[83] D. XXII, 5, 3; 3; *Nov.* XC, 3; XC, 5.

[84] *Cf. Msi.* I, 743, 744; c. 2, *de iudiciis,* II, 1, in VI°; c. 7, *de officio ordinarii,* I, 16, in VI°.

[85] Canon 1770, § 1.

[86] *Cf.* Reiffenstuel, *Ius Canonicum Universum,* lib. II, tit. XX, nn. 502, 503.

witnesses anywhere in his jurisdiction,[87] especially if he considers that it is opportune to combine the testimony with a personal visit to a locality (*accessus*).

B. *Exceptions to the General Rule*

The legislator exempts some persons from the general rule. Testimony can be accepted outside the place of the tribunal from the following persons on account of the dignity of their position or due to a physical, mental or moral state which prevents their personal appearance in court:

1. Cardinals, bishops, even titular, and illustrious personages who are exempt from appearing in court by reason of their civic prerogatives. These may select a place convenient to them for giving testimony, but should acquaint the judge with this fact.[88] The ecclesiastical judge who receives attestations from cardinals and bishops must, in the opinion of Archbishop Muniz,[89] invite them by an official citation and a notary is obliged to go where these witnesses choose to testify, unless there be an act pertaining to their official life which is no secret. In the latter case, a letter suffices, which thereby becomes documentary evidence.

2. All persons prevented from appearing in court by illness or for any other physical or mental reason, or by their state of life, as cloistered nuns, may testify in their respective residences.[90] For

[87] *Cf.* Canon 1636.

[88] Canon 1770, § 2, 1°. In the former law, bishops, priests and clerics, illustrious persons, physicians, soldiers and religious women were exempt. *Cf.* Reiffenstuel, *Ius Canonicum Universum* lib. II, tit. XX, nn. 505-507. The sick, the weak and the very poor were heard at their homes. *Cf. Glossa ad* c. 8, X, *de testibus et attestationibus,* II, 20. Before the Revolution in Spain, the king, queen, hereditary prince and regent of the kingdom were exempted from appearing for testimony in court. *Cf.* Muniz, *Procedimientos Eclesiásticos,* III, n. 315, note 2, p. 250; Jimenez, Iuan Aguilar, *Procedimientos Canonico-Civiles Respecto a Las Causas De Divortio Y Nulidad De Matrimonio* (Madrid, 1923), I, n. 431, p. 179.

[89] Muniz, *Procedimientos Eclesiásticos,* III, n. 315, p. 250; *cf.* Roberti, *De Processibus,* II, n. 345, p. 57.

[90] Canon 1770, § 2, 2°.

physical reasons, the sick, the aged, cripples,[91] prisoners, nuns with solemn vows [92] and, in accordance with different customs, those in mourning, are exempt from going to court.[93] The judge or his representative together with a notary, receive the oaths and attestations of these witnesses.[94]

3. Residents outside the diocese who cannot conveniently return and appear in court without grave inconvenience must, according to Canon 1572, § 2, be heard by the local tribunal where they live in accordance with the formulary of interrogation and the instructions sent to it by the judge in the case.[95] In such cases, letters called *litterae rogatoriae seu remissoriae* are forwarded to the respective diocesan courts,[96] which are obliged to give the desired information and proceed according to judicial rules. But if the witnesses can be called from the other diocese the judge can summon them to his tribunal.[97] In the opinion of A. Coronata [98] the law also applies to the tribunal of religious. Consequently, if a tribunal of religious province needs the testimony of those not under its jurisdiction, it seeks it through the tribunal of the diocese where the witness is staying.

[91] *Cf.* c. 8, X, *de testibus et attestationibus,* II, 20.

[92] *Cf.* Canon 488, 7°. *Instructio Austriaca,* §§ 146, 160; Roberti, *De Processibus,* II, n. 345, p. 57.

[93] *Cf.* Muniz, *Procedimientos Eclesiásticos,* n. 315, p. 250.

[94] Reiffenstuel, *Ius Canonicum Universum,* lib. II, tit. XX, n. 506; Lega, *Praelectiones,* I, n. 485, p. 425. Roberti states that the judge or his representative and a notary are required. *Cf.* Roberti, *De Processibus,* II, n. 345, p. 58. Compare A Coronata, *De Processibus,* III, n. 1298, n. 7, p. 211. In exceptional cases, in causes involving non-consummation of marriage, witnesses can be interrogated without a notary. *Cf. Regulae Servandae in Processibus Super Matrimonio Rato et Non Consummato,* n. 24—*A. A. S.,* XV (1923), 397.

[95] Canon 1770, § 2, 3°, *cf. Instructio Austriaca,* § 224; S. C. EE. et RR., Instr., 11 Junii, 1880 (de modo procedendi oeconomice in causis disciplinaribus et criminalibus clericorum), n. 19—*Coll.,* n. 1534; S. C. de Prop. Fide, Instr. (causae matrimoniales), a. 1883, n. 15—*Coll.,* n. 1587; S. C. de Prop. Fide, Instr. (cum magnopere), a. 1883, n. 19—*Coll.,* n. 1586.

[96] Canon 1570, § 2; *cf.* Reiffenstuel, *Ius Canonicum Universum,* lib. II, tit. XX, n. 437.

[97] Roberti, *De Processibus,* II, n. 345, p. 58 and note 2.

[98] A. Coronata, *De Processibus,* III, n. 1298, p. 212. *Cf.* Muniz, *Procedimientos Eclesiásticos,* III, n. 321, 5ª, p. 256.

4. Residents of the diocese who live so far from the court that it would be expensive for them to come to court, or for the judge to reach them. In such cases the judge shall appoint some worthy and suitable priest to take the testimony with the assistance of another person who may act as clerk. The interrogatories and instructions which are believed necessary must be forwarded to the priest.[99] In those regions of the United States where automobiles are common and easily available it seems that persons living in such circumstances should be expected to appear in person.[100] If the witness had died,[101] or his parents, family or neighbors object to giving testimony, or the witness has gone to a distant region,[102] these facts are to be recorded in the acts of the trial.

Article 4. Presence of the Litigants at the Legal Examination

Canon 1771. Examine testium partes assistere nequeunt, nisi iudex eas admittendas censuerit.

The litigants are not permitted to be present when the witnesses are examined unless the judge give them permission to assist. The judge, a notary, the defender of the bond in marriage causes or the promoter of justice in criminal causes,[103] are present in the court. This prudential and juridical criterion was the traditional legislation of the Church found in the classical collections of the Decre-

[99] Canon 1770, § 2, 4°.

[100] An Instruction of 1883 prudently added the phrase "nec tribunali se sistere posse." *Cf.* S. C. de Prop. Fide, Instr., a 1883, n. 15—*Coll.*, n. 1587. The hazards of travel in the East prompted the Holy Office to state merely that witnesses living in the Orient may be examined in the country. *Cf. Ad Orientales locorum ordinarios*, Instr., Ex. S. Congr. S. R. U. Inquisitionis (De Status libertate ante nuptias probanda)—*A. S. S.*, XXIII (1890), 191.

[101] "Si vero contingit aliquem examini subiiciendum e vita migrasse, mortis documentum inter acta recenseatur."—S. C. de Prop. Fide, Instr., a. 1883, n. 15—*Coll.*, n. 1587.

[102] S. C. S. Off., Instr., a. 1858—*Fontes*, n. 946; *Coll.*, n. 1153.

[103] Wernz-Vidal, VI, *De Processibus*, n. 472, n. 52, p. 410.

tals.[104] The parties are to be excused when the witnesses are examined in criminal causes.[105] Canonists before the Code did not agree regarding their admission in contentious causes.[106] Prior to the Code, the custom of receiving the testimony of witnesses with the adverse party present existed in the ecclesiastical tribunals of some European countries, especially in France. It was also permitted in the ecclesiastical courts of the United States provided that the judges of commissions of investigation thought it prudent and the witnesses were willing.[107] The common law permitting the personal presence of the litigant against whom testimony was to be produced during the examination of the witnesses was regulated by the particular legislation of respective countries. Personal confrontation was not allowed in Austria.[108] The practice was permitted in the United States, unless grave inconvenience would result. Should the judge deem it fitting, he could admit the adverse party, or exclude him and admit his

[104] *Cf.* "Ecce admonendus est semper adversarius ut ad audiendos testes veniat; quod quia hic omissum est, necesse est ut quod contra legem actum est non habeat firmitatem."—C. 2, X, *de testibus et attestationibus,* II, 20; *cf.* c. 41, X, *de testibus et attestationibus,* II, 20. These texts admitting them applied to criminal causes. The parties may be present at the oath of but not at the examination of witnesses. *Cf. Instructio Austriaca,* § 226; Jimenez, *Procedimientos Canonico-Civiles,* I, n. 441, p. 183.

[105] S. C. EE. et RR., Instr. (in causis disciplinaribus et criminalibus clericorum), 11 Junii, 1880, nn. 17, 18—*Coll.,* n .1534.

[106] There were three opinions: (a) The parties must be removed. *Glossa ad* c. 52, X, *de testibus et attestationibus,* II, 20. *Cf.* Reiffenstuel, *Ius Canonicum Universum,* lib. II, tit. XX, n. 499; Schmalzgrueber, *Ius Ecclesiasticum Universum,* lib. III, tit. XX, n. 94; Wernz, *Ius Decretalium,* V, n. 60, p. 467. (b) The party who introduced the witness, but not the adverse party, must be admitted. *Cf.* Pellegrini, *Praxis Vic. De Testium Productione,* n. 30, as cited in Roberti, *De Processibus,* II, n. 346, n. 4, p. 58. (c) Either party must be admitted for if neither is present the attestations are valueless. *Cf.* Crotus, Ioannes, *Tractatus de Testibus* (Venetiis, 1508), pars VI, n. 34, fol. 267.

[107] "Consentientibus testibus, et dirigente prudentia Concilii, repetatur testimonium coram rectore missionario, qui et ipse testes si voluerit interroget per praesidem."—S. C. de Prop. Fide de Commissione Investigationis, Instr., 20 Julii, 1878, n. 12; *cf. Concilii Plenarii III, Acta et Decreta,* p. 296.

[108] "Examen testium partibus remotis et singillatim instituendum est ac, antequam omnino terminatum sit, testium depositiones haud publicentur."—*Instructio Austriaca,* § 164.

advocate.[109] Confrontation of defendant and witnesses was employed only in extraordinary cases through fear of the danger to which the witnesses and the tribunal might be exposed. The view expressed by Cardinal Lega [110] that both litigants can be present at the examination of witnesses in civil causes was accepted. Nevertheless, in order that witnesses be not influenced or disturbed by numerous exceptions or by specious objections,[111] they can be examined after the judge has ordered the parties to depart. The Rules of the Roman Rota accepted this opinion with regard to patrimonial causes but forbade their presence in causes involving the public good. The Roman Rota also established the rule that the party who occasioned the interrogatory cannot be present at the replies unless the Instructor had decreed that an agreement be effected between the principals.[112] As a general rule the Code prohibits the presence of the pincipals, but concedes discetionary power to the judge, enabling him to admit them or exclude them in causes involving either private welfare or the public good.[113] Hence, it cannot be said that testimony will be of no force whatever if the party against whom they testify is not present, unless the party, bearing in mind what was said under Canon 1764, §§ 2, 3, was not able to object against the admission of witnesses if he choose.

[109] S. C. de Prop. Fide, Instr. (De Modo Servando ab Episcopis Foederatorum Septentronalis Americae Statuum in Cognoscendis et Definiendis Causis Criminalibus et Disciplinaribus Clericorum), n. 11—Smith, S. B., *Elements of Ecclesiastical Law* (New York, 1882), II, *Ecclesiastical Trials,* n. 1529, p. 420.

[110] "Quia nullo certo iure prohibetur, iudici fas est, si hoc opportunam ducat, excepere examen testium *in civilibus,* adstante parte producente eiusque adversario. Sed ob plures exceptiones aut cavillationes, quae moveri possunt ab adversario et ab ipso producente, quoties ipsis non satis faverent responsiones testis, ut plurimum magis expedit, examine excipi remotis partibus, aut saltem, remoto adversario."—Lega, *Praelectiones,* I, n. 487, p. 426; *cf.* Augustine, *A Commentary,* VII, p. 224.

[111] *Cf.* S. R. R., *Impedimenti ad Matrimonium et Damnorum,* 31 Augusti, 1912, *Coram R. P. D., Aloisio Sincero,* dec. XXXVII, n. 2—*Decisiones,* IV (1912), 430, 431.

[112] *Regulae Servandae in Iudiciis apud S. R. Rotae Tribunal,* § 114, 6; § 146, 3.

[113] Canon 1771.

The reason for the negative norm of the canon is that in any system it has advantages and disadvantages. From the point of view of the litigant who introduced a witness it is advantageous to him and to the judge to suggest opportune questions to the witness he introduced. From the point of view of the adverse party, it is an advantage to be able to contradict falsehood immediately. On the contrary, exclusion of the principals is a disadvantage to both of them. From the point of view of the litigant who produced a witness, he suffers grave disadvantages if he does not know until after the publication of the testimony, when he can not lawfully introduce new witnesses, that he has introduced useless or insufficient evidence. For (a) he must either produce all available witnesses before examination of witnesses begins or resort to the reprobation of the testimony in order to refute attestations which were made; (b) also, a litigant who is in good faith and a little scrupulous can be worse off than the adverse party who may introduce witnesses for the purpose of violating a secret.[114] In the other hypothesis, in which the parties are excluded from the examination of the witnesses, greater liberty is given to the judge enabling him to make inquiry and to the witnesses who may tell the truth. Roberti [115] observes that this is perhaps the principal reason why the Code considered it quite expedient to remove the parties from the examination of witnesses. In spiritual ecclesiastical causes, things of a very delicate nature come up which, perhaps, a witness would not dare to mention with the litigants present. But if this difficulty is not present and quarrels or captious criticism should not be feared, the judge must, in order to conduct a fair and undelayed administration of justice, be persuaded to admit the parties at the examination of witnesses.

[114] Jimenez, *Procedimientos Canonico-Civiles*, n. 443, p. 184; *cf.* Roberti, *De Processibus*, II, n. 347, pp. 59, 60.

[115] Roberti, *De Processibus*, II, n. 346, p. 60. *Cf.* S. C. EE. et RR., Instr., (De modo procedendi oeconomice in causis disciplinaribus et criminalibus clericorum), 11 Junii, 1880—nn. 17, 18; *Coll.*, n. 1534; *cf.* Lega, *Praelectiones*, I, n. 489, pp. 428, 429.

Article 5. The Manner or Practice of Examining Witnesses

Canon 1772, § 1. Testes seorsim singuli examinandi sunt.

§ 2. Prudenti tamen iudicis arbitrio relinquitur post edita testimonia testes inter se aut cum parte conferre, seu, vulgo, *confrontare.*

§ 3. Id autem fieri poterit si haec omnia simul concurrant, scilicet:

1°. Si testes inter se aut cum parte in re gravi et causae substantiam attingente dissentiant;

2°. Si nulla alia facilior ad veritatem detegendam suppetat via;

3°. Si scandali vel dissidiorum periculum non sit ex collatione pertimescendum.

This canon specifies two directive norms for the guidance of a judge in the examination of witnesses. The first of these is that the witnesses be separated and examined singly. The second is that in some circumstances the witnesses may be allowed to confront one another.

A. The Sequestration of Witnesses

Witnesses cannot be present at the examination of other witnesses. Each must be examined separately.[116] This rule, reminiscent of trial of the two old men who had coveted and borne false witness against Susanna, has been regularly invoked in Canon Law.[117] It was said

[116] Canon 1772, § 1.

[117] C. 52, X, *de testibus et attestationibus,* II, 20; Zallinger, *Institutiones Iuris Ecclesiastici,* lib. II, tit. XX, § 245, p. 181: "Iterim dum pars erit examinanda ipse Cancellarius exscribet in processu primam interrogationem, et deinceps *singulas ex ordine,* post quas scribet responsiones a Iudice dictandas . . . Liberum erit coniugibus testes bonae famae ac de re instructos inducere, qui omnes *seorsum* et methodo hactenus praescripta erunt examini subiiciendi."—S. C. Concilii, Instr. (De causis matrimonialibus recte pertractandis), 22 Augusti, 1840—*Coll.,* n. 911; *Instructio Austriaca,* § 164; S. C. S. Off., Instr., a. 1858—*Coll.,* n. 1153; *Fontes,* n. 946; S. C. de Prop. Fide de Commissione Investigationis, Instr., 20 Julii, 1878, n. 11—Acta et Decreta Concilii Plenarii Baltimorensis III, 295; S. C. EE. et RR., Instr., 11 Junii, 1880—*Coll.,* n. 1534, n. 17; *Fontes,* n. 2005; S. C. de Prop. Fide, Instr., a. 1883—*Coll.,* n. 1587, n. 13;

that the rule was "regularly" invoked in Canon Law because Campegius, the jurisconsult of Bologna testifies [118] that he witnessed the contrary practice in the case of many country people who simultaneously testified. He also states elsewhere [119] that the general rule of examining witnesses separately should be followed. The witnesses are to be kept separate until they are examined. An order from the bench causes them to withdraw; it may be accompanied with notice that if they remain or converse with other witnesses they will not be examined. The purpose to be subserved in obliging witnesses to conform to this rule is that they may not testify to greater advantage by being afforded an opportunity to strengthen their testimony in accord with their bias, or to influence the attestations of other witnesses. It is a legitimate argument against the veracity or fairness of a witness to allege that his attestation was colored by the opportunity he had, from listening to other witnesses, to contradict them or to give a more detailed explanation to conform to the exigencies of the trial.[120] To surmount any difficulty which may arise from the objection of litigants and witnesses who may resent being separated, the judge may prudently divide the examination into different sessions.[121] The rule, however, must not be interpreted so strictly that the validity of the examination is impaired in case that it is not observed.[122]

S. C. S. Off., Instr. (ad Ep. Rituum Orient.), a. 1883—*Coll.*, n. 1588; *Fontes*, n. 1076, nn. 13, 18; *Regulae Servandae in Iudiciis apud S. R. Rotae*, § 114, n. 5; *Instr. Pro Causis Matrimonialibus, ex Indulto, in Sinis Servandis*, § B—Payen, *De Matrimonio*, III, p. 993.

[118] "Vidi tamen aliquando contrarium obseruatum, atque multi rustici simul fuerunt interrogati et omnes simul responderunt."—Campegius, *Tractatus et Regulae De Tesibus*, Regula CXXIV, fol. 45.

[119] *Ibid.*, Regula CCXX, fol. 80.

[120] *Cf.* Kerne's Trial (1679, 7 How. St. Tr. 707, 709): Charge of being a Roman Catholic priest; Golden *v.* State. (1858 Arkansas, 19 Ark. 590); Louisville & Nashville R. Co. *v.* York. (1902, Alabama, 128 Ala. 305); Laughlin *v.* State Supreme Court of Ohio, 1849, 18 Oh. 99, 102; Wigmore, *A Treatise on the Anglo-American System of Evidence in Trials at Common Law*, III, § 1837, § 1840, § 1842.

[121] *Cf.* Lega, *Praelectiones*, I, n. 488, p. 427.

[122] A Coronata, *De Processibus*, III, n. 1300, p. 213; Augustine, *A Commentary*, VII, p. 224.

B. *The Confrontation of Witnesses*

After the publication of the testimony, it is left to the prudent decision of the judge to confront the witnesses with one another and with the parties.[123] This is called the "confrontation." The main purpose of confrontation is to obtain the opportunity of questioning witnesses through the judge and obtaining immediate answers. A secondary advantage to be derived from the personal appearance of witnesses is that it enables the ecclesiastical tribunal to get an impression which is made by the deportment of a witness while testifying. It has also a subjective effect on a witness to be brought face to face with his opponent in the presence of the tribunal. The phrase, "aut cum parte conferre," suggests what has already been said in the previous article regarding the presence of litigants at the legal examination. Considering the confrontation of witnesses with one another and with the principals, the Code[124] admits it under the following conditions: (a) If the witnesses disagree among themselves or with the party on behalf of whom they testify, in a serious and substantial matter; (b) If, in the opinion of the judge, there is no other easier way to discover the truth; (c) If there is no danger of scandal or quarrel arising from a comparison of statements. When it is considered expedient to examine the witnesses confronting one another,[125] they are simultaneously cited, they are sworn in and the judge elicits declarations from each regarding the points which are controverted. Because this process is secret, persons to whom it does not pertain are excluded from the examination.[126] The judge is himself restricted by the phrase, "prudendi iudicis arbitrio," so that there are rare cases in which the judge can permit confrontation of party and witnesses licitly, for the three conditions are laid down by the law and must concur simultaneously. These conditions are new in the positive Canon Law.

[123] Canon 1772, § 2, 1°.

[124] Canon 1772, § 3.

[125] "Remittitur prudenti iudicis arbitrio comparationem inter testes instituere."—*Regulae Servandae in Iudiciis apud S. R. Rotae Tribunal*, § 149.

[126] Roberti, *De Processibus*, II, n. 346, p. 61; Wernz-Vidal, VI, *De Processibus*, n. 474, pp. 413, 414; Jimenez, *Procedimientos Canonico-Civiles*, I, n. 446, pp. 187, 188.

C. *Who Examines the Witnesses*

Canon 1773, § 1. Examen fit a iudice, vel ab eius delegato aut auditore, cui assistat oportet notarius.

§ 2. In examine interrogationes non ab alio quam a iudice vel ab eo qui iudicis locum tenet, testibus deferendae sunt. Quapropter si partes, vel promotor iustitiae, vel defensor vinculi examini intersint et novas interrogationes testi faciendas habeant, has non testi, sed iudici vel eius locum tenenti proponere debent, ut eas ipse deferat.

The examination of witnesses must be conducted by the judge, or by his delegate or auditor, with the assistance of the notary,[127] and if the case call for it, of the promoter of justice or the defender of the bond.[128]

The questions or interrogatories are to be put to the witnesses by the judge or the one who takes his place. If the principals, or the promoter of justice or the defender of the bond should wish to ask questions, the interrogatories must be proposed to the witness not directly but through the judge or the one delegated to replace him.[129] If the questions are addressed to some one whose tongue is foreign to that of the members of the tribunal, the judge will designate an interpreter, against whom a legitimate exception has not been proposed by either party. The interpreter must take an oath to fulfill his duty well.[130]

[127] *Cf.* c. 11, X, *de probationibus,* II, 19; S. C. de Prop. Fide, Instr., a. 1883—*Coll.,* n. 1587, n. 13; S. C. S. Off., Instr. (ad Ep. Rituum Orient.), a. 1883—*Coll.,* n. 1588; *Fontes,* n. 1076; *Regulae Servandae in Iudiciis apud S. R. Rotae Tribunal,* § 114, n. 7. Women examined about *"sollicitatio in confessio"* must be heard separately and may be examined in a sacristy or other non-suspected place in the presence of an appointed judge and notary who are priests. *Cf.* S. C. S. Off., Instr., 20 Julii, 1890—*Coll.,* n. 1732.

[128] Canon 1773, § 1.

[129] Canon 1773, § 2; *cf.* "Si quod interrogatorium, sit superius monitum est, addatur ex officio a Iudice vel a Defensore matrimonii, Cancellarius interrumpet ordinem progressum, et adnotabit 'interrogativa ex officio.' "—S. C. Concilii, Instr., 22 Augusti, 1840—*Coll.,* n. 911.

[130] Canon 1641; *cf.* Muniz, *Procedimientos Eclesiásticos,* III, n. 317, 5ª, p. 252; Roberti, *De Processibus,* II, n. 348, pp. 62, 63.

Cross-examination as understood in the Anglo-American system of evidence for the past two centuries is not, as the negative form of Canon 1773, § 2, indicates, permitted in ecclesiastical courts. The many possible deficiencies, suppressions and sources of untrustworthiness which may be hidden under an untested utterance of a witness are brought out by the confrontation which has been explained. The original and fundamental object of the process of confrontation in the Anglo-American system is the opponent's cross-examination. The witness is confronted with a litigant that he may cross-examine him.[131]

Cross-examination, properly so called, has been discarded in ecclesiastical courts.[132] Instead, questions are to be put to the witnesses by the judge or the one who takes his place. If the parties through their procurators, or the defender of the bond or the promoter of justice should wish to ask questions, the questions must be put to the witness through the judge or his delegate, not directly. Experience has shown that too frequently the purpose of cross-examination was to destroy adverse testimony. It is not employed in ecclesiastical tribunals lest its use defeat the purpose of a trial inasmuch as important witnesses would be reluctant to appear in court and be adjudged contumacious due to their refusal to face a cross-examination which is often interpreted by a witness as an attack upon himself. Hence, as a policy of law expressed in the Code, every examination of witnesses by the parties, the promoter of justice or by the defender of the bond must be done by cross-questions. The questions must be submitted first to the presiding judge in writing and through him to the witness or the party to whom the question, if relevant and fair, may be directed by the judge. The judge, who is also an arbitrator in the Roman Law sense of the word, has the right and sometimes the duty to ask other pertinent questions.

D. *The Nature of the Questions and Answers*

Canon 1774. Testis primo interrogari debet non modo de generalibus personae adiunctis, hoc est, de

[131] *Cf.* Wigmore, *A Treatise on the Anglo-American System of Evidence in Trials at Common Law,* III, §§ 1361, 1382.

[132] *Cf.* Droste-Messmer, *Canonical Procedure,* 67*, p. 115.

> **nomine, cognomine, origine, aetate, religione, conditione, domicilio, sed etiam quae ipsi cum partibus in causa sit necessitudo; deinde deferendae sunt interrogationes quae causam ipsam respiciunt et sciscitandum unde et quomodo ea quae asserit, habeat cognita.**

This canon has the twofold purpose of identifying a witness who is actually in the presence of the tribunal and of unfolding to the judge the generic traits of personality which, made apparent from his answers, affect the probative value of the testimony. In matrimonial trials, witnesses should be interrogated about themselves and regarding the particular diriment impediment which allegedly calls the validity of the marriage in question and about all circumstances connected with the marriage. The questions naturally depend on the nature of the particular impediment. An understanding of this canon entails a consideration of what a judicial interrogation is and the subject matter of the questions.

1. *The Nature of Interrogations.* Canon Law accepted a principle found in Roman Law which governs the questions which a judge is empowered to ask. The principle states that, "Ubicumque iudicem aequitas moverit, aeque oportere fieri interrogationem dubium non est." [133] This principle became written law in 1910 with the publication of the *Rules to be Observed in Trials before the Sacred Roman Rota.*[134]

Canonists before the Code distinguished between the questions put by the judge (*interrogationes*), the facts to be proved (*articuli*) and assertions of fact which do not require proof always (*positiones*).[135] The legislator presupposes a knowledge of these distinctions. The interrogatories are the series of questions which are directed to the witnesses or to either party through the judge.[136]

[133] D. XI, 1, 21.

[134] S. C. De Disciplina Sacram., *Regulae Servandae in Iudiciis apud S. R. Rotae Tribunal,* §§ 140, 146.

[135] Reiffenstuel, *Ius Canonicum Universum,* lib. II, tit. XVIII, nn. 186, 189, 211. *Cf.* Noval, *De Processibus,* n. 436, pp. 303, 304.

[136] *Cf.* Reiffenstuel, *Ius Canonicum Universum,* lib. II, tit. XVIII, nn. 213, 214; Lega, *Praelectiones,* I, n. 443, pp. 393, 394; Muniz, *Procedimientos Eclesiásticos,* III, n. 270, pp. 211, 212; Canon 1742, § 2.

2. *Subject Matter of the Questions.* The subject matter of the examination of witnesses comprises two things: (a) the general personal circumstances bound up with a person, and (b) controverted facts.

(a) *General Personal Circumstances.* Turning attention to the general circumstances surrounding a person, the first object of examination, it is observed that generally speaking there are generic human traits which affect the probative value of testimonial evidence. Hence preliminary inquiries pertain to the general personal circumstances of a witness. In ecclesiastical courts, the witness must be asked his full name, parentage, age, religion, condition or profession, domicile or residence, and also about his connection with the parties in the case.[137] The judge can also ask officially other questions. These are to be consigned to writing and noted as official questions.[138]

Writers on testimony distinguish *questions of a general nature* from *special questions* which more directly pertain to the merit of the case under consideration. The special questions are considered at length in the following chapter. The general questions can be proposed in this way: Does the witness know the parties? If so, how long? Is the witness a blood relative or a relative by marriage of both or of one of the parties? If so, in what grade? Did the witness agree beforehand concerning the answers given? Was the witness suborned or corrupted? Was he an interested party in the cause? etc.[139]

The topics precisely enumerated in the Code [140] were indicated in the Instruction of the Sacred Congregation of the Holy Office, March 8, 1882,[141] in the Instruction issued by the Sacred Congregation of

[137] Canon 1777.

[138] *Cf.* Wernz-Vidal, VI, *De Processibus,* n. 472, p. 411.

[139] *Cf.* Reiffenstuel, *Ius Canonicum Universum,* lib. II, tit. XX, n. 510; Schmalzgrueber, *Ius Ecclesiasticum Universum,* lib. II, pars III, tit. XX, n. 97; Augustine, *A Commentary,* VII, p. 226; A Coronata, *De Processibus,* III, n. 1303, pp. 214, 215.

[140] The Decretals merely intimated these. *Cf.* especially cc. 37, 47, X, *de testibus et attestationibus,* II, 20.

[141] S. C. S. Off., Instr. (ad. Ep. Rituum Orient.), a. 1883, n. 13—*Fontes,* n. 1073; *Coll.,* II, n. 1588; *cf. A. S. S.,* XVIII (1885), 344-368.

the Propagation of the Faith in 1883,[142] and in the Instruction for Matrimonial Causes in China.[143] These three instructions omitted the words parentage (*origo*), religion (*religio*) and residence (*domicilium*) found in the canon. They include, however, two testimonial elements worthy of at least passing notice which were omitted by the Code. These are the word "status" (*status*) which is included by the Code under the term "condition" and the word "country" (*patria*) which indicated the nationality of a witness. The addition of these two last criteria to those enumerated in the canon gives eleven generic criteria which are quite exhaustive. The Code prudently eliminates *status* as a testimonial quality because, although status can have other connotations, it was formerly associated with servile status arising out of slavery. Nationality is also omitted from the common law because first, scientific and professional observation have contributed little useful information regarding the influence of race on veracity; secondly, because any preference for the testimony of witnesses of one race or nation rather than another is likely to be incorrect; and thirdly, because the oath is an external sanction for the veracity of all witnesses.

Canon 1774. " . . . de generalibus personae adiunctis . . . "

Looking at the topics enumerated in the canon more closely, it is to be observed that testimony is affected not merely by the three preliminary conditions of any witness, perception, retention and narration, but also by the general traits which are common to human beings. Experience has enabled men to generalize from them. These generic conditions affecting the reliability of testimony to the human traits influencing the capacity of witnesses for testimony are restricted to those which are found in the canon itself. There are circumstances such as character, religion, bias and the like which increase or diminish the force of a proposed inference. Without philosophizing upon the logical process involved in the use of the various

[142] S. C. de Prop. Fide, Instr., a. 1883—*Coll.*, n. 1587, n. 13.

[143] *Instr. Pro Causis Matrimonialibus, ex Indulto, in Sinis Servanda*—Payen, *De Matrimonio*, II, p. 993, n. 13.

circumstances, it may be stated that there are internal conditions which embrace general truths pertaining to age, sex, religion and emotion. For example, strong emotion disturbs the power of making exact perceptions and recollections. Moral unscrupulousness casts doubt on the correctness of a narration.

a. Full name—"*De nomine, cognomine.*" Witnesses must give their full name. This serves the necessary purpose of identification. Furthermore, if the witness be a woman, the judge is to discount much of what is said about the testimonial capacity of women in Roman Law [144] and in the works of the older canonists.[145] These entertained a poor opinion of the veracity and reliability of the testimony of women. There appears to be no appreciable difference between man and woman from the aspect of perception. It has been observed that women are more inclined to confuse what they perceived with what they wanted to have taken place or imagined to have occurred. From the aspect of narration, it is thought by some that women are apt to excel in facility and positiveness of speech but are less candid and honest than men. The dishonesty with which ecclesiastical tribunals have to deal is for the most part negative. It consists in suppressing a phase of the truth which leads to deceptions and confusions. This has been considered a characteristic of women. In the published decisions of the Roman Rota since 1908, this tribunal calls attention to many evasions and suborning on the part of men. No one, either man or woman, is presumed a perjurer unless it is proved.[146]

[144] D. 28, 1, 20, 6.

[145] "Creditur quoque et magis duobus testibus masculis quam mulieribus ratione instabilitatis quam per se habent. . . . Item praeferuntur duo testes masculi."—Papiensi, Franciscus Curtius, *De Testibus Tractatus Practicabilis ac Necessarius valde tabellionibus, causidicis, iudicibus, et omnibus legalis normae professoribus* (Venetiis, 1508), Conclusio, XVIII, n. 38, fol. 319; *cf.* Crotus, *Tractatus De Testibus*, pars IV, n. 61, fol. 225.

[146] S. R. R., *Nullit. Matrim.*, 29 Julii, 1911, *Coram R. P. D., Francisco Heiner*, dec. XXXVI, n. 4—*Decisiones*, III (1911), 408, 409. Regarding collusion between a plaintiff and her mother the Roman Rota stated, "Factum vero collusionis necessario iubet praesumere qui colludere intendunt, veritati vim facere, cum qua eorum attestationes."—S. R. R., *Nullit. Matrim.*, 1 Augusti, 1913, *Coram R. P. D., Michaele Lega*, dec. XLII, n. 18—*Decisiones*, V (1913),

b. Age—"*Aetas.*" The testimony of children who have not arrived at the age of puberty was considered in the last chapter. A reason for this exclusion is found in Roman Law. "Infants," wrote Gaius, "and those bordering on infancy do not differ much from insane persons, not being capable of judging for themselves." [147] It is possible to offer merely generalizations concerning those of youthful age who have arrived at the age of puberty. The perceptive ability of intelligent boys is thought by some to be better than that of girls of the same age, whereas, apart from strong exaggerations and pure inventions that are to be feared, the girl of approaching maturity discovers more rapidly the petty carryings-on and intrigues of her neighbors.[148]

The influence of advanced age upon the reliability of oral evidence is not, even at this time, determined with scientific exactness. The senses are disposed to become less keen with the advance of old age. Recollection of remote events is easier than the remembrance of more recent occurrences.

In matrimonial procedure, for the proof of the existence of consanguinity the best witnesses are old members of the family who are worthy of credence, religious, God-fearing, who obey the laws of the Church and who know the evil they cause by suborning themselves. If these circumstances do not surround their testimony, relatives are the least reliable witnesses.[149]

c. Origin and Domicile—"*Origine . . . domicilium.*" The parentage and residence of a witness must be given as aids in identifying him. The questions "Who were your parents?" "Where do you live?" may also lead to the discovery of blood relationship to one of the litigants.

497. If many witnesses suborn themselves, the principle is, regardless of their sex, "si plures testes fuerunt subornati, omnes pariter praesummuntur subornati." —S. R. R., *Nullit. Matrim.*, 1 Augusti, 1913, *Coram R. P. D., Michaele Lega*, dec. XXXIX, n. 18—*Decisiones Coram Lega*, 486.

[147] G. 3, 109; *Inst.* III, 19, 10; Mommsen, *Le Droit Penal Romain*, I, pp. 86, 87.

[148] *Cf.* McGeogh, John A., "The Influence of Sex and Age Upon the Ability to Report," *Journal of Comparative Psychology*, XL (1928), 458.

[149] *Cf.* Muniz, *Procedimientos Eclesiásticos*, II, n. 318, p. 387.

The word "origin" (*origo*) in the canon could denote nationality (*patria*) as well as parentage.

d. Religion—*"Religio."* Non-Catholics are excluded from taking the part of a litigant (*actor*) in matrimonial causes, unless they have obtained the power of doing this from the Sacred Congregation of the Holy Office. This faculty is necessary for the validity of the sentence. By virtue of Canon 1892, 2°, a sentence is incurably null (*insanabilis nullitas*) when it has been pronounced on parties at least one of whom was not entitled to stand in an ecclesiastical court.[150] Gasparri [151] voices the opinion that this prohibition seems to extend only to matrimonial causes properly so called, and, therefore, non-Catholics can accuse a marriage in the cases referred to in Canons 1990-1992.

e. Condition—*"Conditio."* In the two Instructions of 1883 [152] the word status was used instead of condition. The Code substituted the term condition. The term connotes the juridical standing of a person with reference to the rights that are recognized and maintained by the law.[153] Practically, however, condition denotes ecclesiastical or lay status, and, in laymen, vocation. It includes character as a witness,[154] inasmuch as persons whose profession is disreputable are disqualified from testimony.[155] They are presumed to be destitute of the moral qualifications necessary for testimony. To this class belong those whose profession makes them infamous in fact.

Canon Law, having adopted the conception of personality found in the Roman social system, legislated that the unbaptized, with the exception of catechumens, have no capacity for the exercise and enjoyment of legal rights.

150 Canon 1892, 2°. *Cf.* Canons 1646-1654.

151 Gasparri, *De Matrimonio,* II, n. 1260, p. 293.

152 S. C. de Prop. Fide, Instr., a. 1883—*Coll.,* n. 1587; S. C. S. Off., Instr. (ad Ep. Rituum Orient.), a. 1883—*Fontes,* n. 1073; Coll., n. 1588.

153 "Conditione, si liber, non servus. Nam saepe servus metu dominantis testimonium supprimit veritatis."—S. Isidorus Hispalensis, *Etymologiarum sive Originum,* c. 15, lib. XVIII—*M.P.L.,* 82, 5, col. 650; *cf.* Canons 87, 1239, § 2; 1149.

154 *Cf.* Augustine, *A Commentary,* VII, 226, 237.

155 Canon 1757, § 2, 2°.

f. Relationship—" . . . *sed etiam quae ipsi cum partibus in causa sit necessitudo* . . . " This phrase of the canon directs attention to those persons who may know and be willing to state truthfully the facts pertaining to a marriage case with reference to some persons and causes, but not with regard to other causes and persons. Their emotions, or affections, or interests may be so strong in the case submitted to the court that they are hindered from telling the truth. For a witness may be a friend or enemy, a servant, a business partner or a neighbor [156] of the litigant against or on behalf of whom he is called to testify.

The feeling, and not necessarily the strong emotion of a witness, may affect his perception, his memory and his narration.[157] Without going into the psychological aspects of the effect of desire on belief, it is a commonplace in psychology that emotion is a source of illusion which gives vividness and persistence to the ideas which are associated with it.

(b) *Controverted Facts.* Looking at controverted points as the proper matter for examination, the second object of the examination of witnesses, the questions which are asked can turn upon all facts pertaining to an action or an exception. The value of the testimony concerning these things depends on whether the information is first-hand (*de visu*) or from hearsay or rumor. Facts irrelevant to a case or elements which do not need legal proof, *e. g.*, a *presumptio iuris et de iure* [158] or facts excluded from a case, or things which a witness cannot know, are not subject matter for the examination of a witness.[159]

3. *Qualities to be Found in Questions:*

Canon 1775. Interrogationes breves sunto, non plura simul complectentes, non captiosae, non subdolae, non

[156] *Cf.* Wernz-Vidal, VI, *De Processibus,* n. 472, note 53, p. 411.

[157] C. 12, C. III, q. 5.

[158] Haec praesumptio iuris et de iure inde sumpsit nomen. Nam praesumptio iuris dicitur quia lege introducta est; et de iure, quia super tali praesumptione lex inducit firmum ius et habet eam pro veritate."—Menochius, *De Arbitriis,* lib. I, Quaestio 3, § 18.

[159] *Cf.* Roberti, *De Processibus,* II, n. 347, p. 61.

suggerentes responsionem, remotae a cuiusve offensione et pertinentes ad causam quae agitur.

Having seen the general character of interrogations and pointed out that general questions must first be asked, the Code ascends to the more particular rules which govern the more definite questions to be asked on the matters or facts pertaining to the case. The ecclesiastical court must adhere to the following regulations which govern the questions to be put to witnesses. The interrogations must be:

a. *Brief,* without unnecessary repetitions, amplifications and inane use of words.[160]

b. *Simple,* that is, easily understood by and kept in the mind of the witness. Questions are not to combine many things in one, lest a doubtful witness be satisfied with one equivocal reply.[161] The rule "never ask him a question to which he is at all likely to give an answer adverse to your case,"[162] obviously cannot be employed in ecclesiastical procedure. The questions, furthermore, must

c. Not be captious, that is, without discourtesy, still less without a brutal attitude toward a witness even though he may have lied. The questions are not to be worded too precisely so that, for example, the titles of anyone mentioned are added.[163] In practice it will sometimes be difficult to conform to this rule, especially with regard to suspect witnesses.[164]

d. Not be crafty, that is, expressed in words that are susceptible of more than one meaning.

160 Canon 1775; *cf.* Iimenez, *Procedimientos Canonico Civiles,* I, n. 451, p. 190; Osborn, Albert S., *The Problem of Proof Especially as Exemplified in Disputed Document Trials* (2 ed., N. J., 1926), 384.

161 Canon 1775; *cf.* Roberti, *De Processibus,* II, n. 347, p. 62; Augustine, *A Commentary,* VII, 228.

162 Reynolds, *Trial Evidence,* § 144, p. 337.

163 *Cf.* Jimenez, *Procedimientos Canonico Civiles,* I, n. 451, pp. 190, 191.

164 *Cf.* "Si testis non suspectus fuerit interrogatus captiose, et de pluribus circumstantiis, et variatione: numquid illa variatio infringet ejus dictum."—Sciaccia, Sigismundus, *Tractatus de Iudiciis Causarum Civilium Criminalium et Haerecticorum* (Coloniae Agrippinae, 1738), lib. II, cap. VIII, n. 903. *Cf. ibid.,* n. 905, in which Sciaccia admits that in practice it is difficult to verify his dictum.

e. Not be a leading question, that is, during the examination no questions are to be so framed as to indicate the answer desired.[165] Leading questions mention names and qualities of persons as well as other circumstances which surround facts in order to inveigle a witness to reply according to a preconceived idea. By taking advantage of a witness, these questions tend to embarrass him and curtail his freedom of response.[166] It is, nevertheless, with difficulty that leading questions can be avoided in the reëxamination of witnesses.[167]

Witnesses are to be examined by questions according to articles.[168] But when the same witness is to be questioned on the same articles the judge may fall into this error unwillingly. He must take care lest a witness plainly perceive from the tenor of the questions addressed to him what the nature of the reply should be as far as its juridical value is concerned.[169] A judge is obliged to refrain from the use of questions which suggest the answer [170] whether the interrogations are made openly or in a covered but ingratiating manner.[171]

165 S. R. R., *Nullit. Matrim.*, 17 Januarii, 1912, *Coram R. P. D., Michaele Lega,* dec. V, n. 10—*Decisiones,* IV (1912), 39.

166 Reiffenstuel, *Ius Canonicum Universum,* lib. II, tit. XX, nn. 516-521; *cf.* Eichmann, *Das Prozessrecht des Codex Iuris Canonici,* § 46, IX, 6, p. 147; Muniz, *Procedimientos Eclesiásticos,* III, n. 317, 2a, p. 252; Roberti, *De Processibus,* II, n. 347, p. 62.

167 S. R. R., *Nullit. Matrim.*, 17 Januarii, 1912, *Coram R. P. D., Michaele Lega,* dec. V, n. 11—*Decisiones,* IV (1912), 40.

168 S. C. Concilii, Instr., 22 Augusti, 1840—*Coll.*, n. 911; S. C. de Prop. Fide, Instr., a. 1883—*Coll.*, n. 1587; Instr. Pro Sinis . . . Payen, *De Matrimonio,* 994; S. R. R., *Diffamationis, Sententia Interlocutoria,* 12 Decembris, 1913, *Coram R. P. D., Michaele Lega,* dec. XLIII, n. 13—*Decisiones Coram Lega,* 539; S. R. R., *Nicien. Nullit. Matrim.*, 15 Martii, 1915, *Coram R. P. D., Gulielmo Sebastianelli,* dec. X, n. 3—*Decisiones,* VII (1915), 113. Questions, not the articles themselves, must be proposed to the witness. *Cf.* S. R. R., *Diffamationis,* 12 Decembris, 1913, *Coram R. P. D., Michaele Lega,* dec. LI, n. 13—*Decisiones,* V (1913), 635.

169 *Cf.* S. R. R., *Nullit. Matrim.*, 17 Januarii, 1912, *Coram R. P. D., Michaele Lega,* dec. XX, n. 11—*Decisiones Coram Lega,* 254.

170 S. R. R., *Nullit. Matrim.*, 17 Januarii, 1912, *Coram R. P. D., Michaele Lega,* dec. V, n. 10—*Decisiones,* IV (1912), 39, 40; *cf.* D. XLVIII, 18, 1, 21.

171 S. R. R., *Parisien. Nullit. Matrim.*, 23 Junii, 1921, *Coram R. P. D., Petro*

To avoid the suggestion of replies, the one who interrogates must proceed from general considerations to things that are specific not by a description of the facts with which an interrogation is concerned, but by imposing the description on the witness by fitting questions.[172] When a question involves the narration of a fact, which frequently happens, the interrogation must not be couched in a "yes" and "no" form, but in such a manner that the witness must relate the whole thing. For example, the question, "Did John call Teresa a wicked woman?" is faulty. It is preferable to ask, "Did John at some time call Teresa a disparaging name? What did he say of her? Why did he say this? When? Where? How do you know this?" In practice, it is well not to let anything indefinite pass that it may be evaluated at a later time.

A leading question does not render a whole process null. As a rule, such questions deprive the answers obtained in this manner of juridical value.[173] Following a review of a case submitted to its consideration, the Roman Rota expressed the view that the substance and value of a matrimonial case was not diminished by reason of leading questions as the defect was accidental and, moreover, because the Curia accepted the mandate to eliminate the testimony which was elicited from questions which could be interpreted as having been suggested to the witnesses.[174] It was said that leading questions as a rule render the replies obtained in that manner valueless from a probative aspect because in a cause involving conditioned consent tried before the Roman Rota, the leading questions put by a defender of the marriage bond to the mother of a plaintiff were considered to have been asked not without merit or reason.[175] Notes added by the judge

Rossetti, dec. XV, n. 11—*Decisiones,* XIII (1921), 149. *Cf.* Reg. 64, R. J., in VI°.

172 *Cf.* Muniz, *Procedimientos Eclesiásticos,* III, n. 317, note 1, p. 252; A Coronata, *De Processibus,* III, n. 1304, p. 215.

173 S. R. R., *Remotionis,* 11 Maii, 1909, *Coram R. P. D., Michaele Lega,* dec. V, n. 7—*Decisiones,* I (1909), 40.

174 S. R. R., *Nullit. Matrim,* 1 Augusti, 1913, *Coram R. P. D., Michaele Lega,* dec. XXXIX, n. 20—*Decisiones Coram Lega,* 487.

175 *Cf.* S. R. R., *Romana. Nullit. Matrim.,* 27 Maii, 1911, *Coram R. P. D., Aloisio Sincero,* dec. XVII, n. 5—*Decisiones,* III (1911), 174, 175.

to the questions asked without the knowledge of the witness himself are extra-judicial. By themselves they lack juridical value. If, however, some circumstances must be noted, the annotation should not be made unknown to the witness. The fact that the comment was made must be consigned to writing and comprehended in the text of the examinations which was made.[176]

f. Witnesses are to be examined in a manner which is *inoffensive*. Witnesses are not to be badgered, browbeaten or treated with scant courtesy so that they may be intimidated, confused and embarrassed. They have a right to be protected from improper questions, and from an insulting demeanor.

g. Finally, the questions asked should *pertain to the cause* which is being tried. The Code recognizes that it is a right of the witness to be safeguarded from irrelevant or immaterial questions.

Besides these rules contained in the canon under consideration it should be remarked that the witnesses are to be examined in *as quick succession* as possible. With a brief interval separating the taking of their attestations, expedition, so much desired in matrimonial causes, is obtained. This not only insures an undelayed dispatch of justice,[177] but it also, by preventing conversations between witnesses and the principals, renders collusion more difficult.

4. *Questions are not to be Communicated Beforehand.* Canon 1776 expresses something new in the present law. Its purpose is to prevent the witnesses who are introduced from suborning themselves. The judge should not acquaint the witnesses beforehand with the questions that are going to be asked them on the witness stand, but

[176] In criminal causes, if prudence dictate, this is sometimes left to the conscience of the judge to whom the final judgment belongs. *Cf.* S. R. R., *Nullit. Matrim.*, 1 Augusti, 1913, *Coram R. P. D., Michaele Lega,* dec. XXXIX, n. 20—*Decisiones Coram Lega,* 487.

[177] S. C. Concilii, Instr., 22 Augusti, 1840—*Coll.*, n. 911; S. C. S. Off., Instr., a. 1858—*Coll.*, n. 1153; S. C. EE. et RR., Instr., 11 Junii, 1880—*Coll.*, n. 1534, n. 17; S. C. de Prop. Fide, Instr., 20 Julii, 1878, n. 11—*Acta et Decreta Concilii Plenarii Baltimorensis Tertii,* 295; S. C. de Prop. Fide, Instr., "Cum Magnopere," a. 1883, n. 17—*Coll.*, n. 1586; S. C. de Prop. Fide, Instr., "Causae Matrimoniales," a. 1883, n. 13—*Coll.*, n. 1587; *Regulae Servandae in Iudiciis Apud S. R. Rotae Tribunal,* § 114, n. 5.

should only indicate their object in a general way.[178] Acquainting a witness with the questions beforehand might lead to collusion and induce a witness to make mental reservations when taking the oath.[179] Hence, under no pretext of refreshing the memory of a witness is it licit for the tribunal to intimate before the oath is taken the things about which the testimony is to be given, unless there be some questions which are so dependent on the memory that they could not be answered easily and truthfully without preparation. The danger of fraud or of collusion must be avoided always.[180]

5. *Answers or Statements are to be Oral.* Witnesses are to make their attestations orally. They must not read them off a paper unless numbers, dates or calculations of a mathematical nature are involved, in which case they may refresh their memory with the notes which they brought with them.[181] The reason for the first part of this canon is that what is written can easily be not the expression of the true mind of a witness, but of the one intending to commit perjury or be a deposition of one of the litigants. The exception in favor of mathematical calculations is prompted by the difficulty of retaining them in mind.

The canon prescribes that the testimony be oral, not written.[182] When a witness is unable to appear in person before the judge, the judge, as has been explained, cannot be content with his written state-

[178] Canon 1776, § 1; *cf. Regulae Servandae in Iudiciis Apud S. R. Rotae Tribunal,* § 114, n. 8.

[179] *Cf.* Roberti, *De Processibus,* II, n. 348, p. 63.

[180] Canon 1776, § 2; *cf.* Muniz, *Procedimientos Eclesiásticos,* III, n. 317, 3a, p. 252; Augustine, *A Commentary,* VII, p. 228; S. C. Concilii, Instr., 22 Augusti, 1840—*Coll.,* n. 911: according to § *Praefinita die,* the defender of the marriage bond is obliged to write out all his questions previous to the examination and hand them sealed to the judge, in open court, in order that they may be then and there opened and asked the witnesses and the litigants.

[181] Canon 1777; *cf. Regulae Servandae in Iudiciis Apud S. R. Rotae Tribunal,* § 114, n. 8. This is the constant doctrine and jurisprudence of ecclesiastical tribunals.

[182] The comparative worth of oral and written testimony is indicated in *Instructio Austriaca,* § 159: "Testimonium personaliter ferendum est. Scripta absentium testimonia probationem haud faciunt, sed praesumptionem tantum fundant."

ment, even though sworn to, but must either go to the witness with a notary or delegate another priest who resides near the witness to take down the testimony in the presence of another witness.

Underlying this canon is a rule that a "witness cannot make evidence for himself." Ecclesiastical courts, applying the principle that a man cannot make evidence for himself, does not make this exclusion complete. The evidence is to be treated on the two grounds or principles of necessity and of a circumstantial guarantee that the witness is trustworthy. The notes of the witness may be admitted in evidence as proof: (a) when he takes an oath that he made the observations; because, as a general rule, the statement of an unsworn witness does not prove anything which is either to the disadvantage of another or cannot be connected with a judicial assertion.[183] (b) Upon proof that he is usually correct in his computations; (c) upon inspection of his memoranda by the judge to ascertain that the notes of the witness are free from any suspicion of collusion or trickery. Evidence of mutilation or alteration of the memoranda requires a satisfactory explanation.

If there be question of statements of a deceased person, before they can be rightfully admitted, the judge must make a preliminary finding of the existence of the facts which alone renders such declarations admissible. The burden of proving these preceding facts is on the party who offers such declarations as evidence. Another of the essential facts is that the declarations were made in good faith. Unless the judge is certain of this, the attestations must be excluded. The judge is to determine the capacity of witnesses to comprehend what was observed and to narrate it with accuracy. The judge is also to come to a conclusion regarding the actual knowledge of the declarant and all the factors bearing upon his understanding, and honesty of purpose.

6. *Replies of Witnesses are to be Consigned to Writing.* Answers

[183] S. R. R., *Londonen. Incardinationis,* 9 Januarii, 1912, *Coram R. P. D., Antonio Perathoner,* dec. II, n. 9—*Decisiones,* IV (1912), 19; S. R. R., *Trincomalien, Nullit. Matrim.,* 1 Februarii, 1913, *Coram R. P. D., Aloisio Sincero,* dec. VIII, n. 2—*Decisiones,* V (1913), 85; S. R. R., *Nullit. Matrim.,* 1 Augusti, 1913, *Coram R. P. D., Michaele Lega,* dec. XXXIX, n. 7—*Decisiones Coram Lega,* 4.

of witnesses respecting either the general traits of their person or the merit of the case are to be set down in writing by the notary. The replies are to be consigned to writing not merely as substantially but as verbally given, unless the judge, taking cognizance of the small importance of the matter, considers that a note summarizing the testimony would suffice.[184] The notary does not necessarily record the questions.[185] It is desirable to have the questions drawn up in typewritten form leaving sufficient space between the lines for the insertion of replies in the pertinent places. The notary must immediately record the answers. The witness should neither answer what is irrelevant to the question nor volunteer to provide testimony lest he become a spontaneous and, consequently, a suspect witness.

The same notary or clerk must likewise state in the minutes immediately the circumstances surrounding the attestations, namely, (a) whether the oath was taken, refused by, or not asked of the witness; (b) whether the parties were present; (c) whether other questions were officially asked by the litigants, the defender of the marriage bond or the promoter of justice; (d) and, generally, everything worth recording which was uttered during the examination.[186] The judge is not allowed to make additions to some of the attestations on his own initiative after the witness has signed them in order to clarify them. Such a practice is reprobated as extra-judicial.[187] If, however, additions are made to attestations by the judge after the witness has signed them they do not in any way obstruct the validity of the attestations which were made.[188]

Before the witness leaves the stand the minutes of testimony must

[184] Canon 1778; *cf.* Roberti, *De Processibus,* II, n. 349, p. 65.

[185] *Cf.* Muniz, *Procedimientos Eclesiásticos,* III, n. 320, p. 254.

[186] Canon 1779.

[187] *Cf. Canons* 1643, § 2; 1585, § 1; S. R. R., *Nullit. Matrim.*, 11 Maii, 1909, *Coram R. P. D., Michaele Lega,* dec. V, n. 7—*Decisiones,* I (1909), 40; S. R. R., *Nullit. Matrim.*, 1 Augusti, 1913, *Coram R. P. D., Michaele Lega,* dec. XLII, n. 20—*Decisiones,* V (1913), 497; S. R. R., *Diffamationis,* 12 Decembris, 1913, *Coram R. P. D., Michaele Lega,* dec. LI, n. 13—*Decisiones,* V (1913), 635; Eichmann, *Das Prozessrecht des Codex Iuris Canonici,* § 46, IX, 9, p. 148.

[188] S. R. R., *Remotionis,* 11 Maii, 1909, *Coram R. P. D., Michaele Lega,* dec. V, n. 7—*Decisiones,* I (1909), 40.

be read to him. The witness may add, suppress, correct or change any statement that he made. Thereupon, the witness is to sign his attestation. The judge and the notary should likewise sign their names.[189]

The declarations of witnesses must, in the first place, be received in judicial form whenever the validity of a marriage is attacked. In the second place, another form is used when a question is to be asked for the purpose of clarifying some point. The questions may, if it be considered opportune, be put to the witnesses under oath. The Ordinary or a pastor who makes the interrogation has the choice of either writing the replies or not consigning the result of the investigation to writing. The signature of a witness is not required for this second form of investigation. In the third place, another way in which to receive the statements of witnesses is used when documents are necessary in order to petition for a dispensation. In these cases, the person whom the Ordinary has delegated follows a specified questionnaire. The formula which is employed for this purpose of securing the desired information is signed by two witnesses under oath. The witnesses are obliged to answer the questions put to them and must sign the formula separately.

7. *Reëxamination of Witnesses.* It is a procedural rule that after witnesses have been heard and their attestations published, they should not be heard again regarding the same articles or be produced directly to give testimony contrary to them on account of the danger of suborning themselves.[190] Canon 1781 permits a new examination of witnesses who have been examined already in the three following circumstances: (a) When the attestations were not yet published, with the exception of the cases of extraordinary presentation of witnesses who can be, as explained, reëxamined; (b) when the examination is conducted at the request of a litigating party in causes involving private welfare, and at the request of the parties or officially in causes

[189] *Cf.* Canon 1780.

[190] S. R. R., *Nullit. Matrim.*, 17 Januarii, 1912, *Coram R. P. D., Michaele Lega,* dec. V, n. 9—*Decisiones,* IV (1912), 39. This applies to matrimonial causes, *quantumvis privilegiatis, Cf.* S. R. R., *Baltimoren. Nullit. Matrim.* (Reid-Parkust), 29 Novembris, 1911, dec. XLIII, n. 6—*Decisiones,* III (1911), 504.

pertaining to the public weal; (c) if the judge esteems that it is necessary or useful, it will be imperative to reëxamine witnesses for the purpose of correcting a substantial error in a declaration and to clarify an obscurity in a declaration; (d) when there is danger of collusion or of corruption, the judge takes the fact into consideration according to the quality of the collusion or the corruption of a witness.[191] Repeated hearings are permitted. According to Haring [192] special and exact attention is to be paid to the facts and circumstances upon which a complaint is based. This also concerns witnesses. In matrimonial causes, new witnesses can be produced or ones who previously gave testimony can again be produced and new proofs admitted. The judge is to decide from a consideration of attending circumstances regarding the juridical value of these attestations.[193]

Article 6. Publication of the Testimony

The attestations are published *ipso facto* when they are received by the auditors whom the judge appointed, if the parties and their procurators are present at the time. They must be estimated as having been published from that time on when the parties were permitted to assist even though they were not present. In this case, however, the attestations must be at the disposal of the parties in order that they may examine them or in order that they may be given an opportunity to hear or read what they did not hear themselves.

When the litigants are not allowed to be present, the publication of the testimony can take place after the verification of the entire proof or immediately after the declaration made by the last witness.[194] It seems highly advisable in practice to admit the procurators and

[191] *Cf.* Canon 1781.

[192] "Wiederholte Einvernahme ist zulässig. Besonders genau sind die Tatsachen und deren Umstände, auf welche die Klage sich stützt, zu erforschen (gilt auch für die Zeugen)."—Haring, *Der Kirchliche Eheprozess,* 83.

[193] S. R. R., *Parisien. Nullit. Matrim.,* 12 Junii, 1919, *Coram R. P. D., Petro Rossetti,* dec. XI, n. 15—*Decisiones,* XI (1919), 107, 108.

[194] *Cf.* Canon 1782, § 1.

advocates to the examination of all witnesses introduced by both parties. This in many instances will save much time and prevent much unnecessary delay. Should the testimonial evidence be the most important of the trial, it may be convenient to publish it as soon as possible. Likewise, whenever this proof by witnesses has shown itself to be either so weak that the proof provided by the oath was required or so obscure or complicated that it was necessary to resort to ocular inspection, it may be useful to publish the testimony as soon as possible. This observation applies to matrimonial procedure with the exception of processes *super rato et non-consummato,* in which causes, as there is no publication of the process, there is no publication of testimony.

Among the canonists the doctrine was generally held that the publication of the testimony did not belong to the essence of a trial because the proofs are intended to instruct the judge, and not the litigants. But if the publication was asked and the judge refused, the principals could appeal against the denial. In a certain way this left the parties without defense.[195] This doctrine cannot be accepted today as a trial is declared null by the Code [196] when proofs are admitted which were unknown to an adverse party. Cardinal Lega [197] entertained the view that the publication must take place at the instance of the party. It must be done officially when the attestations of witnesses summoned by the judge are received. The judge can proceed to the publication of the testimonial evidence when it is verified. It would, however, be convenient for the judge to do this upon the request of one of the parties. He is obliged to do this even though he be not requested at the time of the publication of the process.[198]

[195] *Cf.* Reiffenstuel, *Ius Canonicum Universum,* lib. II, tit. XX, n. 523.

[196] Canon 1861, § 2; *cf.* Muniz, *Procedimientos Eclesiásticos,* III, n. 329, p. 264.

[197] Lega, *Praelectiones,* I, n. 483, p. 424.

[198] Canon 1858; *cf.* Muniz, *ibid.* For the form of the publication, *cf.* Schmalzgrueber, *Ius Ecclesiasticum Universum,* lib. II, tit. XX, n. 116; Muniz, *Procedimientos Eclesiásticos,* III, n. 330, p. 265.

Article 7. The Rejection of Witnesses and the Impugning of Their Testimonies

A judgment for the reprobation of witnesses and for the impugning of their testimony consists in the presentation, examination and definition of the exceptions made against (1) the person of a witness; (2) the form according to which his examination was conducted, or (3) against his attestation.[199]

1. The exceptions made against the person of a witness were developed in the previous chapter. These exceptions are to be proposed before the examination and must be proved during the trial.

2. Schmalzgrueber [200] enumerated ten exceptions which could be taken against the form of an examination. The following which conform to the Code are selected from these: a. An examination conducted by an incompetent judge.[201] b. A witness presented and examined before the answer to the petition is received.[202] c. The presentation of a witness was not made known to the contrary party, unless the judge prudently considers that this cannot be done without grave difficulty.[203] d. The witness did not take an oath nor was he dispensed from it by either the parties or the law itself.[204] e. The witness was examined after he knew the content of the testimony of others or after the questions were made known to him.[205] f. The presentation and examination took place after the end of the probatory period, as was explained in Chapter VI. g. The witness read his answers, instead of stating them orally.[206] h. The witnesses were not examined singly but in globo.[207]

3. With respect to exceptions that can be made against the attestations, the following, selected from the Code and the enumeration of Schmalzgrueber referred to above, can be taken because: a. A wit-

[199] *Cf.* Canon 1783.

[200] Schmalzgrueber, *Ius Ecclesiasticum Universum,* lib. II, tit. XX, n. 113.

[201] Canons 1609, § 1; 1610, 1611.

[202] *I. e.* ,against Canon 1730.

[203] *Cf.* Canon 1763.

[204] Canons 1758, 1767.

[205] Canons 1776, 1786.

[206] Canon 1777.

[207] Canon 1772, § 1.

ness made a declaration which was false. b. The testimony vacillates, is obscure, or contradicts other statements of the same witness or the attestations of others;[208] c. A Witness says something alone, which is not controverted by others; d. He does not affirm anything with certainty and decision, but in a hesitant manner and with confusion;[209] e. A witness either gives no reason for his knowledge or his knowledge is not his own but is derived from rumor or what was heard from another;[210] f. A witness declares what is unworthy of credence.[211]

These considerations suggest another question which involves the manner of proceeding in these incidents. In trial procedure for the rejection of witnesses whose testimony is valueless and in the impugning of their testimony one must resort to the following distinctions. In the first place, a distinction is to be made between what was stated before the citation and what has been attested after it. Secondly, one must distinguish whether the parties were present during the examination of the witnesses and whether they knew about the attestations because of the decree which published them.

In any event, the judgment of reprobation or the impugning of the testimony of a witness follows the manner of an incidental cause which the judge can reject if he adverts that the litigants are merely striving to prolong the trial.[212] Should a judgment of reprobation or the "impugning of the testimony" be admitted, the party who submits the exceptions can present witnesses for two purposes. The first of these is for the rejection of other witnesses. The second is for the purpose of introducing witnesses who can prove something contrary to the statements of the witnesses who are present but which is in favor of an exception.

This testimonial and additional proof is not always necessary. It is inadmissible without a just cause. Nevertheless, whenever a litigant desires to prove that a witness who was admitted into court is disqualified, it is permissible to impugn the qualification of such a witness to testify.

[208] Canon 1783, 2°.

[209] Canon 1789, 3°.

[210] Canon 1789, 2°.

[211] Canon 1783, 2°.

[212] *Cf.* Canon 1784.

Had the litigants not been present at the examination the judge, at the publication of the testimony, appoints a brief time during which the parties must present the exceptions which were not submitted previously.[213] Had the principals been present during the examination of witnesses, the judge can wait until the parties request a "judgment for the reprobation or impugning of witnesses." If the day on which the probatory period ends has come, and the litigants have not requested that the aforementioned judgment take place, the judge declares that the time for the presentation and verification of proofs has terminated. The judge will not admit exceptions which could have been presented on time. In other cases the term of the probatory period must be prolonged if the judgment for reprobation or for the impugning of witnesses was asked in an opportune time and it was admitted by the judge. Ordinarily, there is no interlocutory sentence [214] in a judgment of reprobation or for the impugning of witnesses, because the judge can handle everything in the definitive sentence. However, the exceptions that demand a return of an act which was wrongly posited must be taken care of before the sentence.[215]

213 *Cf.* Canon 1785.

214 *Cf.* Canons 1868, § 1; 1875.

215 In the Spanish courts the reprobation takes place after the discussion of the proof. *Cf.* Muniz, *Procedimientos Eclesiásticos,* III, n. 333, pp. 266-268.

CHAPTER IX

METHOD OF ESTIMATING THE VALUE OF TESTIMONY IN MATRIMONIAL CAUSES

Canon 1789. In aestimandis testimoniis iudex prae oculis habeat:

1°. Quae conditio sit personae, quaeve honestas et an aliqua dignitate testis praefulgeat;

2°. Utrum de scientia propria, praesertim de visu et auditu proprio testificetur, an de credulitate, de fama, aut de auditu ab aliis;

3°. Utrum testis constans sit et firmiter sibi cohaereat; an varius, incertus, vel vacillans;

4°. Denique utrum testimonii contestes habeat, an sit singularis.

ARTICLE 1. THE JUDGE IS TO ESTIMATE THE PROBATIVE VALUE OF TESTIMONY

"In aestimandis testimoniis iudex prae oculis habeat":

These words are an observation by the legislator concerning the four criteria for estimating testimonial evidence which immediately follow. They suggest two legal concepts which have an intimate relation to one another.

A. In aestimandis testimoniis

The Code employs these words, which are found in Roman Law, merely to state the principle that testimony must be duly estimated.[1]

[1] Roman Law imposed no rule which required judges to weigh testimony. They were left free to establish the weight of testimony. D. XXII, 3, 5: Hadrain admonished Varius, a legate to Sicily, "Tu magis scire potes quanta fides habenda sit testibus: qui et cuius dignitatis et cuius aestimationis sint: et qui simpliciter visi sint dicere, utrum unum eumdemque meditatum sermonem attulerint: an ad ea quae interrogaveras, ex tempore versimilia responderit."

The word "estimation" as it is employed by the Code denotes the weighing or the evaluating of the testimony of each witness in a court of law. The value or the weight of testimony does not mean nor does it connote in legal usage any comparison that may be made between circumstantial and testimonial evidence. Reputable canonists use the expression "value of testimony" to indicate the probative force (*vis*) which testimony has in the proof of controverted facts.[2] Consequent-

Cf. D. XII, 3, 5: Hadrian wrote to Valerian Verus, "Ex sententia animi tui te aestimare oportere, quid aut credas aut parum probatum tibi opiniaris." One cannot, however, conclude from these texts alone that the Code restored the principle of Roman Law requiring moral certitude in a judge about the thing to be defined in a sentence and commanding him to estimate proofs from his conscience. *Cf.* Roberti, *De Processibus*, n. 354, p. 74.

[2] *Cf. Instructio Austriaca* (Cardinal Rauscher), §§ 162, 165; *Regulae Servandae in Iudiciis apud S. R. Rotae Tribunal*, § 116, n. 3; *Regulae Servandae in Processibus Super Matrimonio Rato et Non Consummato*, n. 60, n. 1; S. R. R., *Nullit. Matrim.*, 17 Januarii, 1910, *Coram R. P. D., Michaele Lega*, dec. XX, n. 8—*Decisiones*, I (1910), 252, 253; S. R. R., *Nullit. Matrim.*, 21 Decembris, 1912, *Coram R. P. D., Michaele Lega*, dec. XLI, n. 4—*Decisiones*, I (1912), 355; S. R. R., *Nullit. Matrim.*, 1 Augusti, 1913, *Coram R. P. D., Michaele Lega*, dec. XXXIX, n. 20—*Decisiones Coram Lega*, 487; S. R. R., *Nullit. Matrim.*, 1 Julii, 1911, *Massilien, Coram R. P. D., Gulielmo Sebastienelli*, dec. XXIX, n. 4—*Decisiones*, III (1911), 327; S. R. R., *Nullit. Matrim.*, 17 Januarii 1912, *Coram R. P. D., Michaele Lega*, dec. V, n. 23—*Decisiones*, IV (1912), 48; S. R. R., *Nullit. Matrim.*, 18 Augusti, 1916; *Coram R. P. D., Seraphino Many*, dec. XXVIII, n. 8—*Decisiones* VIII (1916), 318; S. R. R., *Nullit. Matrim.*, 18 Augusti, 1916, *Coram R. P. D., Seraphino Many*, dec. XXVIII, n. 19—*Decisiones*, VIII (1916), 324; S. R. R., *Trissonialien Nullit. Matrim.*, 1 Februarii, 1913, *Coram R. P. D., Aloisio Sincero*, dec. VIII, n. 2—*Decisiones*, VIII (1913), 85; S. R. R., *Finium Parochialium*, 5 Maii, 1913, *Coram R. P. D., Michaele Lega*, dec. XXVI, n. 10—*Decisiones*, V (1913), 303; S. R. R., *Nullit. Matrim.*, 19 Julii, 1913, *Coram R. P. D., Iosepho Alberti*, dec. XXXIX, n. 6—*Decisiones*, V (1913), 468. S. R. R., *Cappellaniae Laicalis*, 6 Decembris, 1916, *Coram R. P. D., Ioanne Prior*, dec. XXXI, n .16—*Decisiones*, VIII (1916), 360; S. R. R., *Buscoducen*, 15 Maii, 1915, dec. XX, n. 20—*Decisiones*, VII (1915), 223; compare Lega, *Parelectiones*, I, n. 479, pp. 419, 420; n. 491, p. 430; Mansella, *De Impedimentis Matrimonium Dirimentibus*, 189, 190; Roberti, *De Processibus*, II, n. 353, p. 72; n. 353, p. 74; Augustine, *A commentary*, VII, 235, 237; Wernz-Vidal, VI, *De Processibus*, n. 466, p. 402; n. 481, p. 420; n. 483, note (74), p. 423; A Coronata, *De Processibus*, n. 1286, p. 196; n. 1291, n. 3, p. 203; n. 1293, p. 204; n. 1294, p. 206; n. 1295, p. 209; n. 1321, p. 226; Muniz, *Pro-*

ly, after the examination of witnesses and the hearing of exceptions taken to them, the judge is to weigh the probative force of the attested facts. Since the essential requirement of legitimate testimony is knowledge of the truth, the judge must sedulously inquire whether the witnesses have testified from their own knowledge, or have been ready to believe on slight evidence (*credulitas*) from what they have learned by hearsay or rumor. Moreover, in estimating probative value it is essential that the judge ascertain whether the witnesses who have testified are immune from any suspicion.[3]

B. *Iudex prae oculis habeat*

This legal formula is found in all the Roman Rota cases heard and published by Cardinal Lega. He used the expression in summarizing cases submitted to his consideration.[4] The phrase is not a mere introductory remark. It suggests that in contentious and in criminal causes in which ecclesiastical judges act on presumptions, they should require conclusive proof so as to beget moral certainty before a declaration that any contract is invalid or that a culprit has broken the law. This teaching is in conformity with the practice of the Church courts. It is a practice founded on both civil and Canon law. Reiffenstuel sustained the common and most received teaching that whenever one of the litigants to a lawsuit has on his side a more probable opinion, it is by no means lawful for the judge, provided

cedimientos Eclesiásticos, III, n. 303, p. 241; n. 314, 1°, g), p. 249; n. 314, p. 249; n. 333, p. 268; n. 337, pp. 337, 338; n. 1286, p. 196; n. 1294, p. 206.

[3] C. 1, X, *de consanguinitate et affinitate,* IV, 14; Zallinger, *Institutiones Iuris Ecclesiastici,* lib. II, tit. XX, § 257, p. 190; Wernz-Vidal, VI, *De Processibus,* n. 481, p. 420.

[4] *Cf.* also S. R. R., *Florentia. Finium Parochialium.,* 5 Maii, 1913, *Coram R. P. D., Michaele Lega,* dec. XXVI, n. 10—*Decisiones,* V (1913), 303: "In hoc examine prae oculis habenda est regula tria in foro, nempe: 'magis creditur duabus testibus affirmantibus, quam mille negantibus': qu[a]ia affirmans aliquid, scire vel cognoscere asserit: dum negans, dumtaxat se nescire ait. *Cf. Decis. Recent.* 272, n. 2, part. 2; 141, n. 7; 54, n. 13, part. 4, tom. 2; 294, n. 11, part. 5, tom. 1, etc., in Lega, *loc. cit.* Compare S. R. R., *Nullit. Matrim.,* 17 Januarii, 1912, *Coram R. P. D., Michaele Lega,* dec. V, n. 24—*Decisiones,* IV (1912), 49.

that he recognizes that the opinion or the question is really the more probable, to neglect it and to decide in conformity with a less probable opinion.[5]

It is induitable, by reason of the decree of Innocent XI [6] and the Code itself [7] that a judge may not give a sentence in accordance with a less probable claim, or with more probability but with moral certitude. The moral certitude demanded [8] must result from proof which is sufficient to convince a judge of the rightfulness of the cause. Every sentence opposed to a clear and express text of the law would be null and void by the very fact, inasmuch as the judge is obliged not to reverse but to uphold the law.[9]

For instance, in the proof of affinity which arises out of illicit marital relations, the Roman Rota considered that inasmuch as the proof of this concerned a delict which was committed secretly, it is proved from circumstances (*indicia*) and presumptions which give moral certitude to the judge.[10] The proof of simulated consent, that is of a substantial discrepancy between internal consent and its external expression in words or signs, is difficult. There are no direct proofs of what happened secretly. Canonists unanimously teach that when there is a question of the validity of a marriage the judges may

[5] Reiffenstuel, *Ius Canonicum Universum,* lib. 1, tit. XXXII, nn. 52-60.

[6] Decree of 2 March, 1679, condemned the proposition: "Probabiliter existimo, judicem posse judicare juxta opinionem etiam minus probabilem," as quoted in Reiffenstuel, *ibid.*, n. 51.

[7] Canon 1869, § 1: "Ad pronuntiationem cuiuslibet sententiae requiritur in iudicis animo moralis certitudo circa rem sententiae definiendam." The rule is that testimony being equally strong on both sides, the decision should be in favor of the one in possession because "melior est conditio possidentis." *Cf.* c. 3, X, *de probationibus,* II, 19.

[8] S. R. R., *Nullit. Matrim., Colonien.,* 27 Augusti, 1910, *Coram R. P. D., Gustavo Persiani,* dec. XXXI, n. 15—*Decisiones,* II (1910), 326, 327.

[9] C. 1, X, *de sententia et re iudicata,* II, 27: "Sententia contra leges canonesve prolata, licet non sit appellatione suspensa, non potest tamen subsistere ipse iure. *Postquam tamen ex abundanti, et appellationem tibi constat esse porrectam, mirati sumus, cur nec homines, qui tui iuris potuissent rationem reddere transmisisti.*" *Cf.* c. 1, X, *de constitionibus,* I, 2; c. 1, *de sententia et re iudicata,* II, 14 in VI°.

[10] S. R. R., *Nullit. Matrim.,* 3 Augusti, 1922, *Coram R. P. D., Francisco Solieri,* dec. XXVI, n. 4—*Decisiones,* XIV (1922), 244, 245.

not give a sentence based only on presumptive and conjectural proofs, but, owing to the difficult nature of an accusation of nullity, concede that the judges can draw moral certitude from conjectures, which is required for the giving of a sentence. With respect to testimony, one does not have infallible, but moral certitude. For it is the golden doctrine of St. Thomas,[11] that with respect to testimony, one does not have infallible, but moral certitude.[12] This is the common teaching which all canonists who consider this matter, especially Farinacius, Mascardus, Menochius, Sperellus, Baldus, Decius, Cardinal Tuschus, Bartolus and Leurenius.[13]

Nevertheless, the canon under consideration does not establish rules stating what testimony is evidence. The Code here restricts the wide power of the judge to a few rules of a general or special character.[14] They are the result of experience. By the use of them a judge can and ought to estimate the credibility of witnesses.[15] The criteria which follow are tentative or relative rather than absolute. They are not entirely conclusive in each instance. Because based on a practice of long duration, the directive norms which follow cannot be overlooked by the judge.[16]

The judge himself must evaluate the testimony presented to him; for it is the judge who estimates the sufficiency of proofs in each case.[17] From an examination of the testimony he forms his con-

[11] "Respondeo dicendum quod testimonium, sicut dictum est art. praec., non habet infallibilem certitudinem, sed probabilem. Et ideo quidquid est quod probabilitatem afferat in contrarium, reddit testimonium inefficax."—S. Thomas, *Summa,* 2-2ae, LXX, 3 c.

[12] *Cf.* S. R. R., *Nullit. Matrim.,* 21 Decembris, 1912, *Coram R. P. D., Michaele Lega,* dec. XXXI, n. 4—*Decisiones Coram Lega,* 354.

[13] *Cf.* B. Pellegrini, *De Intentione Boni Sacramenti Adversa Ejusdem Probatione In Iudicio Ad Normam,* Canon 1086, *Ius Pont.,* X (1930), 58, 59.

[14] Roberti, *De Processibus,* II, n. 354, p. 74.

[15] Eichmann, *Das Prozessrecht des Codex Iuris Canonici,* § 46, XII, p. 150.

[16] *Cf.* Augustine, *A Commentary,* VII, 236.

[17] S. R. R., *Nullit. Matrim.,* 17 Januarii, 1912, *Coram R. P. D., Michaele Lega,* dec. V, n. 24—*Decisiones,* IV (1912), 49: "In aestimando vero sufficientia probationis, plurimum relinquitur arbitrio iudicis, non quidem absoluto, sed

science not in an arbitrary manner but in accordance with rules dictated by the law and common sense.[18]

The Code reduced the criteria by which the value of testimony is measured to four: (1) the moral criterion, which directs attention especially to the subjective element of honesty which is necessary in every witness; (2) the mental criterion, which is also subjective, which seeks to find out especially the source of the knowledge of a witness; (3) the material criterion, which is objective, and focuses attention on the manner in which a witness gives his testimony; and (4) the numerical criterion, which is likewise objective. This ascertains whether a witness be alone in his testimony or others agree with him. The subjective as well as the objective testimonial elements must be considered as a person who is truthful can err without perceiving it himself.

Subjectively, the value of testimony accrues from a more or less perfect agreement between the observations really made by a witness concerning facts and the manifestations of them in court. By reasoning especially from the person of a witness and the way in which he testifies one infers the subjective value of an attestation.[19] These general norms, as indicated in the historical synopsis, are found in Roman Law, in the Decretals [20] and in the works of the canonists.

regulato, per textum notabilem, . . . Eum qui iudicat magis scire posse quanta fides habenda sit testibus." For an application of the principle to *vis et metus* cases, *cf.* S. R. R., *Nullit. Matrim.*, 16 Maii, 1912, *Coram R. P. D., Michaele Lega,* dec. XXII, n. 10—*Decisiones,* IV (1912), 270; S. R. R., *Avenionen., Nullit. Matrim.*, 14 Julii, 1914, *Coram R. P. D., Aloisio Sincero,* dec. XXV, n. 2—*Decisiones,* VI (1914), 271. For an application of the principle to a case involving adoption, *cf.* S. R. R., *Adoptionis,* 10 Junii, 1911, *Coram Patriarcatus Ritus Graeci-Catholici in Aegypto,* dec. XXIII, n. 19—*Decisiones,* III (1911), 252. *Cf.* also S. R. R., *Nullit. Matrim.*, 31 Martii, 1922, *Coram R. P. D., Maximo Massimi,* dec. IX, n. 3—*Decisiones,* XIV (1922), 79; S. R. R., *Nullit. Matrim,* 1 Augusti, 1913, *Coram R. P. D., Michaele Lega,* dec. XXXIX, n. 10—*Decisiones Coram Lega,* 484.

[18] A Coronata, *De Processibus,* III, n. 1316, p. 223.

[19] *Cf.* Roberti, *De Processibus,* II, n. 354, p. 74.

[20] *Cf.* also c. 33, X, *de testibus et attestationibus,* II, 20; S. C. de Prop. Fide, Instr., a. 1883—*Coll.*, n. 1587.

Atricle 2. Criteria to be Used by the Judge in Estimating the Value of Testimony

Canon 1789. In aestimandis testimoniis iudex prae oculis habeat:

1°. Quae conditio sit personae, quaeve honestas et an aliqua dignitate testis praefulgeat;

2°. Utrum de scientia propria, praesertim de visu et auditu proprio testificetur, an de credulitate, de fama, aut de auditu ab aliis;

3°. Utrum testis constans sit et firmiter sibi cohaereat; an varius, incertus, vel vacillans;

4°. Denique utrum testimonii contestes habeat, an sit singularis.

A. Condition as a Moral Criterion of the Value of Testimony

1. *Legal Meaning of Condition*—"Quae conditio sit personae . . . " The first of the subjective criteria for evaluating testimony is the condition of a witness. As the character and dignity of a person should, according to this canon, be taken into consideration, the subjective element pointed out by the legislator is a moral one.

The word "condition" is indefinite. It has been interpreted to mean the following:

a. *Condition as Status.* Both Augustine [21] and A Coronata [22] are of the opinion that status means ecclesiastical or lay, and in laymen vocation. Attention is here restricted to this interpretation of the word.

It is observed that there are copious examples found in the authors and in the practice of the Roman and Spanish Rotae which have a bearing on the value of the attestations of persons whose status presupposes a greater intelligence and consequently a more exact knowledge of the facts on which they base their testimony. In practice, however, the testimonial element of condition is not isolated and

[21] *Cf.* Augustine, *A Commentary,* VII, 237.

[22] *Cf.* A Coronata, *De Processibus,* III, n. 1317, p. 223. A Coronata adds that status also means the celibate or the matrimonial. As this may be confusing and as he merely states this without explaining his meaning, it is omitted.

considered by itself. It becomes merely incidental to the procedure. Hence, from a practical point of view, in the matrimonial process the testimony of a witness who is viewed from the aspect of his status is not entirely considered from that viewpoint in the procedure of proof. When a priest, for example, testifies that an interpellation or a dispensation was granted or when he testifies about a marriage contracted before him which is impugned, his testimony is usually secondary to the proof of impediment, dispensation or interpellation which is found in the registers of the parish.

b. *Condition as Character.* The moral criterion of "condition" for determining the probative value of testimony has been thought to suggest whether a witness be cultured or rude, and adult or a minor, etc.[23] It has also been considered to mean whether a witness be man or woman,[24] of noble rank or a plebeian, rich or poor.[25] Augustine [26] and Haring [27] properly observe that the word "condition" also includes character as a witness.

Under character are included all the tendencies of a person's mind which, originally existing in or developed from his personality, are made known to himself by the thoughts, feelings and volitions which those tendencies reveal to his consciousness. These tendencies can be known by other persons only by observing the effects of them in the words which a person utters and the acts which he does. Character is contrasted with either habit or mere emotion and feeling in that character is permanent whereas habit and emotion or feeling are not necessarily permanent. In judicial proof habit and character, although they are not sharply distinguished, represent distinct qualities.

2. *Condition According to the Wording of the Canon*—" . . . quaeve honestas et an aliqua dignitate testis praefulgeat . . . " Because the term "condition" may have various meanings, the canon

[23] *Cf.* Roberti, *De Processibus,* II, n. 354, p. 74. The topic "*aetas*" was considered under Canon 1774.

[24] Sex as a testimonial criterion was considered under Canon 1774.

[25] *Cf.* Noval, *De Processibus,* IV, n. 509, p. 351. For practical purposes this was considered under the word *dignitas.*

[26] Augustine, *A Commentary,* VII, p. 237; *cf.* Canon 1757, §§ 1, 3.

[27] Haring, *Der Kirchliche Eheprozes,* p. 32.

adds the elements honesty and dignity, thereby directing the judge to take cognizance of the honesty and the dignity of a witness.

a. *Honesty as Evidence of Human Condition.* Honesty properly refers to the moral qualities of the person. The law itself, as already seen in the chapter on the qualifications of witnesses in Canon Law, not merely excludes some persons from being witnesses because of their dishonesty and condition, but also states that were such witnesses perchance admitted, they do not enjoy full credibility.[28] The testimony of a witness whose moral reputation is irreproachable is manifestly superior in value to that of a person with a bad reputation.

The Code does not restrict the judge to establish a defendant's character by his specific acts which are considered decisive of tendency and which are attested by witnesses. Evidence of specific acts is admissible; but the judge may enter into a collateral inquiry regarding the circumstances surrounding the acts, so that he will not be led to conclude unfairly that because of a single past act the person necessarily has a bad disposition. It is the practice of the Roman Rota, for example, to require that in the proof of simulated consent resultant from "force and fear" there should be witnesses present who testify to the character of the person or persons alleged to have employed force and fear to bring about a marriage. Conjectures and other circumstances are necessary to the proof of such simulated consent.[29]

As the testimonial proof of "force and fear" will be referred to repeatedly, the following outline may help one to see at a glance the procedure of the testimonial proof of vitiated consent due to force and fear:

Cause of it to be proved first, *i. e.*, as expressed before pastor and witnesses.

[28] *Cf.* Canons, 1757, 1758.

[29] S. R. R., *Nullitatis vel Dispensationis Matrimonii*, 27 Aprilis, 1915, *Coram R. P. D., Iosepho Mori*, dec. XIX, n. 4—*Decisiones*, VII (1915), 209, 210; S. R. R., *Nullit. Matrim.*, 19 Junii, 1915, *Coram R. P. D., Friderico Cattani Amadori*, dec. XXIII, n. 4—*Decisiones*, VII (1915), 245-256; S. R. R., *Nullit. Matrim., Nicien.*, 30 Decembris, 1915, *Coram R. P. D., Petro Rossetti*, dec. XLII, n. 4—*Decisiones*, VII (1915), 468.

This impossible, prove by conjectures or circumstances before, during, after marriage.

On part of Parents, etc.

Threats, entreaties,

Hostile actions.

On part of Plaintiff,

Constant opposition.

Proof of Cause. For the proof of simulated consent its cause must be first proved. In the external forum the proof of conditioned consent is difficult unless the condition were expressed before the pastor and witnesses.[30] To establish the cause or reason for simulating, fear itself would not suffice to annul a marriage already contracted.[31] To prove the simulation, however, the cause for simulating which has to be established, must be proportionate,[32] for a woman is presumed to possess juridical liberty and not to be obsessed by reverential fear if she be no longer a child. Moreover, a pious and honest mother with only one daughter is not to be considered as desirous of forcing her daughter into a marriage because she wants what money she has.[33]

Proof by Conjectures or Circumstances. Secondly, besides proving the cause of the simulation, the simulation itself is proved by conjectures, or by circumstances. Ordinarily, the gravity of reverential fear is proved by the threats, upbraidings, importunate entreaties, the indignation of parents, and the like.[34] There are so many varieties of these conjectures that the law has not certainly de-

[30] *Cf.* S. R. R., *Nullit. Matrim.*, 20 Maii, 1912, *Coram R. P. D., Ioanne Prior*, dec. XX, n. 12—*Decisiones*, IV (1912), 12, 13.

[31] *Cf.* S. R. R., *Nullit. Matrim.*, 22 Februarii, 1919, *Coram R. P. D., Ioanne Prior*, dec. IV, n. 3—*Decisiones*, XI (1919), 38.

[32] S. R. R., *Nullit. Matrim., Oregonopolitana*, 6 Julii, 1914, *Coram R. P. D., Ioanne Prior*, dec. XXII, n. 5—*Decisiones*, VI (1914), 246.

[33] S. R. R., *Nullit. Matrim.*, 1 Augusti, 1913, *Coram R. P. D., Michaele Lega*, dec. XXXIX, n. 12—*Decisiones Coram Lega*, 485.

[34] S. R. R., *Nullit. Matrim.*, 29 Novembris, 1913, *Coram R. P. D., Ioanne Prior*, dec. L, n. 6—*Decisiones*, V (1913), 614, 615; S. R. R., *Nullit. Matrim., Transylvanien*, 1 Maii, 1912, *Coram R. P. D., Ioanne Prior*, dec. XVIII, n. 5—*Decisiones*, IV (1912), 216; S. R. R., *Avenionen., Nullit. Matrim.*, 14 Julii, 1914, *Coram, R. P. D., Aloisio Sincero*, dec. XXV, n. 2—*Decisiones*, VI (1914), 269-271.

fined them. The quality of the conjectures and the value of their proof is left to the judge.[85] As a simple juridical rule to be followed cannot be given in a concrete case, the judge forms his opinion by considering circumstances antecedent to, concomitant with and subsequent to the simulation itself. From the total complex of circumstances he reasons to a conclusion about the state of the person's mind who allegedly married under the influence of fear.[86] The simulated consent is proved by definite statements and precise conjectures or circumstances that preceded, which accompanied and which followed the marriage.[87]

Turning from these observations concerning the proof of simulated consent to honesty as evidence of human condition, with regard to such persons as the excommunicated, the infamous, perjurers, and the like, these may not be excluded from testifying before a sentence has been passed concerning them.[88] It is left to the

[85] S. R. R., *Nullit. Matrim., Nicien.*, 11 Junii, 1920, *Coram R. P. D., Petro Rossetti*, dec. XV, n. 6—*Decisiones*, XII (1920), 132; S. R. R., *Parisien. Nullit. Matrim.*, 1 Julii, 1920, *Coram R. P. D., Ioanne Prior*, dec. XIX, n. 2—*Decisiones*, XII (1920), 181.

[86] S. R. R., *Nullit. Matrim.*, 22 Februarii, 1919, *Coram R. P. D., Ioanne Prior*, dec. IV, n. 10—*Decisiones*, XI (1919), 43-45; S. R. R., *Parisien. Nullit. Matrim.*, 1 Julii, 1920, *Coram R. P. D., Ioanne Prior*, dec. XIX, n. 2—*Decisiones*, XII (1920), 181; *cf.* S. C. S. Off., Instr., *ad Ep. Rituum Orient.*, a. 1883—*Fontes*, n. 1076.

[87] S. R. R., *Nullit. Matrim.*, 9 Julii, 1911, *Coram Ioanne Prior*, dec. XXII, n. 8—*Decisiones*, III (1911), 241; S. R. R., *Massilien, Nullit. Matrim.*, 1 Julii, 1911, *Coram R. P. D., Gulielmo Sebastianelli*, dec. XXIX, nn. 6, 7, 8—*Decisiones*, III (1911), 329, 330; S. R. R., *Nullit. Matrim.*, 9 Aprilis, 1921, *Coram R. P. D., Ioanne Prior*, dec. VII, n. 2—*Decisiones*, XIII (1921), 72, 73; S. R. R., *Parisien., Nullit. Matrim.*, 10 Martii, 1920, *Coram R. P. D., Friderico Cattani Amadori*, dec. VII, n. 2—*Decisiones*, XII (1920), 47, 48; S. R. R., *Nullit. Matrim.*, 16 Martii, 1920, *Coram R. P. D., Maximo Massimi*, dec. IX, n. 6—*Decisiones*, XII (1920), 66; S. R. R., *Nullit. Matrim.*, 18 Maii, 1922, *Coram R. P. D., Iulio Grazioli*, dec. XVII, n. 13—*Decisiones*, XIV (1922), 147; S. R. R., *Nullit. Matrim.*, 16 Augusti, 1922, *Coram R. P. D., Maximo Massimi*, dec. XXXIII, n. 3—*Decisiones*, XIV (1922), 309.

[88] The excommunicated publicly designated by a declaratory or condemnatory sentence can appear in court personally only to impugn the justice and legitimacy of his excommunication. *Cf.* Canons 1654, § 1; 1628, § 3. As

judge to decide from circumstances and from the nature of the cause whether such enjoy any credibility and how far it extends.[39]

b. *Dignity as Corroborative Evidence of Human Condition.* Dignity as evidence of human quality or condition refers not merely to ecclesiastical but also to civic dignity.[40] The legal relevancy of this criterion rests on the assumption that those who, especially by reason of their own merit, have been promoted to an exalted position are both better qualified to perceive and to relate what came under their observation, and are also more deserving of belief when they assert something. In order to prove the credibility of a witness it was permitted to indicate the standing or rank of a witness in the extraordinary period of Roman Law [41] and in the *Corpus Juris Canonici.*[42]

Viewed from a positive aspect, the credibility of a witness is enhanced the higher his position or station in life is.[43] The judge can, nevertheless, require more evidence if the importance of the matter demands it or if there are indications which insinuate doubt regarding what has been asserted. One person furnishes full evidence when he

a witness such a one is repelled as suspect. *Cf.* Canon 1757, § 2, Chelodi, *Ius Poenale,* n. 38, p. 47.

[39] *Cf.* Ferraris, *Bibliotheca Canonica,* VII, v. "Testis," art. I, n. 7, pp. 459, 460.

[40] *Cf.* Augustine, *A Commentary,* VII, 237; Noval, *De Processibus,* IV, n. 510, p. 351; A Coronata, *De Processibus,* III, n. 1317, pp. 223, 224.

[41] "Testium fides diligenter examinanda est. Ideoque in persona eorum exploranda erunt in primis condicio cuiusque, *utrum quis decurio an plebeius sit:* et an honestae et inculpatae vitae an vero notatus quis et reprehensibilis: an locuples vel egens sit, ut lucri causa quid facile admittat: vel an inimicus ei sit, adversus quem testimonium fert, vel amicus ei sit, pro quo testimonium dat. Nam si careat suspicione testimonium vel propter personam a quo fertur (quod honesta sit) vel propter causam (quod neque lucri neque gratiae neque inimicitiae causa fit) admittendus." *Callistratus,* D. XXII, 5, 3. "In testimoniis autem dignitas fides mores gravitas examinanda est: et ideo testes, qui adversus fidem suae testationis vacillant, audiendi non sunt."—*Modestinus,* D. XXII, V. 2.

[42] ". . . utrum decurio an plebeius sit."—c. 3, C. IV, q. 2 et 3. *Cf.* "Conditione, si liber, non servus. Nam saepe servus metu dominantis testimonium supprimit veritatis."—Isadori Hispalensis, *Episcopi Etymologiarum sive Originum, M.P.L.,* XVIII, 15, col. 551.

[43] Eichmann, *Das Prozessrecht des Codex Iuris Canonici,* § 46, XII, p. 150.

is qualified to testify about official business. Provided that rules of law do not forbid, the judge is at liberty to estimate the evidence.[44]

Viewed, however, from a negative aspect, no single witness enjoys full credence unless he testify as a qualified witness against whom no exception can be taken.[45] The rule, nevertheless, suffers exception when applied to the narrative words of the Roman Pontiff regarding things done by himself. Direct proof should not be admitted against such facts if the Holy Father establishes His intention upon them.[46] What was said applies to utterances of a king, an emperor, a civil prince.[47] From a negative aspect, a pastor, although he has a juridical status, is not a credible witness when testifying on his own behalf. In the practice of the Roman Rota, such a witness derives no advantage from his station when he attests that he had questioned the spouses before their marriage or states something else pertaining to the validity of it. The practice of the Roman Rota is thus summarized:

> Nam longissime distat agere causam propriam, in eaque testimonium ferre a testimonio lato de actu a se gesto. Quodsi officialis aut minister publicus testimonium ferens de actu ab ipso gesto, ratione officii sui, esset testis in causa propria, iam actum esset de publicis muneribus seu officiis.[48]

[44] Canon 1869, § 3; *cf.* Haring, *Der Kirchliche Eheprozess,* 31.

[45] Canons 1791, § 1; 239, § 1, 17°. *Cf.* A Coronata, *De Processibus,* III, n. 1318, p. 224; Ferraris, *Bibliotheca,* "Testis," art. II, n. 5, p. 459; Wernz-Vidal, VI, *De Processibus,* n. 483, p. 423.

[46] If words and the fact are only incidental, the fact is referred to the Roman Pontiff, *e. g.,* an excommunicated or suspended person is not absolved because he was saluted in a letter, nor is exemption conceded because a rescript incidentally referred to a church as exempt. *Cf.* Reiffenstuel, *Ius Canonicum Universum,* lib. II, tit. XIX, nn. 103-111; lib. II, tit. XX, n. 278; A Coronata, *De Processibus,* III, n. 1317, p. 224.

[47] *Cf.* Reiffenstuel, *Ius Canonicum Universum,* lib. II, tit. XIX, n. 112; lib. II, tit. XX, n. 279.

[48] S. R. R., *Nullit. Matrim.,* 28 Augusti, 1911, *Coram R. P. D., Aloisio Sincero,* dec. XXXIX, n. 19—*Decisiones,* III (1911), 439.

B. *Source of Knowledge as a Mental Criterion of the Value of Testimony*

Canon 1789, 2°. Utrum de scientia propria, praesertim de visu et auditu proprio testificetur, an de credulitate, de fama, aut de auditu ab aliis.

The mental or intellectual value or weight of testimony must be measured according to suggestions contained in this canon. There are, however, two things which should be considered before one comments upon what is alluded to in the words of the legislator. The questions proposed to a witness are partly general and partly special.

Inquiries of a general nature pertain to the preliminary questions about the personal circumstances of a witness. They are made for the purpose of identifying the witness and to obtain an idea of his condition. Inquiry must be made regarding his full name, parentage, age, religion, profession or job, residence and his connection with the litigants. The last question will aid in ascertaining whether the witness has an "interest" in the cause or is a blood relative. Consequently, questions must be asked, such as: "Do you know the parties? How are you related to them?" etc.

Inquiries of a special nature pertain to the cause itself. The witness is to be asked for the source of his knowledge and how he derived a knowledge of the facts.[49] These special questions lead the judge into a further investigation, the topics of which are provided by the canon under consideration.

1. *Witnesses Testifying from Their Own Knowledge*

Witnesses who testify from their own knowledge are those who make an attestation about a thing which they perceived with their own senses. They are witnesses in the proper sense of the word and it is only they who properly bear witness to the truth.[50] Witnesses who testify from their own immediate knowledge are called wit-

[49] *Cf.* Canon 1774; Augustine, *A Commentary,* VII, p. 226.

[50] Reiffenstuel, *Ius Canonicum Universum,* lib. II, tit. XX, nn. 342, 343; *ibid.*, n. 342: "Testes de scientia dicuntur illi, qui deponunt, proprio sensu corporeo, *v. g.*, visu, vel auditu eam perceperint."

nesses "de visu vel de auditu proprio" inasmuch as they testify to what they have seen or heard.[51]

In matrimonial procedure, witnesses should have not only veracity but knowledge.[52] Witnesses who have perceived something with their own senses enjoy excellent credibility.[53] On the other hand, witnesses testifying to a fact that came within the scope of their personal observation must not be believed and their attestations do not have value in the following circumstances: First, when their testimony suffers many exceptions.[54] Secondly, when they testify about an occurrence which happened at some remote time.[55] Archbishop Muniz provides an illustration of this principle. Writing about the proof of the impediment of disparity of cult he refers to the caution to be taken in the proof of a baptism. He provides the following practical case.[56] Some peddlers left a girl named Jane, who was about six years of age, when they abandoned a town. Nobody claimed

[51] *Cf.* A Coronata, *De Processibus,* III, n. 1318, p. 224; Noval, *De Processibus,* IV, n. 510, p. 351; Eichmann, *Das Prozessrecht des Codex Iuris Canonici,* § 46, XII, p. 150.

[52] S. R. R., *Nullit. Matrim.,* 30 Novembris, 1921, *Coram R. P. D., Ioanne Prior,* dec. XXIX, n. 6—*Decisiones,* XIII (1921), 276.

[53] *Cf.* S. R. R., *Nicien., Nullit. Matrim.,* 30 Decembris, 1915, *Coram R. P. D., Petro Rossetti,* dec. XLII, n. 9—*Decisiones,* VII (1915), 469. A woman servant in a force and fear case testified to what she saw and heard and to having been struck for speaking to plaintiff. *Cf.* S. R. R., *Nullit. Matrim.* 16 Maii, 1912, *Coram R. P. D., Michaele Lega,* dec. XXIV, n. 3—*Decisiones Coram Lega,* 294. In an affinity case from *copula illicita,* eye witnesses testified. *Cf.* S. R. R., *Nullit. Matrim.* (day and month not mentioned), 1909, *Coram R. P. D., Seraphino Many,* dec. III, n. 3—*Decisiones Coram Lega,* 25, 26. In a *turpis conditio* case, witness *de scientia* testified. *Cf.* S. R. R., *Nullit. Matrim.,* 17 Januarii, 1912, *Coram R. P. D., Michaele Lega,* dec. XX, n. 17—*Decisiones Coram Lega,* 256, 257. Eyewitnesses of an immemorial custom aid to prove the fact of it. *Cf.* S. R. R., *Segusina. Iuris Canendi Missas Adventuias,* 12 Julii, 1913, *Coram R. P. D., Antonio Parathoner,* dec. XXXVI, n. 3—*Decisiones,* V (1913), 434.

[54] S. R. R., *Nullit. Matrim.,* 25 Februarii, 1911, *Coram R. P. D., Iosepho Mori,* dec. X, n. 12—*Decisiones,* III (1911), 101.

[55] *Ibid.:* "Omisso enim quod testificatio in themate respicit factum remotissimi temporis seu fere a vicennio secutum, de quo facile praesumitur oblivio in teste iuxta Rotam Oriolo, dec. 86, n. 7 . . ."

[56] Muniz, *Procedimientos Eclesiásticos,* II, n. 204, 2°, pp. 242, 243; *cf. ibid.,* II, n. 270, pp. 326, 327.

her. Twenty years having passed by, she wanted to marry. It had occurred to nobody that she was not baptized. When the pastor needed the baptismal record for the marriage the case was submitted to the curia. The Ordinary ordered an investigation. Jane was asked what she recalled regarding her parents, place of birth, Godparents, places she had been in, the classes of persons who left her, the reasons for the abandonment and all other circumstances of her former life. The woman herself did not know what to say. She testified that she had been called Jane, that she had visited many towns, small and large, and that those who abandoned her frequently abused her. The ill treatment which she had received led her to suspect that those who kept her were not her parents.

The Ordinary directed that the persons who took the girl and the neighbors with whom she was associated during her childhood he questioned. The neighbors added no more details. They attested that the peddlers were not seen in the town before or since that time. What the woman said regarding herself was so vague that, in the opinion of Archbishop Muniz, cases similar to this one should be settled as cases of exposed children. Conditional baptism is to be administered to persons who were foundlings and whose early life is unknown. The baptism is to be recorded as the baptism of unknown parents. The circumstances of the abandonment and the approximate age are also to be put in the record.

Thirdly, witnesses must not be believed and their testimony is without value when they testify not about the facts which they perceived but about any legal element involved in the case. The Roman Rota called the attention of a diocesan curia to the fact that it had asked questions not only regarding controverted facts personally known by the witnesses but had even inquired about the opinion of witnesses on the validity of a marriage and liberty of the woman's consent. This, observed the Rota, was a violation of a fundamental rule in law, "testes fidem facere de *factis,* sed non esse iudices de *merito* causae." [57]

So much for the rules guiding a judge in estimating the value of

[57] S. R. R., *Petrocoricen. Nullit. Matrim.,* 27 Augusti, 1912, *Coram, R. P. D., Michaele Lega,* dec. XXVIII, n. 8—*Decisiones Coram Lega,* 339.

witnesses who testify from their own knowledge or experience. Matrimonial procedure affords many examples of the application of the principles.[58]

2. *Witnesses Testifying from What They Believe to be True*

a. *Testimony Based on Credulity*—" . . . an de credulitate . . . " Witnesses whom the canon refers to as *de credulitate* attest that they believe something is a fact or that something is to be concluded from conjectures and circumstantial evidence the value of which is enhanced by presumption in favor of it. Those persons who rashly believe anything are not reliable witnesses,[59] because they testify that they believe something happened in such a way and their belief arises from various arguments and presumptions.[60] As these persons derive their knowledge mediately, that is by deducation from reasoning or from conjectures,[61] the question how they obtained their information naturally suggests itself. The judge is entitled to know the source from which a witness obtained his knowledge; asked concerning it, a witness is obliged to answer.[62]

The testimony of witnesses who rashly believe anything is devoid of probative value because their information is not derived from their own knowledge or observation. Durandus and Johannes Andreae expressed the principle in these words: "Itaque qui deposuit de credulitate, non de scientia, unde non valet: ut in praecedente

[58] "D'une manière générale, les temoins *de scientia,* dans les affaires de non-consummation, sont ceux qui ont su, en temps utile, de l'un ou l'autre des conjoints, ou des deux, que le mariage n'etait pas consommeé pour telle ou telle raison, et qui connaissent plus ou moins complètement les faits et circonstances du mariage, de la vie commune, de la séparation, etc."—Lanier, Henri, *Guide Pratique De La Procédure Matrimoniale En Droit Canonique* (Paris, 1927), p. 41. For an application of the principles to the presumed death of a spouse, see Chapter X, supra.

[59] *Cf.* c. 37, X, *de testibus et attestationibus,* II, 20; Reiffenstuel, *op. cit.,* lib. II, tit. XX, n. 345; Augustine, *A Commentary,* VII, 227; A Coronata, *De Processibus,* III, n. 1318, p. 224.

[60] S. R. R., *Nullit. Matrim.,* 10 Decembris, 1914, *Coram, R. P. D., Ioanne Prior,* dec. XXXIII, n. 26—*Decisiones,* VI (1914), 353.

[61] *Cf.* Noval, *De Processibus,* IV, n. 510, p. 351.

[62] Reiffenstuel, *Ius Canonicum Universum,* lib. II, tit. XX, nn. 511, 512.

capite relatum . . . : quia non valet testimonium de alieno auditu . . . "[63] The general principle expressed by Durandus and Johannes Andreae is borne out in the present practice of the Roman Rota to such an extent that generally speaking the testimony of such persons does not enjoy credence. Witnesses attesting to what they believe took place do not enjoy any more credence than the unimportant incidents or circumstances upon which the testimony rests.[64]

b. *Testimony Based on Rumor*—" . . . de fama . . . " Rumor is a possible source of inaccuracy and untruthworthiness. The judge is, therefore, reminded by the words *"de fama"* to test the assertion of a witness, if it be deemed necessary, to find out whether it is based on an unfounded rumor or upon an ultimate fact.

For practical purposes, rumor means the common opinion regarding some person or fact entertained by all or by the majority of the people of a city or town.[65] With Reiffenstuel [66] one should distinguish two kinds of rumor. The first, which is properly called rumor (*fama*), exists when a whole city, village or majority of the populace asserts something. The second kind (*rumor*) is present when a minority, whether a half, or a third, or a fourth of the people say that something is so. The first kind, rumor properly so called, proceeds usually from definite and reliable persons who tell a group of people that they were present when something took place. The second kind originates from an uncertain source or author. It proves less than rumor in the strict meaning of the term. Rumor (*fama*) in the better denotation of the word is an assertion which is common to the majority of persons in a city or town. Rumor (*rumor*) in the wider connotation of the word, being something said by a few persons, proves nothing if there is absolutely no positive value to their evidence. It merely induces a suspicion and a presumption.

[63] Gulielmus Durandus cum Ioannes Andreae Baldi, *Speculum Iuris* (Venetiis, apud Iuntas, 1577), lib. I, part IV, *de Teste,* n. 58.

[64] *Cf.* S. R. R., *Nicien. Nullit. Matrim.,* 30 Decembris, 1915, *Coram R. P. D., Petro Rossetti,* dec. XLII, n. 9—*Decisiones,* VII (1915), 469, 470.

[65] *Cf.* "Fama est communis opinio voce manifestata, ex suspicione proveniens."—Reiffenstuel, *Ius Canonicum Universum,* lib. II, tit. XX, n. 384; A Coronata, *De Processibus,* III, n. 1318, p. 224.

[66] *Cf.* Reiffenstuel, *Ius Canonicum Universum,* lib. II, tit. XX, n. 392.

In the present Canon Law, rumor by itself merely creates a presumption and not full proof if it is spread by and among prudent men.[67] In either case the origin of the rumor must be investigated. If the person or persons who started it cannot be found out, the rumor is to be disregarded.[68]

Regarding the value of the testimony resting on rumor, it may be said that the credibility of a witness is enhanced "when the witness testifies to what he saw and heard and not merely to what he believes and heard from hearsay or rumors and probabilities and provided that the witness is steadfast and unwavering in his assertions."[69] As a general rule, rumor is not a valid reason with which to establish anything. Nevertheless, it may be used in certain circumstances and especially in matters difficult to prove,[70] provided that the source of the rumor is traced and is legitimately established and proved; in which case the rumor fully proves what is difficult of proof.[71] In matrimonial procedure, proof afforded by rumor must, to constitute juridical proof, be uniform, constant and perpetual. The rumor must not be vague or contrary.[72] The rumor can be truly consistent, common, constant and indicative of the public judgment. It can be an opinion which can be substantiated by at least two witnesses against whom no exception can be taken (*omni exceptione maiores*). The rumor has the force of full proof when two witnesses testify that the community believed the fact existed from what they had heard.[73] The value of the proof afforded by a rumor attested to by

[67] S. R. R., *Impedimenti ad Contrahendum.*, 11 Martii, 1910 *Coram R. P. D., Gustavo Persiani,* dec. X, n. 13—*Decisiones,* II (1910), 100. *Cf.* Crotus, Ioannes a Monteferrato, *Tractatus De Testibus,* Pars VII, nn. 121-124, fol. 284.

[68] *Cf.* Wernz-Vidal, VI, *De Processibus,* n. 484, pp. 425, 426; A Coronata, *De Processibus,* III, n. 1318, p. 225; Augustine, *A Commentary,* VII, 227, 228.

[69] Translated from Eichmann, *Das Prozessrecht des Codex Iuris Canonici,* § 46, XII, 150.

[70] S. R. R., *Nullit. Matrim.,* 23 Decembris, 1922, *Coram R. P. D., Raphaele Chimenti,* dec. XXXIX, n. 11—*Decisiones,* XIV (1922), 359.

[71] S. R. R., *Nullit. Matrim.,* 12 Novembris, 1921, *Coram R. P. D., Ioanne Prior,* dec. XXVIII, n. 4—*Decisiones,* XIII (1921), 265.

[72] *Ibid.,* pp. 265, 266.

[73] S. R. R., *Impedimenti ad Contrahendum.,* 11 Martii, 1910, *Coram R. P. D.,*

two such witnesses makes half proof (*semi-plena probatio*) when the witnesses give the reason for their knowledge and their statement; when other circumstances (*adminicula*) are added to the rumor it makes full proof.[74] The rumor is weakened in value if contrary proof brought against it is stronger than the proof of the rumor itself.[75]

Having seen what is meant by rumor and indicated the principles used for the evaluation of testimonial evidence relying upon it, the application of the principles to matrimonial procedure will now be briefly indicated.

(1) *Impediment of Ligamen.* The impediment of previous and existing bond is mentioned in Canon 1069, § 1.[76] That the impediment of *ligamen* arise, the marriage must have been objectively and certainly valid and still remain undissolved. Canon 1069, § 2, states the manner in which one should proceed with reference to this impediment in the case of the presumed death of a married party, which subject is again considered from the aspect of testimony resting on rumor.[77] The ecclesiastical law requires that in every case the invalidity or dissolution of the previous marriage be certainly established before another marriage is contracted. The invalidity or disso-

Gustavo Persiani, dec. X, n. 13—*Decisiones,* II (1910), 100; *cf.* also Reiffenstuel *Ius Canonicum Universum,* lib. II, tit. XX, nn. 393-395; S. R. R., *Nullit. Matrim.,* 12 Novembris, 1921, *Coram R. P. D., Ioanne Prior,* Dec. XXVIII, n. 4—*Decisiones,* XIII (1921), 265. *Cf.* Crotus, Ioannes a Monteferrato, *Tractatus De Testibus,* Pars VIII, nn. 13, 14, 16, fol. 306, 307.

[74] S. R. R., *Nullit. Matrim.,* 22 Februarii, 1921, *Coram R. P. D., Ioanne Prior,* dec. I, n. 6—*Decisiones,* XIII (1921), n. 7; S. R. R., *Nullit. Matrim.,* 12 Novembris, 1921, *Coram R. P. D., Ioanne Prior,* dec. XXVII, n. 4—*Decisiones,* XIII (1921), 265. Public rumor with other circumstances by themselves are incomplete or half-full proof, but united are full proof of affinity from *copula illicita. Cf.* S. R. R., *Nullit. Matrim.,* 10 Februarii, 1912, *Coram R. P. D., Friderico Cattani Amadori,* dec. VIII, n. 6—*Decisiones,* IV (1912), 87, 88.

[75] *Cf.* S. R. R., *Imperimenti ad Contrahendum,* 11 Martii, 1910, *Coram R. P. D., Gustavo Persiani,* dec. X, n. 15—*Decisiones,* II (1910), 102, 103. *Cf.* Reiffenstuel, *Ius Canonicum Universum,* lib. II, tit. XII, nn. 233-237.

[76] Canon 1069, § 1: "Invalide matrimonium attentat qui vinculo tenetur prioris matrimonii, quanquam non consummati, salvo privilegio fidei."

[77] *Cf.* Canon 1069, § 2: "Quamvis prius matrimonium sit irritum aut solutum qualibet ex causa, non ideo licet aliud contrahere, antequam de prioris nullitate aut solutione legitime et certo constiterit."

lution ought to be legitimately or legally established by either a dispensation from a marriage ratified and unconsummated or by the death of one of the spouses. To contract a second marriage it is necessary that the death of the first spouse be established. This is done by a declaration of the legally competent authority of the Church. It is expedient that the investigation of the presumed death be conducted by the diocesan curia in an administrative manner. Nothing, however, prevents it from being done in a judicial way. Nevertheless, when the investigation is conducted in an administrative manner, or when the fact of death or the declaration of the fact is thrashed out judicially, strict adherence to the rigid regulations of evidence need not be necessary. Although the defender of the marriage bond is present, his presence is not necessary,[78] and he is not obliged to appeal as he must do in matrimonial causes.

A special rule for the proof of the presumed death of a spouse which properly belongs in this place is that the proof afforded by rumor is not very strong by itself to prove the presumed death of an absent spouse. Nevertheless, together with some other proofs which may even be incomplete (*semi-plena*), the proof by rumor can be a sufficient motive for the declaration of the death of the married person. The existence of the rumor or a general belief that the spouse is dead has to be strengthened by the attestations of two credible witnesses who also make a declaration regarding what they consider is the reasonable source of the rumor. If they heard it from a majority of people who are prudent, credence is given to the rumor provided that it was not spread by persons who are themselves parties interested in the death of the spouse, *e. g.*, the surviving spouse or the person with whom the living spouse wants to contract marriage.[79]

[78] *Cf. Sacra C. Concilii,* 14 Decembris, 1889, *Wratislavien, Dubium Matrimonii—A. S. S.,* XXII (1889-1890), 546-554, esp. 553, 554, which are the conclusions of the editor, *viz.*—"Exquibus colliges: I. Defensorem s. vinculi requiri quando res de causis, quae aguntur super matrimoniorum validitate, seu nullitate; seu quando aliquis ex coniugibus instantiam porrigit super nullitate matrimonii; non autem de eorum existentia. II. Probationem status liberi faciendam esse sine strepitu iudicii a iudice ecclesiastico, prudenti iudicio, attentis omnibus circumstantiis locorum et personarum." *Cf.* Linneborn, *Gundriss Des Eherechts,* § 24, III, 1, p. 233; Knecht, *Handbuch,* § 32, b, p. 380.

[79] Muniz, *Procedimientos Eclesiásticos,* II, n. 262, p. 313.

Should doubt regarding the death of the spouse remain and the Ordinary should not want to declare the death of the missing spouse, the information gathered on the case must be forwarded to the Sacred Congregation of the Sacraments. If, however, the cause was considered in a judicial way the appeal is taken to the metropolitan.[80]

(2) *Impediment of Violent Abduction.* In the impediment of abduction (*raptus*),[81] the crime of rape is to be distinguished from the impediment of abduction.[82] A criminal action resultant from violent abduction may cease in five years by prescription [83] whereas the impediment may remain.[84] Hence, there is a difference between criminal rape and the term employed by the Code. Moreover, although some authors do not clearly state it, the Code extends the force of the impediment of rape to the sequestration of a woman, which is not, properly speaking, rape. Violence alone suffices for the existence of the impediment. Consequently, it makes little difference whether the woman consent so long as there are conditions which constitute the impediment.

The proof of this impediment presents serious difficulty in the external forum. This is due to the necessity of establishing a relation between the intention to contract marriage and the violent abduction or the detention of the woman in a place that is not safe. If the woman did not return to the place from which she was abducted, it is presumed that some violence was used to restrain her notwithstanding anything that may be adduced to the contrary.

It was pointed out that the confession of the principals is worthless unless the woman be placed in a safe place. The abduction or the violent retention can be established in the following manner:

(a) If the woman affirms it. Her statement about the first union is believed without the need of any more proofs.

[80] *Ibid.*, n. 263, pp. 313, 314.

[81] *Cf.* Canon 1074.

[82] *Cf.* Canon 2353; Reiffenstuel, *Ius Canonicum Universum,* lib. V, tit. XVII, n. 58; Chelodi, *Ius Poenale,* n. 81, 2, p. 109; n. 82, 2, p. 110; Augustine, *A Commentary,* V, pp. 192, 193.

[83] *Cf.* Canon 1703, 2°.

[84] *Cf.* Canon 1074, § 2.

(b) If the witnesses worthy of credence testify to the existence of the abduction, credence is given to them. In this case, if both the one who perpetrated the abduction and the victim of the abduction deny the fact, they must fulfill the requirements contained in the second paragraph of Canon 1074.[85] These requirements are that the woman and her abductor have separated, that the woman remains in a safe place, and according to the judgment of the Ordinary, or of the pastor or of witnesses worthy of credence, that she is actually free. When the woman is in a safe place and is free she must be examined regarding her willingness to contract the marriage.

(c) If there be no witnesses, but ony presumptions. Facts which may provide a basis for such a presumption are that the woman is away from the home of her parents or the place where she customarily lives; that there was flight, even though it does not appear to have been an abduction; that certain precautions are taken in the house where the woman is staying to prevent free communication between her and somebody outside that place. Public rumor circulating the information that the woman was forcibly detained is sufficient to lead to the presumption of abduction. Nevertheless, all of these and even more circumstances will be insufficient to affirm the existence of the impediment. These and kindred circumstances will be sufficient to fulfill the second paragraph of the canon to which reference was made.[86]

(3) *Impediment of Crime.* The impediment of crime [87] has been considered as either a penal or an inhabilitating law. Lest one be deceived, it is an inhabilitating law having a certain penalty annexed to it. Consequently, as it is to be considered also as a penal law, ignorance does not excuse from it. This is deduced from Canon 16, the common opinion of canonists and the mode of acting in the Roman curia, the Sacred Congregation of the Sacraments.

Briefly, there are four species of this impediment: (a) Adultery with promise of marriage; (b) Adultery with attempt at marriage;

[85] Canon 1074, § 2: "Quod si rapta, a raptore separata et in loco tuto ac libero constituta, illum in virum habere consenserit, impedimentum cessat."

[86] *Cf.* Muniz, *Procedimientos Eclesiásticos,* II, n. 294, pp. 352, 353. For the burden of proof in these cases, *cf.* Chapter VI.

[87] Canon 1075.

(c) Adultery with conjugicide; and (d) Conjugicide without adultery.[88] Attention is restricted to the second species of the impediment, adultery with attempt at marriage, to ascertain when rumor suffices for the proof of the impediment. The adultery of the contracting parties can be established because one of them was sentenced for adultery or by reason of the fact that they had lived in public concubinage. It can also be proved by the testimony of persons worthy of credence even though it had not been public. It is, likewise, proved either by the fact that their children were recorded as illegitimate or by strong presumptions. One must establish that this promise and the adultery existed simultaneously with the legal, legitimate marriage.

For this purpose one must consider that the promise of a future marriage can exist or may not exist when an adultery is a casual occurence. One must pay attention both to what the contracting parties said under oath before the celebration of the marriage and to the testimony of witnesses worthy of credence who testify to what they had heard the contracting parties say.

In habitual adultery, on the other hand, it is very probable that a promise of future marriage existed. This is a presumption of fact which is not destroyed by the oath of the contracting parties made *before* the celebration of the marriage. Some other proofs which destroy the presumption that a promise was made or which strengthen the oath of the parties are necessary. This is especially the case if the innocent spouse could not live very long because of age and illness. Among those proofs are the declaration of witnesses who affirm the absence of any indication of a promise and rumor.[89]

(4) *Impediment of Consanguinity.* This impediment is not defined in the Code. Various authors have given the traditional definition of it.[90] Marriage between any persons in the direct line is null and void. Legitimate and illegitimate children are embraced

[88] Canon 1075. *Cf.* Müssener, Herm., *Das Katholische Eherecht in Der Seelsorgspraxis* (Düsseldorf, 1933), p. 68.

[89] *Cf.* Muniz, *Procedimientos Ecclesiásticos*, II, n. 306, 2°, pp. 366, 367.

[90] "Vinculum personarum ab eodem stipite descendentium carnali propagatione contractum."—*Hostiensis, Commentaria,* lib. IV, tit. XIV, n. 1.

in the prohibition. In the collateral line, the impediment extends to and embraces those in the third degree.[91] The impediment exists even though only one of the parties is baptized.[92] Should one party be in the fourth degree, the relationship does not invalidate the marriage,[93] as long as there is no closer relationship.

The first part of the proof of this impediment is merely mechanical. If the baptismal records of the contracting parties show the names not only of the parents, but of the grandparents, it is frequently easy to establish the impediment by a comparison of the names and surnames. The two baptismal records are insufficient proofs if the impediment is in the remote degrees. Sometimes the records are not indications of the proof, because the surnames may be lost. This happens especially when the relationship comes through the female line. In such cases the parochial registers must be examined to identify the great-grandparents. Public rumor, uncommon surnames, and the small number of inhabitants in a town, in which almost all may easily be relatives are sufficient indications with which to begin the proofs. Public rumor that the contracting parties are relatives can also be the motive justifying the asking for records from other parishes. If no public rumor exists, or if there be no other circumstances which are grounds for suspicion, one can proceed to marry the persons.[94]

(5) *Impediment of Affinity.* According to the Code, affinity arises only from a valid marriage, whether it is ratified only, or ratified and consummated. It arises as well from a *matrimonium ratum tantum* as from a *matrimonium ratum et consummatum.* The impediment exists only between the husband and the blood relations of the wife, and between the wife and the blood relations of the husband. The blood relations of one of the parties are not related by affinity to those of the other party. The line and degree of relation-

[91] *Cf.* Canon 1076; Wahl, Francis X., *The Matrimonial Impediments of Consanguinity and Affinity* (The Catholic University of America Canon Law Studies, No. 90, 1934), pp. 20, 21.

[92] *Cf.* Canon 1036, § 3.

[93] Blat, Albert, *Commentarium Textus Codicis Juris Canonici* (Romae, 1921-1927), III, 590.

[24] *Cf.* Muniz, *Procedimientos Eclesiásticos,* II, n. 318, pp. 387, 388.

ship between the husband and the blood relations of the wife, are determined by the line and degree of consanguinity by which the wife and her blood relatives are related. This is also true of the relationship between the wife and the blood relations of the man.[95]

It was pointed out that documents and witnesses establish the proof of the presence of this impediment. The absence of the impediment, however, is established by general proofs. These are the negative results of the banns of marriage, the declaration of the spouses, the attestations of witnesses of the contracting parties, the sentence of nullity passed concerning the first marriage, the marginal note of the sentence which must be written in the marriage record and can be a particular proof. There are also other proofs which are provided by public rumor. Instructions published by the Holy See [96] state that public rumor can be of no light foundation in the proof of affinity. The origin of the rumor, and the reasons upon which it rests must, however, be carefully ascertained.[97]

(6) *Impediment of Legal Relationship Arising from Adoption.* In countries where legal parentage resulting from adoption renders a marriage illicit or invalid, Canon Law also declares the marriage illicit or invalid.[98] Whenever the proof of the impediment of legal relationship is to be established outside of a trial, in cases which concern a marriage which is going to be contracted, usually the impediment is so apparent that special proof for the demonstration of its absence is superfluous. Public rumor can be an indication which is sufficient to require an investigation of the existence of the impediment. Public rumor suffices for the postponement of a marriage until the investigation has been completed. In practice, however, one need not be preoccupied with this too much, as adoption is a rather rare

[95] *Cf.* Canon 97; *cf.* Payen, *De Matrimonio,* I, nn. 1485, 1486, pp. 1041-1045.

[96] *Cf.* S. C. S. Off., Instr. (*ad Ep. Rituum Orient.*), a. 1883—*Fontes,* n. 1076, n. 31, n. 32; S. C. de Prop. Fide, Instr., a. 1884—*Coll.,* n. 1587; *Instr. Pro Causis Matrimonialibus, Ex Indulto, In Sinis Servanda,* n. 31—Payen, *De Matrimonio,* II, p. 999.

[97] *Cf.* Muniz, *Procedimientos Eclesiásticos,* II, n. 328, p. 402.

[98] *Cf.* Canons 1059, 1080; Payen, *De Matrimonio,* I, nn. 843, 844, pp. 598, 599; n. 1591, p. 1111.

occurrence, and the cases in which it takes place with the solemnities necessary to constitute the impediment are very rare.[99] Therefore, if the existence and legality of the impediment are doubtful, the person intending to contract a marriage may be permitted to contract the marriage without a dispensation in a particular case.

(7) *Proof of Liberty of Parties in Marriages of Conscience.* A marriage of conscience is a marriage contracted in legitimate form before a priest and two witnesses, but without publication of the banns, and secretly, moreover, with a promise and grave obligation on all of keeping it secret.[100] In gathering the proofs of the liberty of conscience enjoyed by the contracting parties there exists some danger of the defamation of the parties concerned by reason of the secret celebration of the marriage. When it is urgent that the celebration take place,[101] it seems that the declaration under oath made by the contracting parties that they were baptized, and are bound by no canonical impediment is sufficient proof of liberty. One can and must add to this a declaration under oath of those who are to be witnesses of the celebration. These declarations can be estimated as sufficient proof because the parties are supposed to be legitimately married, make a declaration that they are living in concubinage, and petition for a legitimization of their status, which results from a valid marriage. According to the conscience of the judge, these statements deserve more credence than do a dozen witnesses against whom no exception can be taken (*omni exceptione maiores*). This argument appears to have insuperable strength by reason of two circumstances. The parties were commonly considered to be married, as they lived together as man and wife for a long time. They also had their children recorded as legitimate. It is not, however, denied that sometimes these proofs and arguments can fail, as public rumor can exist which dissipates the contention that the parties were ever married.[102]

[99] Muniz, *Procedimientos Eclesiáticos,* II, n. 355, pp. 429, 430.

[100] Canons 1104, 1105; *cf.* Payen, *De Matrimonio,* II, nn. 1934, 1935, pp. 306-308.

[101] In other cases, the proof of liberty must be established by documentary evidence and by a secret investigation by the bishop or his delegate.

[102] *Cf.* Muniz, *Procedimientos Eclesásticos,* I, n. 627, p. 581.

c. *Testimony Based on Hearsay of Others.* " . . . aut de auditu ab aliis." Hearsay witnesses relate what they have heard from others (*de auditu alieno vel de auditu auditus*). Hence, this phrase of the canon implies an admonition suggesting that the judge ascertain the origin of an opinion expressed by those testifying about what they heard. For the witness may say that he heard something said or done, or state that he heard a rumor from trustworthy persons that an incident happened. Hence, Linneborn [103] aptly states that the judge must ascertain whether the testimony of a witness is based on his own knowledge of an occurrence, such as that provided by experience and sense perception, or merely on the hearsay of others, perhaps even on that of the plaintiff; for those who are not direct witnesses testifying from their own knowledge are not true witnesses, and do not produce true proof.[104] It can be said, in the main, that witnesses who rely on others for their testimony do not enjoy full credibility, but provide an excellent foundation for an assumption, excepting in causes in which they give full credibility by reason of other attending circumstances.[105] It is well to test the truth of what a witness who spoke from hearsay said by insisting that he particularize when he has spoken in general terms of many persons. It is a test of the truth of a witness' evidence to ask him to give the names of some persons, or the name of even one person who told him a fact, for much depends on the number of those who heard that something was so.

The testimony of a group of hearsay witnesses is excluded if their attestations are not founded on some fact which came under the observation of a witness, but upon the mere word of a third party. In some matrimonial causes this testimony is admissible as corroboratory.[106] If other circumstances (*adminicula*) and conjectures are

[103] Linneborn, *Grundriss Des Eherechts*, III, p. 464.

[104] S. R. R., *Nullit. Matrim.*, 19 Junii, 1909, *Coram R. P. D., Gulielmo Sebastianelli*, dec. VIII, n. 3—*Decisiones*, I (1909), 70.

[105] Reiffenstuel, *Ius Canonicum Universum*, lib. II, tit. XX, nn. 344-359.

[106] *Cf.* S. R. R., *Nullit. Matrim.*, 6 Aprilis, 1914, *Coram R. P. D., Seraphino Many*, dec. XV, n. 4—*Decisiones*, VI (1914), 183, 184; S. R. R., *Nullit. Matrim.*, 11 Aprilis, 1911, *Coram R. P. D., Iosepho Mori*, dec. XVI, n. 15—*Decisiones*, III (1911), 169, 170; S. R. R., *Massilien. Nullit. Matrim.*, 1 Julii, 1911, *Coram R. P. D., Guilelmo Sebastianelli*, dec. XXIX, n. 4—*Decisiones*, III (1911), 327.

present and there are grave presumptions, hearsay evidence may be admitted if there is sufficient proof to give moral certitude to the judge.[107] In other matrimonial causes, especially if direct witnesses are lacking, hearsay witnesses are admissible, especially in causes difficult to prove.[108] If a report or story was spread by one person, the story possesses the probative value of the testimony of one witness, even though forty other persons repeated it from hearsay. Hearsay witnesses who relate what somebody else said can be admitted only if the original narrator is dead or cannot be found.[109]

Hearsay witnesses (*de auditu alieno*) provide legitimate proof when they testify to a fact which happened at a time which is not suspect, which is attested by persons worthy of credibility because of the known principle that such witnesses are admissible in things difficult to prove.[110] A patent application of the principles stated may be found in the proof of the presumed death of a spouse,[111] the testimonial proof of which is developed in Chapter X. The declarations of hearsay witnesses are admissible when there are no direct witnesses who can declare anything which they themselves observed. However, in the case of these hearsay witnesses the following things should be established. First, that the direct witnesses who were present at the death (*testes de visu*) cannot make a declaration because they died, or are absent and cannot be produced, or, cannot be found because of some other reasonable cause which should be proved. If, however, it were possible to take their attestations

[107] S. R. R., *Nullit. Matrim.*, 9 Januarii, 1922, *Coram R. P. D., Iosepho Florczak*, dec. I, n. 13—*Decisiones*, XIV (1922), 6.

[108] S. R. R., *Parisien. Nullit. Matrim.*, 11 Decembris, 1916, *Coram R. P. D., Seraphino Many*, dec. XXXII, n. 12—*Decisiones*, VIII (1916), 370; *cf.* S. R. R., *Nullit. Matrim.*, 17 Januarii, 1912, *Coram R. P. D., Michaele Lega*, dec. V, n. 10—*Decisiones*, IV (1912), 39; S. R. R., *Nullit. Matrim.*, 17 Januarii, 1912, *Coram R. P. D., Michaele Lega*, dec. XX, n. 8—*Decisiones Coram Lega*, 252, 253.

[109] *Cf.* c. 47, X, *de testibus et attestationibus*, II, 20; Zallinger, *Institutiones Iuris Ecclesiastici*, lib. II, tit. XX, § 260, VII, p. 191; Augustine, *A Commentary*, VII, 227.

[110] *Cf.* Reiffenstuel, *Ius Canonicum Universum*, lib. II, tit. XX, nn. 464, 465. For an application to the proof in court of an intention contrary to the good of the sacrament, *cf. Ius Pont.*, X (1930), 58.

[111] *Cf.* Canon 1069.

through the ordinary of the place where they live, their declarations must be obtained.

Second, that the hearsay witnesses heard of the death from eye-witnesses. In this case, the definite circumstances surrounding the death of the spouse must have been known at a time which is not suspect, namely, the witness must have heard about the missing spouse before he knew that it was necessary to establish the fact of death, and before he was cognizant of the fact that the surviving partner intended to contract another marriage.

Third, that the declaration of hearsay witnesses possesses the appearance of truth, the testimony should coincide with other circumstances that are known. If all these conditions are together in the case, the ordinary can declare that the missing spouse is dead.[112]

C. *Conduct of Witness as a Material Criterion of Testimony*

Canon 1789, 3°. "Utrum testis constans sit et firmiter sibi cohaereat; an varius, incertus, vel vacillans."

The material value of testimony lies in the manner in which the testimonial evidence is produced. Much depends on whether a witness is consistent, contradictory, variable or uncertain. The Code does not define these terms.

The material evaluation of an attestation suggests two considerations of a practical nature to an ecclesiastical judge: What facts can be used to prove that feeling or emotion, which was discussed as a generic human trait, is manifesting itself or has displayed itself in a witness? Whenever emotion is shown, how can the degree of its intensity or influence be determined?

External circumstances are the data which can be utilized in the proof of the existence of an emotion. The conduct of a witness while he is testifying, or the words which he employs indicate the stress of feeling. There does not appear to be any decisive rule for estimating what definite circumstances have had a tangible effect on an individual.

The conduct of a witness while on the stand frequently indicates

[112] Muniz, *Procedimientos Eclesiásticos,* II, n. 260, p. 312.

his emotion. There are no exact rules for interpreting the various manifestations that are known. The faculties of memory and speech may be affected by habits and temperament, which constitute personality. These tendencies are to be taken into consideration during the narration of facts, in order to evaluate the testimony of a witness. In judicial proceedings the judge must seek to overcome the obstacle of temperament. Practical precepts have resulted from the experience of those canonists and writers on evidence who have examined many classes of witnesses.

1. *Consistent Witnesses.* "Utrum testis constans sit et firmiter sibi cohaereat . . . " In estimating the testimony of witnesses one should ascertain whether a witness adheres to what he says and is absolutely consistent with himself. The rule must be understood regarding the attestation of one witness. One must prescind from other attending circumstances (*adminicula*) and indications which, in a particular case, can, if taken into consideration simultaneously with the attestation of the same witness, morally evince the truth of some fact.[113]

2. *Variable Witnesses.* ". . . . an varius . . . " A variable witness is inconsistent with himself, or gives utterance to different statements on the same subject during the same trial, in which case he is properly called a contrary witness (*testis contrarius*); or makes one statement in a "stage" or instance, or the examination which is followed by other different and contradictory assertions.[114] In matrimonial procedure, a varying witness is usually one who does not give his testimony in an unshaken, stable and firm manner.[115] An exception to the credibility of a witness who varied in his testimony was

[113] *Cf.* Wernz-Vidal, VI, *De Processibus,* n. 483, p. 423.

[114] Reiffenstuel, *Ius Canonicum Universum,* lib. II, tit. XX, nn. 313-315; *Encyclopedie de La Théologie Catholique,* Traduit de L'Allemand, Pars I, Goschler (Paris, 1865), XXIII, 162; Augustine, *A Commentary,* VII, p. 237. A Coronata, *De Processibus,* III, n. 1319, p. 225; *cf.* D. XXII, 5, 16. Others maintain that a varying witness testifies not about contrary but regarding the same things, but in a different way by adding or eliminating something.

[115] S. R. R., *Nullit. Matrim.,* 17 Januarii, 1912, *Coram R. P. D., Michaele Lega,* dec. V, n. 12—*Decisiones,* IV (1912), 40. For a treatment of the ways in which testimony varies, *cf.* Osborn, *The Problem of Proof,* p. 385; *cf.* S. R. R.,

not sustained by the Roman Rota in a force and fear case. A witness testified in the court of first instance that the father of the plaintiff did not strike his daughter. In a subsequent trial he testified that he himself saw the woman beaten by her father. It seemed that the witness was a perjurer because other witnesses agreed that the woman was abused by her father. The witness provided the court with a probable reason for his varying testimony. He had great respect for the mother and family of the plaintiff. The Rota adverted to the fact that the reason prompting the witness to act was not praiseworthy, but it was well that fear lest the honor of a principal family be wounded dominated the whole cause. The facts which were asserted were not deprived of credence, in spite of the fact that a witness contradicted himself.[116] Hence, testimony which is called varying or contrary, which contradicts another statement made by the same witness, is inadmissible and lacks probative value, unless it admits of correction. As a rule, it must be held that the first of the contradictory answers to the same question holds unless the error is corrected immediately, and the second attestation seems more probable.[117] If a witness should contradict in court a statement made by him extra-judicially, the judicial attestation is to be accepted because of the oath which was taken and the authority of the presiding judge.[118] In estimating the value of the testimony of witnesses who vary or contradict themselves, it is a practical rule to exact from them the material circumstances of fact about which they testify, and in so far as these facts were attested in a spontaneous and certain

Nullit. Matrim., 17 Januarii, 1912, *Coram R. P. D., Michaele Lega,* dec. XX, n. 22—*Decisiones Coram Lega,* 261.

[116] S. R. R., *Vesprimien. Nullit. Matrim.* (videntibus omnibus), 2 Junii, 1911, *Coram R. P. D., Michaele Lega,* dec. XIII, n. 18—*Decisiones Coram Lega,* 181, 182.

[117] *Cf.* Reiffenstuel, *Ius Canonicum Universum,* lib. II, tit. XX, n. 327; Muscat, *Institutiones Canonici,* lib. II, tit. XX, nota 3, p. 747; Augustine, *A Commentary,* VII, p. 238.

[118] Pirhing, *Ius Canonicum,* lib. II, tit. XX, Sec. III, § 5, nn. 161-163. *Cf.* Campegius, *De Testibus,* Reg. CXXVI, fol. 42. Campegius assigns six reasons for this rule. *Cf.* Crotus a Monteferrato, *Tractatus De Testibus,* Pars VII, n. 183, fol. 297.

manner.[119] Regarding the defects found in testimony in matrimonial procedure, especially in causes involving conditioned consent, an observation of the Signatura Apostolica stated: "Testium depositiones, in actis relatae quoad appositionem conditionis turpis ex parte Actoris, deficientes et non raro incertae apparent. Iudex enim in testium interrogationibus et excussione non videtur rem funditus inquisivisse."[120]

3. *Uncertain Witnesses.* ". . . incertus . . ." An uncertain witness makes a deposition in a hesitant manner, which betrays a doubting frame of mind. He makes contradictory answers during the same instance or stage of a trial.[121] This type of witness is the opposite of a positive witness, who usually finds it difficult to unsay anything which was said, however mistaken the witness was. The attestation of such a witness has no probative force, because the doubt in the mind of the witness makes him uncertain on which side the truth lies.[122]

Canonists, looking at an uncertain witness from another aspect, consider a witness who contradicts a previous statement made by himself during a trial or an examination (*testis contrarius*). Such testimony is inadmissible. It lacks probative value, unless the error shall have been corrected. Moreover, from the manifest contrariety, the witness is rendered suspect, and becomes a perjurer since he took an oath to tell the truth, and both contradictory statements cannot be true.[123] A judicial attestation affirmed in court has probative

[119] *Cf.* S. R. R., *Nullit. Matrim.*, 17 Januarii, 1912, *Coram R. P. D., Michaele Lega,* dec. XX, n. 12—*Decisiones Coram Lega,* 254.

[120] S. R. R., *Nullit. Matrim.*, 17 Januarii, 1912, *Coram R. P. D., Michaele Lega,* dec. XX, n. 7—*Decisiones Coram Lega,* 252.

[121] Reiffenstuel, *Ius Canonicum Universum,* lib. II, tit. XX, n. 316; A Coronata, *De Processibus,* III, n. 1319, p. 225. Augustine observes that an uncertain witness is also called a contrary witness (*testis contrarius*). *Cf.* Augustine, *A Commentary,* VII, p. 237. "Testis contrarius dicitur, qui deponit duo, vel plura inter se repugnantia."—Reiffenstuel, *Ius Canonicum Universum,* lib. II, tit. XX, n. 313.

[122] *Cf.* Reiffenstuel, *Ius Canonicum Universum,* lib. II, tit. XX, n. 317. A witness who testifies in an obscure manner is to be re-examined. *Cf.* c. 53, X, *de testibus et attestationibus,* II, 20.

[123] *Cf.* Reiffenstuel, *Ius Canonicum Universum,* lib. II, tit. XX, nn. 326, 327.

value, although it is denied outside of court; nevertheless, the judge should acquaint himself with the reason which prompted the utterance of a contradictory extra-judicial statement.[124]

4. *Vacillating Witnesses.* " . . . vel vacillans." A vacillating witness speaks in an apprehensive, hesitant manner.[125] This descriptive definition of a vacillating witness refers to the wavering, uncertain mode of answering, which appears to indicate some doubt or disbelief. If this hesitant manner of speaking betrays doubt or disbelief, the credibility of the witness is, consequently, removed, and his testimony should not be accepted.[126]

Nevertheless, all witnesses who speak in an apprehensive, or nervous, or hesitant manner do not necessarily doubt or disbelieve what they themselves say. A witness who simply vacillates merits some, but not full, credibility, if the hesitation or trembling is a mere concomitant or indication of a nervous disposition and it does not produce a positive doubt inasmuch as it is strengthened by other conjectures. The judge should endeavor to ascertain the cause of the apprehension or the nervousness.[127] (a) The fact that a witness is hesitant may manifest itself in the furtive aspect of the witness, or in his unduly timid and self-conscious manner. The fear or apprehension may be occasioned by the novelty of the experience of being subjected to an examination before an ecclesiastical court. A hesitating witness may be a great liar, or a truthful and cautious witness. It is not uncommon for Catholics to consider that their testimony given in an ecclesiastical tribunal is akin to what they say under the seal of the confessional. They dread to commit perjury, and lie in the presence of priests, and fear to say anything that will

[124] A Coronata, *De Processibus,* III, n. 1319, note 8, p. 225.

[125] *Cf.* S. R. R., *Nullit. Matrim.,* 28 Augustii, 1911, *Coram R. P. D., Aloisio Sincero,* dec. XXXIX, n. 20—*Decisiones,* III (1911), 440; S. R. R., *Nullit. Matrim.,* 17 Januarii, 1912, *Coram R. P. D., Michaele Lega,* dec. V, n. 12—*Decisiones,* IV (1912), 40; A Coronata, *De Processibus,* n. 1319, p. 225.

[126] "In testimoniis autem dignitas fides mores gravitas examinanda est: et ideo testes, qui adversus fidem suae testationis vacillant, audiendi non sint."—D. XXII, 5, 2; *cf.* Reiffenstuel, *Ius Canonicum Universum,* lib. II, tit. XX, n. 317; Noval, *De Processibus,* IV, n. 510, p. 352; Augustine, *A Commentary,* VII, p. 237.

[127] Reiffenstuel, *Ius Canonicum Universum,* lib. II, tit. XX, nn. 318-320.

occasion the abuse of the sacrament of matrimony. Bearing this in mind, the judge must be on his guard against an apprehensive witness, who hesitates between the answer he should give, and the effect of a truthful reply upon either himself or the case. Fear may lead a witness to color facts, to suppress truth, to omit saying something unconsciously. (b) A nervous witness, described by canonists as a trembling witness (*testis tremens*) either does not answer at all, or gives expression to opposites in close succession, or makes answers such as "yes" and "no" simultaneously, which may be followed by a laconic "I do not know." One must be careful not to wound the sensibilities of a nervous witness. If trembling or perspiration is a mere indication of a nervous disposition, and does not insinuate a positive doubt, the testimony is admissible, if it is fortified by conjectures and other proofs.[128] When the witness is uncertain in making an attestation, the testimony either merits no belief or little credence, according to the diverse circumstances or that present themselves in cases.[129] Not infrequently it happens that a natural suggestion made to a witness, like a question directed to exhaust some circumstance connected with a fact, influences the imagination of a witness. The witness, as a consequence, may think that he retains in his memory, or knows what he actually did not hear or perceive, at least under the aspect about which he is questioned.[130] Finally, it may happen that a witness who says, "I do not know," before an ecclesiastical tribunal, betrays the fact that he is suborning himself, or that he was coached by circumstances surrounding what he has already said (*adminicula*), and by his insistence on one point upon which he would establish his contention. In ecclesiastical courts the humorous or flippant witness and the canting hypocrite should be made to confine their testimony to the specific questions which are put to them. Judges of ecclesiastical courts are indulgent toward rambling, dull and

[128] *Cf.* Augustine, *A Commentary,* VII, pp. 237, 238; S. R. R., *Nullit. Matrim.,* 17 Januarii, 1912, *Coram R. P. D., Michaele Lega,* dec. XX, n. 14—*Decisiones Coram Lega,* 254, 255.

[129] S. R. R., *Nullit. Matrim.,* 17 Januarii, 1912, *Coram R. P. D., Michaele Lega,* dec. V, n. 13—*Decisiones,* IV (1912), 41.

[130] S. R. R., *Nullit. Matrim.,* 17 Januarii, 1912, *Coram R. P. D., Michaele Lega,* dec. XX, n. 10—*Decisiones Coram Lega,* 253.

stupid witnesses, whose apparent deficiencies arise from emotional and intellectual defects.

The portion of the canon which was explained provides the judge with general indications to warn him about the tendency of some witnesses toward untruthfulness. There are many other such indications. As many of them are in the realm of conjecture, the following which are considered more important are mentioned: (a) A defensive smile and a nervous laugh unwarranted by circumstances, but apparently used unconsciously, with a desire to cover deceit; (b) avoidance of looking at the question, except for an occasional quick glance, and keeping the eyes fixed in an unnatural manner on a distant object; (c) an almost inaudible voice, and an indication in many ways of a desire to be elsewhere. Some witnesses try to cover the mouth or face while testifying; (d) repetition of plain and audible questions in what appears to be an unconscious effort to recall testimony and frame a good reply; (e) unnecessary and minute accuracy to show that the whole truth is being told; (f) repeated avowal of a desire to tell the truth; (g) unnatural emphasis on one point with a reluctance to be questioned regarding the source of information and the logical result of premises.[131] (h) Whereas, a witness who makes an attestation with circumspection, diligently and subtly distinguishing what he saw from what he learned as a hearsay witness, or can give no account of, shows his veracity.[132]

D. Number of Witnesses Required as Numerical Criterion of Testimony

Canon 1789, 4°. Denique utrum testimonii contestes habeat, an sit singularis.

The number of witnesses who agree in their assertions has a logical bearing on proof. The cumulation of a number of witnesses as-

[131] Four hundred and forty-one rules for estimating the value of testimony are systematically arranged in Campegius, *De Testibus,* fol. 1-176. The rules of testimonial evidence are reduced to one hundred and twenty in Papiensi, Franciscus Curtius, *De Testibus Tractatus,* reg. 1-120.

[132] S. R. R., *Osnabrugen. Nullit. Matrim.,* 11 Januarii, 1912, *Coram R. P. D., Francisco Heiner,* dec. III, n. 6—*Decisiones,* IV (1912), 23.

serting the same thing possesses a value only in so far as the testimonial status of the witnesses who agree is substantially the same. If something that might lead into error is common to all or several witnesses, their agreement loses value. Canon Law has long recognized that proof resting fundamentally on a quantitative or numerical system does not necessarily have logical value in favor of it.[133] No specific general rule of reasoning exists for estimating the inferential value of a group of witnesses who disagree or contradict one another.[134] Hence, the Code has not figured out a scale of numerical values. It makes no declaration that a preponderance of numbers has logical force on the side of the greater number. Nevertheless, as men do sense a difference of values in the coincidence of varius numbers of persons who agree about something, the Code reminds the judge in this canon to take this fact under advisement. Relative to its probative force, the numerical value of testimony is dependent on whether several witnesses agree with one another (*contestes*) or differ from one another (*singulares*).

1. *Corroboration of Witnesses.* "Denique utrum testimonii contestes habeat . . . " When two or more witnesses testify alike regarding one and the same fact, they are said to be witnesses who agree among themselves (*testes contestes*).[135] An example of this is found when two witnesses state that on a certain day they saw the father of a family strike his daughter and heard him upbraid and threaten her for not consenting to marry a man of his choice.[136] If a litigant procure ten witnesses, of whom nine agree and one contradicts them,

[133] *Cf.* D. XXII, 5, 21, 3; c. 3, C. IV, q. 2 et 3; c. 10, X, *de verborum significatione,* V, 20; S. Isadorus, *Etymologiarum sive Originum,* lib. XVIII, c. 15—*M.P.L.*, 82, col. 650; Zallinger, *Institutiones Iuris Ecclesiastici,* lib. II, tit. XX, § 261, IX, p. 191. When it is possible the judge must restrict the number of witnesses—*cf.* S. R. R., *Remotionis,* 11 Maii, 1909, *Coram R. P. D., Michaele Lega,* dec. V, n. 5—*Decisiones,* I (1909), 39.

[134] An approximation of such a rule is found in Zallinger, *ibid.*

[135] A Coronata, *De Processibus,* III, n. 1280, p. 188; n. 1321, p. 226.

[136] *Cf.* S. R. R., *Nullit. Matrim,* 16 Maii, 1912, *Coram R. P. D., Michaele Lega,* dec. XXIV, n. 3—*Decisiones Coram Lega,* 295, 296; S. R. R., *Petrocoricen. Nullit. Matrim.,* 27 Augustii, 1912, *Coram R. P. D., Michaele Lega,* 27 Augustii, 1912, dec. XXVII, n. 7—*Decisiones Coram Lega,* 338, 339.

the testimony of the majority has value, in spite of the fact that the witness who is contradictory, weakens the testimony somewhat.[137] If, on the other hand, all the witnesses coincide, the Code adheres to the rule that two or three witnesses who agree produce entire proof (*plena probatio*).

2. *Discordance of Witnesses.* " . . . an sit singularis." Individual witnesses who differ from one another (*testes singulares*), make an attestation regarding different facts in such a manner that each gives his individual testimony and does not coincide, at least perfectly, with the others.[138] The value of the testimony of individual witnesses who do not agree with others, at least perfectly, is weighed according to Canon 1790.

> **Canon 1790. Si testes inter se discrepent, iudex perpendat utrum edita ab eis sibi invicem adversentur, an sint dumtaxat diversa vel adminiculativa.**

This canon expresses the concept that if witnesses disagree with one another, it is the function of the judge to weigh carefully whether their attestations conflict with one another, or are merely adverse or corroborative. In the terminology employed by the older canonists,[139] the word singular or individual (*singularis*) was employed in the following three senses. A witness was individual with either adverse (*adversativa, vel obstativa*), or diverse (*diversificativa*), or corroboratory (*adminiculativa*), individuality.

a. *Adverse singularity* (*singularis adversativa vel obstativa*) is present when attestations conflict with one another, so that the utter-

[137] *Cf.* Reiffenstuel, *Ius Canonicum Universum,* lib. II, tit. XX, nn. 321-326.

[138] *Cf.* Jimenez, *Procedimientos Canonico-Civiles,* I, n. 502, p. 213; A Coronata, *De Processibus,* III, n. 1321, p. 226. Canonists also deduce that two legitimate witnesses are sufficient to prove that something was entrusted to a person on condition that he should give it up to some other person. Two individual (*singulares*) witnesses stating there was a gift made in trust of a whole inheritance or a particular thing to a pious cause is full proof against the heir (*fiduciarius*) denying it. *Cf.* Reiffenstuel, *Ius Canonicum Universum,* lib. III, tit. XXVI, § 6, n. 157; *Ius Pont.,* VI (1926), 86-91.

[139] *Cf.* Pirhing, *Ius Canonicum,* lib. II, tit. XX, sec. III, § 2, n. 142; Muschat, *Institutiones Canonicae,* lib. II, tit. XX, note 3, p. 745.

ances of one witness contradict those of another in such a way that the testimony of both cannot be true at the same time.[140] As a general rule, contradictory witnesses prove nothing, and eliminate the value of the testimony of one another.[141] Individual witnesses generally prove nothing, because each of them is but one witness who, as a rule, does not fully prove anything,[142] and they mutually exclude one another when their assertions do not agree. A classic illustration of this principle is found in the story of Susanna, who was accused of adultery by two old men, one of whom alleged that the crime was committed under a mastic tree, whereas the other declared that it had taken place under a holm tree.[143]

[140] *Cf.* "Ad reprobandum vero quosdam testium ecclesiae Ravennatensis etsi ex parte Faventinorum quidam sint testes inducti plures tamen illorum reprobantur, quia sibi invicem evidentissime contradicunt."—c. 9, X, *de probationibus,* II, 19; Lega, *Praelectiones,* I, n. 492, p. 432.

[141] *Cf.* Reiffenstuel, *Ius Canonicum Universum,* lib. II, tit. XX, nn. 285, 286, 293; Augustine, *A Commentary,* VII, p. 238; Wernz-Vidal, VI, *De Processibus,* n. 485, p. 426.

[142] *Cf.* Canon 1791, § 1; S. R. R., *Nullit. Matrim.,* 24 Martii, 1922, *Coram R. P. D., Petro Rossetti,* dec. VIII, n. 7—*Decisiones,* XIV (1922), 74. One witness induces a presumption in causes involving simulated consent. *Cf.* S. R. R., *Massilien. Nullit. Matrim.,* 1 Julii, 1911, *Coram R. P. D., Gulielmo Sebastianelli,* dec. XXIX, n. 4—*Decisiones,* III (1911), 327, 328. One witness provides full proof of baptism, ordination, or that a church or place is consecrated. *Cf.* Canons 742, § 1; 779, 1010, 1011, 1159, § 1—S. R. R., *Nullit. Matrim.,* 25 Februarii, 1911, *Coram R. P. D., Iosepho Mori,* dec. X, n. 9—*Decisiones,* III (1911), 100. Adultery and *copula carnalis* are proved by one eyewitness although many hearsay witnesses testify otherwise. *Cf.* S. R. R., *Nullit. Matrim.,* 29 Julii, 1911, *Coram R. P. D., Francisco Heiner,* dec. XXVI, n. 4—*Decisiones,* III (1911), 407, 408. A pastor testifying officially merits credibility. Nevertheless, "Quodsi officialis aut minister publicus testimonium ferens de actu ab ipso gesto, ratione officii sui, esset testis in causa propria, iam actum esset de publicis muneribus seu officiis."—*Cf.* S. R. R., *Nullit. Matrim.,* 28 Augustii, 1911, *Coram R. P. D., Aloisio Sincero,* dec. XXXIX, n. 19—*Decisiones,* III (1911), 439; S. R. R., *Mediolanen. Nullit. Matrim.,* 23 Februarii, 1910, *Coram R. P. D., Ioanne Prior,* dec. VII, n. 17—*Decisiones,* II (1910), 66. Individual testimony with certain indications (*indicia*) is sufficient for the proof, however, of *copula illicita. Cf.* S. R. R., *Nullit. Matrim.,* 11 Aprilis, 1911, *Coram R. P. D., Iosepho Mori,* dec. XVI, n. 13—*Decisiones,* III (1911), 169.

[143] *Dan.,* XIII, 54, 58.

The practice of the Sacred Roman Rota requires that a lack of conformity between the statements of witnesses must be proved, and not merely stated. The Rota does not presume that witnesses individually contradict one another. When considering what appear to be contradictions between various witnesses it will not be amiss to keep in mind, especially in causes pertaining to force and fear, the following principle of jurisprudence. The attestations of witnesses should be reconciled with one another, and as far as it can be done, one should not call the good faith of witnesses into question.

> Si vero—dixerunt Domini—hactennus adlaboravimus, quasi inter se conciliare discordantes attestationes, distinguendo varia tempora et variam intentionem minarum . . . et quantum fieri poterat non in discrimen adducenda erat testium bona fides, hoc factum est quia testes, etiam qui validitati adversantur, exhibentur ut probi et honesti.[144]

Some contradictions apparent in the utterances of witnesses are not difficult to reconcile, as they exclude the danger of collusion in witnesses.[145] There are other facts, however, that may force upon one the presumption that the witnesses intended to conspire fraudulently, since their attestations do not agree. If many witnesses, testifying on one side, were suborned, all are presumed to be suborned.[146]

The Castellane-Gould case, which was submitted to the Rota three times, and finally went to a specially selected group of Cardinals, provides an example of witnesses who are individual with adverse singularity. The case involved an error of law about an essential property of marriage.

Such an error of law concerns the right itself over the body. It is present when a contracting party, for example, is of the opinion that

[144] S. R. R., *Nullit. Matrim.*, 1 Augustii, 1913, *Coram R. P. D., Michaele Lega*, dec. XXXIX, n. 10—*Decisiones Coram Lega*, 484.

[145] "Collusionis enim labes maior est ubi maxima est in testibus concordia, potissimum quum agitur de factis referendis iam a viginti et amplius annis praeteritis. Ita passim haec regula confirmata est iurisprudentia H. S. O. . . . "—S. R. R., *Nullit. Matrim.*, 21 Decembris, 1912, *Coram R. P. D., Michaele Lega*, dec. XXXI, n. 6—*Decisiones Coram Lega*, 356.

[146] S. R. R., *Nullit. Matrim.*, 1 Augustii, 1913, *Coram R. P. D., Michaele Lega*, dec. XXXIX, nn. 18, 19—*Decisiones Coram Lega*, 486, 487.

the purpose of marriage is not for the procreation of children, but for social reasons, and consent is given to it as such. Marital consent is not present in this case.[147] This error is not presumed in the external forum after the age of puberty.[148] The error may be quite difficult to prove. An error of law regarding an essential property of marriage exists in the three following instances: If the person contracting marriage thinks that the bond can be broken under some circumstances; if the person thinks that he can have a second partner simultaneously; or if he thinks that the marriage is not a sacrament. A marriage is valid in the three cases mentioned, even though the error is present, and it was a motivating cause for marriage.[149] But if the contracting party should exclude an essential property by an explicit act of the will, or by a "true condition of the mind," the marriage would be invalid.[150] But as the presumption of law is against this last supposition, it must be proved.

With these preliminary notions in mind, it is observed that in the Castellane-Gould case a group of witnesses testified that Anna Gould said that she would leave her husband if he should be unfaithful. They testified that the defendant, Anna Gould, spoke of divorce before her marriage. Nevertheless, two brothers of the defendant attested that their sister freely accepted the conditions required by the Church for a mixed marriage, readily acceded to all the consequences which followed upon the engagement, and loved her fiancé very much. The Rota concluded that it could not be admitted easily that Anna had spoken of getting a divorce, and if a word about divorce fell on the day of the marriage, or a little before or after it, it must be said that Anna had made the remark lightly and jocosely.[151] Other examples of witnesses who contradict one another are found in the decisions of the Roman Rota.[152]

[147] Canon 1081, § 2.

[148] Canon 1082, § 2; *cf.* Gasparri, *De Matrimonio,* II (1932), n. 805, p. 27.

[149] *Cf.* Canon 1084.

[150] *Cf.* Gasparri, *De Matrimonio,* II, n. 807, p. 28.

[151] S. R. R., *Neo-Eboracen. Nullit. Matrim.,* 9 Decembris, 1911, *Coram R. P. D., Michaele Lega,* dec. XIX, n. 2—*Decisiones Coram Lega,* 240.

[152] For example, in an alleged force and fear case, *cf.* S. R. R., *Nullit. Matrim.,* 1 Augustii, 1913, *Coram R. P. D., Michaele Lega,* dec. XXXIX, n. 8—

b. *Diverse singularity* (*singularis diversificativa*). Whenever attestations are not contrary, but pertain to distinct facts or circumstances, so that one witness testifies to the exisence of one fact, and another to a separate fact, which has no connection with the other fact, and both statements do not contradict one another, their testimony is called diverse.[153] Individual witnesses who compare their attestations with one another are frequently included under this category.

An example of this testimony is found in the Castellane-Gould case, to which reference was made. A group of witnesses provided concordant testimony that the defendant, Anna Gould, spoke of divorce before her marriage. The Roman Rota admitted the validity of this testimony. Nevertheless, the Rota pointed out that she wished to contract and consented to a Christian marriage, although the marriage was entered into with an error of law. Hence, the Rota made the following observation regarding the witnesses who expressed in various ways what all except one agreed upon, but who were oblivious of the meaning of the word "condition":

> Neque dicatur quaestionem non esse de verbo, sed de re, et praefatos testes, utpote de iure canonico penitus ignaros, etsi in testimonio perhibendo, verbo *conditionis* usi non fuerint, adhibuisse tamen locutiones eidem verbo aequipollentes. Etenim vera sumenda sunt prout sonant: propositum autem aliquid agendi non secumfert consensum conditionatum; et in dubio, quis praesumitur pure contraxisse, nisi aperte liqueat de *conditione*, praesertim si conditio substantiae contractus opponatur, uti considerat Benedictus XIV loco citato.[154]

Decisiones Coram Lega, 482. The credibility of physicians is not destroyed by a less number of doctors who are not so expert. *Cf.* S. R. R., *Nullit. Matrim.*, 11 Augustii, 1910, *Coram R. P. D., Antonio Perathoner*, dec. XXX, n. 3—*Decisiones* (1910), 302. In vitiated consent cases, *cf.* S. R. R., *Nullit. Matrim.*, 23 Martii, 1914, *Coram R. P. D., Gulielmo Sebastianelli*, dec. XII, n. 9—*Decisiones*, VI (1914), 150; S. R. R., *Osnabrugen. Nullit. Matrim.*, 11 Januarii, 1912, *Coram R. P. D., Francisco Heiner*, dec. III, n. 6—*Decisiones*, IV (1912), 23.

153 *Cf.* Lega, *Praelectiones*, I, n. 492, p. 432.

154 S. R. R., *Neo-Eboracen. Nullit. Matrim.*, 9 Decembris, 1911, *Coram*

There was but one witness, a Prince John Del Drago, who testified not to simple error, but to an express condition, which was elicited and rendered the marriage null. His individual and contradictory testimony was insufficient to obtain a declaration of nullity because the Rota applied the principle, "Testis unus nullus testi," or "unicus testis non probat," inasmuch as the other witnesses testified to other and different facts. The Rota decided that one witness was insufficient to prove that a condition against an essential property of marriage had been made by the defendant.

> Et in themate quia alii testes, cum primis, Annae huiusmodi voluntatem perceperunt ex relatione Ioannes Del Draco, praesumendum est ita tunc significatam a Ioannes fuisse, uti hodie eam referunt iidem testes. Iamvero hi non loquuntur de propria ac vera conditione ab Anna contractui apposita; sed de intentione libere et libenter utendi divertendi facultate quam illi dabant placita sectae protestanticae.[155]

Another case before the Roman Rota involved the proof of simulated consent to a marriage.[156] Internal consent is always supposed to correspond to the words or signs used during the celebration of marriage. But if one of the parties, or both of them, would exclude either marriage itself or all right to the conjugal act, or an essential property of marriage by a positive act of the will, the contract would be null.[157] There is simulation when a contracting party pronounces words expressive of a willingness to contract marriage while he has not the internal intention of entering into a marriage contract.[158] Simulated consent is likewise present when there is a positive act of the will excluding all right to the conjugal act or some essential property of marriage—unity (*fides*), indissolubility or sacramental

R. P. D., Michaele Lega, dec. XIX, n. 6—*Decisiones Coram Lega,* 245. *Cf.* Benedictus XIV, *De Synodo Diocesana* (Romae, 1806), I, 13, c. 22, n. 7.

[155] S. R. R., *Neo-Eboracen. Nullit. Matrim.,* 9 Decembris, 1911, *Coram R. P. D., Michaele Lega,* dec. XIX, n. 7—*Decisiones Coram Lega,* 246.

[156] Defects which render marriage consent null are enumerated in Canons 1082, § 1; 1083, § 1, § 2; 1086, § 2; 1087, § 1; 1092, 2°, 4°.

[157] Canon 1086.

[158] Chelodi, *Ius Matrimoniale,* n. 115, p. 125.

dignity (*sacramentum*).[159] Whether the exclusion is due to substantial ignorance, substantial error or takes place intentionally (*ex industria*) is irrelevant. All these can give rise to nullity and actions for declaration of the nullity of the marriage. Total simulation is concerned with the subject of consent, whereas partial pertains to the object of consent, *e. g.*, the right over one's body (*jus in corpus*). Consequently, they are of distinct natures.[160] The proof of simulated consent is difficult. An outline of the proof of simulated consent is indicated by the following sentence from the Roman Rota:

> Necesse est, igitur, in primis probare causam simulationis, curnam scilicet Titius ficte contraxerit, ac deinde ipsa simulatio evinci debet ex circumstantiis antecedentibus, concomitantibus, subsequentibus, quae adeo praecisae et urgentes sint, ut certum moraliter reddant iudicem de hoc ficto consensu.[161]

What directly pertains to individual statements which have no connection with one another, but do not exclude one another is that conjectures are generally sufficient to prove fictitious consent if witnesses show that a man or woman immediately after marriage appeared to have consented fictitiously, and there are witnesses who attest that before the marriage was celebrated, he or she had shown constant repugnance to the marriage.

In a case involving fictitious consent all of the witnesses did not agree about the circumstances surrounding the flight of the bride. All were unanimous in their narration of the substantial fact that there had been flight. The individual witnesses coalesced in their

159 Canon 1086, § 2; Chelodi, *Ius Matrimoniale*, n. 116, p. 125.

160 *Cf.* Fourneret, Pierre, *Le Mariage Chretien* (Paris, 1925), 118; Gugnard, Armdando, *Tractatus De Matrimonio* (Mechliniae, 1931), n. 31, pp. 149, 150; Roberti, in *Appolinaris*, VI (1933), 105.

161 S. R. R., *Nullit. Matrim.*, 18 Julii, 1911, *Coram R. P. D., Ioanne Prior*, dec. XXXII, n. 2—*Decisiones*, III (1911), 347. *Cf.* Gasparri, *De Matrimonio* (1932 ed.), n. 819, pp. 39, 40; Sanchez, *De Sancto Matrimonio Disputationum*, lib. II, disp. XLV, nn. 1-3; Ayrinhac, H. A.-Lydon, P. J., *Marriage Legislation in the New Code of Canon Law* (New York, 1932), 202-204.

testimony that there had been, but there was no agreement as to the time when the flight took place.[162]

c. *Cumulative Individuality* (*singularitas adminiculativa*). Witnesses who testify about different facts or circumstances which coincide with one another, and pertain to the same fact, are "singular in their testimony with cumulative individuality."[163] For example, a priest testified in a force and fear case, that his father, who had a violent character, boxed the ears of his sister, upbraided and threatened her to such an extent that she shut herself in a room to avoid a beating. A woman servant attested that she saw the girl resist her father and run away. The mother of the girl said that her daughter did not want to marry the man chosen by her father, so that she ran away. As a result of the flight, scenes were multiplied in the home and the girl was treated brutally by her father.[164] In criminal causes individual witnesses stating different facts which coincide with one another establish only a presumption, because entire proof is an absolute requisite for condemnation.[165] It is commonly held that in civil causes witnesses of this description may be admissible to provide entire proof, as they are equivalent to a group of witnesses to

[162] S. R. R., *Nullit. Matrim.*, 18 Julii, 1911, *Coram R. P. D., Ioanne Prior*, dec. XXXII, n. 11—*Decisiones*, III (1911), 351.

[163] *Cf.* Lega, *Praelectiones*, I, n. 492, p. 432; A Coronata, *De Processibus*, III, n. 1321, p. 226; Crotus, Ioannes, a Monteferrato, *Tractatus De Testibus*, Pars VII, n. 140, fol. 286. *Cf.* S. R. R., *Vic. Apost. Tonkin Orientalis. Nullit. Matrim.*, 18 Augustii, 1921, *Coram R. P. D., Friderico Cattani Amadori*, dec. XXVI, nn. 4, 6—*Decisiones*, XIII (1921), 252-255.

[164] S. R. R., *Nullit. Matrim.*, 16 Maii, 1912, *Coram R. P. D., Michaele Lega*, dec. XXIV, n. 3—*Decisiones Coram Lega*, 295, 296; *cf.* S. R. R., *Varsavien. seu Lublinen. Nullit. Matrim.*, 21 Julii, 1910, *Coram R. P. D., Gulielmo Sebastianelli*, dec. XXVIII, n. 7—*Decisiones*, II (1910), 293; S. R. R., *Vesprimien. Nullit. Matrim.*, 2 Junii, 1911, *Coram R. P. D., Michaele Lega*, dec. XIII, n. 9—*Decisiones Coram Lega*, 178, 179; S. R. R., *Petrocoricen. Nullit. Matrim.*, 27 Augustii, 1912, *Coram R. P. D., Michaele Lega*, dec. XXVII, n. 7—*Decisiones Coram Lega*, 338, 339; S. R. R., *Nullit. Matrim.*, 29 Novembris, 1913, *Coram R. P. D., Ioanne Prior*, dec. L, n. 27—*Decisiones*, V (1913), 625.

[165] *Cf.* c. 9, X, *de probationibus*, II, 19; Reiffenstuel, *Ius Canonicum Universum*, lib. II, tit. XX, nn. 297-312; Wernz-Vidal, VI, *De Processibus*, n. 485, p. 426.

state the same fact (*contestes*).[166] The witnesses under consideration are called witnesses who agree (*contestes*) when viewed as a group, who attest some fact with one accord.[167] When the same aggregate is considered individually, and it is seen that the testimony of each mutually completes and aids the others,[168] it is called individual with cumulative singularity.

The judge, having been reminded by Canons 1789 and 1790, to pay attention to the credibility and sources of the knowledge of witnesses, and having been advised to ascertain whether witnesses are uniform or contradictory in their utterances, may take advantage of the following practice. In criminal causes and, if the judge think it prudent, in contentious causes, the judge can officially, or at the instance of the parties, confront opposing or contradictory witnesses with one another when (a) witnesses disagree between themselves or with the party in a matter which is grave and pertains to the substance of the cause; (b) when there is no easier way to detect the truth; (c) when scandal or danger of dissensions do not result from the confrontation.[169] The auditor cites those who contradicted one another. When they are present in the tribunal, he reminds them to tell the truth, and takes their oath. Thereupon, the notary reads the

[166] *Cf.* Reiffenstuel, *Ius Canonicum Universum,* lib. II, tit. XX, n. 287.

[167] S. R. R., *Nullit. Matrim.,* 30 Junii, 1910, *Coram R. P. D., Michaele Lega,* dec. IX, n. 7—*Decisiones Coram Lega,* 135; S. R. R., *Separationis quoad thorum et mensam,* 5 Julii, 1910, *Coram R. P. D., Michaele Lega,* dec. X, n. 7—*Decisiones Coram Lega,* 150; S. R. R., *Nullit. Matrim.,* 11 Augustii, 1910, *Coram R. P. D., Antonio Perathoner,* dec. XXX, nn. 6, 8—*Decisiones,* II (1910), 303, 305; S. R. R., *Nullit. Matrim.,* 30 Augustii, 1911, *Coram R. P. D., Michaele Lega,* dec. XVII, n. 16—*Decisiones Coram Lega,* 228; S. R. R., *Nullit. Matrim.,* 13 Februarii, 1913, *Coram R. P. D., Michaele Lega,* dec. XXXIV, n. 1—*Decisiones Coram Lega,* 411, 412; S. R. R., *Separationis quoad thorum et cohabitationis,* 20 Aprilis, 1912, *Coram R. P. D., Michaele Lega,* dec. XXII, n. 4—*Decisiones Coram Lega,* 277; S. R. R., *Nullit. Matrim.,* 1 Augustii, 1913, *Coram R. P. D., Michaele Lega,* dec. XXXIX, n. 4—*Decisiones Coram Lega,* 478; S. R. R., *Nullit. Matrim.,* 8 Aprilis, 1921, *Coram R. P. D., Raphaelo Chimenti,* dec. VI, n. 3—*Decisiones,* XIII (1921), 65.

[168] *Cf.* Roberti, *De Processibus,* II, n. 354, p. 75.

[169] *Cf.* Canon 1772, § 3; Muniz, *Procedimientos Eclesiásticos,* III, n. 334, p. 268.

respective declarations. Should the witnesses admit what they said, the auditor points out the contradictory statements one by one. Then he invites the individual witnesses who contradicted one another to explain the discrepancies, and to come to an agreement. The notary records all that the witnesses say and do. When he considers that the explanations have been exhausted, he states that the "incident" is completed, whether or not the contrary attestations were reconciled.

CHAPTER X

FULL PROOF BASED ON TESTIMONY

CANON LAW recognizes that the probative value of the testimony of a witness is utterly incapable of being measured by arithmetic. The personal element behind an attestation is a vital one, which cannot be appraised exactly by rules. A single witness to a fact is, in general, not sufficient. One witness, however, legally suffices as evidence under certain conditions. One or more witnesses with corroboration may produce entire juridical proof in the circumstances which it is attempted to indicate in the three following articles.

ARTICLE 1. THE VALUE OF THE TESTIMONY OF ONE WITNESS

Canon 1791, § 1. Unius testis depositio plenam fidem non facit, nisi sit testis qualificatus qui deponat, de rebus ex officio testis.

This canon expresses a rule of law. The first part of it expresses a general rule. The second part indicates an exception to it.

The general rule contained in this canon is that one witness does not afford complete proof. The regulation rests on the principle, "Vox unius, vox nullius." The testimony of one witness, although it is admissible, is not sufficient to form the basis of a decision or a verdict.[1]

The Roman Rota has repeatedly referred to this basic principle that "One witness is no witness."[2]

[1] *Cf.* Deut. xvii, 6; Matt. xviii, 16; c. 8, C, XXXIII, q. 2; cc. 10, 23, 47, *de testibus et attestationibus,* II, 20; Reiffenstuel, *Ius Canonicum Universum,* lib. II, tit. XX, nn. 247-249; Zallinger, *Institutiones Iuris Ecclesiastici,* lib. II, tit. XX, § 259, VII, p. 191.

[2] *Cf.* S. R. R., *Mediolanen. Nullit. Matrim.,* 23 Februarii, 1910, *Coram R. P. D., Ioanne Prior,* dec. VII, n. 18—*Decisiones,* II (1910), 66; S. R. R., *Nullit. Matrim.,* 25 Februarii, 1911, *Coram R. P. D., Iosepho Mori,* dec. X, n. 9—*Decisiones,* III (1911), 99, 100; S. R. R., *Nullit. Matrim.,* 17 Januarii, 1912,

Nevertheless, the basic principle whether stated, "Vox unius, vox nullius" or "Testis unus, nullus testis," is not found in the Code. The dictum of the Code that one witness alone does not suffice to make entire proof qualifies the old rule that one witness is no witness. The legislator, taking cognizance of the doctrine of eminent canonists and the jurisprudence of the Roman Rota before the promulgation of the Code, settles by this rule of law, which is laid down in the canon under consideration, that one witness provides some proof, and at times produces complete evidence.

There is one exception to the rule of law in the paragraph when one witness alone does provide complete proof. The exception is stated in the second paragraph: one qualified witness may give full proof when he makes an attestation regarding acts which he himself performed *ex officio*. The exception is called qualification whenever a witness gives testimony about acts performed by himself in his official capacity.[3]

A public official is a qualified witness about what pertains to his official acts. In the classification of public officials are the following:

1. The Roman Pontiff is a qualified witness concerning things done by himself. Direct proof should not be admitted against these facts, if the Roman Pontiff establishes his intention on them.[4]

2. The utterances of a king, an emperor or a civil prince which are official likewise enjoy full credence.[5]

Coram R. P. D., Michaele Lega, dec. V, n. 23—*Decisiones,* IV (1912), 49; S. R. R., *Limburgen. Nullit. Matrim.,* 2 Januarii, 1913, *Coram R. P. D., Antonio Perathoner,* dec. I, n. 8—*Decisiones,* I (1913), 7; S. R. R., *Londonen. Incardinationis,* 9 Januarii, 1912, *Coram R. P. D., Antonio Perathoner,* dec. II, n. 9—*Decisiones,* IV (1912), 19.

[3] *Cf.* c. 25, X, *de electione et electi potestate,* I, 6.

[4] *Cf.* Reiffenstuel, *Ius Canonicum Universum,* lib. II, tit. XIX, nn. 103-111; lib. II, tit. XX, n. 278; A Coronata, *De Processibus,* III, n. 1317, p. 224. Contrary proof is not admitted against Letters of the Roman Pontiff which bear his signature. *Cf.* Cicognani, Amleto G., *Canon Law* (Philadelphia, 1934), p. 628, note 5.

[5] *Cf.* Reiffenstuel, *Ius Canonicum Universum,* lib. II, tit. XIX, n. 112; lib. II, tit. XX, n. 279.

3. Cardinals are also in the classification of public officials who are qualified witnesses.[6]

4. Pastors are official witnesses when they testify about acts which they performed *ex officio*.[7] The juridical value of the testi mony of a pastor in matrimonial causes is considered in Article 3 below.

5. A witness who occupies an eminent position of trust gives complete proof when he discusses matters which pertain to events which came under his official observation. For example, the opinion of a Russian consul regarding the danger attendant on travel during perilous times was accepted by the Roman Rota. His opinion on the Canon Law involved in a case was rejected as devoid of juridical value in so far as he expressed an opinion regarding something with reference to which he was not a qualified witness.[8]

6. A physician expert in his profession who testifies about a fact which came under his personal observation is a qualified witness when he has been called upon to testify, especially if he is honest and conspicuous for his practice of religion and piety.[9] Provided that no legitimate exception can be taken such a medical or surgical expert his testimony gives complete proof. This rule of jurisprudence has been expressed in a decision of the Roman Rota in these words:

> Quin ex adverso opponatur quod perito in arte et testanti de facto proprio uti testi qualificato semper fides sit praestanda, praesertim cum a Curia medicus Anicius renunci-

[6] A cardinal's attestation regarding a statement by the Pope carries the weight of full proof in the external forum. *Cf.* Canon 239, § 1, 17°.

[7] S. R. R., *Nullit. Matrim.*, 11 Maii, 1910, *Coram R. P. D., Michaele Lega*, dec. VIII, nn. 8, 13—*Decisiones Coram Lega*, 127, 129; S. R. R., *Nullit. Matrim.*, 30 Junii, 1910, *Coram R. P. D., Michaele Lega*, dec. IX, n. 8—*Decisiones Coram Lega*, 138.

[8] *Cf.* S. R. R., *Nullit. Matrim.*, 11 Maii, 1910, *Coram R. P. D., Michaele Lega*, dec. VIII, nn. 4, 5—*Decisiones Coram Lega*, 128. *Cf.* Crotus, Ioannes, a Monteferrato, *Tractatus De Testibus*, Pars VII, n. 126, fol. 285.

[9] *Cf.* Canon 1795, § 1; Roberti, *De Processibus*, II, n. 358, p. 82; S. R. R., *Nullit. Matrim.*, 11 Augustii, 1910, *Coram R. P. D., Antonio Perathoner*, dec. XXX, n. 2—*Decisiones*, II (1910), 302; S. R. R., *Nullit. Matrim.*, 29 Julii, 1920, *Coram R. P. D., Petro Rossetti*, dec. XXIII, n. 12—*Decisiones*, XII (1920), 223.

> atur uti medicus honestissimus et religione seu pietatis laude conspicuus. Omisso enim quod testificatio in themate respicit factum remotissimi temporis seu fere a vicennio secutum, de quo facile praesumitur oblivio in teste iuxta Rotam coram Oriolo *dec. 86, n. 7,* illud insuper expendendum venit, quod Doctor Anicius non refert tamquam peritus in arte de baptismo, quia minister ordinarius huius sacramenti est tantum parochus, ideoque dici ipse nequit testis qualificatus: quod autem testetur de facto proprio, hoc nihil refert, cum eius testimonium pluribus impetitum appareat exceptionibus, quae omnem fidem ei auferunt, et ad nihilum reducunt amplum Curiae praeconium de medici honorabilitate.[10]

On the other hand, the testimony of a physician about matters which do not come under his observation as a doctor but pertain to something else do not carry the same weight. Thus, for example, the testimony of a doctor regarding the difficulty of practicing the Catholic religion under the Latin rite in Russia does not necessarily have any probative value because the witness is not competent in those matters.

7. Official messengers, court-clerks, public notaries, obstetricians, architects, pharmacists, and the like, furnish complete proof about what they observed in their official capacity. Being qualified witnesses, each provides entire proof and enjoys full credibility as there is a presumption of law in favor of these persons until the contrary is proved.[11] It should be observed, however, that civil lawyers who defend their clients in a civil case for divorce are not thereby considered competent or qualified before an ecclesiastical tribunal. The mental agility of an accomplished lawyer in a civil court does not necessarily equip him with competence to testify with regard to Canon Law in an ecclesiastical court. The testimony of the lawyer which pertained to the marriage law involved in the case was considered valueless by the Roman Rota.[12]

[10] S. R. R., *Nullit. Matrim.,* 25 Februarii, 1911, *Coram R. P. D., Iosepho Mori,* dec. X, n. 12—*Decisiones,* III (1911), 101.

[11] *Cf.* c. 13, X, *de testibus et attestationibus,* II, n. 26; Reiffenstuel, *Ius Canonicum Universum,* lib. II, tit. XX, nn. 271-278.

[12] *Cf.* S. R. R., *Colonien. Nullit. Matrim.,* 27 Augustii, 1910, *Coram R. P. D., Gustavo Persiani* dec. XXXI, nn. 12, 13—*Decisiones,* II (1910), 325, 326.

The general rule of law expressed in the Code is that the attestation of one witness does not provide complete proof unless the witness testifies about acts which he performed himself *ex officio*. This rule will now be examined with reference to Canon 1789. In the first place, the negative form of Canon 1791, § 1, does not imply that one witness who is not qualified is devoid of all credibility. Canon 1791, § 1, concedes that one witness against whom no lawful exception can be taken, can afford incomplete or half proof (*semi-plena probatio*). In the second place, a single witness may, by reason of the presence or the lack of the criteria mentioned in Canon 1789 give either no proof or incomplete proof or, in certain circumstances provide complete proof.

In the first place, the general rule that one witness against whom no exception can be taken can produce incomplete proof [13] suffers an exception. There are occasions when one witness alone merits entire credence and produces full proof. The present jurisprudence of the Roman Rota and older canonists induce one to maintain that a single witness against whom no legal exception can be taken suffices for the decision of causes which involve no prejudice to others. Hence, one witness may give full proof not only regarding questions pertaining to whether a person was baptized,[14] confirmed [15] or received sacred orders, but also to prove that a person is a doctor, or that a church was consecrated, or that somebody who was denounced is innocent of an alleged crime. An individual witness is capable of providing full proof that a person who is dead manifested signs of repentance.[16]

In the second place, from a consideration of the criteria specified in Canon 1789 together with dispositions found in the decisions of

[13] *Cf.* Reiffenstuel, *Ius Canonicum Universum*, lib. II, tit. XX, nn. 250-252; Zallinger, *Institutiones Iuris Ecclesiastici*, lib. II, tit. XX, § 259, VII, p. 191.

[14] *Cf.* Canon 779.

[15] *Cf.* Canon 800.

[16] *Cf.* S. R. R., *Nullit. Matrim.*, 25 Februarii, 1911, *Coram R. P. D., Iosepho Mori*, dec. X, n. 9—*Decisiones*, III (1911), 100; Reiffenstuel, *Ius Canonicum Universum*, lib. II, tit. XX, nn. 254-270, 280; Roberti, *De Processibus*, II, n. 354, p. 75, note 5.

the Roman Rota it may be said that a single witness can provide incomplete evidence and, together with other attending circumstances (*adminicula*), may produce complete proof. Neither the Code nor modern writers on evidence have figured out a scale of values to determine the probative value of the testimony of one or more witnesses. Professor Wigmore has written that for estimating the inferential force to be given to cumulative or contradictory witnesses, there is no more tangible general rule of reasoning than for circumstantial evidence. The problem is really only a part of the greater and general problem of the ultimate effect to be given to any mass of opposing evidence. Logically this problem is the same for both kinds, testimonial and circumstantial, alone or mixed. It cannot be solved for either class independently of the other. No systematic guidance has yet been discovered by science.[17] One does, however, sense a difference of values, and theoretically each witness, at the time one is ready to draw his final inference, can be valued respectively.

Without a systematic guidance from modern science, one turns to Canon 1789 to ascertain the probative value of the testimony of one witness by himself or when he is in a group. It may be stated briefly first, that the party who produced a witness may not reject him. But he may enter an exception provided that new reasons for the exception have arisen and produce witnesses in rebuttal of his testimony.[18] Secondly, against the full proof provided by positive evidence the mere denial made by several witnesses is insufficient to overthrow it. Thirdly, if evidence is positive on both sides the judge must find a solution by either confronting the witnesses with one another or by summoning other witnesses to weaken, or strengthen, the testimony on either side. Fourthly, proofs are not to be estimated mathematically or without the production of new witnesses when there is conflicting evidence. If certain definite circumstances are known conformable witnesses to even unessential factors would be decisive. Having exhausted the means for discriminating between the conflicting proofs, the judge will be obliged in a case involving the validity of a marriage to decide "non constare de nullitate."

[17] Wigmore, *The Principles of Judicial Proof*, § 153, p. 276.

[18] *Cf.* Canon 1764, § 3.

ARTICLE 2. THE VALUE OF THE TESTIMONY OF TWO OR THREE WITNESSES

Canon 1791, § 2. Si sub iuramenti fide duae vel tres personae, omni exceptione maiores, sibi firmiter cohaerentes, de aliqua re vel facto in iudicio testificentur de scientia propria, sufficiens probatio habetur; nisi in aliqua causa iudex ob maximam negotii gravitatem, vel ob indicia quae dubium de veritate rei assertae ingerunt, necessariam censeat pleniorem probationem.

The attestations of two or three witnesses are, as a rule, considered full proof. The above paragraph applies the word of Christ, "that in the mouth of two or three witnesses every word may stand" as a principle of Canon Law.[19] The principle is found in Roman Law [20] and in the *Corpus Juris Canonici*.[21] The dictum that two or three witnesses as a rule produce complete proof must, however, by no means be considered as a prohibition to admit many witnesses. It merely specifies that at least two witnesses are required to produce full credibility[22]

Two or three witnesses provide full proof when the following conditions are verified:

1. When they testify in court.[23]
2. When exception cannot be taken to them (*omni exceptione*

[19] Matt. xviii, 16; John viii, 17. *Cf.* Deut. xix, 15.

[20] "Ubi numerus testium non adiicitur, etiam duo sufficient: pluralis enim locutio numero contenta est."—Ulpianus, D. XXII, 5, 12.

[21] Reg. 40, R. J., in VI°.

[22] *Cf.* Reiffenstuel, *Ius Canonicum Universum*, lib. II, tit. XX, nn. 236-239, 249.

[23] *Cf.* Augustine, *A Commentary*, VII, 239. S. R. R., *Solutionis et Refectionis Damnorum*, 7 Decembris, 1914, *Coram R. P. D., Iosepho Mori*, dec. XXXII, n. 2—*Decisiones*, VI (1914), 333; S. R. R., *Nullit. Matrim.*, 3 Martii, 1922, *Coram R. P. D., Ioanne Prior*, dec. X, n. 8—*Decisiones*, XIV (1922), 88. Perjured testimony is devoid of probative value. *Cf.* S. R. R., *Parisien. Nullit. Matrim.*, 12 Junii, 1919, *Coram R. P. D., Petro Rossetti*, dec. XI, n. 16—*Decisiones*, XI (1919), 108, 109.

maiores). This quality is possessed by witnesses when doubt regarding any assertion made by them cannot be entertained because of their knowledge and inasmuch as they are of unquestioned probity and would abhor the commission of perjury. No suspicion is engendered regarding either their persons, the mode of their examinatin or against their attestations.[24]

3. When their testimony is consistent. Two witnesses whose testimony dovetails generally produces sufficient or full proof in the possession of which the judge can pass sentence. The rule is verified in causes in which two or three witnesses who corroborate one another testify on behalf of one litigant, whereas one credible witness against whom no exception can be taken attests the opposite. Full proof is generally produced by the coincidence of two or three witnesses. It is diminished when there are indications contrary to their testimony. In such cases a judge can in his prudent judgment require full proof in these cases and in other similar ones. Ultimately, the judge decides how credible each witness is. The rules provided by the Code and interpreted by canonists should aid the judge in forming his conscience and in coming to a decision.[25] He will not necessarily accept the testimony of two consistent witnesses as full proof, unless there are circumstances which corroborate their attestations.[26]

4. When witnesses make a judicial attestation about a thing

[24] Reiffenstuel, *Ius Canonicum Universum,* lib. II, tit. XX, nn. 10, 11. Witnesses who may not be *omni exceptione maiores* can provide full credibility but the qualities which are lacking must be supplied by the number of those who agree. *Cf.* Reiffenstuel, *Ius Canonicum Universum,* lib. II, tit. XX, n. 231; Wernz-Vidal, VI, *De Processibus,* n. 484; A Coronata, *De Processibus,* III, n. 1322, p. 227, note 5; Mansella, *De Impedimentis Matrimonium Dirimentibus,* 188. Rumor used in proof of affinity is provided by two witnesses *omni exceptione maiores. Cf.* S. R. R., *Nullit. Matrim.*, 22 Februarii, 1921, *Coram R. P. D., Ioanne Prior,* dec. I, n. 6—*Decisiones,* XIII (1921), 7; S. R. R., *Nullit. Matrim.*, 12 Novembris, 1921, *Coram R. P. D., Ioanne Prior,* dec. XXVIII, n. 4—*Decisiones,* XIII (1921), 265. Two such witnesses produce full proof of force (*metus*) to elicit marital consent. *Cf.* S. R. R., *Nullit. Matrim.*, 15 Februarii, 1919, *Coram R. P. D., Gulielmo Sebastianelli,* dec. II, n. 2—*Decisiones,* XI (1919), 10, 11.

[25] *Cf.* A Coronata, *De Processibus,* III, n. 1322, pp. 227, 228.

[26] *Cf.* S. R. R., *Nullit. Matrim.*, 11 Maii, 1910, *Coram R. P. D., Michaele Lega,* dec. VII, n. 9—*Decisiones Coram Lega,* 130.

which they themselves have witnessed and know from their own immediate knowledge.[27]

5. When there are no contrary indications which engender a doubt about what has been asserted.[28]

6. When the gravity of what is under consideration does not postulate fuller proof. In matrimonial causes of non-consummation, for example, the testimony of the seventh hand is required.[29]

ARTICLE 3. AN APPLICATION OF RULES REQUIRING ONE OR MORE WITNESSES TO MATRIMONIAL CAUSES

Considering Canon 1791, § 1, from the aspect of matrimonial causes it is observed that a pastor is an authorized witness of the Church. He supplies the defects of other witnesses.[30] Should a pastor be called upon to testify about a parochial record in his custody, his attestation that he had inspected the records and found that they were written in legal form is *usually* accepted but an unsigned record is doubted. In one case before the Roman Rota the attestation of a pastor was accepted in spite of the fact that the register of the ordinariate was incomplete. The Rota decided that despite the fact that for a period of eleven years only the number of dispensations granted was known, each dispensation granted during the specified number of years was valid and the testimony of the pastor regarding one of them was accurate.[31]

In another Rota case the defects and omissions in a marriage register were, in doubt of law, efficaciously supplied by the sworn affirmation of the pastor in whose parish they should have been recorded. A defect in the register pertaining to the description of the

[27] *Cf.* S. R. R., *Nullit. Matrim.*, 31 Martii, 1922, *Coram R. P. D., Ioanne Prior*, dec. X, n. 8—*Decisiones*, XIV (1922), 88.

[28] *Cf.* Roberti, *De Processibus*, III, n. 1322, pp. 227, 228.

[29] *Cf.* Canon 1975.

[30] S. R. R., *Nullit. Matrim.*, 28 Maii, 1909, *Coram R. P. D., Aloisio Sincero*, dec. VI, n. 2—*Decisiones*, I (1909), 52; S. R. R., *Nullit. Matrim.*, 11 Maii, 1910, *Coram R. P. D., Michaele Lega*, dec. VIII, nn. 3, 13—*Decisiones*, I (1910), 127, 131.

[31] *Cf.* S. R. R., *Nullit. Matrim.*, 30 Junii, 1910, *Coram R. P. D., Michaele Lega*, dec. IX, n. 7—*Decisiones Coram Lega*, 137.

spouses or the marriage itself does not eliminate the proof provided by the testimony of the pastor. The negligence of a pastor in these matters should not conduce to the disadvantage of the person seeking a declaration of nullity. However, the testimony of a pastor regarding a baptism performed by himself is to be accepted.[82]

On the other hand, when a pastor testifies as a private individual and not as a qualified witness his testimony does not derive any special force from his office.[83] Direct proof against the testimony of a pastor cannot well be adduced against one who himself administered a sacrament. Although a baptismal record be not written, a pastor is, according to Canon 779, a witness against whom no exception can be taken. Should a baptismal record be missing the testimony of a pastor as a qualified witness is sufficient to establish complete proof of the fact of the baptism which is questioned. If, however, a baptismal record is missing and the pastor should testify about the baptism as a mere individual giving a personal opinion about it and not as a pastor testifying *ex officio,* his testimony gives no complete proof when prejudice to a third party may arise as a result of the attestation. There are examples of this practice found in cases tried before the Roman Rota. Two examples may be cited as illustrative of the practice.

Exception was taken to a pastor because of his forgetfulness. He had not recorded a dispensation in the matrimonial register lest it displease a non-Catholic who was considered to be baptized. He felt that inasmuch as the fact of non-baptism was recorded in the ordinariate of the archbishop it was sufficient. Two curates (*coadiutores*) attested that in spite of the fact that the pastor was forgetful, he was and had been constant in affirming the validity of the marriage as it was a juridical principle that the fact which had been recorded was a legitimate one.[84]

[82] S. R. R., *Nullit. Matrim.,* 11 Junii, 1910, *Coram R. P. D., Michaele Lega,* dec. IX, nn. 19, 20—*Decisiones Coram Lega,* 144.

[83] *Cf.* S. R. R., *Nullit. Matrim.,* 28 Augustii, 1911, *Coram R. P. D., Aloisio Sincero,* dec. XXIX, n. 19—*Decisiones,* III (1911), 439.

[84] *Cf.* S. R. R., *Nullit. Matrim,* 30 Junii, 1910, *Coram R. P. D., Michaele Lega,* dec. IX, n. 20—*Decisiones Coram Lega,* 145, 146; *Decis.* 434, n. 7, p. 1, *Recent.,* c. Calcagnin,—"Quando aliquid est factum, semper praesumitur legitime

Regarding the second point, when a pastor speaks as an individual and not as a qualified witness, his testimony is devoid of the special juridical value of a qualified witness in two circumstances, first, when he was not present at the marriage regarding which he testifies [85] and secondly, when his attestation, although substantiated by other witnesses, is a mere personal opinion or a private observation about matters which have a bearing upon his own act but are not directly connected with it. In such circumstances, the Roman Rota has applied the aphorism, "nostra existimatio rerum veritatem non mutat." [86]

Turning from the consideration of a pastor as a qualified witness in matrimonial procedure to other individual witnesses who appear in causes involving the marriage process, the general abstract rule regarding the value of the testimony of one witness which was explained must be rigidly adapted to individual circumstances. An assistant priest or a deacon who administered solemn baptism is a witness against whom no exception can be taken. In the case of a private baptism the pastor has to decide on the personal qualities and truthfulness of the witness. When the pastor examines witnesses with respect to the fact of baptism he must give attention to the validity of the sacraments which were not conferred by clerics.[87]

The fundamental proof of the existence or the absence of the impediment of disparty of worship [88] is identical with the proof of baptism. One witness against whom no objection can be registered as well as an oath of the person himself that he received baptism in adult age [89] is sufficient proof of baptism when no prejudice exists

factum, potius quam illegitime, praesertim ad tollendam delictum Parocho viro probo et literato."

[85] *Cf.* S. R. R., *Nullit. Matrim.*, 23 Martii, 1914, *Coram R. P. D., Gulielmo Sebastianelli*, dec. XII, n. 9—*Decisiones*, VI (1914), 150.

[86] S. R. R., *Nullit. Matrim.*, 11 Maii, 1910, *Coram R. P. D., Michaele Lega*, dec. VIII, n. 13—*Decisiones Coram Lega*, 131. *Cf.* S. R. R., *Matrimonii*, 13 Februarii, 1913, *Coram R. P. D., Michaele Lega*, dec. XXXIV, nn. 5, 7—*Decisiones Coram Lega*, 417.

[87] *Cf.* Muniz, *Procedimientos Eclesiásticos*, II, n. 204, p. 241.

[88] *Cf.* Canon 1070.

[89] Canon 779.

against another person. Gasparri is more specific. He observes that [40] the testimony of either the godmother or the godfather is worthy of credence, or an authentic document attesting to the reception of first communion may be used. Testimony to the reception of confirmation may be, as Gasparri remarked, confirmatory. In this country, however, it is not accepted as such. In order to exact further proof because there is prejudice against a third person, it is necessary that the prejudice arise from the fact of the baptism or an annotation of filiation in the record. These are independent of the proof of baptism.[41]

As the general rule the testimony of a nurse to the baptism of a child is acceptable. Nevertheless, a practical case may suggest itself when a baptismal record is requested and it cannot be found. Archbishop Muniz [42] presents the case of a child whose nurse told its mother that she took the boy to a church where it was baptized. When the case was proposed to the Ordinary the investigation showed (a) that the mother suspected that the nurse who was light-fingered stole the money. The mother did not believe that the child was baptized. (b) An investigation showed that the baptismal records of neighboring parishes during the year of the alleged baptism provided no full name and identical filiation with the person who was supposed to have been baptized about that time. (c) The declarations of two credible witnesses were taken to the effect that the child was born on the day which was stated, within the limits of the parish, and that the nurse was not careful about the practice of her religion. (d) Together with this information and the testimony of the pastor and the assistants of the parish was added. They testified that they did not recall any fact for or against the baptism. The baptism could be accepted as proved as far as the marriage is concerned because there were indications that it was administered, but the proof is insufficient for the baptism itself. Therefore, the Ordinary in this and in kindred cases should declare that the baptism must be administered conditionally. The fact is to be recorded in the parochial

[40] *Cf.* Gasparri, *De Matrimonio,* I, n. 141, p. 89.

[41] *Cf.* Muniz, *Procedimientos Eclesiásticos,* II, n. 204, pp. 240, 241; n. 270, p. 326.

[42] Muniz, *Procedimientos Eclesiásticos,* II, n. 204, pp. 242, 243.

book. The place and the time of the conditional administration are to be noted together with a further annotation in the place where the record should have been but is not found.[43]

In the proof of the death of a spouse who has been absent a long while, some positive fact is required which points to the likelihood of the death. There must first of all be circumstantial evidence of a negative character. There must, in other words, be no reason for a prolonged absence of the spouse, *e. g.*, there must have been no discord in the family to warrant the disappearance or no business reasons for the non-appearance of the mission person or no felony or crime committed which prompts the missing person to remain away. Secondly, there must be one or more positive reasons for the disappearance of the spouse. A positive reason or fact sufficient for the establishment of the death would be a battle in which the person is known to have engaged or a hazardous journey which was taken by him. Thirdly, other circumstances may be added to prove the death of the missing party. One of these may be that the missing person continued a correspondence with his wife which was abruptly terminated. Witnesses may add other corroborative details.[44]

In the proof of the death of a spouse who has been absent for a long while, as a rule one witness does not furnish complete proof. Due to the importance of this subject from a procedural aspect, the general rules for the establishment of the testimonial proof of the death of a husband or wife will first be indicated and then, the special rules applying to witnesses who testify from their own knowledge will be considered.

General Rules Regarding Presumed Death of a Spouse. Before another marriage can be permitted the evidence of the death of the former spouse must be both positive and in conformity with the regulations expressed in law.[45] If it be said that a marriage was disssolved

[43] *Cf.* Muniz, *Procedimientos Eclesiásticos*, II, n. 204, 1°, p. 242. For the procedure in the case of a non-Catholic who supposes that he is baptized, *cf.* Muniz, *Procedimientos Eclesiásticos*, II, n. 204, 3°, p. 243.

[44] For a summary of the proofs of the death of a husband or wife, *cf.* Schaaf, Valentine, O.F.M., "*Proof of the Death of Husband or Wife,*" *American Ecclesiastical Review*, LXXXIX (1933), 282-286.

[45] Compare Canon 1069, § 2.

by the death of another party, the probability of death is not sufficient. Moral certitude is required. One is presumed to be living until death is proved. In doubt, a spouse should not do anything which would prejudice the right of another and expose a new marriage to the danger of nullity.[46]

A certificate of the death is always the first requisite. Such a certificate is not usually issued by the ecclesiastical authorities who officially attest to and record deaths in the obituary. In this country and elsewhere, when the Church is unable to furnish a death certificate, the law permits a civil one.[47] In particular, the authenticity and certitude of such documents are, remarks Linneborn,[48] to be examined and their certitude strengthened in times of accidents and above all in times of war.[49] One cannot proceed to the celebration of

[46] Gasparri, *De Matrimonio* (1932), I, n. 561, p. 346.

[47] *Cf.* Linneborn, *Grundriss Des Eherechts,* § 24, III, 2, p. 233.

[48] *Ibid.,* p. 234: "Insbesondere wären derartige Zeugnisse bei allgemeinen Unglücksfallen und vor allem bei Kriegszeiten auf ihre Zuverlassigkeit zu prüfen und die Gewissheit duch andere Nachforschungen zu verstärken."

[49] The Holy Office applied the rules of evidence contained in previous instructions to the following instances: Italian soldiers killed in the battle of Adona (Adua) in Africa—S. C. S. Off., decretum, 20 Julii, 1898—*A. S. S.,* XXXI (1898-1899), 252 and *A. A. S.,* II (1910), 198; III (1911), 28. *Cf.* Acta Sacrorum Congregationum, *Sacra Congregatio de Disciplina Sacramentorum, Praesumptae Mortis Coniugis* in the following cases: After the "Messanensa-Rheginensem" earthquake the reply of the Sacred Congregation was "Expendendos esse ab Ordinario casus particulares juxta instructionem *Matrimonii* vinculo a S. C. Sancti Officii datam anno 1868." *Cf.* S. C. de Sacram., *Messanen. seu Rhegenen.,* 12 Martii, 1910—*A. A. S.,* II (1910), 196-199.

After the Russo-Japanese War, the Sacred Congregation referred to replied regarding the Russians lost in the battle of. Mukden, "Applicandum esse responsum a S. O. die 20, Julii, 1898, quoad viros qui adstiterunt pugnae de Adua," *cf.* S. C. de Sacram., *Mohilovien.,* 16 Decembris, 1910—*A. A. S.,* III (1911), 26-29. Other applications of presumed death of a spouse by the S. Congr. de Disciplina Sacra. follow: 18 Decembris, 1914—*A. A. S.,* VII (1915), 40-44; 29 Aprilis, 1915—*A. A. S.,* VII (1915), 235, 236; 25 Junii, 1915—*A. A. S.,* VII (1915), 476-479; 25 Februarii, 1916—*A. A. S.,* VIII (1916), 151-153; 19 Januarii, 1917—*A. A. S.,* IX (1917), 120-122; 18 Novembris, 1920—*A. A. S.,* XIV (1922), 96, 97; compare with the last, *De Praesumpta Morte Coniugis—Jus Pont.,* I (1921), 28, in which the writer observed that the reply pertains more to practice

another marriage even though the civil authority has made a declaration in legal form that the missing person is dead. The ecclesiastical authority can make use of the fact that the ecclesiastical authorities have recorded the death in the obituary and the fact that the civil authority has made a declaration of the demise of the party for the purpose of indications, conjectures or presumptions of the death. Some of the older instructions were guides in the procedure for presenting evidence whenever one of the married persons was alleged to be dead and the surviving spouse desired to remarry.[50] Nevertheless, the ecclesiastical authorities must today establish the proofs of a presumed death in accordance with the rules laid down in an instruc-

than to doctrine. See *Decretum-lex* d. d. 15 Augustii, 1919, n. 1467 et *Reg.* Decr. d. d. 11 Januarii, 1920, n. 40, quoted in Chelodi, Ioanne, *Ius Matrimoniale*, p. 78, note 1: This was a special law for those not returning for a year after the end of the World War, whether they fought on land or sea. It stated that a declaration of presumed death is made by the tribunal at the instance of the interested party. The second marriage is declared null, although it was valid due to an error in stating the time of the death if the absent party returns and accuses it. *Cf.* Kaas, *Kriegsverschollenheit und Wiederverheiratung*, 68-73.

[50] *Cf.* (1) 21 Augustii, 1670—C. Congr. S. R. U. Inquisitionis *"Cum alias"* Decretum, in *Coll.*, II, 192 p. 64; *AFKK*, II (1857), 317-320;

(2) 23 Junii, 1671—S. Congr. S. Off. Decretum, in *Coll.*, I, n. 196, p. 66;

(3) 21 Aprilis, 1788—Rescriptum, Propaganda, in *Coll.*, I, n. 595, p. 370;

(4) 1792—Instructio, Propaganda, in *Coll.*, I, n. 606, p. 379;

(5) 22 Junii, 1822—S. C. S. Off., Instr., *"Ingentes bellorum clades,"* in Feije, *De Impedimentis et Dispensationibus Matrimonialibus*, 816-822; *cf. AFKK*, XXII (1869), 186; XXVII (1872), 116; LIII (1885), 426;

(6) 24 Februarii, 1847—S. C. S. Off., rescriptum Circa decretum *"Cum alias,"* 21 Augustii, 1670, de statu libero comprobando, in *Coll.*, I, n. 1011, p. 549;

(7) 12 Februarii, 1851—S. C. S. Off., rescriptum in *Coll.*, I, n. 1057, p. 572;

(8) 6 Februarii, 1861—S. C. S. Off. rescriptum—*A. S. S.*, XXIV (1891-1892), 747; *cf.* S. C. de Sacram., *Mohilovien. Praesumptae Mortis Coniugis*, 16 Decmbris, 1910—*A. A. S.*, III (1911), 26-29;

(9) 22 Martii, 1865—S. C. S. Off., rescriptum in *Coll.*, I, n. 1272, p. 701;

(10) 28 Junii, 1865—S. C. S. Off., rescriptum in *Coll.*, I, n. 1073, p. 701; *cf.* Martii, 1910, in causa Messan. et Reghionen.—*A. A. S.*, II (1910), 198;

(11) 1 Februarii, 1865—*Ex S. Congr. S. R. U. Inquisitionis*, Instr., *"Se il Vescovo"*—*A. S. S.*, XXXI (1898-1899), 408, 409.

tion issued by the Sacred Congregation of the Holy Office in the year 1868.[51]

The proofs are of three kinds, testimonial, proof by presumptions and rumor. These proofs cannot be taken into consideration unless the documentary evidence is lacking. The proofs derived from presumption cannot be taken up if testimonial proof is possible. The proof from rumor cannot be considered if the other proofs are possible. However, the second and third proofs, namely, from presumption and rumor, can be given attention for the purpose of confirming the first, that is, the testimonial.[52]

The proof when a certificate of the death is not obtained must begin with a declaration under oath made by the living party. This deposition should describe in detail the date of and the reasons for the absence of the missing spouse. Any news which the surviving spouse has received regarding the missing person must be communicated. The letters which have been received are to be produced and copied among the documents covering the case. Likewise, the motives which lead the living party to believe that the missing spouse is dead must be copied among the documents.[53]

Other rules found in the Instruction of 1868 are not considered here as they do not apply directly under consideration.

Special Rules Applying Principle to Presumed Death of Spouse. After the examination of the relatives of the parties, which phase of the subject was treated under the topic of the value of the testimony of relatives, one observes that in the testimonial proof three situations may occur: (1) When at least two witnesses may testify from their own knowledge; (2) when only one eyewitness can be obtained; (3) when only hearsay witnesses can be produced. In all

[51] This instruction of 13 Maii, 1868, entitled "Instructio ad probandum obitum aliciuus coniugis" is found in *A. S. S.*, VI (1870), 436-442; S. C. S. Off., Instr., a. 1868—*Fontes,* § 1002; *cf. AFKK,* XLVIII (1882), 56; see also Triebs, *Praktisches Handbuch des geltenden Kanonischen Eherechts,* II, 311-314; Gasparri, *De Matrimonio,* II, nn. 723, 724, pp. 507-509; *A. A. S.,* II (1910), 199-203, which is a reprint as a reply of the S. C. of Sacraments; *Acta Et Decreta Concilii Plenarii Baltimorensis Tertii* (1884), pp. 258-261.

[52] Muniz, *Procedimientos Eclesiásticos,* II, n. 259, p. 310.

[53] *Ibid.*

three of these situations the witnesses have to be first of all, worthy of credence. If the Ordinary does not himself know them, he will procure information about their credibility through an investigation from other persons in whom he has confidence and whom he knows personally; secondly, the witnesses must be above suspicion, namely, they must not come under Canon 1757 which has been explained. Thirdly, the witnesses, if it be possible, should be relatives of the dead person. According to the circumstances of the case, a witness should be somebody who had accompanied the missing person on the last journey which he took, been with him in the army or navy, or been associated with him as a business partner or workman. Fourthly, the witness must be under oath.

With these special rules for testimony in mind, one turns in the first place to the case in which it is possible to gather the declarations of at least two witnesses who make an attestation from what came under their own observation. When the witnesses have all the conditions enumerated in the previous paragraph and, moreover, knew the dead spouse personally [54] and give testimony which harmonizes about the fact of death, the place it occurred, its cause, whether from sickness, ship-wreck, accident or homicide, and testify that they were present at the burial, the Ordinary, guided by this testimony and because of other substantial circumstances, will declare that the death of the spouse is sufficiently established.[55] In the second case, if there be but one witness who testifies from his own knowledge about the things mentioned in the first case, and the Ordinary is certain of his truthfulness, as when the witness is a serious man of grave aspect, and when the Ordinary is sure of his disinterestedness, the death of the spouse can be declared in either of the two following circumstances: (a) If other grave indications of the death of the spouse are present;[56] (b) if these indications are lacking, and it is absolutely certain that there is nothing in the attes-

[54] *Cf. S. C. S. Off., Instr.*, a. 1868, "Instructio ad probandum obitum aliciuus coniugis," n. 13—*Fontes*, n. 1002.

[55] *Cf.* Muniz, *Procedimientos Eclesiásticos*, II, n. 260, p. 311; *cf.* Linneborn, *Grundriss Des Eherechts*, § 24, III, p. 234.

[56] *Cf. S. C. S. Off., Instr.*, a. 1868—"Instructio ad probandum obitum aliciuus coniugis," n. 4; *cf.* Linneborn, *Grundriss Des Eherechts*, § 24, III, p. 234.

tation of the only witness which does not possess the appearance of truth by itself and with relation to the person, place and other circumstances of the case.[57] Thirdly, whenever there are no witnesses present who can declare from their own knowledge (*ex scientia propria*) that the missing spouse is dead, the attestations of hearsay witnesses (*de auditu*) are admissible. Three things should be established before these hearsay witnesses are admitted to prove the alleged death. These are: (a) The principle witnesses (*de visu*) cannot make a declaration because they themselves are either dead or absent and cannot come to the court or because they have some other reasonable excuse that should be proved. If, however, it is possible to record their declarations through the Ordinary of the place where they reside, the attestations cannot be omitted. (b) The hearsay witnesses learned about the death of the spouse from those who were present at it (*de visu*) in such a manner that the nature of the death is certain and the time during which they heard of it is non suspect. For example, the witness must have known that the death occurred before he knew that it was necessary to establish the fact and before the surviving spouse intended to contract a second marriage. (c) The testimony of the hearsay witnesses must have the appearance of truth, so that it conforms with at least most important circumstances of the case. If these conditions are present together the Ordinary can declare that the absent spouse is dead.[58]

It was asserted that there is complete proof when there are two or more witnesses who have the qualities mentioned in Canon 1791, § 2.[59] This rule applies in matrimonial causes. At least two witnesses against whom no exception can be taken must substantiate the depo-

[57] Muniz, *Procedimientos Eclesiásticos,* II, n. 260, 2°, p. 312.

[58] *Cf.* Muniz, *Procedimientos Eclesiásticos,* II, n. 260, p. 312.

[59] *Cf.* S. R. R., *Londonen. Incardinationis,* 9 Januarii, 1912, *Coram R. P. D., Antonio Perathoner,* dec. II, n. 9—*Decisiones,* IV (1912), 19; S. R. R., *Nullit. Matrim.,* 17 Januarii, 1912, *Coram R. P. D., Michaele Lega,* dec. V, n. 23—*Decisiones,* IV (1912), 48, 49; S. R. R., *Limburgen. Nullit. Matrim.,* 2 Januarii, 1913, dec. I, n. 8—*Decisiones,* V (1913), 7; S. R. R., *Proprietatis,* 16 Augustii, 1916, *Coram R. P. D., Gulielmo Sebastianelli,* dec. XXVI, n. 2—*Decisiones,* VIII (1916), 279; S. R. R., *Transilvanian. Nullit. Matrim.,* 5 Julii, 1921, *Coram R. P. D., Raphaele Chimenti,* dec. XVI, n. 7—*Decisiones,* XIII (1921), 160-163.

sitions of the principals in matrimonial causes although both parties plainly agree on things pertaining to the invalidity of the marriage.[60] Turning to the application of the rule that "two or more witnesses who are consistent in their testimony produce full proof" it is first of all to be observed that the Sacred Roman Rota has repeatedly invoked the rule in the adjudication of causes affecting the marriage bond.[61] A summary application of the principle to matrimonial procedure in the case of diriment impediments to which it directly applies follows:

Age. Males who have not completed their sixteenth and females who have not completed their fourteenth year cannot marry validly. The ordinary proof for the existence or the non-existence

[60] S. R. R., *Parisien. Nullit. Matrim.*, 17 Aprilis, 1915, *Coram R. P. D., Friderico Cattani Amadori,* dec. XVI, n. 3—*Decisiones,* VII (1915), 163.

[61] *Cf.* in the proof of force and fear used to elicit matrimonial consent, S. R. R., *Veszprimien. Nullit. Matrim.*, videnibus omnibus—2 Junii, 1911, *Coram R. P. D., Michaele Lega,* dec. XIII, n. 17—*Decisiones Coram Lega,* 181; S. R. R., *Veszprimien. Nullit. Matrim.* (Andrassy-Szechenyi), 2 Junii, 1911, *Coram R. P. D., Michaele Lega,* dec. XXI, n. 17—*Decisiones,* III (1911), 235; S. R. R., *Nullit. Matrim.*, 29 Novembris, 1913, *Coram R. P. D., Ioanne Prior,* dec. L, n. 16—*Decisiones,* V (1913), 619; S. R. R., *Nullit. vel Dispensationis Matrim.*, 27 Aprilis, 1915, *Coram R. P. D., Ioanne Prior,* dec. XIX, n. 4—*Decisiones,* VII (1915), 210; S. R. R., *Parisien. Nullit. Matrim.*, 4 Martii, 1916, *Coram R. P. D., Gulielmo Sebastianelli,* dec. V, n. 8—*Decisiones,* VIII (1916), 64; S. R. R., *Pitilianen. Nullit. Matrim.*, 20 Octobris, 1916, *Coram R. P. D., Gulielmo Sebastianelli,* dec. XXIX, n. 7—*Decisiones,* VIII (1916), 332: "Quare iure meritoque admittitur plus valere duos testes de metu in specie deponentes, quam mille de libertate testantes." S. R. R., *Parisien. Nullit. Matrim.*, 12 Junii, 1919, *Coram R. P. D., Petro Rossetti,* dec. XI, n. 17—*Decisiones,* XI (1919), 108. In the proof of invalidating conditions contrary to the *bonum prolis, cf.* S. R. R., *Nullit. Matrim.*, 17 Januarii, 1912, *Coram R. P. D., Michaele Lega,* dec. V, n. 23—*Decisiones,* IV (1912), 48, 49. In the proof of the valid form of marriage, *cf.* S. R. R., *Parisien. Nullit. Matrim.*, 22 Aprilis, 1923, *Coram R. P. D., Antonio Perathoner,* dec. XXIII, n. 2—*Decisiones,* V (1923) 264. Compare the proof of a particular custom. *Cf.* S. R. R., *Segusina. Iuris Canendi. Missas Adventicias,* 12 Julii, 1913, *Coram R. P. D., Antonio Perathoner,* dec. XXXVI, n. 3—*Decisiones,* V (1913), 434; S. R. R., *Vincentina. Exemptionis et Funerum,* 9 Martii, 1915, *Coram R. P. D., Aloisio Sincero,* dec. IX, n. 9—*Decisiones,* XII (1915), 98; S. R. R., *Bergomen., Iuris Funerandi,* 25 Februarii, 1919, *Coram R. P. D., Petro Rossetti,* dec. V, n. 4—*Decisiones,* XI (1919), 52.

of the impediment of age among Christians is a certificate which contains a record of the birth. When this is lacking one can try to obtain a civil record in the registry of vital statistics. The impediment is a public one if it is known either with notoriety of fact or notoriety of law. It is a public impediment when it can be proved in the external forum by a record or by at least two witnesses against whom exception cannot be taken (*omni exceptione maiores*).[62] Hence, if the approximate age of the person intending to contract a marriage is well known, two credible witnesses may testify regarding the probable age. Likewise, if the appearance of the party does not indicate that he is very young or that he is quite old the testimony of two witnesses worthy of credence suffices. When the party, however, is a member of a well known family and a certificate of baptism or a birth record from the civil authorities is not found, the testimony of the family suffices for the determination of the age provided that there are not presumptions against the fact.[63]

Previous and Existing Marriage. Marriage, with the exception of the privilege of the faith, is rendered invalid by the bond of a previous marriage, even though it was only ratified. Although the first marriage be null or dissolved for whatsoever reason, it is unlawful to contract another marriage before the nullity or dissolution of the first be established legitimately and certainly.[64] There are six proofs of the absence of this impediment which the pastor can accept himself.[65] The proofs of the impediment which must be established by the diocesan curia, however, have a more direct bearing on the subject under consideration. The first of these pertains to the establishment of the freedom of a person who has resided in another place for six months, or when there is a suspicion that the contracting party is not at liberty to marry, even for a briefer time. In this case the Ordinary possesses the right to decide: (a) that the banns of marriage be published in the place or places in which the person has

[62] *Cf.* S. R. R., *Parisien. Nullit. Matrim.*, 12 Januarii, 1919, *Coram R. P. D., Petro Rossetti,* dec. XI, n. 4—*Decisiones,* XI (1919), 96.

[63] *Cf.* Muniz, *Procedimientos Eclesiásticos,* II, n. 239, p. 284.

[64] Canon 1069, §§ 1, 2.

[65] These are briefly outlined in Muniz, *Procedimientos Eclesiásticos,* II, n. 257, pp. 306-308.

lived for six months or whenever there exists a suspicion that the party could have contracted a previous marriage;[66] (b) that each of the pastors of those places where the person resided certify that he has known the party sufficiently to certify to his freedom to marry; (c) that sworn declarations be received from two or more credible witnesses. As a general rule the letters of credibility provided by their pastors which testify to the probity and credibility of these witnesses should suffice.[67] The three proofs or one of them can be established according to the circumstances of the case and the judgment of the Ordinary. Archbishop Muniz [68] makes the observation that in many dioceses of Spain the pastors are authorized to correspond with one another in their respective dioceses with reference to this impediment. This practice precludes the necessity of going to the Ordinary for the establishment of the freedom to contract marriage

Sacred Orders and Solemn Vows. A marriage when attempted by clerics in sacred orders is invalid.[69] A marriage is also null when attempted by religious who have taken solemn vows, or simple vows which have that annulling power by a special disposition of the Apostolic See.[70] The *ordinary proof* of the existence of the impediment

[66] Canon 1023, §§ 2, 3; *cf.* Gasparri, *De Matrimonio,* I, nn. 158-168, pp. 97-103; Chelodi, *Ius Matrimoniale,* nn. 25-27, pp. 21-24.

[67] *Cf.* S. C. S. Off., Instr., a. 1858—*Fontes,* n. 946; *Coll.,* I, n. 1153; S. C. S. Off., Instr., (ad Ep. Rituum Orient.), a. 1883—*Fontes,* n. 1076, n. 16; Instr. S. C. de Prop. Fide, a. 1883—*Coll.,* n. 1587, n. 16; *Instr. . . . Pro Sinis.,* nn. 19, 20, 37—Payen, *De Matrimonio,* II, pp. 994, 995, 1003; *S. C. de Disc. Sacram.* (Regulae Servandae In Processibus Super Nullitate Sacrae Ordinationis vel Onerum Sacris Ordinibus Inhaerentium), V, § 16—*Ius Pont.,* XII (1932), 149. The testimony of a pastor to the credibility of the mother of a plaintiff was rejected by the Roman Rota because maternal affection rendered her suspect. *Cf.* S. R. R., *Colonien. Nullit. Matrim.,* 27 Augustii, 1910, *Coram R. P. D., Gustavo Persiani,* dec. XXXI, n. 10—*Decisiones,* II (1910), 322, 323. The curia of Warsaw requires the testimony of the pastor to the probity and credibility of a witness and that a witness approach a confessor before the examination. *Cf.* S. R. R., *Varsavien. seu Lublinen. Nullit. Matrim.,* 21 Julii, 1910—*Coram R. P. D., Gulielmo Sebastianelli,* dec. XXVIII, n. 5—*Decisiones,* II (1910), 291.

[68] Muniz, *Procedimientos Eclesiásticos,* II, n. 258, 1°, p. 308.

[69] Canon 1072.

[70] Canon 1073.

of sacred orders is a document or certificate which is issued in some dioceses in the United States. It provides documentary evidence of the reception of sacred orders. When this is lacking or has not been issued, the record of ordinations which is kept by the diocesan curia [71] and the marginal note appended to the record of the baptism in the baptismal register are used.[72] This last proof can be impugned by a certificate of the curia which states that the person did not receive sacred orders and that, consequently, the marginal note is wrong. The curia of the locality in which the marriage is to be celebrated must conduct a special investigation to ascertain whether the marginal note be faulty regarding the place of ordination but not about the ordination itself. The investigation will be very simple if the person and his previous life are sufficiently known. Special care has to be exercised if the person comes from a foreign country and his life is unknown [73] or if he has been absent for a long time. The permission to contract marriage cannot be granted unless the curia of the place in which the baptism was recorded does not certify that the ordination to major orders did not take place in spite of the marginal note.

An *extraordinary proof* of the impediment of sacred orders which directly refers to two or more witnesses is the testimonial evidence with which sacred ordination is established. This proof, however, is insufficient by itself if the interested party challenge it. The proof becomes worthless when challenged because the absence of any record in the register of sacred orders is a very strong presumption in favor of the party. This presumption should be destroyed. The ordinary proofs of the absence of this impediment are the negative result of the publication of the banns of marriage, the declaration under oath of two or three credible witnesses that the party is not well known, a declaration made by the interested person himself and the absence of any marginal note in the baptismal register. These proofs are enough if the party is not a foreigner with a dubious reputation.

[71] Canon 1010.

[72] *Cf.* Canons 470, § 2; 1011.

[73] *Cf.* S. C. Consist., 30 Decembris, 1918, Decretum (De clericiis in certas quasdam regiones demigrantibus)—*A. A. S.*, XI (1918), 11-39; *Period.*, X (1918), 42,

What has been said regarding the impediment of sacred orders applies to the ordinary and extraordinary proofs of the impediment of solemn vows. The original document establishing the proof of solemn profession must be in the archives of the convent in which the profession took place. A notification of the fact of solemn profession must be forwarded to the pastor of the place where the baptism took place for the purpose of making a marginal annotation beside the baptismal record.[74]

Consanguinity. It was stated previously that the proofs of consanguinity are a baptismal record and sometimes the matrimonial record. A document from the civil registry of vital statistics can be used as a suppletory proof together with the declarations of witnesses but it is insufficient by itself. Attestations of witnesses will be received for the following purposes: (a) To eliminate a doubt or to confirm a suspicion; (b) to prove or to establish the absence or the presence of the impediment when it is impossible to secure the records mentioned because they either do not exist or because it is very difficult to obtain them; (c) to prove and establish consanguinity which was illegitimate and is not found in the parish register because the parents are unknown; (d) to correct a mistake that was made in the records either for or against the impediment;[75] (e) to make sure that no other impediment than the one indicated by the record exists.[76]

[74] Canons 470, § 2; 576, § 2; *cf.* Muniz, *Procedimientos Eclesiásticos,* II, n. 286, pp. 342, 343. For extraordinary proofs of the absence of these impediments see Chapter VII, supra.

[75] This does not imply that the two or more witnesses can actually fabricate a new document or record when one has been lost.

[76] *Cf.* Muniz, *Procedimientos Eclesiásticos,* II, n. 318, p. 387.

BIBLIOGRAPHY

SOURCES

Acta Apostolica Sedis, Romae, Typis Polyglottis Vaticanis. 1909.

Acta et Decreta Sacrorum Conciliorum Recentiorum (Collectio Lacensis), 7 vols. Friburgi Brisgoviae. 1870-1890.

Acta et Decreta Concilii Provincialis Portlandensis in Oregon Quarti, Portlandiae, 1932.

Acta Sanctae Sedis, 41 vols., Romae, Ex Typographia Polyglotta, 1865-1908.

Codex Iuris Canonici Pii X Pontificis Maximi iussu digestus Benedicti Papae XV auctoritate promulgatus, Romae, Typis Polyglottis Vaticanis. 1918.

Codex Theodosianus, Ed. P. Krueger, Th. Mommsen, 3 vols. Berolini. 1905.

Codicis Iuris Canonici Fontes, Cura Emi. Petri Card. Gasparri editi, 6 vols. Romae, Typis Polyglottis Vaticanis. 1923-1933.

Codicis Justiniani a Gratissimi Principis Ex Repetita ad Vetustissimorum Exemplarium, Atque Ad Ipsius Noricae Editionis, 5 vols. Lugduni, Apud Hugonem à Porta. 1553.

Collectanea S. Congregationis de Propaganda Fide, 2 vols. Romae, ex Typographia Polyglotta, Romae. 1907.

Concilii Plenarii Baltimorensis I, Acta et Decreta (1852), Baltimorae, Typis Joannes Murphy et Sociorum. 1853.

Concilii Plenarii Baltimorensis II, Acta et Decreta (1866), Baltimorae, Typis Joannes Murphy et Sociorum. 1868.

Concilii Plenarii Baltimorensis III, Acta et Decreta (1884), Baltimorae, Typis Joannes Murphy et Sociorum. 1886.

Coram Lega Habitae S. R. Rotae Decisiones Sive Sententiae Quas Nempe Emus. Cardinalis Michaelis Lega Annis 1909-1914 Eiusdem Sacri Auditorii Deacanus Exaravit, Romae, Typis Polyglottis Vaticanis. 1926.

Corpus Iuris Canonici, Editio Lipsiensis II, Richter-Friedberg, 2 vols. Lipsiae. 1922.

Corpus Iuris Civilis, 3 vols. Berolini. 1928-1929.

Institutiones, quas recognovit P. Krueger.

Digesta, quae recognovit T. Mommsen et retractavit P. Krueger.

Codex Iustinianus, quem recognovit et retractavit P. Krueger.

Novellae, quas recognovit R. Schoell, et absolvit G. Kroll.

Decreta Authentica Congregationis Sacrorum Rituum, 6 vols. Romae. 1898.

Decretum Gratiani emendatum et notionibus illustratum, una cum glossis, Gregorii XIII Pont. Max. iussu editum, 2 vols. Romae. 1852.

Fontes Iuris Romani Antejustiniani in Usum Scholarum, ediderunt S. Riccobono, J. Baviera, C. Ferrini. Iuris Antecessores Leges, Auctores, Leges Saeculares. Florentia. Apud G. Barbera. 1908.

Fragmenta Interpretationis Gai Institutionum Augustodunensia.
Fragmenta Quae Dicuntur Vatciana.
Gai Institutionum Commentarii Quattuor.
Gai Institutionum Epitome.
Iulii Pauli Quinque Sententiarum ad Filium.

Glossarium ad Scriptores Mediae et Infimae Latinitatis, Cardus Dufresne, Du Cange, Rege a Consiliis, et Franciae apud Ambianos Quaestore, Ed. nova, 6 vols., Parisiis, Sub Oliva Caroli Osmont, 1733.

Harduinus, Joannes, *Acta Conciliorum et Epistolae Decretales ac Constitutiones Summorum Pontificum,* 12 vols., Parisiis, 1714-1715.

Hinchius, Paulus, *Decretales Pseudo-Isidorianae et Capitula Angelramni,* Lipsiae, Ex Officina Bernhardi Tauchnitz, 1863.

Lauchert, Friedrich, *Die Kanones Der Wichtigsten Altkirchlichen Concilien nebst Den Apostolischen Kanones,* Freiburg i B. und Leipzig. 1896. Akademische Verlagsbuchhanglung von J. C. B. Mohr. 1896.

Mansi, Joannes, *Sacrorum Conciliorum Nova et Amplissima Collectio,* Joannes Dominicus Mansi et post ipsius mortem Florentinus et Venetianus Editores. Paris. H. Welter. 1901—53 vols.

Migne, Jacques, *Patrologiae Cursus Completus seu Bibliotheca Universalis,* Series Graeca. 161 vols; Series Latina. 221 vols. Parisiis. 1858-1864.
Eusebius, *Historia Ecclesiastica—M. P. G.* 20, 45-906.
Irenaeus, *Adversus Haereses—M. P. G.* 7, 431-1224,
Hieronimus, References to passages in his works as in *M. P. G.* 39, 217-226.
Socrates, *Historia Ecclesiastica—M. P. G.* 67, 29-841.
Sozomen, *Historia Ecclesiastica—M. P. G.* 67, 843-1630.

Monumenta Germaniae Historica.
Auctores Antiquissimores, edidit Societas Aperiendis Fontibus Rerum Germanicarum Medii Aevi. Berolini. Apud Weidmannos. 1877-1919. 15 vols.
Leges, Georgius Henricus Pertz, 5 vols, edidit, Hannoverae. 1925-1929.

Quinque Compilationes Antique Nec Non Collectio Canonum Lipsiensis, Recognovit et adnotatione critica instruxit Aemilius Friedberg, Lipsiae, Ex Officina Bernhardi Tauchnitz, 1882.

Regulae Servandae In Iudiciis Apud Sanctae Romanae Rotae Tribunal, Romae, Typis Polyglottis Vaticanis. 1910.

Regulae Servandae In Processibus Super Matrimonio Rato et Non Consummato, Cum Appendice Praecipuorum Actorum Formularum, Quae Utiliter et Opportune Adhibentur in His Causis, Romae, Typis Polyglottis Vaticanis. 1923.

Rerum Gallicarum et Francicarum Scriptores (Recueil des historiens des Gaules et de la France). Edited by M. Bouquet and others. Paris. 1738-1904. 24 vols. Vol. XIV, Introduction. Edit., H. Welter.

Sacrae Romanae Rotae Decisiones seu Sententiae, Romae, Typis Polyglottis Vaticanis. 1912-1930. 15 vols.

Works

A Coronata, P. Matthaeus Conte, ***Institutiones Iuris Canonici Ad Usum Utriusque Clerici et Scholarum***, Vol. III, ***De Processibus***, Taurini (Italia) ex Officina Libraria Marietti. 1933.

Ayrinhac, H. A., ***Penal Legislation in the New Code of Canon Law*** (Liber V). New York, Benziger Brothers.

Ayrinhac, H. A.—Lydon, P. J., ***Marriage Legislation in the New Code of Canon Law***. New York, Benziger Brothers. 1933.

[Bachofen] Augustine, Charles, O.S.B., ***A Commentary on Canon Law***, 4th ed., 8 vols. St. Louis, B. Herder Book Co. 1920.

Bangen, Joannes, ***Instructio Practica in Sponsalibus et Matrimonio***, Monasterii. 1858.

Basu, Nrisinha Das, ***The Law of Evidence in British India***, Calcutta, Eastern Law House. 1931.

Benedictus XIV, ***De Synodo Diocesana***, 2nd Parmensis ed., 2 vols., Parmae. 1764.

Bentham, Jeremy, ***Rationale of Judicial Evidence, Specially Applied to English Practice***, 5 vols. From Manuscripts of Jeremy Bentham. London, Hunt and Clarke. 1827.

Berardi, Carolus Sebastianus, ***Gratiani Canones Genuini ab Apocryphis Discreti, Corrupti ad Emendationum Codicum Exacti, Difficiliores Commoda Interpretatione Illustrati***, 3 vols. in 4. Venetiis, Ex. Typ. P. Valnasensis. 1777.

Best, William M., ***The Principles of the Law of Evidence, with Elementary Rules for Conducting the Examination and Cross-examination of Witnesses***, 11th ed. London, Sweet & Maxwell. 1911.

Bethmann-Hollweg, ***Der Civilprozess des gemeinen Rechts in geschichtlicher Entwickelung***, 6 vols. Bonn. 1864-1870.

Blat, Albertus, ***Commentarium Textus Codicis Iuris Canonici***, 6 vols. Romae, Ex Typographia Pontificia in Instituto Pii X. 1921-1927.

Bouix, Marie Dominique, ***Tractatus De Iudiciis Ecclesiatsicis Ubi Et De Vicario Generali Episcopi***, 3d ed., 2 vols. Parisiis, Apud Perisse Fratres Catholicos Bibliopolas. 1883.

Bright, William, ***The Canons of the First Four General Councils of Nicaea, Constantinople, Ephesus and Chalcedon with Notes***, 2 ed. Oxford, at the Clarendon Press. 1892.

Brunnehemanni, Johannis, ***Commentarius In Codicem Justinianeum***, 1 vol. Lipsiae, Sumptibus Johannis Christophori Tarnorii, Litteris Andreae Zeidleri. 1659.

Buckland, W. W., ***A Text-Book of Roman Law from Augustus to Justinian***, 2 ed. Cambridge, at the University Press. 1932.

Campegius, Ioannes, Iurisconsult Bononiensis, ***Tractatus et Regulae de Testibus, Cum Ampliationibus, ut Dicitur, Limitationibus et Sallentiis***. Venetiis, Apud candentis Salamandre insigne. 1508.

Cappello, Felix M., *Tractatus Canonico-Moralis de Sacramentis,* Vol. II, *De Poenitentia,* Romae, Apud Aedes Univ. Gregorianae. 1929. Vol. III, *De Matrimonio,* Romae, Apud Aedes Univ. Gregorianae. 1933.

Catholic Encyclopedia, The. Edited by Charles G. Herberman, Edward A. Pace, Conde B. Pallen, Thomas J. Shahan, John J. Wynne, assisted by numerous collaborators. New York, Robert Appleton Co. 1907. 15 vols.

Cerato, Prosdocimi, *Censurae Vigentes Ipso Facto A Codice Iuris Canonici Excerptae Cum Suspensionibus Ferendae Sententiae Poenis Vindicativis Remediis Poenalibus Poenitentiss et Irregularitatibus,* 2 ed. Patavii, Typis Seminarii. 1921.

Chelodi, Ioannes, *Ius Matrimoniale Iuxta Codicem Canonici,* 3 ed., Tridenti. Libreria Moderna Ed. A. Ardesi & C. 1921.

——— *Ius Poenale et Ordo Procedendi In Iudiciis Criminalibus Iuxta Codicem Iuris Canonici,* 3 ed., Tridenti. Libreria Moderna Ed. A. Ardesi & C. 1933.

Chrysostomus, Joannes, *De Sacerdotio Libri Sex Graece et Latine,* Opera J. A. Bengelii. Erhardum. 1725.

Cicognani, Amleto G., *Canon Law.* Philadelphia, The Dolphin Press. 1934.

Claeys-Bouuaert-G. Simeon, *De Secramentis.* Liége, Grandae et Leodii, Desain. 1931.

Cocchi, Guidus, *Commentarium In Codicem Iuris Scholarum,* Vol. V, *De Delictis Et Poenis.* Taurin, Libraria Marietti. . 1928.

Colinet, Paul, *La Procédure Par Libelle,* Études Historiques Sur Le Droit De Justinien, Tome Quatrème. Paris, Librarie Du Recueil Sirey. 1934.

Conran, Edward James, *The Interdict,* The Catholic University of America Canon Law Studies, Number 56, Washington, D. C. 1930.

Continental Legal History Series, The.

Cornelius, Ascher Lynn, *The Cross-examination of Witnesses,* Rules, Principles and Illustrations. Indianapolis, The Bobbs-Merrill Co. 1929.

Cosci, Christophorus, *De Separatione Tori Coniugalis tam nullo existente seu soluto, quam salvo vinculo matrimonii, euisque effectibus.* Florentiae, Ex Typis Magnae Ducalis Typographiae. 1856.

Croti, Dominus Ioannes a Monteferrato, *Tractatus de Testibus.* Venetiis, Apud candentis Salamandre insigne. 1508.

D'Annibale, Josephus Cardinalis, *Summula Theologiae Moralis,* 3 ed., 3 vols. Romae, 1892.

De Becker, Julius, *De Sponsalibus et Matrimonio Praelectiones Canonicae.* Lovanii, Polleunis et Centerick. 1903.

De Lugo, Joannes, *Disputationes Scholasticae et Morales,* 6 vols. Parisiis, Ludovicus Vives. 1869.

De Meester, A., *Juris Canonici et Juris Canonico-Civilis Compendium,* 3 vols. Bruges, 1921-1928.

Devoti, Joannes, *Institutionum Canonicarum Liber IV,* 3 vols. Venetiis, Sebastianus Valle Typ. et Edit. 1860.

Donohue, John F., *The Impediment of Crime,* The Catholic University of America Canon Law Studies, Number 69, Washington, D. C. 1931.

Droste, Francis, *Canonical Procedure In Disciplinary and Criminal Cases of Clerics.* Edited by Sebastian G. Messmer. New York, Benziger Brothers. 1887.

Duchesne, Louis, *Le Liber Pontificalis,* Texte, Introductio et Commentaire. Edited by Ernest Thorin. 2 vols. Paris. 1886.

Durandus, Gulielmus cum Ioannes Andreae Baldi, *Speculum Iuris.* Venetiis, Apud Iuntas. 1577.

Eichmann, Eduard, *Das Prozessrecht des Codex Iuris Canonici.* Paderborn, Ferdinand Schöningh. 1921.

Encyclopaedia Brittanica, The, 24 vols, 14 ed. London. 1929.

Encyclopédie de La Theologie Catholique, Traduit de L'Allemand Par I. Goschler, 26 vols. Paris. 1926.

Esmein, A., *Le Mariage en Droit Canonique,* 2 ed., Tome Priemier. Paris, Sirey. 1929.

Farrar, Frederick W., *Lives of the Fathers. Sketches of Church History in Biography,* 2 vols. Edinburgh, Adam and Chas. Black. 1889.

Farrugia, Nicolaus, *De Matrimonio et Causis Matrimonialibus Tractatus Canonico-Moralis iuxta Codicem Iuris Canonici,* Taurini, Romae. 1924.

Feije, Henricus J., *Impedimentis et Dispensationibus Matrimonialibus.* Lovanii, Carolis Peeters. 1885.

Ferraris, F. Lucius, *Bibliotheca Canonica Iuridica Moralis Theologica nec non Ascetica Polemica Rubricistica Historica,* Ed. novissima, 9 vols. Romae, Ex Typographia Polyglotta S. C. de Propaganda Fide. 1891.

Ferrini, Contardo, *Pandette,* Romae. 1927.

Ford, Edmond John, *Massachusetts Evidence and Trials,* 4 vols. Chicago, Callaghan and Company. 1931.

Fourneret, Pierre, *Le Mariage Chrétien Principes—Guide Pratique—Formulaire,* 5 ed. Paris, Gabriel Beauchesne, Editeur. 1925.

Freisen, Joseph, *Geschichte des Canonischen Eherechts bis zum Verfall der Glossenlitteratur,* 2 ed. Paderborn, Ferdinand Schöningh. 1893.

Fresquet, R. de, *Traité Élementaire De Droit Romain,* 2 vols. Paris, Etienne Giraud, Libraire, no date.

Fulton, John, *The Laws of Marriage, Containing the Hebrew, Roman and New Testament Law,* New York. 1883.

Gasparri, Petrus, *Tractatus Canonicus De Matrimonio,* 3 ed., 2 vols. Edited by Beauchesne, Paris. 1904.

——— *Tractatus Canonicus De Matrominio,* 2 vols. Romae, Typis Polyglottis Vaticanis. 1932.

Gibbon, Edward, *The History of the Decline and Fall of the Roman Empire,* edited by Dr. William Smith, with notes by Milman, Guizot and Wenck, 6 vols. New York, Charles C. Bigelow & Co., Inc.

Gonzale, Emmanuel . . . Tellez, *Commentaria Perpetua in Singulos Textus Quinque Librorum Decretalium Gregorii IX,* 5 vols. Lugduni, Anisson et T. Posuel, 1715.

Gosselin, M., *Power of the Popes During the Middle Ages,* translated by Matthew Kelley, 2 vols. London, C. Dolman. 1853.

Gross, Hans Gustav Adolf, *Criminal Psychology;* a manual for judges, practitioners and students, Hans Gross. Translated from the 4th German ed. by Horance M. Kallen . . . with an introduction by Joseph Jastrow. Boston, Little, Brown and Company. 1911.

Gugnard, Armandus, *Tractatus De Matrimonio,* 7 ed. Mechliniae, H. Dessain. 1931.

Hageman, John F., *Privileged Communications as a Branch of Legal Evidence.* New Jersey, Honeyman & Co. 1889.

Haring, Johann, *Der Kirchliche Eheprozess mit Einen Anhang über Den Weiheprozess Eine Praktische Anleitung Für Kirchliche Richter.* Graz, Ulrich Moser. 1932.

Hefele-Leclercq, *Histoire des Conciles D'Après Les Documents Originaux,* 9 vols. Paris. 1907-1930.

Henry, William J., and Harris, William L., *Ecclesiastical Law and Rules of Evidence,* with special reference to the jurisprudence of the Methodist Episcopal Church. Cincinnati, Hitchcock & Walden. 1879.

Hostiensis (Henricus de Segusio), *Commentaria in Quartum Librum Decretalium,* Venetiis. 1581.

——— *Summa Aurea.* Lugduni. 1568.

Jiménez, Juan Aguilar, *Procedimientos Canónico-Civiles Respecto a Las Causas De Divorcio y Nullidad De Matrimonio.* Madrid, Imprenta Del Instituto nacional De Sordomudos y De Cregos. 1923. Tomo I.

Kadushin, J. L., *Jewish Code of Jurisprudence,* 4 ed., 3 vols. New Rochelle, N. Y.

Kass, Ludwig, *Kriegsverschollenheit und Wiederverheiratung nach staatlichem und kirchlichem Recht.* Paderborn, Ferdinand Schöningh. 1919.

Kirsch, P. J., *Kirchengeschichte,* Vol. I, *Die Kirche in Der Antiken Grieschisch-Römischen Kulturwelt.* Freiburg im Breisgau. 1930.

Koeniger, Albert M., *Katholisches Kirchenrecht mit Berücksichtigung Des Deutschen Staatssirchenrechts.* Freiburg im Breisgau. 1926.

Jewish Encyclopedia, The, Isadore Singer, Projector and Managing Editor, 12 vols. New York, Funk and Wagnalls Co. 1906.

Knecht, August, *Handbuch Des Katholischen Eherechts auf Grund Des Codex Iuris Canonici Und Unter Berücksichtigund Des Bergurlichen Eherechts Des Deutschen Reiches, Österreichs, Ungarns Der Tschechoslowakei Der Schweiz.* Freiburg im Breisgau, Herder & Co. 1928.

Lanier, Henri, *Guide Pratique de la Procédure Matrimoniale en Droit Canonique.* Paris, Pierre Teque. 1927.

Larson, John A., Haney, George W., and Keeler, Leonarde, *Lying and Its Detection*, a Study of Deception and Deception Tests. Chicago, The University of Chicago Press. 1932.

Lea Henry, *Superstition and Force*. Philadelphia. 1892.

Leach, William Barton, *Massachusetts Cases on Evidence*. Chicago, The Foundation Press, Inc. 1934.

Leccisi, Giacinto, *La Prova Testimoniale nel Codice Di Diritto Canonico*. Romae, Desclée & C. 1926.

Lega, Michael, *Praelectiones In Textum Iuris Canonici De Iudiciis Ecclesiasticis In Scholis Pont. Sem. Rom. Habitae*, Vol I, *De Iudiciis Ecclesiasticis Civilibus*, 2 ed. Romae, Ex Typographia Polyglotta S. C. de Propaganda Fide. 1905.

Lehmkuhl, Augustinus, *Theologia Moralis*, 12 ed. Freiburg im Breisgau, B. Herder & Co. 1914.

Leitner, Martin, *Handbuch des Katholischen Kirchenrechts*. Regensburg, Josef Kosel & Frederich Pustet. 1922.

Liguori, St. Alphonsus, *Theologia Moralis*, 2 vols. Augustae Taurinorum. 1891.

Lindsay, W. M., *Isadori Hispalensis Episcopi Etymologiarum sive Originum*. Oxonii. 1910.

Lingard, John, *Antiquities of the Anglo-Saxon Church*. Philadelphia. 1841.

Linneborn, Johannes, *Grundriss Des Eherechts Nac Dem Codex Iuris Canonici*. Paderborn, Ferdinand Schöningh. 1933.

Livius, Titus, *Titi Livii Patavini historiarum ab urb condita libri qui supersunt XXIV*, 7 vols. Parisiis, Barbau. 1775.

Mansella, Joseph, *De Impedimentis Matrimonium Dirimentibus ac De Processu Iudiciali in Causis Matrimonialibus*. Romae, Ex Typographia Polyglotta S. C. De Propaganda Fide. 1881.

Maroto, Philippus, *Institutiones Iuris Canonici*, 3 ed., 2 vols. Romae, Apud Commendarium pro Religiosis. 1921.

Marshall, Francis W., *Common Legal Principles*, 2 vols. New York and London. 1929.

Mascardi, Giuseppe, *Conclusiones Omnium Probationum quae in Utroque Jure Quotidie Versantur*, 2 vols. Venetiis. 1588.

Meile, Joseph, *Die Beweislehre des Kanonischen Prozesses In Ihren Grundzügen Unter Berucksichtigung Der Modernen Prozessrechtswissenschaft*. Paderborn, Ferdinand Schöningh. 1925.

Memoirs de l'Institute National de France Academie des Inscriptions et Belles-Lettres (Juxtà Cabrol: Memoirs de l'Acadamie des Inscriptions et Belles-Lettres), Vol. 32. 1886-1891.

Menochius, Jacobus, *De Arbitrariis Judicum Quaestiones et Causae*. Venetiis. 1569.

——— *De Praesumptionibus, Coniecturis, Signis et Indicus*. Coloniae Allobrogum, Samuel de Tournes. 1686. Lib. I.

Mommsen, Theodore, *Le Droit Penal Romain,* Traduit de L'Allemand par J. Duquesne, 3 vols. Paris. 1907.

Mourret, Fernand, *Histoire Général de l'Église,* 9 vols. Paris, Libraire Bloud et Gay. 1920-1928.

Muniz, T., *Procedimientos Eclesiásticos,* 2 ed., 3 vols. Sevilla, Lib. de Sobrino de Izquierdo, no date.

Munsterberg, Hugo, *On the Witness Stand;* essays on psychology and crime. New York, Clark Boardman Co. 1923.

Muscat, Remigius, *Institutiones Canonicae.* Romae. 1707.

Müssener, Herm., *Das Katholische Eherecht in der Seelsorgspraxis.* Düsseldorf, L. Schwann. 1933.

Noldin, Henricus, *Summa Theologiae Moralis Iuxta Codicem Iuris Canonici,* 3 vols., III, *De Secramentis.* Ratisbonae, Fredericus Pustet. 1928.

Norman, Edwin Gates and Houghton, Arthur Stillman, *Massachusetts Trial Evidence Including Citations from Massachusetts Reports,* Vols. 1-205. New York, Baker Voorhis & Co. 1911.

Noval, P. Josephus, *Commentarium Codicis Iuris Canonici,* IV, *De Processibus,* Pars I, *De Iudiciis,* Augustae Taurinorum. Romae, Petrus Marietti. 1920.

Osborn, Albert S., *The Problem of Proof Especially as Exemplified in Disputed Document Trials,* 2 ed. Newark, N. J., The Essex Press. 1926.

Panormitanus (Nicholas de Tudeschio), *Commetaria,* 8 vols. Venetiis. 1588.

Papiensi, Franciscus Curtius, *De Testibus Tractatus Practicabilis ac Necessarius valde Tabellionibus, Causidicis, Iudicibus, et Omnibus Legalis Normae Professoribus.* Venetiis, Apud Candentis Salamandre Insigne. 1508.

Papiensis, Bernardus, *Summa Decretalium,* Laspeyres *ed.* Ratisbonae. 1860.

Payen, G., *De Matrimonio in Missionibus ac Potissimum in Sinis Tractatus Practicus et Casus,* 3 vols. Zi-ka-wei, in Topographia T'OU-SE-WE. 1928-1929.

Petrovits, Joseph J. C., *The New Church Law on Matrimony,* 2 ed. Philadelphia, McVey. 1919.

Pirhing, Henricus, *Ius Canonicum in V Libros Decretalium,* 5 vols. Dilingae. 1674-1678.

Prümmer, Dominicus M., *Manuale Theologiae Moralis Secundum Principia S. Thomae Aquinatis in Usum Scholarum,* 6 ed., 3 vols. Friburgi Brisgoviae, B. Herder & Co. 1928.

Reiffenstuel, Anacletus, *Ius Canonicum Universum,* 7 vols., Parisiis. 1864-1870.

Reynolds, William, *Trial Evidence. The Rules of Evidence and of the Examination of Witnesses in Trials at Common Law and in Equity as Established in the United States, with the Reasons for Them.* Chicago, Callaghan & Co. 1912.

Rittershutii, Cunradi, *Expositio Methodica Novellarum Imperatoris Justiniani,* ed. novissima. Florentia. 1839.

Roberti, Franciscus, *De Processibus,* 2 vols. Romae, Apud Aedes Facultatis Iuridicae ad S. Apollinaris. 1926.

Roskovány, Augustinus, *De Matrimonio in Ecclesia Catholica.* Augsburg. 1837.

Ross, W. D., *The Works of Aristotle.* Oxford. 1924.

Sanchez, Thomas, *De Sancto Matrimonio Disputationum,* 3 vols., Tomi Tres. Lugduni. 1669.

Santi, Franciscus, *Praelectiones Juris Canonici Quas Juxta Ordinem Decretalium Gregorii IX,* 4 ed., 5 vols. Ratisbonae. 1885.

Santi-Leitner, *Praelectiones Juris Canonici,* 5 vols. Ratisbonae, Pustet. 1905.

Savigny, Frederich C. von, *Geschichte des römischen Rechts im Mittelalter,* 2 ed., 7 vols. Heidelberg. 1834-1851.

——— *System des Heutigen romischen Rechts.* Berlin. 1841.

Schenk, Francis J., *The Matrimonial Impediments of Mixed Religion and Disparity of Cult,* The Catholic University of America Canon Law Studies, Number 51, Washington, D. C. 1929.

Schmalzgrueber, Franciscus, *Ius Ecclesiasticum Universum,* 12 vols. Romae, Ex Typographia Rev. Cam. Apostolicae. 1884.

Sciaccia, Sigismundus, *Tractatus de Iudiciis Causarum Civilium Criminalium et Haereticalium,* 2 vols. Coloniae Agrippinae, Viduae Wilh, Mellernich & Filii. 1738.

Smith, S. B., *The Marriage Process in the United States.* New York, Benziger Brothers. 1893.

Socrates, Scholasticus, *The Ecclesiastical History of Socrates.* London. 1853.

Soglia, Joannis Cardinalis, *Institutiones Juris Publici et Privati Ecclesiastici,* 10 ed., 2 vols in 1. Boscocia, A. N. Verhieven. 1842.

Sole, Jacobus, *De Delictis et Poenis Praelectiones in Lib. V Codicis Iuris Canonici.* Cincinnatensis, Fredericus Pustet. 1920.

Steinwenter, A., Universität Graz: *Gesta collationis carthaginiensis* (411 p. ch. n.) *ut fons iuris romani,* Acts of International Juridical Congress, November, 1934.

Stephen, Sir James Fitzjames, *A Digest of the Law of Evidence,* from 5 ed., 1899, of Sir Herbert Stephen, bart. By George E. Beers. Hartford, Conn., Dissell Publ. Co. 1901.

Strickler, Louis Julius, *The Doctrine of Privileged Communications between Attorney and Client,* Sayler prize essay at the Cincinnati Law School. Cincinnati. 1921.

Tacitus, Cornelius, *Agricola et Germania.* Edited on the basis of Draeger's Agricola and Schweizer—Sidler's Germania with introduction and maps by A. Grosvenor Hopkins, Leach, Shewell and Sanborn. Boston. 1893.

Taft, Henry Waters, *Witnesses in Court,* with some criticisms of court procedure. With a foreword by Frederick Evan Crane. New York, The Macmillan Co. 1934.

Tesoro, Giorgio, *La psicologia della testimonianza.* Con prefazione di Enrico Ferri. Torino, Fratelli Bocca. 1929.

Thayer, James Bradley, *A Preliminary Treatise on Evidence at the Common Law,* 1 ed. Cambridge. 1893.

Theiner, Augustinus, *Disquisitiones Criticae.* Romae. 1836.

Thomas Aquinas, *Summa Theologica,* Romae, 1894 and 1928; Parame, 1855; Taurini, 1922, 6 vols., ed. Frette, Parisiis, 1873-1879.

Timlin, Bartholomew Thomas, *Conditional Matrimonial Consent,* The Catholic University of America Canon Law Studies, Number 89, Washington, 1934.

Triebs, Franz, *Praktisches Handbuch des geltenden kanonischen Eherechts,* in Verleichung mit dem deutschen staatlichen Eherecht, 2 ed., 4 vols. Breslau, Ostdeutsche Verlagsanstalt. 1929.

Ugarter, José M., *Manual De Formularios Referentes A Las Distinctas Causas De Divorcio De Que Trata El Codex Juris Canonici,* 1 ed., Manuales Reus De Derecho, Vol. L. Madrid, Editorial Reus, S. A. 1930.

Van Espen, Z., *Ius Ecclesiasticum Universum Ceteraque Scripta Omnia.* Venetiis. 1769.

Vecchiotti, Septimus M., *Tractatus Canonicus de Matrimonio.* Taurini. 1868.

Vermeersch, Arthurus, *Theologiae Moralis. Principia-Responsa-Consilia,* 3 vols. Brugis, Firme Charles Beyaert. 1926.

Vermeersch, A.-Creusen, J., *Epitome Iuris Canonici cum Commentariis ad,* altera editio, *Scholas et ad Usum Privatum.* Romae. 1926.

Vinogradoff, P., *Roman Law in Medieval Europe,* 2 ed., by F. De Zulueta. Oxford. 1929.

Vives, *Compendium Iuris Canonici,* 4 ed, 3 vols. in 1. Romae. 1905.

Vlaming, T., *Praelectiones Juris Matrimonii,* 3 ed., 2 vols. Bussum, Edit. Anon. 1919.

Vromant, G., *Ius Missionariorum,* Vol. V, *De Matrimonio.* Louvain, Museum Lessianum. 1931.

Wahl, Francis X., *The Matrimonial Impediments of Consanguinity and Affinity,* The Catholic University of America Canon Law Studies, Number 90, Washington, 1934.

Wenger, Leopold, *Institutionen Des Romischen Zwilprozessrechts.* München, Verlag der Hochschulbuchhandlung Max Hueber. 1925.

Wernz, Franciscus, *Ius Decretalium,* 6 vols. Romae. 1908-1913.

Wernz-Vidal, *Ius Canonicum ad Codicis Normam Exactum, Apud Aedes Universitatis Gregorianae,* VI, *De Processibus;* II, *De Personis.* Romae. 1927.

Westermarck, Edward, *The History of Human Marriage,* 5 ed., 3 vols. New York, Allerton Book Co. 1922.

Wigmore, John H. *A Treatise on the Anglo-American System of Evidence in Trials at Common Law,* compiled and edited by John Henry Wigmore, 2 ed. Boston, Little, Brown & Co. 1923.

——— *The Principles of Judicial Proof as Given by Logic, Psychology and*

General Experience and Illustrated in Judicial Trials. Boston. 1913. Same publisher.

——— *Select Cases on the Law of Evidence,* 3 ed. Boston. 1932. Same publisher.

Wouters, L., *De Forma Promissionis et Celebrationis Matrimonii,* 5 ed. Bussum in Hollandia. 1919.

Woywod, Stanislaus, *A Practical Commentary on the Code of Canon Law,* 3 ed. New York. 1929.

Zallinger, Jacobus Ant., *Institutiones Iuris Ecclesiastici Maxime Privati Ordine Decretalium.* Romae, Typis Antonii Bouzaler. 1823.

Zollman, Carl, *American Church Law.* St. Paul, West Publishing Co. 1933.

Periodical Articles

American Ecclesiastical Review, Philadelphia. 1889.

Apollinaris Commentarium Iuridico-Canonicum, Romae. 1928.

Archiv für Katholisches Kirchenrecht, Mainz. 1889.

Catholic University Bulletin, Washington. 1894.

English Historical Review, London. 1886.

Homiletic and Pastoral Review, The, New York. 1900.

Irish Ecclesiastical Record, Dublin. 1864.

Ius Pontificium, Romae. 1921.

Monitore Ecclesiastico, Il, II, Romae. 1888.

Periodica de Re Canonica et Morali, Romae et Brugis. 1905.

Theologische Praktische Quartalschirft, Linz. 1832.

Theologische Quartalschrift, Tübingen. 1819.

Zeitschrift der Savigny—Stiftung für Rechtsgeschichte, 51 vols., Weimar, Hermann Bohlaus Nächfolger. 1880-1931.

ABBREVIATIONS

A. A. S.—*Acta Apostolica Sedis.*
AKKR—*Archiv für Katholisches Kirthenrecht.*
A. S. S.—*Acta Sanctae Sedis.*
Cod.—*Codex Iustinianus.*
Coll.—*Collectanea.*
C. Th.—*Codex Theodosianus.*
D.—*Digesta.*
Fontes—*Codicis Iuris Canonici Fontes.*
F. V.—*Fragmenta Quae Dicuntur Vaticana.*
G.—*Gai Institutiones.*
H. E.—Hefele-Leclercq, *Histoire des Conciles.*
Hrd.—*Harduinus, Acta Conciliorum et Epistolae Decretals ac Constitutiones Summorum Pontificum.*
Inst.—*Institutiones.*
M. G. H.—*Monumenta Germaniae Historica.*
M. P. G.—Migne, *Patrologiae Cursus Completus,* Series Graec.
M. P. L.—Migne, *Patrologiae Cursus Completus,* Series Latin.
Msi.—Mansi, *Sacrorum Conciliorum Nova et Amplissima Collectio.*
Nov.—*Novellae.*
Z. s. s.—*Zeitschrift der Savigny-Stiftung für Rechtsgeschichte.*

Universitas Catholica Americae

WASHINGTON, D. C.

Facultas Juris Canonici

No. 99

1934

INDEX

VITA

Donald William Whalen was born in 1899 at Beverly, Massachusetts. After his elementary instruction he attended St. John's Preparatory School in Danvers, Massachusetts, and Boston College, at Chestnut Hill, Massachusetts. His seminary course was made at St. John's Seminary, Brighton, Massachusetts. He was ordained to the Priesthood on May 7, 1926. He received a degree of Bachelor of Philosophy from St. John's Seminary and the degree of Master of Arts from the Graduate School of Boston College in 1930. In September, 1932, he enrolled in the School of Canon Law at the Catholic University of America from which he received the degrees of J. C. B. in 1933 and J. C. L. in 1934.

CANON LAW STUDIES

1. FRERIKS, REV. CELESTINE A., C.PP.S., J.C.D., Religious Congregations in Their External Relations, 121 pp., 1916.
2. GALLIHER, REV. DANIEL M., O.P., J.C.D., Canonical Elections, 117 pp., 1917.
3. BORKOWSKI, REV. AURELIUS L., O.F.M. De Confraternitatibus Ecclesiasticis, 136 pp., 1918.
4. CASTILLO, REV. CAYO, J.C.D., Disertacion Historico-canonica sobre la Potestad del Cabildo en Sede Vacante o Impedida del Vicario Capitular, 99 pp., 1919 (1918).
5. KUBELBECK, REV. WILLIAM J., S.T.B., J.C.D., The Sacred Penitentiaria and Its Relations to Faculties of Ordinaries and Priests, 129 pp., 1918.
6. PETROVITS, REV. JOSEPH, J. C., S.T.D., J.C.D., The New Church Law on Matrimony, X-461 pp., 1919.
7. HICKEY, REV. JOHN J., S.T.B., J.C.D., Irregularities and Simple Impediments in the New Code of Canon Law, 100 pp., 1920.
8. KLEKOTKA, REV. PETER J., S.T.B., J.C.D., Diocesan Consultors, 179 pp., 1920.
9. WANNENMACHER, REV. FRANCIS, J.C.D., The Evidence in Ecclesiastical Procedure Affecting the Marriage Bond, 1920. (Not Printed.)
10. GOLDEN, REV. HENRY FRANCIS, J.C.D., Parochial Benefices in the New Code, IV-119 pp., (Printed 1925.)
11. KOUDELKA, REV. CHARLES, J., J.C.D., Pastors, Their Rights and Duties According to the New Code of Canon Law, 211 pp., 1921.
12. MELO, REV. ANTONIUS, O.F.M., J.C.D., De Exemptione Regularium, X-188 pp., 1921.
13. SCHAAF, REV. VALENTINE THEODORE, O.F.M., S.T.D., J.C.D., The Cloister X-180 pp., 1921.
14. BURKE, REV. THOMAS JOSEPH, S.T.B., J.C.D., Competence in Ecclesiastical Tribunals, IV-117 pp., 1922.
15. LEECH, REV. GEORGE LEO, J.C.D., A Comparative Study of the Constitution "Apostolicae Sedis" and the "Codex Juris Canonici," 179 pp., 1922.
16. MOTRY, REV. HUBERT LOUIS, S.T.D., J.C.D., Diocesan Faculties According to the Code of Canon Law, II-167 pp., 1922.
17. MURPHY, REV. GEORGE LAWRENCE; J.C.D., Delinquencies and Penalties in the Administration and the Reception of the Sacraments, IV-121 pp., 1923.
18. O'REILLY, REV. JOHN ANTHONY, S.T.B., J.C.D., Ecclesiastical Sepultuae in the New Code of Canon Law, II-129 pp., 1923.
19. MICHALICKA, REV. WENCESLAS CYRILL, O.S.B., J.C.D., Judicial Procedure in Dismissal of Clerical Exempt Religious, 107 pp., 1923.

20. Dargin, Rev. Edward Vincent, S.T.B., J.C.D., Reserved Cases According to the Code of Canon Law, IV-103 pp., 1924.
21. Godfrey, Rev. John A., S.T.B., J.C.D., The Right of Patronage According to the Code of Canon Law, 153 pp., 1924.
22. Hagedorn, Rev. Francis Edward, J.C.D., General Legislation on Indulgences, II-154 pp., 1924.
23. King, Rev. James Ignatius, J.C.D., The Administration of the Sacraments to Dying Non-Catholics, V-141 pp., 1924.
24. Winslow, Rev. Francis Joseph, A.F.M., J.C.D., Vicars and Prefects Apostolic, IV-149 pp., 1924.
25. Correa, Rev. Jose Servelion, S.T.L., J.C.D., La Potestad Legislativa de la Iglesia Católica, IV-127 pp., 1925.
26. Dugan, Rev. Henry Francis, M.A., J.C.D., The Judiciary Department of the Diocesan Curia, 87 pp., 1925.
27. Keller, Rev. Charles Frederick, S.T.D., J.C.D., Mass Stipends, 167 pp., 1925.
28. Paschang, Rev. John Linus, J.C.D., The Sacramentals According to the Code of Canon Law, 129 pp., 1925.
29. Piontek, Rev. Cyrillus, O.F.M., S.T.B., J.C.D., De Indulto Exclaustrationis necnon Saecularizationis, XIII-289 pp., 1925.
30. Kearney, Rev. Richard Joseph, S.T.B., J.C.D., Sponsors at Baptism According to the Code of Canon Law, IV-127 pp., 1925.
31. Bartlett, Rev. Chester Joseph, A.M., LL.B., J.C.D., The Tenure of Parochial Property in the United States of America, V-108 pp., 1926.
32. Kilker, Rev. Adrian Jerome, J.C.D., Extreme Unction, V-425 pp., 1926
33. McCormick, Rev. Robert Emmett, J.C.D., Confessors of Religious, VIII-266 pp., 1926.
34. Miller, Rev. Newton Thomas, J.C.D., Founded Masses According to the Code of Canon Law, VII-93 pp., 1926.
35. Roelker, Rev. Edward G., S.T.D., J.C.D., Principles of Privilege According to the Code of Canon Law, XI-166 pp., 1926.
36. Bakalarczyk, Rev. Richardus, M.I.C., J.U.D., De Novitiatu, VIII-208 pp., 1927.
37. Pizzuti, Rev. Lawrence, O.F.M., J.U.L., De Parochis Religiosis, 1927. (Not Printed.)
38. Bliley, Rev. Nicholas Martin, O.S.B., J.C.D., Altars According to the Code of Canon Law, XIX-132 pp., 1927.
39. Brown, Brendan Francis, A.B., LL.M., J.U.D., The Canonical Juristic Personality with Special Reference to its Status in the United States of America, V-212 pp., 1927.
40. Cavanaugh, Rev. William Thomas, C.P., J.U.D., The Reservation of the Blessed Sacrament, VIII-101 pp., 1927.
41. Doheny, Rev. William J., C.S.C., A.B., J.U.D., Church Property: Modes of Acquisition, X-118, pp., 1927.

42. Feldhaus, Rev. Aloysius H., C.PP.S., J.C.D., Oratories, IX-141 pp., 1927.
43. Kelly, Rev. James Patrick, A.B., J.C.D., The Jurisdiction of the Simple Confessor, X-208 pp., 1927.
44. Neuberger, Rev. Nicholas J., J.C.D., Canon 6 or the Relation of the Codex Juris Canonici to the Preceding Legislation, V-95 pp., 1927.
45. O'Keeffe, Rev. Gerald Michael, J.C.D., Matrimonial Dispensations, Powers of Bishops, Priests, and Confessors, VIII-232 pp., 1927.
46. Quigley, Rev. Joseph, A.M., A.B., J.C.D., Condemned Societies, 139 pp., 1927.
47. Zaplotnik, Rev. Ioannes Leo, J.C.D., De Vicariis Foraneis, X-142 pp., 1927.
48. Duskie, Rev. John Aloysius, A.B., J.C.D., The Canonical Status of the Orientals in the United States, VIII-196 pp., 1928.
49. Hyland, Rev. Francis Edward, J.C.D., Excommunication, Its Nature, Historical Development and Effects, VIII-181 pp., 1928.
50. Reinmann, Rev. Gerald Joseph, O.M.C., J.C.D., The Third Order Secular of Saint Francis, 201 pp., 1928.
51. Schenk, Rev. Francis J., J.C.D., The Matrimonial Impediments of Mixed Religion and Disparity of Cult, XVI-318 pp., 1929.
52. Coady, Rev. John Joseph, S.T.D., J.U.D., A.M., The Appointment of Pastors, VIII-150 pp., 1929.
53. Kay, Rev. Thomas Henry, J.C.D., Competence in Matrimonial Procedure, VIII-164 pp., 1929.
54. Turner, Rev. Sidney Joseph, C.P., J.U.D., The Vow of Poverty, XLIX-217 pp., 1929.
55. Kearney, Rev. Raymond A., A.B., S.T.D., J.C.D., The Principles of Delegation, VII-149 pp., 1929.
56. Conran, Rev. Edward James, A.B., J.C.D., The Interdict, V-163 pp., 1930.
57. O'Neil, Rev. William H., J.C.D., Papal Rescripts of Favor, VII-218 pp., 1930.
58. Bastnagel, Rev. Clement Vincent, J.U.D., The Appointment of Parochial Adjutants and Assistants, XV-257 pp., 1930.
59. Ferry, Rev. William A., A.B., J.C.D., Stole Fees, X-107 pp., 1930.
60. Costello, Rev. John Michael, A.B., J.C.D., Domicile and Quasi-Domicile, VII-201 pp., 1930.
61. Kremer, Rev. Michael Nicholas, A.B., S.T.B., J.C.D., Church Support in the United States, VI-136 pp., 1930.
62. Angulo, Rev. Luis, C.M., J.C.D., Legislación de la Iglesia sobre la intención en la applicación de la Santa Misa, VII-104 pp., 1931.
63. Frey, Rev. Wolfgang Norbert, O.S.B., A.B., J.C.D., The Act of Religious Profession, VIII-174 pp., 1931.
64. Roberts, Rev. James Brendan, A.B., J.C.D., The Banns of Marriage, XIV-140 pp., 1931.
65. Ryder, Rev. Raymond Aloysius, A.B., J.C.D., Simony, IX-151 pp., 1931.

66. CAMPAGNA, REV. ANGELO, PH.D., J.U.D., Il Vicario Generale del Vescovo, VII-205 pp., 1931.
67. COX, REV. JOSEPH GODFREY, A.B., J.C.D., The Administration of Seminaries, VI-124 pp., 1931.
68. GREGORY, REV. DONALD J., J.U.D., The Pauline Privilege, XV-165 pp., 1931.
60. DONOHUE, REV. JOHN F., J.C.D., The Impediment of Crime, VIII-110 pp., 1931.
70. DOOLEY, REV. EUGENE A., O.M.I., J.C.D., Church Law on Sacred Relics, IX-143 pp., 1931.
71. ORTH, REV. CLEMENT RAYMOND, O.M.C., J.C.D., The Approbation of Religious Institutes, 171 pp., 1931.
72. PERNICONE, REV. JOSEPH M., A.B., J.C.D., The Ecclesiastical Prohibition of Books, XII-267 pp., 1932.
73. CLINTON, REV. CONNELL, A.B., J.C.D., The Paschal Precept, IX-108 pp., 1932.
74. DONNELLY, REV. FRANCIS B., A.M., S.T.L., J.C.D., The Diocesan Synod, VIII-125 pp., 1932.
75. TORRENTE, REV. CAMILO, C.M.F., J.C.D., Las Processiones Sagradas, V-145 pp., 1932.
76. MURPHY, REV. EDWIN J., C.PP.S., J.C.D., Suspension Ex Informata Conscientia, XI-122 pp., 1932.
77. MACKENZIE, REV. ERIC F., A.M., S.T.L., J.C.D., The Delict of Heresy in its Commission, Penalization, Absolution, VII-124 pp., 1932.
78. LYONS, REV. AVITUS E., S.T.B., J.C.D., The Collegiate Tribunal of First Instance, XI-147 pp., 1932.
79. CONNOLLY, REV. THOMAS A., J.C.D., Appeals, XI-195 pp., 1932.
80. SANGMEISTER, REV. JOSEPH V., A.B., J.C.D., Force and Fear as Precluding Matrimonial Consent, V-211 pp., 1932.
81. JAEGER, REV. LEO A., A.B., J.C.D., The Administration of Vacant and Quasi-Vacant Episcopal Sees in the United States, IX-229 pp., 1932.
82. RIMLINGER, REV. HERBERT T., J.C.D., Error Invalidating Matrimonial Consent, VII-79 pp., 1932.
83. BARRETT, REV. JOHN D. M., S.S., J.C.D., Comparative Study of the Third Plenary Council and the Code, IX-221 pp., 1932.
84. CARBERRY, REV. JOHN J., PH.D., S.T.D., J.C.D., The Juridical Form of Marriage, X-177 pp., 1934.
85. DOLAN, REV. JOHN L., A.B., J.C.D., The Defensor Vinculi, XII-157 pp., 1934.
86. HANNAN, REV. JEROME D., A.M., S.T.D., LL.B., J.C.D., The Cannon Law of Wills, VI-517 pp., 1934.
87. LEMIEUX, REV. LELISLE A., A.M., J.C.D., The Sentence in Ecclesiastical Proceduce, IX-131 pp., 1934.
88. O'ROURKE, REV. JAMES J., A.B., J.C.D., Parish Registers, IX-109 pp., 1934.

89. Timlin, Rev. Bartholomew, O.F.M., A.M., J.C.D., Conditional Matrimonial Consent, X-381 pp., 1934.
90. Wahl, Rev. Francis X., A.B., J.C.D., The Matrimonial Impediments of Consanguinity and Affinity, VI-125 pp., 1934.
91. White, Rev. Robert J., A.B., LL.B., S.T.B., J.C.D., Canonical Ante-Nuptial Promise and the Civil Law, VI-152 pp., 1934.
92. Herrera, Rev. Anthony Parra, O.C.D., J.C.L., Legislacion Ecclesiastica sobre el Ayuno y la Abstinencia, 1935.
93. Reilly, Rev. Peter, J.C.L., Residence of Pastors, 1935.
    Cases of Evident Nullity, 1935.
94. Manning, Rev. John J., A.B., J.C.L., Presumption of Law in Matrimonial Procedure, 1935.
95. Moeder, Rev. John M., J.C.L., The Proper Bishop for Ordination and Dimissorial Letters, 1935.
96. O'Mara, Rev. William A., Canonical Causes for Matrimonial Dispensations, 1935.
97. Reilly, Rev. Peter, J.C.L., Residence of Pastors, 1935.
98. Smith, Rev. Mariner T., O.P., S.T.Lr., J.C.L., The Penal Law for Religious, 1935.
99. Whalen, Rev. Donald W., A.M., J.C.L., The Value of Testimonial Evidence in Matrimonial Procedure, 1935.

www.ingramcontent.com/pod-product-compliance
Lightning Source LLC
LaVergne TN
LVHW050257080826
844660LV00012B/650
* 9 7 8 0 8 1 3 2 2 2 8 8 2 *